Charlie Barnet

Charlie Barnet

An Illustrated Biography and Discography of the Swing Era Big Band Leader

by Dan Mather

McFarland & Company, Inc., Publishers
Jefferson, North Carolina, and London

For Karyl

Publisher's note: Dan Mather died on March 26, 2001, after writing this book. His friend Frank Rutter was of great help in completing its proofreading and indexing.

The present work is a reprint of the illustrated case bound edition of Charlie Barnet: An Illustrated Biography and Discography of the Swing Era Big Band Leader, *first published in 2001 by McFarland.*

LIBRARY OF CONGRESS CATALOGUING-IN-PUBLICATION DATA

Mather, Dan, 1925–2001.
Charlie Barnet : an illustrated biography and discography of the swing era big band leader / by Dan Mather.
p. cm.
Includes bibliographical references (p.) and index.

ISBN 978-0-7864-3761-0
softcover : 50# alkaline paper ♾

1. Barnet, Charlie. 2. Conductors (Music)—United States—Biography. 3. Jazz musicians—United States—Biography. 4. Barnet, Charlie—Discography. 5. Swing (Music)—Discography. I. Title.

ML422.B19 M37 2008
784.4'8'092—dc21
[B] 2001044492

British Library cataloguing data are available

On the cover: Charlie Barnet in 1939 (by arrangement with Wayne Knight)

Manufactured in the United States of America

McFarland & Company, Inc., Publishers
Box 611, Jefferson, North Carolina 28640
www.mcfarlandpub.com

Contents

Preface vii
Acknowledgments ix
Abbreviations xi

1. Sideman, 1913–1932 1
2. Leader, 1933–1937 8
3. Cherokee—The Billy May Band, 1939–1941 32
4. Skyliner—The Andy Gibson Band, 1942–1945 68
5. Things Ain't What They Used to Be, 1946–1948 105
6. Be-bop Spoken Here, 1949 126
7. Barnetology, 1950–1966 137
8. The Last Jump, 1967 173
9. In a Mellow Tone, 1967–1991 177

Between pages 180 and 181 are 16 pages containing 32 photographs.

Postscript 181
Album Listing 183
Pseudo-Charlie 204
Bibliography 209
Recording Units Index 211
Program Index 213
Song Title Index 215
Name Index 221

Preface

A few observations on the subject of this book, Charles Daly Barnet (aka Dale Bennett, The Mad Mab, The Mab, Cherokee Charlie, etc.) and his recordings.

I got interested in Charlie's band during my teens when I bought for 5¢ a used copy of Bluebird B10825, *Pompton Turnpike/I don't want to cry anymore*—which still sounds pretty good after 60 years, at least to my prejudiced ears. The book came about from a desire to document the many recording sessions and the like in as accurate a way as possible thus making it a more enjoyable experience to listen to the music made by Charlie's fine bands.

Charlie was never in the very top tier of bands—Glenn Miller, Harry James, the Dorseys, Duke Ellington, Count Basie—but he did make a contribution to the big band era. Even in the earliest recordings one is aware of a swingy sound not heard in many of the bands from those early 1930s days. His goal was not so much to put together a band that would attract a broad public and make a lot of money by "making sweet music" but rather to form bands with a strong musical content that were somewhere between the out-and-out jazz orchestras and the commercially successful white bands of the day.

The music was made by the players but the players and the arrangements were Charlie's choices—not always easy during the scuffling years 1933–1938—and gradually he was able to put together a good mix of lead men and soloists, rhythm section players and talented arrangers, and with his own solo voices, the band clicked with the more hip part of the dancing and listening public.

Charlie's solos were good for their time and caught the ears of popular music reviewers. They were by turns very rhythmic and driving on the up stuff, and very emotional and lyrical on the ballads—never lacking in integrity and frequently bold and adventuresome. Barnet took his share of risk and often went out on a limb. His tenor playing was in the Bean bag, Coleman Hawkins style; on soprano the Rabbit (Johnny Hodges) takes over, and on alto, somewhere in between but often echoing his idol, Johnny; maybe the alto sax is the real Charlie.

He took up the soprano several years after he had become a working musician, and it's enlightening to compare his first grapples with the instrument (e.g., "Smiles" and "You go to my head" on Thesaurus) to his later mastery of the "fish-horn." The soprano sax is by all accounts a formidable foe when it comes to intonation. No matter the instrument, he had a distinctive sound and was easily identifiable. Although he was not a particularly original soloist, he did exert at least a passing influence on one sax man, George Auld; listen to Auld's chorus on Bunny Berigan's *Frankie and Johnny*.

Charlie Barnet came from a well-to-do background but he was a working musician who scrabbled for jobs both as a sideman and as a leader. If what is often said of him were true, i.e., that he was a millionaire, then his bands wouldn't have broken up and he would not have lost players like Billy May and Chubby Jackson to Glenn Miller and Woody Herman, for example. There were times—probably plenty of them—when he took a handout from his mother, but overall he supported himself, and as he remarked in the 50s, "I have to work." Late in life he inherited a substantial sum of money but, by and large, he earned his living playing his horn, leading bands and combos and collecting royalties on his compositions and recordings.

He left behind a lot of memories as well as a body of excellent big band recordings.

Marital Footnote

Joyce O'Day (chorus girl?)
Married in Boston or NYC ca. March 1934. Annulled ca. 1936.

Shirley Lloyd (singer with Ozzie Nelson)
Married 1936 in Armonk, NY. Annulled shortly after.

Betty Lorraine
Married early 1939. Annulled.

Harriet Clarke
Married November 27, 1940, in Miami. Permanent separation few years later.

Rita Merritt
Married October 5, 1946, in Tijuana. Ended ca. late 1950.

Betty Reilly ("The Irish Señorita")
Married ca. May 1952. Ended ca. 1953.

Linda Joyce Johnson
Married April 25, 1956, in Tijuana. Annulled June 21, 1956.

Joy Windsor
Married May 13, 1957, in Las Vegas. Annulled August 8, 1957.

Betty Thompson
Married May 1, 1958, in Mexicali, and then again in Las Vegas, August 4, 1962.

Acknowledgments

I would like to state at the outset that this book owes much to the several discographers who have pioneered big band discography—especially Brian Rust and Ernie Edwards—and the researchers who have built on the work of these pioneers, Charles Garrod and George Hall.

Special thanks go to Betty Barnet, who has been extremely generous in supplying important pictures and information on her late husband.

Thanks also to these musicians—who were more than willing to search their memories for long-ago events—and collectors, discographers and librarians: Manny Albam, Ray Alexander, Ray Anthony, David Armstrong, Harlow Atwood, Von Babasin, Rod Baum, Carl Benevente, John Best, the late Bill Boyle, John Brechler, Joseph E. Brown, Reny Brown, Peter Burgis, Ed Burke, Donald A. Burns, Earl Butler, Harold Callanan, Mark Cantor, Christine Chang at the University of Charleston (W.Va.) Library, Alfredo R. Coleman, Jack Cullen, Jehangir B. Dalal, Evelyn Darrow at the Western Washington University Library, Don S. Davidson, Barbara Davis at the New Rochelle Historical Society, Vinni Dean, Tony Debonee, Horace Diaz, Jr., Dave Dixon, Lucia Dunn, Stan and Midge Ebin, Thomas Fancy, Carmen Fanzone, Faye Fenske at the Bellingham (Wash.) Public Library, Joe Ferrante, Mike Fitt, Bob Flatter, Lynn (Franklin) Winiecki, Eric Gee, Kathy Giegerich, Brian Gladwell, Keith Grant, Chris Griffin, Ben Hafey, Carl Hällström, Warren Hicks, George Hulme, the IAJRC Library (Bozy White), Bob Inman, Bob Jung, Red Kelly, Judith Kipp at the Tacoma Public Library, Wayne Knight, Bob Koester, Gary Lazare, John Leahy, Tom Lord, Don Manning, Billy May, Ernie McDaniel, Harry McKenzie, Hal Miles, Jack Mirtle (for information from his *The Music of Billy May*, Greenwood, 1999), Bernadette Moore, the late Gerry Murray, Ray Norman, Glenn Osser, Steve Parque, John Payne, Jack Perciful, Etienne Perret, Mike Pettingale, A.F.B. Real, Trudy (Richards) Moreau, Bill Richmond, Tiny Rips, the late Raoul Romero, Frank Rutter, Harry Schmidt, Buddy Schutz, Jim Seidelle, Hal Serra, Joe Showler, Dan Singer (BMI), Ernie Small, the late Bob Thompson, Mario Toscano-Pouchan, Jerry Waddell, Eddie Weid, Dave Wells, Don Whyte, Dale Williams, Phil Woods, and Red Wootten. Unless otherwise indicated, I did the interviews.

Abbreviations

a . . . . arranger
AFM . . . . American Federation of Musicians Local 47 recording contract
AFRS . . . . Armed Forces Radio Service
AFRTS . . . . Armed Forces Radio & TV Service
aka . . . . also known as
as . . . . alto sax
b . . . . string bass
bb . . . . brass bass/tuba/sousaphone
BB . . . . Bluebird
BML . . . . Basic Music Library (AFRS)
Br . . . . Brunswick
btpt . . . . bass trumpet
btbn . . . . bass trombone
bar . . . . baritone sax
c . . . . cello
Cap . . . . Capitol
CCSB . . . . Coca Cola Victory Parade of Spotlight Bands (commercial version)
cel . . . . celesta
Col . . . . Columbia
dec. . . . . deceased
d . . . . drums
fl . . . . flute
frh . . . . french horn
g . . . . guitar
HMV . . . . His Master's Voice (UK); VSM (France); Voce del Padrone (Italy)
JATJB . . . . Jill's All Time Juke Box (AFRS)
JJB . . . . Jill's Juke Box (AFRS)
Jubilee . . . . Jubilee (AFRS)
MC . . . . Magic Carpet (AFRS)
ONS . . . . One Night Stand (AFRS)
p . . . . piano

PMR	Popular Music Replacement (AFRS)
r.n.	real name
SB	Spotlight Bands (AFRS version)
ss	soprano sax
tbn	trombone
tpt	trumpet
ts	tenor sax
USIA-VOA	U.S. Information Agency—Voice of America
v	vocal
Vi	Victor
v-tbn	valve trombone
vla	viola
vn	violin
°	Issued in U.S. and Canada with same release number
#title	Incomplete performance, e.g., #*Cherokee* = top missing
Title	Non-studio performance documented but not recorded
Title	Non-studio performance recorded in some form
Title	Studio performance recorded in some form

Release Media

Col 12345	78 RPM
Col 12345	45 RPM
Col 12345	LP
Col 12345	45 EP
Col 12345	Cassette (or other indicated tape format)
COL 12345	CD
COL 12345	Transcription
(Arg)	Argentina
(Australia)	Australia
(Brazil)	Brazil
(C)	Canada
(Cz)	Czechoslovakia
(Den)	Denmark
(E)	England, UK
(Eu)	Europe
(Fi)	Finland
(Fr)	France
(Ger)	Germany
(In)	India
(It)	Italy
(Ja)	Japan
(N)	Netherlands/Holland
(NZ)	New Zealand
(Nor)	Norway
(Sp)	Spain
(Switz)	Switzerland

Chapter 1

Sideman 1913–1932

Charles Daly Barnet was born in New York City on Oct. 26, 1913 into a well-to-do family. ("I wasn't rich," he said during an interview. "My family was comfortable. It wasn't a question of rolling in wealth. Those things as they get retold always get exaggerated. First you're comfortable, then well off, then rich, then filthy rich.") His maternal grandfather, Charles Frederick Daly, was a prominent man in railroading and banking and was a member of numerous boards of directors. A much honored man, he joined with Will Durant in the automobile business.

Charlie (he was also called Daly) early showed an interest in music and at age 8 or 9 his mother gave him a C-melody saxophone. "You have never suffered unless you have been forced to listen to the first pitiful moans of a new saxophone in the hands of a new player. Unfortunately, after listening to the current sounds created by our rock and roll artists (I use the word 'artist' with poetic license), little progress seems to have been made" (undated manuscript in Charlie's hand, hereafter *MS*). He attended a number of (mostly) private schools including Berkeley-Irving, Rumsey Hall (Sept. 1922–June 1923), Riverdale Country School (1923–4?), Blair Academy (1925–6?), New Trier (Sept.–Dec. 1928) and Berkeley-Irving again in 1929. As he notes in *Those Swinging Years* (hereafter *TSY*), he took school music lessons on piano, tuba and soprano sax.

In "The Golden Age of the American Musical" he saw a number of shows during the 1928/29 season, duly noted in his little black book, including *Hello Daddy* (with the Ben Pollack orchestra), *Blackbirds of 1928* (Bill Robinson, Adelaide Hall) and *Gambols* (Libby Holman). Much further down the road Charlie and Bill Robinson would have another across-the-footlights encounter.

Sometime during this period he developed a crush on Lillian Roth, two

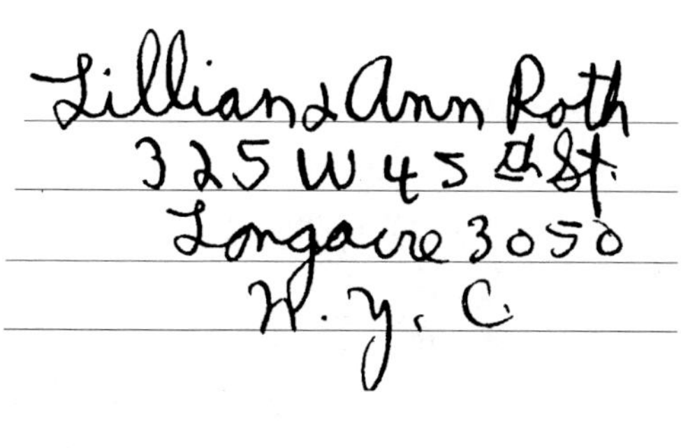
Lillian Ann Roth
325 W 45 St.
Longacre 3050
N.Y.C.

years his senior, and succeeded in at least getting as far as visiting her in her apartment (*TSY*) and getting her telephone number.

In July of 1929 he signed a contract with Louis Booking to provide a band for an Atlantic crossing on the S.S. *Republic.* (This was his second Atlantic trip as his grandfather had taken the family on a cruise in 1927 which included the Mediterranean, Cairo and London, so he was familiar with ocean travel.) The band:

George Tully, tpt; George Cates, saxophone; "Fred," piano, Buzz Meredith, d.

Cates became "the chief of the arranging staff for Lawrence Welk … The drummer was the brother of the famous and talented actor, Burgess Meredith … The trumpet player was a guy from Little Rock … a man of much volume and an unpredictable behavior pattern. Perhaps the real star of the group was the piano player that we will just call "Fred." Fred was a human tank. His capacity for whiskey was only surpassed by his ability to play the wrong chords to anything he attempted." (*MS*) This was the first of 22 crossings Charlie made either as leader or sideman during 1929–1932.

While in school he was playing dance jobs and by the late 1920s "I had absorbed various experiences with my saxophone such as a New Year's Eve job (anybody that can hold an instrument can work on New Year's Eve) and several short-lived dance jobs in non-union Chinese-American restaurants. In those days practically all of these establishments used an orchestra. I had never taken the trouble to read music, and usually I was able, due to a very good ear, to bluff my way for a short time until my deficiency was discovered. This

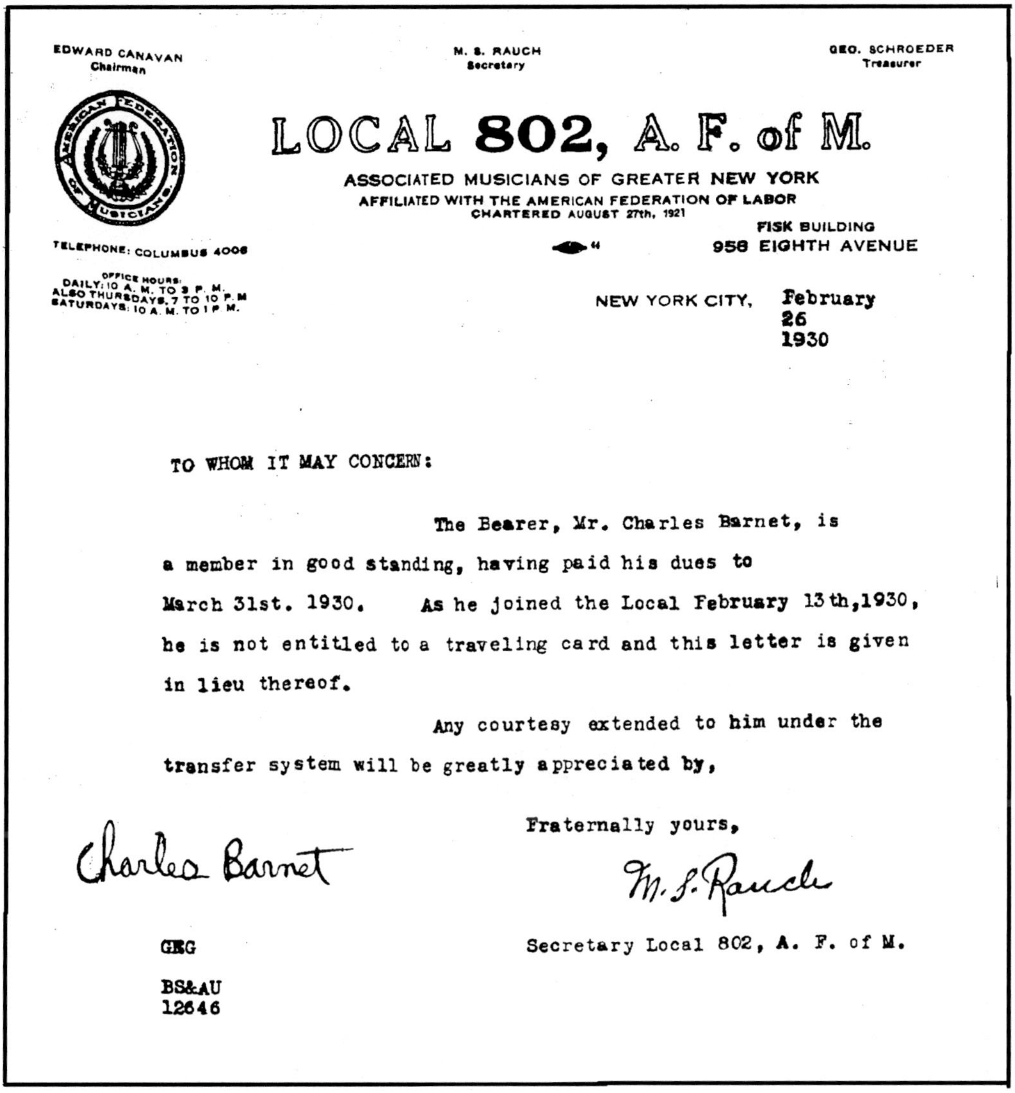

EDWARD CANAVAN
Chairman

M. S. RAUCH
Secretary

GEO. SCHROEDER
Treasurer

LOCAL 802, A. F. of M.

ASSOCIATED MUSICIANS OF GREATER NEW YORK
AFFILIATED WITH THE AMERICAN FEDERATION OF LABOR
CHARTERED AUGUST 27th, 1921

TELEPHONE: COLUMBUS 4006

OFFICE HOURS:
DAILY: 10 A. M. TO 3 P. M.
ALSO THURSDAYS, 7 TO 10 P. M.
SATURDAYS: 10 A. M. TO 1 P. M.

FISK BUILDING
958 EIGHTH AVENUE

NEW YORK CITY, February 26 1930

TO WHOM IT MAY CONCERN:

The Bearer, Mr. Charles Barnet, is a member in good standing, having paid his dues to March 31st. 1930. As he joined the Local February 13th,1930, he is not entitled to a traveling card and this letter is given in lieu thereof.

Any courtesy extended to him under the transfer system will be greatly appreciated by,

Fraternally yours,

Charles Barnet

M. S. Rauch

Secretary Local 802, A. F. of M.

GEG

BS&AU
12646

usually occurred when the band was called upon to accompany an act. I was up on all the tunes of the day, but when it came to the exacting rendition of show music, I was asked to take my talents elswhere."

The extra-curricular activities began to get in the way of the prescribed curriculum and his class attendance began to suffer. At last—probably in early 1930—the family threw in the towel and accepted his decision to follow a musical career. They expressed the hope that he would have a band made up of nice and proper men like those in Guy Lombardo's band (*Charlie to Harlow Atwood*). "I went through two years of high school and didn't pay much attention the last year because I was working in bands." Reports that he was enrolled at Yale and Brown have not been substantiated.

In 1930 Charlie, his mother and his grandmother moved temporarily to Southern California and it was then that he first tried the movies. He appeared in *Playboy of Paris* (which starred Maurice Chevalier) and is on screen several times:

early in the film he's seen briefly riding a bicycle, later he's a barber, and near the middle he's a patron in a restaurant.

A number of writers have incorrectly credited the chimes on Duke Ellington's 1930 recording of *Ring dem bells* to Charlie. "It's one of those things that keeps cropping up in discographies and some of the people that write the books about the big band era, and it just never happened and I have no idea how it ever got started." (*Smithsonian Institution interview of Charlie Barnet by Patricia Willard, 1978*, hereafter *Sm*).

Back on the east coast in about October of 1930, Charlie became a member of the Frank Wine-gar band which was rehearsing at Pelham Heath Inn (NYC). Collective personnel included:

Gordon Tully, Bill Moore, Don McCarter, Eddie Wade, tpts; Huffert "Huff" Allen, tbn; Gable Gelinas, Norman "Pal" Campbell, as; ***Charlie Barnet****, Ralph Spangler, Willard Brady, ts; Horace Diaz, Jr., Norman Sherman, p; "Scoop" Thomson, g; Walt Ottinger, d; Bill Wyder, sousaphone; Evan Young, vn.*

Wine-gar was booked for some Sunday evening performances at the Asbury Park Casino (New Jersey) and the song list for one of their programs has been preserved:

Lingering twilight
Wedding of the birds
Body and soul
It's easy to fall in love
Miss a little miss
Just a little while
Don't send my boy to prison
The toy brigade
Three little words
Medley of famous waltz love ballads
When the organ played at twilight
I lost my gal from Memphis
Violin solo by Evan Young
Baby's birthday party
Trio of outstanding hits of 1930
Victor Herbert medley
Tiger rag

On this particular occasion the band was made up of:

Gordon Tully, Don McCarter, tpts; Huff Allen, tbn; Willard Brady, Norman Campbell, as; ***Charlie Barnet****, ts; Evan Young, vn and arr; Norman Sherman, p; Scoop Thomson, g; Bill Wyder, sousaphone; Walt Ottinger, d*

The Wine-gar band opened at the Village Barn (Greenwich Village) on January 13, 1931 for what turned out to be a long engagement. There was a CBS wire and the band's broadcasts were carried by WABC and WMCA. Charlie later recalled that "One would take him [Winegar] to be a very religious man, as he used to call the band in the dressing room and pray before each of our radio broadcasts. As I think back, this was probably prompted more by fear of the musical atrocities the band was apt to inflict on the innocent listeners, rather than any deep religious fervor." (*MS*) This remembrance may be an embellishment or variant on a story told by Howard Waters in his article on Wine-gar which appeared in *Storyville* (hereafter *Waters*) about two of the band members (Scoop Thomson and Don McCarter) whose behavior put them in jail. Frank got them out and was determined to put an end to their antics. "In a solemn ritual, Frank led a service in an attempt to reform the two waywards. It brought them out of it and McCarter, showing a complete reversal, stopped smoking pot and became so pious that he refused to play on Sunday."

During a concert performance, McCarter fell apart. "He stood up in his chair, shouted, 'Seek ye the Lord' and walked out. He later returned and told Frank, 'You are Jesus and these are your twelve disciples.' ... The next day Charlie and Frank took McCarter to New York to place him in a sanitarium. As they were driving along Broadway, McCarter suddenly jumped out of the car and ran down a subway station ... That is the last anyone saw of Don McCarter." (*Waters*)

"Presently a crisis arose between Frank Wine-gar and myself. The band was scheduled to make some phonograph records. Up to this point Frank had been unaware of my failing in the art of reading music. We arrived at the recording studio and I was confronted by the gentleman in charge of producing the date. His name was Schubert and his knowledge of music was on a par with his illustrious namesake. He was one of those fellows, that if you were to belch, would announce 'that was a B-flat'. In other words, perfect pitch. Half way through the first chorus of the first tune he came charging out of the control room. 'Somebody in the saxophone section is playing a G concert,' he said. 'Run it down again. That G should be an F. I was quickly discovered and of course much to the embarrassment of Frank Wine-gar who certainly looked bad under the circumstances. At first he fired me, but then, considering that I had fooled him for so long, and to his satisfaction, he relented and agreed to keep me on if I would take reading lessons from the violinist in the band. This was how I became a 'reader'." (*MS*) There's the remote possibility that Charlie was part of the band when this session took place.

Frank Wine-gar and his orchestra

NYC, recording session, 1931?

Titles unknown

Late in 1931 Charlie had eyes for getting a band together. He talked Frank into using some of his men for an engagement at Roseland. Further, he persuaded Frank to front the band. Musicians involved included:

Johnny Fisher, tpt; Harold "Red" Saliers, as; Charlie Barnet, Ralph Spangler, ts; Scoop Thomson, g.

Evidently the band was poorly organized and under-rehearsed as the opening night disintegrated into a jam session, "not exactly what the Roseland management and patrons were used to. The band managed to finish the week, but Frank bowed out after the opening night disaster." (*Waters*)

Following his departure from the Wine-gar band—probably in early 1932—Charlie and some buddies bummed their way musically south and west arriving finally in Los Angeles. On the way they got to know Matty Matlock, Beasley Smith, Sonny Clapp, Flem Ferguson, Jack Purvis, Peanuts Holland, Roy Riley, Henry Schreiber, Hank Biagini, Bob Zurke, and Peck Kelly among others. (*TSY*)

Jack Purvis was with Charlie for a good part of this 1932 southwest swing and was a rich source of anecdotes. Jack "succeeded in amassing at least six wives (some say 12) without benefit of divorce. This later proved his undoing as he was remanded to the Texas State penitentiary for this oversight." (*MS*) Charlie and Jack "arrived in El Paso and of course repaired across the Mexican border to Juarez, where sin reigned on unrestricted. We pretty well tapped ourselves out enjoying the delightful attractions of Juarez, so much so that it appeared some work was in order were we to reach California. Jack got a job at Green Lantern No. 2, a night club in Juarez. I was unable to play in the band because of the Mexican labor laws, which only allowed one American. This might have been very lucky for me as things turned out. It seems that Jack was recognized by somebody who remembered his gun running days and he departed in a fusillade of bullets for the safety of the U.S. I fortunately had elected to spend the evening in one of the many bordellos and was not present to witness or possibly become involved in this escapade. However I did have my own troubles. I had a habit of hiding my money in my socks when visiting dens of iniquity. When I emerged at daylight to hail a cab to return across the border, I seated myself in the back seat. I started groping down inside my socks for my money. The driver of the cab, observing this through his mirror and knowing the possibilities for a reward from U. S. Customs, proceeded to describe my actions to the officials at the border. I was promptly ordered from the cab and subjected to a most extensive search. Then as I stood before them in complete disarray, the customs official said, "A wise guy huh?" I was then informed of Purvis' adventure. I couldn't find hide nor hair of Jack so I proceeded on my way to the Coast, after putting in an SOS to my folks in New York." (*MS*)

"I took a job over in the east Texas oil fields in the town of Kilgore, which at that time was nothing but mud and wooden shacks, but it was smack dab in the middle of a big oil boom area. If you've never been in an oil boom town, you have never lived. If you have, you may not live, that is, to tell of it. These towns attracted all the dregs of the world. One day the law rounded up everybody that was on the street at 2 o'clock in the afternoon, some 1,500 people in all and after processing them, had turned up over 700 people with criminal records. I was working in what was called a keg house. This was nothing more than a public dance hall and brawl room. We started to play at 8 o'clock and continued until 3 A.M., continuously, no intermissions. The only time we got off any earlier would be when the inevitable fight got completely out of hand and the county law would close us down for the night.

"It was some band. The manager of the joint played drums and his wife played the piano. The piano looked and sounded like it had been up in the Yukon and she didn't help any. Her husband had a rhythm beat like an army blanket and the rest of us stayed paralyzed on the available $2.00 per gallon sugar whiskey which was all of two hours old. One morning I staggered home to my hotel and got into a beef with the manager of the coffee shop and first thing I knew I had been bopped on the head with a catsup bottle. I jumped over the counter and had him down on the floor when all of a sudden his wife who weighed about 250 pounds sat down on both of us and started screaming. In the melee he squirmed out from under and through the blood running in my eyes from the effects of the catsup bottle, I saw him hovering around with a big bread knife looking for a chance to stick me with it. Things didn't look so good for me, as I couldn't get out from under the female avoirdupois atop of me. However enter the Texas Rangers in the person of the legendary Gonzales who put a stop to the proceedings." (*MS*)

In LA Charlie gigged around, working for Wes Echols' Dixie Rhythm Kings (Buck Clayton was the trumpet) and Everett Hoagland, among others. During this LA sojourn he wrote his first arrangement, Rube Bloom's *Primitive.* (*TSY*) This trek seems to have been a significant part of his dues paying. "My career at this point had been anything but lucrative and I was always in trouble with my leaders. I had an idea of how music should be played and it didn't seem to concur with the gentlemen I had been working for. It was then that I began considering once again becoming a leader, this time with a full orchestra ... I returned to New York [around February 1932] and commenced rehearsals." (*MS*) A fundamental requirement was a library. He discovered that when Jan Garber decided to go the Lombardo route, his library had been given to his former drummer, Ernie Link. "Ernie had not fared well and I was able to buy the whole library for $20 cash. This deal was consummated in the apartment speakeasy operated by a gent called 'Mitch'" who migrated from place to place as he was busted. Another reason for his troubles "was perhaps the presence always of at least one young lady, whose favors were for hire. The gin was home made and not bad. Nobody ever went blind. It was quite reasonable, $2.00 a fifth and you would put a label on the bottle with your name on it and consume it at your own leisure, being sure that Mitch would stow it away for your return." (*MS*) "I talked a bunch of musicians into rehearsing a library I'd picked up from Jan Garber ... Most of the library was written by Spud [Lyle M.] Murphy ... later I found out that Spud hadn't bothered to write out the fourth saxophone parts, because he'd been playing them himself from memory, so the library wasn't much good to anyone else. But we did salvage maybe 15 complete arrangements." (*Down beat* Sept. 21, 1951).

Chapter 2

Leader 1933–1937

"Realizing that a helping hand was needed to launch my band, I told my uncle, E. K. Gordon, executive of the Knott hotel chain, of my plans. My folks had never approved of my activities and I hardly expected the reactions I received. My uncle introduced me to an executive of CBS, Roy Wilson, who had had a band of his own in earlier days. Roy was most sympathetic and encouraging. He in turn introduced me to a lot of people in the business and offered me counsel in my procedure," with the result that an audition recording was made for World Transcriptions.

Charles Barnet and his orchestra
NYC, World Transcriptions, (Feb. 1932?)

Unknown titles

For a time Charlie co-led the Tommy Christian band:

ca. Feb. 1932, De Witt Club, Syracuse
ca. Feb. 1932, Buffalo

"In the end, though, it was my uncle who provided my big break. It seems the Knott chain was operating the Paramount Hotel on West 46th St. in New York. They had leased out the Grill Room to a syndicate which was having trouble making their rent payments. The hotel had threatened to take back the room and put them out. My uncle had arranged that should this come to pass my orchestra and I would take over the bandstand on behalf of the hotel. For two nights in a row we came to the hotel all dressed and prepared for work, waiting in a suite of rooms upstairs for the green light to mount the bandstand. All the time all sorts of negotiations were going on between the syndicate and the hotel. Finally on the third night the negotiations collapsed, the hotel took over the room and 'Charlie Barnet and his orchestra' became a reality.

"When we got the word up in the suite to move down to the bandstand, you never saw a more nervous bunch of guys. We were not only on Broadway in a New York hotel, but we were broadcasting nightly over the Columbia Broadcasting System, Coast to Coast. Two of the CBS announcers that used to do our programs from the hotel were Harry Von Zell and the late Paul Douglas ... Again I must point out that the big break would never

11:15—William O'Neal, Tenor
11:30—Ted Lewis Orch.
12:00—Belasco Orch.
12:30 A. M.—Nelson Orch.
1:00—Barnet Orch.
1:30—Leroy Orch.

Notes on Dance Orchestras—Harold Stern plays in the Supper Room of the Biltmore, Madison at 43 (Murray Hill 2-7920).* . . . Dick Gasparre plays for supper dancing, Sat. Eves. only, in the Ambassador Grill, Park at 51 (Wickersham 2-1000).* . . . Ozzie Nelson is at the Terrace Restaurant, Hotel New Yorker, 8 Ave. at 34 (Medallion 3-1000). . . . You will find Ted Weems at the Pennsylvania Grill, 7 Ave. at 33 (Pennsylvania 6-5000). . . . Bert Lown is at the Park Central Cocoanut Grove, 7 Ave. at 55 (Circle 7-8000). . . . Charles Barnet plays at the Hotel Paramount Grill, 235 W. 46 (Chickering 4-7560).

Broadway Atmosphere—Club Richman, 157 W. 56 (Columbus 5-1470), drawing the late Broadway crowd; with Jerry Freeman's band, Frances Faye, Gilda Gray, and others. . . . Paradise Restaurant, B'way at 49 (Circle 7-1680), with an elaborate, undressed revue and Abe Lyman's orchestra. . . . Hollywood Restaurant, B'way at 48 (Chickering 4-2572), featuring Ted Lewis and a lively show. . . . Hotel Paramount Grill, 235 W. 46 (Chickering 4-7560), with Charles Barnet's orchestra.

have happened without the help of my uncle, E. K. Gordon, and Roy Wilson."

Collective personnel:

Nathan Van Cleave, Johnny Dillard, Bob Cusumano, Dub Shoffner, Jack Purvis, tpts; Wally Barron, tbn; Ray Eberle, as; Stew Anderson, ts; Billy Speer, bar; Bill Long, Horace Diaz, Jr., p; Bill King, b; Billy Gussack, d; Scoop Thomson, g; Evan Young, vn; Harry Wright, instrument unknown (possibly violin); Helen Nugent, voc. Nathan Van Cleave, arr (MS)

March 2–May 31, 1933: NYC, Paramount Hotel Grill

"Of course every band in NYC that was any kind of a band at all had a Benny Carter arrangement in the book. He wrote more arrangements that he was not paid for, because he had a copyist by the name of Jack Maisel and every time Benny would make an arrangement, Jack would make an extra copy for himself. Jack's room was piled to the ceiling with Benny

. . . Charles Barnet plays at the Hotel Paramount Grill, 235 W. 46 (Chickering 4-7560)

Carter arrangements, and other people's arrangements. And he would go around and sell the arrangements. And so any band at all that was playing arrangements, like Benny Carter's *Take my word* or *Lonesome nights* as it was originally called, and let's see his *Nagasaki* and his *Devil's holiday*, oh they were around in all the books." (*MS*) (Harlow Atwood tells a story about *Devil's holiday* being brought to the Bunny Berigan band as a new chart, and as the rehearsal went on, the band had a rest and no one played at all. Atwood, who had played the arrangement many times with other bands, gave Bunny the word that this was a place for a piano solo.)

During the Paramount engagement, "I remember we went over to play the musicians' ball, which was a command performance ... and we completely broke the place up." (*Sm*)

The band embarked on a road trip after closing at the Paramount. Johnny Dillard and Bob Cusumano did not make the trip but Purvis was in the trumpet section (and doing some arranging) and trumpeter and vocalist Joe Hostetter (Hoste), also joined. ("Purvis was the first person I ever saw using heroin," reports Harlow Atwood.)

ca. early June, 1933: Albany, NY, New Kenmore Hotel
ca. June, 1933 (two weeks): Dayton, OH, Greenwich Village
ca. summer 1933: Columbus, OH, Valley Dale

He disbanded due to the lack of bookings and formed a loose association with Red Norvo. "Red and I had an orchestra together when neither one of us could get steady work. When he got the job he'd stand in front of the band, and usually that was when Mildred Bailey would work ... and he'd do his bit with the xylophone, and I would sit down and play saxophone in the section. And when it was my job, Red would play piano. But it was the same band." (*Sm*) Personnel included Eddie Sauter and probably Chris Griffin, tpts, Russ Jenner, tbn, possibly Hymie Schertzer, as, and Bob White, d. The band made a southern tour including Kentucky and Tennessee (*TSY*), traveling part of the way in Charlie's 1933 Auburn sedan. "I had done some dates up at Brunswick for some of those cover labels like Perfect and Melotone, and the kind of dates where you just walk in and meet and carve up a stock orchestration or something and play it." (*Sm*)

Charles Barnett and his orchestra

Frank "Stinky" Davis, Johnny Dillard, Nathan Van Cleave, tpts; Wally Barron, Abe Lincoln, tbns; Ralph Spangler, Stu Anderson, as and flute; Charlie Barnet; Ted Choate, ts and flute; Bill Long, Horace Diaz, Jr., p; Scoop Thomson, g; Bill King, b; Billy Gussak, d. (Garrod 84)

New York City, American Record Corp. recording session, Oct. 9, 1933

14121-1 **What is sweeter (than the sweetness of I love you)** vHarry Von Zell
Banner 32876; Domino 156; Melotone 12818; Oriole 2778; Perfect 15834; Romeo 2151; *Ajax 104*; **LE JAZZ (E) 8102**

14122-1 **I'm no angel** vHelen Heath
Banner 32875; Domino 155; Melotone 12817; Oriole 2777; Perfect 15833; Romeo 2150; EBW (E) W75; Peacock (E) P-176; *Ajax 104*; **LE JAZZ (E) 8102** [Peacock P-176 as "The Fifth Avenue Band." This was a Decca Custom Pressing issued for and distributed by the UK firm, Peacock Stores. The reverse side is untraced (information from Peter A. Lowe).]

14123-1 **I want you—I need you** vHarry Von Zell [Take 1 has a six-bar intro, starting with vibraphone; CB improvises behind part of tbn melody statement.]
Banner 32875; Domino 155; Melotone M 12817; Oriole 2777; Perfect 15833; Romeo 2150; EBW (E) W75

14124-1 **Buckin' the wind** vHelen Heath
Banner 32876; Domino 156; Oriole 2778;

Perfect 15834; Romeo 2151; Melotone M 12818; *Ajax 104*; LE JAZZ **(E) 8102**

As preceding, Oct. 25, 1933

14123-3 **I want you—I need you** vHarry Von Zell [Take 3 has a four-bar intro. No sax under tbn. Guitar audible.]
Banner 32875; Conqueror 8251; Melotone 12817; Oriole 2777; Perfect 15833; Romeo 2150; (EBW (E) W75?) ["It is possible that this take may also have been used for EBW W-75" (Brian Rust)]; *Ajax 104*; LE JAZZ **(E) 8102**

[Note that **LE JAZZ 8102** is a dub of *Ajax 104*, complete with skips and incorrect playback speeds.]

ca. Oct. 25–Dec. 31, 1933: NYC, Roseland Ballroom

> **Fletcher Henderson has moved out of the Roseland Ballroom, Broadway, for a tour of one-nighters up to Jan. 1. Charles Bartnett has the Roseland assignment.**

At Roseland the band first played opposite Claude Hopkins and then Mal Hallett.

John Best recalls hearing the band there when Charlie was playing opposite Claude Hopkins. During one number Charlie hit a high note on the tenor, then trilled it, and several men from Hopkins' band stood up to see how this sound was being made and where it was coming from.

Adrian Rollini and his orchestra (Brunswick issues as by Adrian's Ramblers.)

Pat Circirello, tpt; Jimmy Dorsey, cl, as; ***Charlie Barnet****, ts; Adrian Rollini, bsx; (Charlie Magnante?), pac; Fulton McGrath, p; Carl Kress, g; Gene Krupa, d (Rust JR)*

NYC, Brunswick recording session, February 26, 1934

14857-1 **Keep on doin' what you're doin'** vChick Bullock
Br 6786; Br (E) 01750

14858-1 **Get goin'** vChick Bullock
Br 6786; Br (E) 01750

14859-1 **A hundred years from today** vChick Bullock
Voc 2675

Charles Barnet and his orchestra

Toots Camarata, Benny Carter, Nathan Van Cleave, tpts; Wally Barron, tbn; Nat Brown, Milton Laufer, as; Willard Brady, Ted Choate, ts; Horace Diaz, Jr., p; (Adrian Rollini?), vbs; Marty Britt, g; George Nida or Tex Hurst, b; Joe Dale, d (Garrod 84)

NYC, American Recording Corp. record session, March 23, 1934

14985-1 **Butterfingers** aBenny Carter, vHelen Heath
Rejected

14986-1 **Infatuation** aBenny Carter, vHelen Heath
Banner 33015; Conqueror 8281; Melotone M 12974; Perfect 15912; Romeo 2246; Oriole 2872; *Ajax 104*; LE JAZZ **(E) 8102**

14987-1 **I lost another sweetheart** aBenny Carter, vJackie Martin
Banner 33033; Melotone M 12992; Oriole 2884; Perfect 15923; Romeo 2258; *Ajax 104*; LE JAZZ **(E) 8102**

14988-1 **Emaline** aBenny Carter, vCharlie Barnet
Banner 33033; Melotone M 12992; Perfect 15923; Oriole 2884; Romeo 2258; *Ajax 104*; LE JAZZ **(E) 8102**

"... They had Benny Carter make some arrangements for some of those things and oh, Joe Higgins was in charge of it. He just hit the ceiling. He said, 'What are you trying to do to me? All this doodley doop.' He said, 'We just want the melody.' And he cut one of Benny Carter's arrangements, he just said, 'I won't even issue that.' And it was great you know. And we had to come back and make the stock orchestration of the tune ... about a week later." (*Sm*)

"We had also done another of those

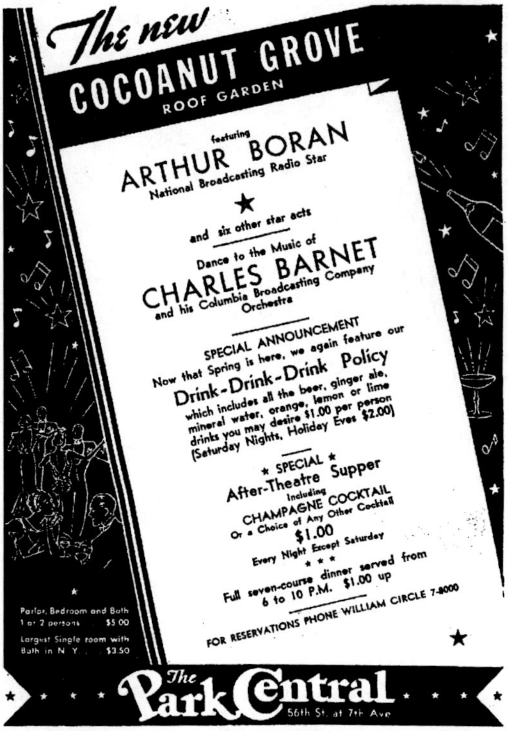

NIGHT CLUB REVIEW

Coconut Grove, New York

Coconut Grove, atop the Park Central Hotel, is one of the better cooling-off spots within the city limits. Food and service are very good, under the management.... Norman does three numbers, last one being a return after a second routine for the Co-Eds. Impersonator's change of voice into his natural baritone, as always, gets a surprise and a good hand.

Music is from Charles Barnett's Orchestra, a crack band. Ruth Robbins, also a CBS act, as is Barnett, is the vocalist. She has a pleasing voice and nice rhythm.

FRANKEN.

10:00—Gray Orch.; Stoopnagle and Budd, Comedians; Connie Boswell, Songs
10:30—Harlem Serenade
11:00—Charles Carlile, Tenor
11:15—News; Barnett Orch.
11:45—Light Orch.
12:00—Bosnik Orch.
12:30 A. M.—Belasco Orch.
1:00—Robbins Orch.

COCOANUT GROVE At Park Central Hotel, 56th & 7th Ave. Charles Barnet's Orchestra and the Tick Tock Girls. Continuous Entertainment. Seven-Course Dinner $1.25. No Cover Charge. No tipping allowed. After 10:30 P. M. minimum charge per person $1.50 Sundays and week nights; $2.00 Friday nights; $2.50 Saturday nights, Holiday evenings and special nights. Phone William, Circle 7-8000.

nothing record dates, on which [Benny Carter] played trumpet and wrote all the arrangements." (*TSY,* p.66)

Charles Barnett and his orchestra

NYC, American Record Corp. recording session, March 29, 1934

14985-3 **Butterfingers** aBenny Carter; vHelen Heath
Banner 33015; Conqueror 8281; Melotone M 12974; Oriole 2872; Perfect 15912; Romeo 2246; *Ajax 104*; LE JAZZ **(E) 8102**

15020-1 **Baby, take a bow** aBenny Carter, vJackie Martin
Banner 33029; Fox Movietone F 112; Melotone M 12988; Oriole 2880; Perfect 15919; Romeo 2254; *Ajax 104*; LE JAZZ **(E) 8102**

15021-1 **This is our last night together** aBenny Carter, vJackie Martin
Banner 33029; Fox Movietone F 112; Melotone M 12988; Oriole 2880; Perfect 15919; Romeo 2254; *Ajax 104*; LE JAZZ **(E) 8102**

(Feb. or March) 1934: NYC, Cocoanut Grove, Park Central Hotel
(substituted for Ozzie Nelson for two week period)

April (2?)–Oct. 1, 1934: NYC, Cocoanut Grove, Park Central Hotel

The band for the Park Central engagement included at various times Eddie Sauter, Toots Camarata, Terry Shand, Mort Dixon, Milt Laufer, Nat Brown, Jackie Martin, Mart Britt, Pete Peterson, Joe Dale, Chris Griffin and possibly Neil Reed. Benny Carter sat in occasionally. Garnet Clark played intermission piano and was also used on one nighters. Ram Ramirez also performed. The girl singer was Ruth Robbins. Known as "The Happy Dozen," the band's theme at this time was *I lost another sweetheart*. The band broadcast on WABC on Friday nights and was heard at midnight on Saturdays and from 11:00–11:30 Sundays on WOR. Harry Salter succeeded Charlie.

Summer 1934: NYC, Saturday Night Swing Session (CBS)

For his appearance on "Saturday Night Swing Session" he played, among other things, *There's a house in Harlem for sale* by James Van Heusen. This was the first time the song was heard on the air.

Baton and Golf Club.

The danceable rhythms of Charlie Barnet's orchestra draws listeners to his WABC - Columbia network programs. Charlie is just twenty years old — and besides wielding a baton he likes to swing a golf club.

Charlie Barnet

Red Norvo and his Swing Septet

Red Norvo, x; Jack Jenney, tbn; Artie Shaw, cl; ***Charlie Barnet****, ts; Teddy Wilson, p; Bobby Johnson, g; Hank Wayland, b; Billy Gussak, d (Rust JR)*

NYC, Columbia recording session, Sept. 26, 1934

16021-A **Old fashioned love**
Col 3059-D; 35688; Col (E) (Eu) DB/MC5102; *Epic JEE 22009, LG/LN3128; Philips (N?) BBL 7077; Time-LifeSTLJ 14; Sounds of Swing LP122*; Col RJ 44118; **Col RK 44118; Hep (E) CD 1044; Giants of Jazz (It) CD 53283; Affinity (E) CDAFS 1017; Classics (Fr) 1085**

16021-B **Old fashioned love**
Meritt LP 3

16021-C **Old fashioned love**
Meritt LP 3

16022-A **I surrender, dear**
Col 2977-D; 35688; Col (E) (Eu) DB/MC 5012; *Epic JEE 22009, LG/LN 3128; Philips (N?) BBL7077; Sounds of Swing LP 122*; Col RJ 44118; **Col RK 44118; Hep (E) CD 1044; Affinity (E) CDAFS 1017; Classics (Fr) 1085**

16022-B **I surrender, dear**
Meritt LP 3

As preceding, October 4, 1934

16033-A **Tomboy**
Col 2977-D; Col (E) MC 3031; Parlophone (E) R-2110; *Epic JEE 22009, LG/LN 3128; Philips (N?) BBL 7077; Sounds of Swing LP 122; BBC (E) REB 666*; Col RJ 44118; **Col RK 44118; BBC (E) REB666; CDS (E) CDS666; CDS (Ger) RPCD 305; Hep (E) CD 1044; Affinity CDAFS 1017; ASV (E) 5431; Classics (Fr) 1085**

16033-B **Tomboy**
Meritt LP 3

16034-A **The night is blue**
Col 3026-D; Parlophone (E) R-2088; *Epic JEE 22009,JSN 6042, LG/LN 3128, BN 24029; Col (E) 33-SX 511; Philips (N?) BBL 7077; Sounds of Swing LP 122*; Col RJ 44118; **Col RK 44118; Affinity (E) CDAFS 1017; Hep (E) CD 1044; Classics (Fr) 1085**

Chris Griffin, Toots Camarata, Eddie Sauter, tpts; Russ Jenner, Neil Reed, tbns; George Bone, Les Cooper, Jack Henderson, Dan Morris, reeds; (Bill Miller?), p; Peter Peterson, b; Rudy De Julius, d; Marion Nichols, voc (TSY, p. 28)

ca. Sept. 1934: NYC, Roseland (opposite Fletcher Henderson; possibly doubling from Park Central?)
ca. Oct. 6-19, 1934: (NYC? Providence, RI?), Arcadia Ballroom
ca. Oct. 1934: Waltham, Mass., Nutting's-on-the-Charles
ca. Oct. 1934: Boston, Roseland State Ballroom
ca. Oct. 1934: Wildwood, NJ, site unknown
Nov. 9-15, 1934: NYC, Apollo Theater

The Fletcher Henderson band was scheduled to break up at about the end of October and Benny Carter had signed a

Maestro

CHARLES BARNET, versatile conductor of a band famous for its dance music and widely popular with radio audiences. On December 29 he will open an engagement in the Blue Room of The Roosevelt, where he promises the same type of orchestration that has gained him fame.

New Year's Eve Party in The BLUE ROOM with CHARLEY BARNET and his CBS Orchestra. $10 per person. Phone MAin 3920 for reservations.

The music of Charley Barnett and his orchestra, usually heard over WDSU at 10:30 p. m., will be heard today at 10:15 p. m. in order that WDSU may broadcast the opening of the President's Birthday Ball.

capacity . . . and he'll have more than that! The Tip Top Inn is being converted into a swanky night club for the night with Mickey Alpert and his orchestra holding forth there along with a complete floor show. Charles Barnet and his New York orchestra (new in the Blue Room) will have a special New Year's Eve show for the $10 customers. . . .

Charles Barnet, new maestro at the Blue Room, won't be a stranger here long...In fact he's made many friends now...he's that type!

CHARLIE BARNETT and his orchestra have had their engagement at the Hotel Roosevelt, New Orleans, extended another four weeks. Vibrant voiced Marion Nichols is vocalist. Combo is broadcasting over local station nightly.

contract to appear at the Apollo intending to use most of the Henderson musicians. However, Henderson secured an engagement at the Graystone Ballroom in Detroit for the first week of November so Benny was left without a band. "Believe it or not there was a shortage of guys that could read … [so] Benny recommended us." (*Sm*) (The headliners were Pigmeat Markham and Ada Brown.) This was very probably the first appearance at the Apollo by a white entertainer. Charlie recalled that amateur night was a highlight of the evening but "If the audience didn't care for one of the amateurs, they were very definite in their reaction which was climaxed by the appearance on stage of one of the stage hands, dressed in a ballet costume or some other ridiculous get up. He was known as Porto Rico and he would lead the offender off stage and there would follow a loud gun shot as Rico would supposedly dispose of the unfortunate and untalented contestant … One of Rico's other talents was being the possessor of the foulest vocabulary in existence, which he generously used upon the slightest provocation. Sometimes without provocation." (*MS*)

"Charlie Barnet, the 'spoilt brat of music' … He introduced me to his mother as 'Lord Calvert', she curtsied and embraced me, an embarassing moment. My 1934–36 years with 'Clap hands here comes Charlie' was a 'doozy', even though I enjoyed the 'swing'." (*DeJ*)

(ca. Dec.?) 1934: Cedar Grove, NJ, Meadowbrook (1 week)

(ca. Dec.?) 1934: Long Island, NY, Pavillon Royal

Dec. 1934: Buffalo, site unknown

"Playing one of his very first engagements [at the Pavillon Royal] was Charlie Barnet who would grow embarrassed when the management would relay a phone wire from his mother insisting that he should be careful to wear his red flannel underwear." (*Variety,* Dec. 1, 1948) Following the Buffalo engagement the band members made their way to New Orleans (Chris Griffin and Marion Nichols took a Greyhound bus). "It was a cooperative band, incidentally." (*Sm*)

> Barnet has been doing unusually well and is improving steadily. His popularity is growing too, due, no doubt, to his anxiety to please . . . and there is none who can come nearer granting all requests than this versatile young maestro. He was asked the other night to play the old Nora Bayes song hit "Just Like A Gypsy." "Never heard it," said Charles, "but if you'll hum the melody, I'll play it." He listened to the humming and went back to the band stand. None of his boys had heard it either (it was popular back in 1917 and 1918) but a few minutes later the orchestra was playing it as if they were reading from a complete orchestration.

Eddie Sauter, Chris Griffin, Toots Camarata, tpts; Russ Jenner, (Bill McVeigh? Frank Llewellyn?), tbns; Les Cooper (lead), George Bone, as; Charlie Barnet, Fred Fellensby, ts; Rupe Biggadike, p; Buford Turner, g; Pete Peterson, b and bb; Rudy DeJulius, d; Marion Nichols, voc (DeJ and Sm)

Dec. 29, 1934–Feb. 8, 1935: New Orleans, Roosevelt Hotel

As Charlie notes in *TSY,* his was the first out-of-town band to play at the conservative and dicty Roosevelt Hotel where they replaced a local group led by Mickey Alpert. They were well received by the management, who let them know that in effect they had the job for as long as they wanted it.

Eli Oberstein recorded the band with Victor's portable equipment, "in some loft up there." Rudy De Julius remembers that Eli intended to record a black band but its intonation was bad, so he asked Charlie if he could record his band. The band regularly broadcast on New Orleans station WDSU at 7:15 from the Fountain Room and usually at 10:30 from the Blue Room, where "vibrant voiced" Marion Nichols was to be heard (*New Orleans Times-Picayune,* Jan. 21, 1935; *Billboard,* Feb. 9, 1935). "We used to play the dinner session in the Fountain Room … and then we'd have to pack the instruments up and go into the Blue Room."

> Charley Barnet thinks he's set a new kind of record. He's broadcasting 35 times a week now on various Blue Room and Fountain Room periods at the Roosevelt.

Huey Long frequented the hotel and there are conflicting stories about his behavior: Charlie says he was a pussy cat, Rudy De Julius says he was a boor. Both observers agree that Huey was always accompanied by his bodyguards. Long always wore a gold toothpick on a chain—also gold—around his neck (*Griffin*). Charlie notes, "He liked *Stars fell on Alabama.* I don't know why, but that and that Jack Benny theme song, *Love in bloom.*" (*Sm*). Will Rogers was often in the audience, and contrary to some reports, he liked the music. (*DeJ*)

Charles Barnet and his orchestra

(Personnel as preceding. No names are listed on Victor session sheet, which notes only "4 saxes, 3 trumpets, trombone, guitar, str. bass, piano & trapman." A violinist who may be Biggadike is heard on "I'm keeping those keepsakes" as is a brass bass.)

New Orleans, RCA Victor recording session, Jan. 21, 1935

87642-1 **Growlin'** aHead
BB B5816; HMV (E) X-4490 [Reverse is

Fats Waller *Alligator crawl*]; *BB AXM2 5526*; *RCA(Fr) PM 45689*; *PM 42401*; Ajax C-712; **RCA 2135554-2; Jazz Archives (Fr) 30; Giants of Jazz (It) CD 53274; Zeta (Ger) ZET 749; Le jazz (E) 8102; Jazz Greats (E) CD 071; RCA (Fr) 74321355542**

87642-2 **Growlin'** aHead
Unissued

87643-1 **Nagasaki** aBenny Carter
BB B5815°; HMV X-4495; *BB AXM2 5526*; *RCA (Fr) PM 45689*; *RCA (Fr) PM 42401*; *RCA (Fr) PM 43259*; Ajax C-712; **RCA 2135554-2; Best of Jazz (Fr) 4039; Jazz Archives (Fr) 30; Giants of Jazz (It) CD 53274; Zeta (Ger) ZET 749; Le Jazz (E) 8102; RCA (Fr) 74321355542; Masters of Jazz (Fr) CD 59**

87643-2 **Nagasaki** aBenny Carter
Unissued

87644-1 **I'm keeping those keepsakes** vMarion Nichols
BB B 5814; *BB AXM2 5526*; Ajax C-712; **Le Jazz (E) 8102**

87644-2 **I'm keeping those keepsakes** vMarion Nichols
Unissued

87645-1 **Fare thee well, Annabelle** aEddie Sauter, vMarion Nichols
BB B5815°; HMV (E) X-4495; Regal Zonophone (E) MR-1762; **Le Jazz (E) 8102**

87465-2 **Fare thee well, Annabelle** aEddie Sauter, vMarion Nichols
BB AXM2-5526; Ajax C-712;

87646-1 **Don't be afraid to tell your mother** vMarion Nichols
BB B5814; Regal Zonophone (E) MR-1642; *BB AXM2 5526*; Ajax C-712; **Le Jazz (E) 8102**

87646-2 **Don't be afraid to tell your mother** vMarion Nichols
Unissued

87647-1 **On a holiday** aBenny Carter
BB B5816; *BB AXM2 5526*; *RCA (Fr) PM 45689*; *RCA (Fr) PM 42401*; *Ajax C-712*; **RCA 2135554-2; Jazz Archives (Fr) 30; Giants of Jazz (It) 53274; Zeta (Ger) ZET 749; Le Jazz (E) 8102; RCA (Fr) 74321355542; Masters of Jazz (Fr) CD 59**

87647-2 **On a holiday** aBenny Carter
Unissued

Interested spectators in the Blue Room one night late in January were members of the Guy Lombardo band who were in town for a series of engagements and who came by after one of their gigs. (*DeJ*)

Charlie's job came to an end early in February following an incident, probably incidents. The circumstances are not at all clear in detail, but there is no doubt that the hotel manager, Seymour Weiss, decided he had to get rid of Charlie and his band. By one account there was some kind of frame up involving musicians and the red light district. By another, the band began playing too loudly, and "we were definitely playing too much jazz for the Blue Room." (*TSY*, 64) Charlie acknowledged that "I culminated and compounded our engagement by appearing in the lobby of the hotel in my bathrobe, a bottle of gin in one hand, and an equally attired blonde, supposedly the property of one of the local politicians on the other arm." (*MS*) By yet another recounting, he was late for a performance so the band played without him. When he finally showed up he was smashed, and accompanied by a handsome black lady with whom he insisted on dancing—a short-lived dance as they both fell to the floor (and as Weiss later told him, the hotel was not ready for integration). (*DeJulius*) "There was a setup of a kind, but the way it happened was Seymour Weiss called Milton Romer and said, 'Look, will you get this band out of here? They're driving me crazy.' So Milton went along. He called me and said, 'Look, I've got a job for you in Miami Beach. Would you like to work there?' And I said, 'Oh, yeah.' He said, 'Well, give your notice.' There wasn't any job in Miami Beach. We gave our notice [another version: Weiss gave them one week to get out of town] and of course, we were out." (*Sm*) Charlie summed it up by saying, "Aside from the public's general animosity, and the fact that I had blown all my loot at the racetrack, I must admit now that the hotel was justified in firing us. The conduct of the band was, ah, not commendable." (*MS*) By conspiracy or whatever, Charlie was through and the band broke up.

Back in New York he gigged around, sometimes using members of his "New Orleans band" and got married, for the first time, to Joyce O'Day, "a young lady who savored of life like I did." This union was ill-fated and within a few days had fallen apart. On the advice of a booker Charlie fronted a band formed in Boston by Vin Gary, and embarked on a southern college tour.

Winter/Spring 1935: Lexington, VA, Washington & Lee Univ.
Spring 1935?: Miami, FL, Gang Plank Club (4 weeks)

He led a five-piece band at the Gang Plank. "Oh, it was a horrible band. They used local Miami musicians, and the only note that came out of the bass player was the slap, and it was terrible." (*Sm*) To stay clear of Joyce, who with her lawyer was looking for a generous alimony settlement, Charlie booked passage on a ship for Havana. "As the boat pulled away from the dock, I stood out on the aft deck as my wife's subpoena servers rushed up. I hollered at them, 'Millions for defense but not one cent for alimony.'" (*MS*)

In Cuba "I kind of worked as a gigolo there ... I met some guys around Sloppy Joe's bar ... these women would come in on these cruise boats ... and you'd take them around and you'd get paid for it ... at the time it was fun, but that's not one of the proudest moments of my life, I'll tell you that ... I stayed in Havana for the better part of four months." (*Sm*)

Following a satisfactory resolution of the Joyce O'Day affair, he set about forming another band in New York City.

Aug. 29, 1935: Claremont, NH, Roseland Ballroom (aka Rose-land Crystal Ballroom)

Charles Barnett and his orchestra

Frank Amaral, Kermit Simmons, tpts; Joe Hostetter, tpt, tbn; Buzz Smith, John Doyle, tbns; George Vaughn, Don Morris, as; Willard Brady, Bob Parks, ts; Horace Diaz, Jr., p; Frank Klinger, g; Sid Weiss, b; Julie Mendelson, d (Edw 65)

NYC, American Record Corp., May 13, 1936

19241-1 **My first thrill** aHorace Diaz, Jr.; vBob Parks [On label as Robert Parkes]
ARC 6-07-12 [Melotone; Oriole]; *Ajax LP 104*; LE JAZZ (E) 8102

19242-1 **The swing waltz** aGlenn Osser, vJoe Hostetter [On label as Joe Host]
ARC 6-07-13 [Melotone; Perfect]; *Ajax LP 104*; LE JAZZ (E) 8102

19243-1 **Cross patch** aGlenn Osser; vCharlie Barnet
ARC 6-07-13 [Melotone; Perfect]; *Ajax 106*; LE JAZZ (E) 8102

19244-1 **Too good to be true** aHorace Diaz, Jr.; vCharlie Barnet
ARC 6-07-12 [Melotone; Oriole]; *Ajax 106*; LE JAZZ (E) 8102

April 1936? Boston, Normandie Ballroom

> JUST-OUT-OF-TOWN—Ben Riley's Arrowhead Inn, Riverdale Ave. at 246 (Kingsbridge 6-2000), with Irving Conn's orchestra. . . . Riviera, at the Jersey end of the George Washington Bridge (Ft. Lee 8-2000), opens Thurs., May 21, with Enric Madriguera's orchestra and a floor show. . . . **Glen Island Casino, off the Shore Road, New Rochelle, N.Y. (Hamilton 4480), opens Thurs., May 21, with Charles Barnet's orchestra.**

Metronome noted that "A dark horse has captured the much sought after Glen Island Casino spot. Charley Barnet's the lad. Story is that Barnet and the operators of the Casino have formed a corporation. Barnet, who used to have a good band in New York's Park Central Hotel a few years back, should do nicely. He, himself, is an excellent tenor sax man, a good enough vocalist, and makes a splendid appearance.

As to be expected, the band, in its formative stage, is still pretty ragged, but Barnet has been around long enough to be successful in whipping an aggregation into good shape." (May 1936)

"I was very fortunate in getting the summer season at the Glen Island Casino, a spot that had been magic for the Casa Loma band and the Dorsey Brothers in projecting them into national popularity … We opened and while business was good, our brand of music was not having the impact that had favored my predecessors." (*MS*)

The Casino closed at 1AM, and often when the place had cleared out, the band would run through a new batch of arrangements for an hour or so.

May 21–ca Sept. 13, 1936: New Rochelle, NY, Glen Island Casino

The band broadcast regularly on WABC (CBS) on Saturdays 5:30PM–6:00, Sunday nights at midnight and Thursdays at either 5:30PM or midnight. It was also carried by WOR.

New Rochelle, NY, Glen Island Casino, WABC b'cast, May 27, 1936

When you're low
Sunshine at midnight vJoe Hoste
Spring in Vienna
Cross patch vCharlie Barnet
In a little wayside inn
Dream lullaby (closing theme)

Charlie Barnet and his Glen Island Casino orchestra

Frank Amaral, Kermit Simmons, Joe Hoste, tpts; Buzz Smith, Johnny Doyle, tbns; George Vaughn, Don Morris, Willard Brady, Bob Parks, reeds; Horace Diaz, Jr., p; Frank Klinger, g, st-g; Sid Weiss, b; Jules Mendelson, d (ViSS)

NYC, RCA Victor recording session, June 1, 1936

101645-1 **I'm an old cowhand** aHorace Diaz, Jr.; vJoe Hoste
BB B6448°; Regal Zonophone (E) MR-2188; *BB AXM2 5526*; Ajax C-712; **Le Jazz (E) 8102**

101645-2 **I'm an old cowhand** aHorace Diaz, Jr.; vJoe Hoste
Unissued

101646-1 **But definitely** aHorace Diaz, Jr.; vLaura Deane
BB B6433°; Regal Zonophone (E) MR-2187; Twin (India) FT-8129; Vi (Arg) JR-63; *BB AXM2 5526*; Ajax C-712

101646-2 **But definitely** aHorace Diaz, Jr.; vLaura Deane
Unissued

101647-1 **Long ago and far away** aHorace Diaz, Jr.; vCharlie Barnet
BB B6432°; Twin (India) FT-8164; *BB AXM2 5526*; Ajax C-712

101648-1 **When I'm with you** aHorace Diaz, Jr.; vBob Parks
BB B6433°; Regal Zonophone (E) MR-2187; Twin (India) FT-8129; Vi (Arg) JR 63; *BB AXM2 5526*; Ajax C-712

101649-1 **Where is my heart** aHorace Diaz, Jr.; vJoe Hoste
BB B6432°; *BB AXM2 5526*; Ajax C-712

101650-1 **Empty saddles** aHorace Diaz, Jr.; vJoe Hoste
BB B6448°; Regal Zonophone (E) MR-2188; Vi(Arg) JR-66; *BB AXM2 5526*; Ajax C-712

101650-2 **Empty saddles** aHorace Diaz, Jr.; vJoe Hoste
Unissued

During June the band was augmented by a singing group which had formerly performed with the Ozzie Nelson band (where they were known as "The Wizards of Ozzie"). There is disagreement as to who came up with the name by which the group became well known—Charlie says he thought it up, Hal "Spook" Dickinson says *he* named them—but be that as it may, the Barnet Modern-Aires became part of Charlie's band for that summer. The singers were Billy Conway, Spook Dickinson and Chuck Goldstein. Jack Lathrop also sang with them, joining in early August. On September 24, Ralph Brewster left the Henry Halstead band and replaced Lathrop.

Charlie and one of his arrangers were driving in Charlie's car and the Mab reminisced about his days in Havana. "I got the worst dose of the clap I ever had from a lady down there." "Well, how did you get rid of it?" "I didn't—I just got used to it," Charlie cracked.

New Rochelle, NY, Glen Island Casino, WOR b'cast (10:45), July 17, 1936

Dear old southland
Stop, look and listen
You're not the kind (vCharlie Barnet?)
Christopher Columbus
Without a shadow of a doubt vJoe Hoste
Stompin' at the Savoy
These foolish things

As preceding, WABC b'cast, 12:30PM, July 23, 1936

Yeah man (aFletcher Henderson?)
Robins and roses vBarnet Modern-Aires
My first thrill
My melancholy baby
You're not the kind vCharlie Barnet
I'm an old cowhand vJoe Hoste
Sophisticated lady
Stop, look and listen vBarnet Modern-Aires
The Dixieland band vCharlie Barnet
King Porter stomp aFletcher Henderson

As preceding, July 30, 1936

'Tain't good (like a nickel made of wood)
My blue heaven
When I'm with you vBarnet Modern-Aires
Down south camp meetin' aFletcher Henderson
These foolish things vCharlieBarnet
Between the Devil and the deep blue sea
Stompin' at the Savoy
Living from day to day vJoe Hoste

Charlie Barnet and his Glen Island Casino orchestra

George Kennedy, Kermit Simmons, Irving Goodman, tpts; Buzz Smith, Johnny Doyle, Joe Hoste, tbns; Willard Brady, Don Morris, George Vaughn, Bob Parks, reeds; Horace Diaz, Jr., p; Buford Turner, g; Sid Weiss, b; Billy Flanagan, d. Barnet Modern-Aires (Ralph Brewster, Billy Conway, Harold "Spook" Dickinson, Chuck Goldstein), voc. (ViSS)

NYC, RCA Victor recording session, August 3, 1936

102406-1 **Until the real thing comes along** aHorace Diaz, Jr.; vCharlie Barnet
BB B6487; *AXM2 5526*; Ajax C-712

102406-2 **Until the real thing comes along** aHorace Diaz, Jr. or; vCharlie Barnet
Unissued

102407-1 **Make believe ballroom** aHorace Diaz, Jr.; vBarnet Modern-Aires
BB B6504°; *BB AXM2 5526*; *Reader's Digest RD4-25-1 (mono and fake stereo)*; *Reader's Digest (Ja) 9S (number?)*; *Bandstand 7123*; Ajax C-712; Reader's Digest RD-3; READER'SDIGEST RD-8 5384, RD-5 025-1/1 (8-track); **READER'S DIGEST RB-7 002, RDD025/CD11; AERO SPACE RACD 7123**

102407-2 **Make believe ballroom** aHorace Diaz, Jr.; vBarnet Modern-Aires
Unissued

102408-1 **Bye-bye, baby** aHorace Diaz, Jr.; vBarnet Modern-Aires
BB B6504°; Regal Zonophone (E) MR-2214; *BB AXM2 5526*; Ajax C-716

102408-2 **Bye-bye, baby** aHorace Diaz, Jr.; vBarnet Modern-Aires
Unissued

102409-1 **A star fell out of heaven** aHorace Diaz, Jr.; vJoe Hoste
BB B6488; Regal Zonophone (E) MR-2195; *BB AXM2 5526*; Ajax C-716

102409-2 **A star fell out of heaven** aHorace Diaz, Jr.; vJoe Hoste
Unissued

102410-1 **When did you leave heaven?** aHorace Diaz, Jr.; vJoe Hoste
Bluebird B6488; Regal Zonophone (E) MR-2213; Twin (India) FT-8170; *BB AXM2 5526*; Ajax C-716

102411-1 **Always** aHorace Diaz, Jr.
BB B6487; *BB AXM2 5526*; *RCA (Fr) PM 45689*; AjaxC-716; **RCA 2135554-2; Jazz archives (Fr) 30;Giants of jazz (It) CD 53274; Zeta (Ger) ZET 749; RCA (Fr) 74321355542**

102411-2 **Always** aHorace Diaz, Jr.
Unissued

New Rochelle, NY, Glen Island Casino, WABC b'cast, 12:30PM, August 6, 1936

Dream lullaby (opening theme)
Always
Until the real thing comes along aHorace Diaz, Jr.; vCharlie Barnet
Bye-bye baby vBarnet Modern-Aires
A star fell out of heaven vJoe Hoste
My melancholy baby
You're not the kind vCharlie Barnet
Make believe ballroom aHorace Diaz, Jr.
These foolish things vCharlie Barnet
My blue heaven
Toodle-oo

As preceding, 5:45PM, August 8, 1936

I'm an old cowhand vJoe Hoste
Robins and roses vBarnet Modern-Aires
When I'm with you vBarnet Modern-Aires
Cross patch vCharlie Barnet
Rosetta
My first thrill
King Porter stomp aFletcher Henderson
Night and day aHead
Anything goes
Bye-bye, baby vBarnet Modern-Aires
Down south camp meetin' aFletcher Henderson

As preceding, 12:30PM, August 13, 1936

King Porter stomp aFletcher Henderson
When I'm with you vBarnet Modern-Aires
Stompin' at the Savoy vBarnet Modern-Aires
You're not the kind vCharlie Barnet
Blue skies
Me and the moon vBarnet Modern-Aires
Down south camp meetin' aFletcher Henderson
A star fell out of heaven

As preceding, August 15, 1936

I've lost another sweetheart (opening theme)
Swingtime in the Rockies aJimmy Mundy
Me and the moon vBarnet Modern-Aires
My melancholy baby
I can't escape from you vJoe Hoste
Until today vJoe Hoste
So nice of you vJoe Hoste
Bye-bye, baby vBarnet Modern-Aires
The Dixieland band vCharlie Barnet
Would you vJoe Hoste
Honeysuckle rose (aHorace Henderson?)
When did you leave heaven vJoe Hoste

As preceding, August 17, 1936

Swingtime in the Rockies aJimmy Mundy
Until the real thing comes along aHorace Diaz, Jr.; vCharlie Barnet
Me and the moon vBarnet Modern-Aires
The darktown strutters' ball
Take my heart
Stop, look and listen vBarnet Modern-Aires
'Way down yonder in New Orleans
Did I remember
Make believe ballroom aHorace Diaz, Jr., vBarnet Modern-Aires
Down south camp meetin' aFletcher Henderson

NYC, "Make Believe Ballroom," WNEW broadcast, 11:30PM, Aug. 20, 1936

Bye-bye, baby vBarnet Modern-Aires
My melancholy baby
When I'm with you vBarnet Modern-Aires
The darktown strutters' ball
Me and the moon vBarnet Modern-Aires
Blue skies
Robins and roses vBarnet Modern-Aires
My first thrill vBarnet Modern-Aires
The Dixieland band vCharlie Barnet
Yeah man (aFletcher Henderson?)
Between the Devil and the deep blue sea
Blue moon vBarnet Modern-Aires
Moonglow vBarnet Modern-Aires
Stompin' at the Savoy vBarnet Modern-Aires
Make believe ballroom vBarnet Modern-Aires

New Rochelle, NY, Glen Island Casino, WABC b'cast, Aug. 22, 1936

Jazz marches on (Charlie Barnet's history of jazz) [duration 7 min.] "Several songs—Africa, Dixieland band, no swing (1929), swing (1936) *Dear old southland.*" (Bob Inman notation, 1936)
Dear old southland (aAndy Gibson?)
Stop, look and listen vBarnet Modern-Aires
'Way down yonder in New Orleans

As preceding, 5:30PM, August 22, 1936

I've lost another sweetheart (opening theme)
Always
So nice of you vCharlie Barnet
Make believe ballroom vBarnet Modern-Aires
A star fell out of heaven vJoe Hoste
Rosetta
Jazz marches on (Charlie Barnet's history of jazz) vCharlie Barnet
Stop, look and listen vBarnet Modern-Aires
My melancholy baby
'Way down yonder in New Orleans

As preceding, 5:30PM, August 29, 1936

Down south camp meetin' aFletcher Henderson
Me and the moon vBarnet Modern-Aires
Three little words
Four or five times
Midnight and you
Sweet misery of love
I can't escape from you
Darktown strutters' ball
She shall have music
Moonglow vBarnet Modern-Aires
A star fell out of heaven vHal Dickinson
'Way down yonder in New Orleans

As preceding, 12:00PM, August 30, 1936

I've lost another sweetheart (opening theme)
Always aHorace Diaz, Jr.
You're not the kind vCharlie Barnet
Bye-bye, baby aHorace Diaz, Jr.; vBarnet Modern-Aires *If we never meet again* vHal Dickinson
King Porter stomp aFletcher Henderson
Jazz marches on (Charlie Barnet's history of jazz) vCharlie Barnet

Stop, look and listen vBarnet Modern-Aires
I'm an old cowhand vHal Dickinson
'Tain't no good (like a nickel made of wood)

As preceding, September 3, 1936

Three little words
Stop, look and listen vBarnet Modern-Aires
Jangled nerves
It's the talk of the town
Four or five times
Stompin' at the Savoy
Yeah man (aFletcher Henderson?)

As preceding, 5:30PM, September 5, 1936

I've lost another sweetheart (opening theme)
Symphony in riffs aBenny Carter
It was a sad night in Harlem vBarnet Modern-Aires
Without a shadow of a doubt
Through the courtesy of love
Riffin'
You're not the kind vCharlie Barnet
It all begins and ends with you

As preceding, 12:00PM, September 10, 1936

Make believe ballroom vBarnet Modern-Aires
If we never meet again
Jazz marches on (Charlie Barnet's history of jazz) vCharlie Barnet
These foolish things vCharlie Barnet
Three little words
It's the talk of the town

Charlie Barnet and his orchestra

George Kennedy, Kermit Simmons, Irving Goodman, tpts; Johnny Doyle, Sonny Lee, tbns; Willard Brady, Don Morris, George Vaughn, Murray Williams, reeds; Horace Diaz, Jr., p; Scoop Thomson, g; Sid Weiss, b; Billy Flanagan, d (ViSS)

NYC, RCA Victor recording session, September 24, 1936

541-1 **The milkmen's matinee** a Horace Diaz, Jr.; vBarnet Modern-Aires
BB B6593°; *BB AXM2 5526*; Ajax C-716

542-1 **Rainbow on the river** aHorace Diaz, Jr.; vCharlie Barnet
BB B6619° [Reverse: Amanda Randolph—*I've got something in my eye*]; Regal Zonophone (E) MR 2363 [Reverse: Dolly Dawn—*There's frost on the moon*]; Twin (India) FT 8225 [Reverse: Shep Fields—*I'm talking through my heart*]; *BB AXM2 5526*; Ajax C-716

543-1 **Did you mean it?** aHorace Diaz, Jr.; vCharlie Barnet
BB B6605 [Reverse: Wingy Manone—*Floatin' down to cotton town*]; BB (C) B6605 [Reverse: Wingy Manone—*I can't pretend*]; *BB AXM2 5526*; Ajax C-716

544-1 **You do the darndest things, baby** aHorace Diaz, Jr.; vCharlie Barnet
BB B6594°; Regal Zonophone (E) MR-2362; Twin (India) FT-8211; Vi (Arg) JR-69; *BB AXM2 5526*; Ajax C-716

545-1 **It's love I'm after** aHorace Diaz, Jr.; vCharlie Barnet
BB B6594°; Regal Zonophone (E) MR-2362; Twin (India) FT-8211; Vi (Arg) JR-69; *BB AXM2 5526*; Ajax C-716

546-1 **Sing, baby, sing** aHorace Diaz, Jr.; vCharlie Barnet
BB B6593°; *AXM2 5526*; Ajax C-716

After closing at the Glen Island Casino, Charlie embarked on a one-nighter tour which "staggered through the fall and winter" (*TSY*, p.73), minus a few members of his regular band, but with the addition of Kurt Bloom and Frank Amaral. Kurt was to be a mainstay of Charlie's various bands down the years, serving as manager, music director, and Charlie's alter ego when it came time for a Barnet solo and he was otherwise engaged.

October 9, 1936: Charleston, WV, Midelburg Auditorium

NYC, "Make Believe Ballroom," WNEW b'cast, 6:15, November 12, 1936

RECORDS RETAILING AT 35c

BLUE BIRD—No. 1	'Let's Get Drunk and Truck,' 'Maybe It's Someone Else You Love' (Tampa Red Orch.)	'Did I Remember?' (Shep Fields Orch.)	'When I'm with You' (Charlie Barnet Orch.)
BLUE BIRD—No. 2	'Knock, Knock,' 'When Lady Meets Gentleman Down South' (Dolly Dawn Orch.)	'Sin to Tell a Lie,' 'Would You?' (George Hall Orch.)	'Did I Remember?' (Shep Fields Orch.)
BLUE BIRD—No. 3	'Bye, Bye, Baby,' 'Make Believe Ballroom' (Charlie Barnet Orch.)	'Sweet Misery of Love' (Shep Fields Orch.)	'Rendezvous with a Dream' (Shep Fields Orch.)

Best selling records, September 1936.

Milkmen's matinee vBarnet Modern-Aires
The Dixieland band vCharlie Barnet
Until the real thing comes along aHorace Diaz, Jr.; vCharlie Barnet
King Porter stomp [tpt solo Irving Goodman]
Make believe ballroom vBarnet Modern-Aires

November 28, 1936: York, PA, Valencia Ballroom

It was probably during 1936-7 that Charlie married Shirley Lloyd, Ozzie Nelson's vocalist, with Claude Thornhill and Artie Shaw as witnesses. Personnel is not known for following January 13 appearance, beyond the fact that it was a small combo.

<u>*Motor Boat Show, WEAF b'cast, January 13, 1937*</u>

Christopher Columbus
Stop, look and listen vBarnet Modern-Aires
Oh say can you swing
Did you mean it vBarnet Modern-Aires
Sailing, sailing (theme)

<u>*NYC, "Make believe ballroom," WNEW b'cast, Feb. 4, 1937*</u>

Milkmen's matinee vBarnet Modern-Aires
'Way down yonder in New Orleans

Charlie has been mentioned as one of three possibilities for the tenor sax part on the following recording session:

Dick McDonough and his orchestra

Bunny Berigan and possibly Manny Klein or Sterling Bose, tpts; Jack

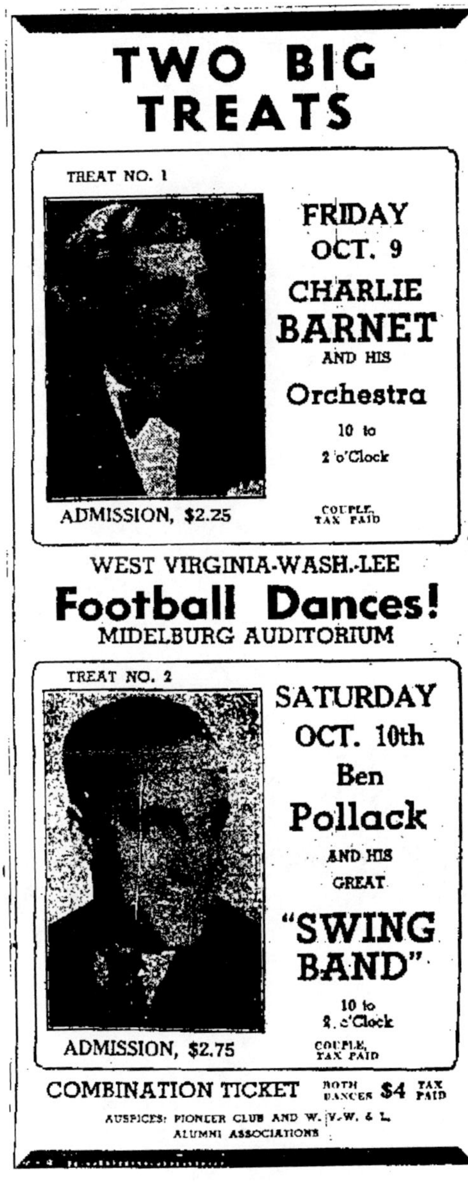

7:30-WEAF—Barnett Orchestra; Modernaires Quartet

Lacey, tbn; Toots Mondello, cl, as; ***Charlie Barnet*** *or Art Drelinger or Fred Fellensby, ts; (Carl Kress?), g; Dick McDonough, g; Claude Thornhill, p; Paul Prince, b; Cozy Cole, d (Rust JR)*

NYC, American Record Corp. recording session, February 16, 1937

20686-2 **The mood that I'm in** vBarry McKinley
ARC 7-05-02
20687-2 **All God's chillun got rhythm** vBarry McKinley
ARC 7-06-14

A report in *Down beat* (February 1937) stated that Henry Red Allen and Tommy Miles, trumpet and drums respectively, were to be part of Charlie's new band which was to begin rehearsals on January 25. There's no evidence that these men became part of the band but it did include Frank Amaral, Buddy Schutz and Sid Weiss and probably Kurt Bloom; Kathleen Lane was the girl singer.

George Frazier wrote on hearing the band in Boston, probably in March, that "a superb trumpet" (Amaral) and "Charlie's weird vocalizing" were in evidence.

Some of Charlie's activities at this time included a series of week-end jobs with a very loosely organized band outside of New York City, often using men who were waiting out their union cards. Among those who took part in these jobs were trumpeters John Best, Barney Zudecoff and Malcolm Crain. Best and Crain, together with others from this informal group, later became members of the Artie Shaw band.

(March?) 1937: Boston, unidentified location
(April?) 1937: Georgian Bay, ON, Wasaga Beach
April 18–24,1937: Barnesville, PA, Lakeside Park
(May?) 1937: Reading, Carsonia Park

California Ramblers (under direction of Ed Kirkeby) [actually Charlie's band]

Al Stuart, Irving Goodman, Frank Amaral, tpts; Bob Fishel, James Curry, tbns; David Gotwalls (lead), Joe Estren, as; ***Charlie Barnet****, Kurt Bloom, Henry Saltman, ts; John Nicolini, p, celesta; Tom Morgan, g; Bob Elden, b; Buddy Schutz, d (Edw 65)*

NYC, Master Records recording session, May 6, 1937

M439-1 **Down south camp meetin'** aFletcher Henderson
Variety VA 577; *Ajax 106*
M440-1 **Swingin' down to Rio** aCharlie Barnet
Variety VA 603; *Ajax 106*
M441-1 **Take my word** aBenny Carter
Variety VA 577; *Ajax 106*
M442-1 **Chris and his gang** aCharlie Barnet
Unissued?
M442-2 **Chris and his gang** aCharlie Barnet
Variety VA 603 [released ca Sept.–Oct. 1937]; *Ajax 106*

Charlie Barnet and his orchestra

NYC, RCA Victor recording session, May 7, 1937

Personnel as preceding except for **He walked right in***: (Frank Amaral?), tpt; Curry or Fishel, tbn; Charlie Barnet, ts; rhythm section as preceding.*

10133-1 **The first time I saw you** vCharlie Barnet
BB B6973°; *BB AXM2 5526*; Ajax C-716
10134-1 **In your own little way** vKathleen Lane
BB B6975°; *BB AXM2 5526*; Ajax C-716
10135-1 **You're looking for romance** vKurt Bloom
BB B6975°; *BB AXM2 5526*; Ajax C-716
10136-1 **Love is a merry-go-round** vKathleen Lane
BB B6973°; *BB AXM2 5526*; Ajax C-716
10136-2 **Love is a merry-go-round** vKathleen Lane
Unissued

10137-1 **A sailboat in the moonlight** vKurt Bloom
BB B6967°; *BB AXM2 5526*
10138-1 **He walked right in** vKathleen Lane, Kurt Bloom
BB B6967°; *BB AXM2 5526*

May 8–(May 22?), 1937: Albany, NY, New Kenmore Hotel

> **Charlie Barnet**
> The other night I caught the Barnet band on the radio, and now I know they could do better if they were given good material. Barnet's four [Bluebird] sides are all pops, and only the tenor (Barnet) and the clarinet get a chance at short passages, what with all the long vocals and ensembles. Part of Barnet's bunch waxed two sides under the name of The California Ramblers. Down South Camp Meetin' follows the original Henderson score, and it is a neat job. Take My Word is, apparently, the new title for Bennie Carter's Lonesome Nights, and á la Henderson, the Ramblers get off a slow but swingy version. Barnet's tenor gets more of a chance here. (Paul Edward Miller, *Down beat* July 1937)

> *NBC—Red—WEAF*
> 12:30 P.M., EDST, Sat. May 15—
> This night's meagre fare came to a welcome end when in played Charlie Barnet from—would you believe it—the new Kenmore Hotel in Albany, N.Y. He's music to the ears and feet! Easy-going swing tempos perfectly cast for dancing, with the swell ride of an outfit pulling together, plus good blending, shading, phrasing, and timing. Nice sustained power in ensemble. Charlie has captured the good of Goodman without imitating! Nice work.
> His open style on *Sweet Is the Word For You* too barren to hold interest. Not a Barnet dish. Good one to sit out for better stuff to come. Whic did, though his *Dear Old Southland* started disappointingly—rough in spots and minus the best Barnet ride. Picked up by the last chrous … Fill-ins done with a flair, and even the slow swings are danceable. Barnet's music is worth the wait anytime. And Charlie himself is in good form. Miss the Modernaires. P.S. Why Albany? (*Metronome* July 1937)

Albany, NY, New Kenmore Hotel, WEAF b'cast, 12:30PM, May 15, 1937

Sweet is the word for you
Dear old southland

As preceding, May 20, 1937

Swing low, sweet chariot aJames Mundy
This is my last affair vKathleen Lane
Night and day aHead
Rockin' chair swing
Clarinet lament
In your own little way vKathleen Lane
Trees
You're precious to me
September in the rain
The you and me that used to be
Dear old southland

May 23, 1937: Jersey City, NJ, unidentified location (band battle with George Hall)
(May) 1937: Boston, Raymor Ballroom (weekend engagement)
(May) 1937: Rochester, NY, unidentified location (one nighter)
May 30, 1937: Lawrenceville, NJ, unidentified location (band battle with George Hall)
(June?) 1937: Princeton, NJ, Huns Prep

Art Lombardi, Al Stuart, Frank Beraidi, tpts; John W. Sarnelli, Bob Fishel, tbns; Dave Gotwalls, Joseph Estren, as; Kurt Bloom, Henry Saltman, ts; John Nicolini, p; Buddy Schutz, d; Bob Elden, b. Gail Reese, Jean Boza and Chester Boone, vocalists (Bob Inman autographs, Hickory Lodge)

June 15–(July 31?) 1937: Larchmont, NY, Hickory Lodge [formerly Post Lodge]

The band was heard on WEAF (*Inman*).

It was probably in the spring of 1937 that Charlie, Buddy Schutz, and one or more other members of the band augmented the all girl orchestra of Rita Rio (Rita Shaw) for a recording session. Rita and Charlie kept one another company during this period. (*Buddy Schutz*). [Rita, "this delicious singing morsel, is now being groomed by Paramount for filmdom's high spots. Did you see her in 'Road to Morocco'?" (*Song hits*, March 1943).]

Barney Bigard and his Jazzopators

Rex Stewart, c; Juan Tizol, vtb; Barney Bigard, cl; Harry Carney, bs; Duke Ellington, p; Fred Guy, g; ***Charlie Barnet****, maracas; Billy Taylor, b; Sonny Greer, d (Rust JR)*

NYC, Master Records recording session, June 16, 1937

M-526-1 **Moonlight fiesta**
CBS (Fr? N) 88210
M-526-2 **Moonlight fiesta**
Variety 626; Vocalion 3834; *CBS (Fr? N) 88210*; *Tax (Swed) m8023*

"Well, [Irving Mills] wanted more of a Latin sound than they were getting there, and of course Sonny was the only percussionist there at the moment, and so he suggested that I play the maracas, and that's how I happened to be in the studio." (*Sm*)

Charlie Barnet and his orchestra

Larchmont, NY, Hickory Lodge, WEAF b'cast, June 21, 1937

Caravan
The you and me that used to be vJean Boza
There's a lull in my life
Never in a million years
The goona goo
They can't take that away from me
Echoes of Harlem
You're looking for romance
High [tide?]

As preceding, June 26, 1937

Somebody loves me
The you and me that used to be vGail Reese
Lullaby to a lamp post
When love is young
A sailboat in the moonlight vKurt Bloom
Rockin' chair swing
Caravan
Carelessly vGail Reese
Admiration
I've lost another sweetheart (closing theme)

As preceding, June 28, 1937

They can't take that away from me vJean Boza
The goona goo
You're looking for romance
Song of India
Honeysuckle rose aHorace Henderson

Metronome (July 1937) carried George T. Simon's review of the band in which he noted that it was potentially a great band, and Charlie potentially a great leader. "Apparently, though, Charlie Barnet lacks just one important qualification, and it's that deficiency which is keeping him from reaching truly great heights. Charlie Barnet seems to have no sense of responsibility ... This writer has interrogated various people who have worked for Charlie, and they've all come through with the same story: 'We could have a swell band, but, man, we have too much fun. We play for ourselves on the stand, and when we're not playing we're usually out someplace knocking ourselves out. You know—weed and whiskey—the usual story!' ... There's no doubt whatsoever in this writer's mind that Barnet, if imbued with a fine sense of responsibility, could come to the top with one of the greatest of all bands in history. He has all the other qualifications, personal, musical, and commercial. Potentially he's about the world's greatest fronter for a band, and that's saying a lot. Here's a fervent prayer that all those potentialities will be realized before it's too late. It's up to you, Charlie Barnet!"

Jack Koven, Jimmy Milazzo, Frank Newton, tpts; John D'Agostino, Bob Fishel, tbns; Harry Carrel, Ernie Diven, as; Kurt Bloom, ts; Ludwig Flato, p except as noted; George Cuomo, g; John Kirby, b (Liner for

Col CG 33557 "John Kirby—Boss of the Bass")

<u>NYC, Master Records recording session, August 5, 1937</u>

M-582-2 **Shame on you** aCharlie Barnet; vCharlie Barnet
Variety VA 627; *Jazz Archives JA 9*; *Ajax 106*; **JAZZ ARCHIVES (FR) 3891092**
M-583-1 **Emperor Jones** aFranklyn Marks
Jazz Archives JA 9; *Col J2 15596*; *Ajax 106*; <u>Col Legacy C3T 52862</u>; **COL LEGACY 52862; JAZZ ARCHIVES (FR) 3891092**
M-583-2 **Jubilesta** aFranklyn Marks
Col CG 33557
M-584-1 **If you're ever in my arms again** aCharlie Barnet; vFour Stars (James Van Heusen, p, in place of Flato)
Variety VA 627; *Ajax 106*
M-585-1 **Admiration** aJuan Tizol
Meritt 8 ; *Franklin Mint 93-96*

On August 10, 1937, Charlie took part in a jam session at the Onyx Club (NYC) with Sal Franzella and the John Kirby band (Frankie Newton, Buster Bailey, Don Frye, Pete Brown, O'Neil Spencer, John Kirby, Leo Watson) from 3 to 3:45 AM. (*Inman*)

As for August 5 except as noted.

<u>As preceding, Aug. 13, 1937</u>

M-590-1 **Surrealism** aFranklyn Marks. (Josef Myrow replaced Flato.)
Variety VA 633; Vocalion 3835; *Ajax 106*
[A bassoon is audible]
M-591-1 **Lullaby to a lamp post** aFranklyn Marks?
Unissued
M-591-2 **Lullaby to a lamp post** aFranklyn Marks?
Unissued
M-592-1 **Overheard in a cocktail lounge** aFranklyn Marks. [2:48] (Josef Myrow replaced Flato.)
Variety VA 633; Vocalion 3835; *Epic BN 24029*; *Epic JSN 6042*; *Col (E) 33SX-1511*; *Ajax 106*
[A bassoon and a bass clarinet are audible]
M-592-2 **Overheard in a cocktail lounge** aFranklyn Marks. [2:43]
Variety VA 633; Vocalion 3835
M-593-1 **Merry widow on a spree** aFranklyn Marks
Ajax 106

Charles Barnet (Variety)

Surrealism. Best artistic record of the month. From the pen of Josef Myrow, who plays the difficult piano passages in the disc. This newest effort is the logical development of the talent foreshadowed in one of his earlier pieces, *Blue Drag*, which Earl Hines waxed some years ago. Both pieces effect an eerie sensation uponthe listener. *Surrealism* was arranged from the piano score by Franklyn Marks, who displays a sense of genuine aptitude for the development of unusual ideas. Both the main theme and the ingenious sub-tone counter-melody are deftly built around the piano passages, each one being preceded by an expertly constructed climax. The score as a whole has unity of form seldom found in jazz; it never gets monotonous. In short, it's good abstract music in the jazz style.

Overheard in a Cocktail Lounge. Also by Myrow, orchestrated by Marks. Here is an attempt at something more descriptive, and immediately we begin to look for familar sounds which we can identify with reality. In this respect the piece falls short of its goal. However, as experimental jazz, the tune, though less intriguing than Surrealism, is nevertheless diverting, and the unusual treatment merits our attention. (Paul Edward Miller, *Down beat* October 1937)

Leith Stevens and his orchestra

(Charlie Barnet was soloist)

<u>NYC, "Saturday Night Swing Club," WABC b'cast, August 21, 1937</u>

It's the talk of the town
Rosetta

At some point in about the fall of 1937 he disbanded and went out to Hollywood aiming once again to try the actor's life. "I wound up working as a glorified extra in a few westerns," as he told Leonard Feather in 1951 (*Down beat*, Sept. 21, 1951) as well as appearing in *Love and hisses* and *Sally, Irene and Mary* as a bandleader. Later on he came back to the east coast and formed another band.

Dec. 25, 1937: Providence, RI, Arcadia Ballroom

(Compiler's note: Barnet discographies have included several collections of songs denoted as airchecks which are in fact items from transcriptions. One such collection was marketed as "Charlie Barnet's rare and unreleased masters." In one somewhat bizarre case, Bunny Berigan's *Devil's holiday* [from Thesaurus 563] is ascribed to one of these Barnet broadcast performances.)

(Providence, RI, Arcadia Ballroom?), (NBC?) b'cast, Jan. 7, 1938

If dreams come true vCharlie Barnet

Band on one-nighter junket (*Variety,* Jan. 26, 1938).

Feb. 26, 1938: Frederick, MD, Hood College
(April?), 1938: Philadelphia, Temple University

The band played "the all dental dance" of Temple University and "the protests haven't died yet. Barnet brought an outfit which spent most of the time in feebly trying to sight-read stock orchestrations. On the other numbers Charley galloped around, blasting into the ears of his individual men the figures he thought of. It took time to serenade each man and more time for the men to catch on to the idea and join in. [Birth of a head arrangement?] The bandstand looked smart, too, with a pitcher of beer on the piano, cases and coats lying around, and chairs being utilized for music stands." (*Metronome* May 1938)

(April?) 1938: Asbury Park, NJ, Reade's Casino
May 13–14, 1938: Williamstown, MA, Williams College Proms

Rhythm Makers Orchestra

Probable personnel: John Mendell, Johnny Owens, Bob Burnet, tpts; Bob Fishel, Ben Hall, Don Ruppersburg, tbns; Joe Estren (lead), Henry Saltman, as; Rocque Dominick, ts; James Lamare, ts, bar; Graham Forbes, p; Bob Elden, b; Wesley Dean, d

NYC, RCA Thesaurus recording session, May 16, 1938

(Each transcription side was assigned a stamper number,e.g., MS 23232-1, with letters identifying the individual songs. The "reissue" transcriptions, such as 1145, also have stamper numbers, e.g., ND3-MM-3193-1)

MS 23232-1 **Prelude in C# minor** aChappie Willett
THESAURUS 537; *First Time FTR 1504*; *Onward to Yesterday OTY 1504*; *Jazz Band (Fr) 8008*; *Alamac/JazzKings QSR 2435*; *Cicala (It) BLJ 8008*; *Joyce 2017*; Ajax C-668; Alamac QSR 2435; **TAX (SWED) CD 3715-2; GIANTS OF JAZZ (IT) CD 53274**

MS 23232-1 **I let a song go out of my heart** aCharlie Barnet
THESAURUS 537, 1145; *First Time FTR 1504*; *Onward to Yesterday OTY 1504*; *Jazz Band (Fr) 8008*; *Alamac/Jazz Kings QSR 2435*; *Cicala (It) BLJ 8008*; *Limited Editions LP 101*; Ajax C-668; Alamac QSR 2435; **TAX (SWED) CD 3715-2; GIANTS OF JAZZ (IT) CD 53274**

MS 23232-1 **You go to my head** aAndy Gibson [CB heard briefly on ss]

THESAURUS 537, 1140°; *First Time FTR 1504*; *Onward to Yesterday OTY 1504*; *Jazz Band (Fr) 8008*; *Cicala (It) BLJ 8008*; Ajax C-668; **TAX (SWED) CD 3715-2**; **GIANTS OF JAZZ (IT) CD 53274**

MS 23232-1 **Stop, look and listen**
THESAURUS 537; *Alamac/Jazz Kings QSR 2435*; *First Time FTR 1504; Onward to Yesterday OTY 1504*; *Jazz Band (Fr) 8008*; *Cicala (It) BLJ 8008*; Ajax C-668; Alamac QSR 2435; **TAX (SWED) CD 3715-2**; **GIANTS OF JAZZ (IT) CD 53274**

MS 23233-1 **Harmony in Harlem** aBob Burnet
THESAURUS 566; 1147; *Alamac/Jazz Kings QSR 2435*; *First Time FTR 1504*; *Onward to Yesterday OTY 1504*; *Jazz Band (Fr) 8088*; *Cicala (It) BLJ 8008*; *Limited Editions LP 101*; Ajax C668, C-708; Alamac QSR 2435; **TAX (SWED) CD 3715-2**; **GIANTS OF JAZZ (IT) CD 53274**

MS 23233-1 **Echoes of Harlem** aDuke Ellington
THESAURUS 566, 1147; **TAX (SWED) CD 3715-2**

MS 23233-1 **Blue, turning grey over you** aAndy Gibson
THESAURUS 566; *Alamac/Jazz Kings QSR 2435*; *First Time FTR 1504*; *Onward to Yesterday OTY 1504*; *Jazz Band (Fr) 8008*; *Cicala (It) BLJ 8008*; Ajax C-668; Alamac QSR 2435; **TAX (SWED) CD 3715-2**; **GIANTS OF JAZZ (IT) CD 53274**

MS 23233-1 **In-a-jam** aBob Burnet
THESAURUS 566, 1147; *Alamac/Jazz Kings QSR 2435*; *First Time FTR 1504*; *Onward to Yesterday OTY 1504*; *Jazz Band (Fr) 8008*; *Cicala (It) BLJ 8008*; Ajax C-668; **TAX (SWED) CD 3715-2**; **GIANTS OF JAZZ (IT)CD 53274**

MS 23234-1 **Chatterbox** a(Andy Gibson?)
THESAURUS 606, 1148°; *First Time FTR 1504*; *Onward to Yesterday OTY 1504*; *Jazz Band (Fr) 8008*; *Alamac/Jazz Kings QSR 2435*; *Cicala (It) BLJ 8008*; Ajax C-668; Alamac QSR 2435; **TAX (SWED) CD 3715-2**

MS 23234-1 **Marie** aBenny Carter
THESAURUS 606; **TAX (SWED) CD 3715-2**

MS 23234-1 **Love is flying high**
THESAURUS 606; Ajax C-668; **TAX (SWED) CD 3715-2**

MS 23234-1 **Swinging down to Rio** aCharlie Barnet
THESAURUS 606, 1147; Ajax C-668; **TAX (SWED) CD 3715-2**

MS 23235-1 **Moonshine over Kentucky**
THESAURUS 538, 1175; Ajax C-668; **TAX (SWED) CD 3715-2**

MS 23235-1 **Rock it for me** aBilly May
THESAURUS 538; *Jazz Band (Fr) 8008*; *Alamac/Jazz Kings QSR 2435*; *Cicala (It) BLJ 8008*; *First Time FTR1504*; *Onward to Yesterday OTY 1504*; Ajax C-668; Alamac QSR 2435; **TAX (SWED) CD 3715-2**; **GIANTS OF JAZZ (IT) CD 53274**

MS 23235-1 **That feeling is gone**
THESAURUS 538, 1175; Ajax C-668; **TAX (SWED) CD 3715-2**

MS 23235-1 **Somewhere with somebody else**
THESAURUS 538, 1175; Ajax C-671; **TAX (SWED) CD 3715-2**

MS 23236-1 **Lullaby in rhythm** aAndy Gibson
THESAURUS 565, 1184°; *Alamac/Jazz Kings QSR 2435*; *Cicala (It) BLJ 8008*; *First Time FTR 1504*; *Onward to Yesterday OTY 1504*; *Jazz Band (Fr) 8008*; Ajax C-671; Alamac QSR 2435; **TAX (SWED) CD 3715-2**; **GIANTS OF JAZZ (IT) CD 53274**

MS 23236-1 **Laugh and call it love** aBilly May
THESAURUS 565; Ajax C-671; **TAX (SWED) CD 3715-2**

MS 23236-1 **Don't let that moon get away** aBilly May
THESAURUS 565; Ajax C-671; **TAX (SWED) CD 3715-2**

MS 23236-1 **Smiles** aSkippy Martin? [Charlie plays soprano sax briefly, and—with marginal intonation—on this recording.]
THESAURUS 565; 1139°; **TAX (SWED) CD 3715-2**

"Skippy Martin had written something for him [requiring soprano] before I made *Pompton*." (*Billy May letter* Dec. 3, 1996). *Smiles* may be it.

May 22, 1938: Bridgeport, CT, Pleasure Beach Park

May 29, 1938: Randall Island, Martin Block Carnival of Swing

Jane Churchill "has been added as vocalist." (*Variety* May 18, 1938)

June 10–23, 1938: Liberty, PA, New Penn Club

"Charlie came through Pittsburgh with a really wild-sounding band and I went out and took my manuscript paper

in my hand and asked him if I could make an arrangement for him, and he said, 'Sure.' So I stayed up all night and wrote one because they rehearsed the next day." (*Billy May interviewed by Stanley Dance, JJI, May 1982*). Charlie recalled,"We were having a rehearsal, and here was this guy waiting there, and his shoes were cut out at the side to make it more comfortable ... I told him, 'As soon as we finish what we're doing here I'll be happy to try it.' So we passed the arrangement out and the guys in the band, it was in the afternoon and they wanted to get out. They started groaning and I said, 'Well, let's try this arrangement.' And they were real drug and bored, and they leaned back and they got through about the first eight bars ... and they all came up in their seats and they were looking at the music, and Mr. Billy May was in." (*Sm*) The song was, apparently, *If it rains, who cares?*

"Plenty of horn tooters were among those present on his opener, and their cheers brought memories to Charlie of his appearances with the Saturday Swing Session." (*Metronome* July 1938)

The band was using *Lazy bug* as its theme song at this time.

June 27–July 3, 1938: Auburn, NY, Enna Jettick Owasco Lake Park
July 4, 1938: Hamilton Square, NJ, Civic celebration
(Summer) 1938: NYC, Famous Door (Sunday night)

The band played twice on Count Basie's night off at the Famous Door. (Basie performed there from July through early November, 1938.)

July 19, 1938: Barnesville, PA, Lakeside Park
July 21, 1938: Mahanoy City, PA, Lakewood Park
July 22, 1938: Budd Lake, NJ, Fordham Club Pavilion
July 23–Aug. 5, 1938: Virginia Beach, VA, Ocean Casino
Aug. 27, 1938: Providence, RI, Narragansett Pier Casino
(Aug?) 1938: Wildwood, NJ, Hunt's Ocean Pier (one week)
Sept. 30, 1938: Ashland, VA, Randolph Macon College
Oct. 28–Nov. (4?), 1938: Washington, DC, Howard Theater (band battle with Lucky Millinder)

Rhythm Makers Orchestra

Note: Thesaurus 1100 series as "The Rhythm Makers."

NYC, RCA Thesaurus recording session, November 5, 1938

MS 28916-1 **You must have been a beautiful baby** aAndy Gibson; vCharlie Barnet (as "Tom Billings")
THESAURUS 594; Ajax C-671
MS 28916-1 **This is madness** vMary McHugh
THESAURUS 594; Ajax C-671
MS 28916-1 **You got me**
THESAURUS 594; *Jazz Band (Fr) 8008*; *Cicala (It) BLJ 8008*; *First Time FTR 1504*; *Onward to Yesterday OTY 1504*; Ajax C-671; **GIANTS OF JAZZ (IT) CD 53274**

MS 28916-1 **After looking at you**
THESAURUS 594, 1184°; Ajax C-671

MS 28917-1 **Prelude to a kiss** aCharlie Barnet
THESAURUS 605, 1145; *Alamac/Jazz Kings QSR 2435*; *Jazz Band (Fr) 8008*; *Cicala (It) BLJ 8008*; *First Time FTR 1504*; *Onward to Yesterday OTY 1504*; *Limited Editions LP 101*; Ajax C-671; Alamac QSR 2435; **GIANTS OF JAZZ (IT) CD 53274**

MS 28917-1 **Jump jump's here** aBenny Carter
THESAURUS 605, 1176°; *Alamac/Jazz Kings QSR 2435*; *Jazz Band (Fr) 8008*; *Cicala (It) BLJ 8008*; *First Time FTR 1504*; *Onward to Yesterday OTY 1504*; Ajax C-671; Alamac QSR 2435; **GIANTS OF JAZZ (IT) CD 53274**

MS 28917-1 **I found my yellow basket** vJudy Ellington (as "Billy Perkins")
THESAURUS 605, 1184°; Ajax C-671

MS 28917-1 **Do you wanna jump, children?** aBenny Carter
THESAURUS 605 ["Do you want to…"], 1138°; *Alamac/Jazz Kings QSR 2435*; *First Time FTR 1504*; *Onward to Yesterday OTY 1504*; Ajax C-671; Alamac QSR 2435

Nov. 11, 1938: Baltimore, McDonough School
Nov. 12, 1938: NYC, Webster Hall
Nov. 15, 1938: NYC, Manhattan Opera House (AFM Medical Fund) (Band finished performing at 5:08AM)
Nov. 24, 1938: Washington, DC, Mayflower Hotel "Charlie and Stuff Smith battle it out for sorority sisters" (*Billboard Nov. 26, 1938*)
Dec. 16, 1938: Springfield, Mass, Auditorium
Dec. 21, 1938: Boston, MIT
Dec. 28, 1938: Red Bank, NJ, Elks' Club

Charlie married Betty Lorraine possibly in early 1939. "I found out she had another husband she hadn't bothered to divorce. We quietly got our divorce by mail from Mexico." (*Down beat* Sept. 21, 1951)

The band was scheduled to appear sometime in January at Raymor Ballroom in Boston but got stuck in snow and didn't make it.

Chapter 3

Cherokee— The Billy May Band 1939–1941

Jan. 3–(Jan. 9?), 1939: NYC, Arcadia Ballroom

Jan. 17–March 22, 1939: NYC, Famous Door (preceded by John Kirby; followed by Woody Herman)

> The *New Yorker* magazine in February listed these "places where you can listen to swing music": The Onyx (John Kirby); Hickory House (Joe Marsala); The Famous Door (Charlie Barnet); Nick's (Bobby Hacket, Pee Wee Russell, Zutty Singleton); Café Society (Frankie Newton, Joe Turner, Billie Holiday, and Ammons and Lewis, "the boogie woogie pianists.")

> . . . **with Jan Savitt going into Hotel Lincoln. CHARLIE BARNETT brings his band this week into 52d street's Famous Door with four NBC remote shots weekly.**

> . . . Charlie Barnett tones down his boys for two grand numbers. NIGHT SONG and IN A MIZZ . . .

Billboard's reviewer, describing an opening night performance at the Famous Door, wrote: "Making another serious attempt to strike a responsive note in ork circles, Barnet, whose solo saxings have always been a lap-up for the cats, brings a socko band of scorchers to this swing street citadel. And if his gang of riders shape up as their preem showed promise, it looks like the musical felines will once again congregate at the Famous Door. Arrangements are all gauged for six brass, whose screaming tends to dissipate some marvelous effects in the scoring; five sax, the maestro making the fifth man with alto and tenor tootling, and four rhythm, in which section Nat Jaffe proves a potent knuckler at the keyboard. Bending backwards from the Fletcher Henderson school of swingo, Barnet has patterned his style along Duke Ellington lines, the first of the paleface bands to adopt that pattern. In fact, Duke's own arrangements figure prominently in the library, with Barnet following suit in his own scorings. It is in those numbers where the band revives the lost art of playing with mutes that achieves a distinction of style. This judicious use of the metal cup lends a definite amount of tonal coloration that promises to distinguish Barnet from other rhythm riders. Barnet, in front, is altogether delirious in his tootling—his tenor

CHARLES BARNET ORCH. (16)
With Judy Ellington
Famous Door, N. Y.

Barnet's crew should make current maestros near the top keep a wary eye on it during the next six months. It's in here for 10 weeks with four network shots per, after which it will probably follow Jan Savitt into the Lincoln Hotel, N. Y. Savitt debuts there Feb. 9.

Current outfit is not Barnet's original. It's been together about a year and is a powerful, hard-riding outfit of 14 pieces, fronted by the personable Barnet. Leader lips plenty of reed when he gets off on either alto or tenor sax, or clarinet, and the crew behind him is sock whether riding clear or on the mutes. Rhythm section seldom stands out, except that it occasionally brings the piano to the fore, drums, etc., being subordinate to the saxes and brass. Fact that it's there, though, is attested to by the unusually enlivening bounce it starts out on a bounce and winds up bouncing the customers.

Outfit's arrangements are handled by Barnet, couple of men from the crew, Duke Ellington (few) and Benny Carter. There are several Andy Gibson writings also to make the conglomeration complete, but the crew is gradually working out its own style, based for the most part on Carter's output. Barring things unforeseen it's a crew that should go places.

Judy Ellington handles the vocals in either ballad or swing style and helps toward creating a good impression for the crew. She's a blonde looker.

sax playing a paleface Hawkins and scintillates as well on the alto. Plenty of instrumental highlights besides Barnet and Jaffe that'll make the pussyfoots lick their chops in a growl trumpeter and the high riding clary and trumpet. Judy Ellington, blond looker, braves the heated swingo for the vocal folderols. Gal can bawl the ballads and dig the ditties with a fine rhythmic sense. Strictly of swing genre, for those who dote on swingeree, Barnet is a sleeper and bears watching." (Jan. 28, 1939)

"Of course we went to the Famous Door … and I sent for Billy. I said, 'I want you to come in and arrange for me,' you know. Oh, it was a ridiculous deal. Something like $15.00 an arrangement. And Billy was not playing in the band, just arranging for it. He and Andy Gibson and Billy Moore, Jr." (*Sm*)

The Famous Door engagement was the big breakthrough for the Barnet band as the Palomar was for Benny Goodman.

Bassist Harlow Atwood came in one night and was able to find a seat near the band (most patrons wanted to distance themselves because of the decibels). During the evening the band was to do an NBC remote, and the young Ivy League–type announcer went into his routine: "The National Broadcasting Company takes pleasure in bringing you music from the Famous Door on 52nd St. and here is Guy Lombardo and his orchestra." Charlie got very upset and threatened the announcer with his tenor sax but was restrained by Atwood, who later remarked, "I may have prevented a murder." This may have been an early appearance of the later famous "V" made by pulsing veins on his forehead when he became upset/enraged/furious.

Charlie Barnet and his orchestra

Bob Burnet, John Mendell, Charles Huffine, tpts; Ben Hall, Bill Robertson, Don Ruppersburg, tbns; Gene Kinsey, Don McCook, as; Jimmy Lamare, ts & bar, Kurt Bloom, ts. Nat Jaffe, p; Bus Etri, g; Phil Stephens, b; Wesley Dean, d (ViSS)

NYC, RCA Victor recording session, January 20, 1939

31536-1 **I get along without you very well**
vJudy Ellington
BB B10119º; Regal Zonophone (E) MR-3079; *BB AXM2 5526*; *Big Band Archives BBA 1209*

31536-2 **I get along without you very well** vJudy Ellington
Unissued

31537-1 **I'm prayin' humble** aBenny Carter
BB B10119°; *BB AXM2 5526*; *RCA (Fr) PM 42401*; *RCA (Fr) PM 45689*; *Sounds of Swing LP 103*; **RCA 2135554-2; JAZZ ARCHIVES (FR) 30; ZETA (GER) ZET 749; RCA (FR) 74321355542**

31538-1 **Tin roof blues** aBenny Carter
BB 10131°; HMV (Australia) EA 2772; *BB AXM2 5577*; *RCA (Fr) PM 45689; Big Band Archives BBA 1209*; BB AXK2 5577; **RCA 2135554-2; JAZZ ARCHIVES (FR) 30; GIANTS OF JAZZ (IT) CD 53274; ZETA (GER) ZET 749; RCA (FR) 74321355542**

31539-1 **Knockin' at the Famous Door** aHorace Henderson, Charlie Barnet
BB B10131°; *AXM2 5577; Sounds of Swing LP 103*; BB 61059-4; BB AXK2 5577; **BB 6273-2-RB; BB 61059-2; GIANTS OF JAZZ (IT) CD 53274; RCA (E) 86273**

31539-2 **Knockin' at the Famous Door** aHorace Henderson, Charlie Barnet
BB AXM2 5590; RCA (Fr) PM 45689; **RCA 2135554-2; ARISTA 886281; JAZZ ARCHIVES (FR) 30; ZETA (GER) ZET 749; JAZZ GREATS (E) CD 071; RCA (FR) 74321355542**

"[*Knockin' at the Famous Door*] was actually an arrangement by Horace Henderson of *Honeysuckle rose* with the melody omitted and renamed in honor of the club." (CB in notes to *"The Complete Charlie Barnet, vol. 2," BB AXM2 5577*)

NYC, Famous Door, NBC b'cast, Jan. 25, 1939

Undecided# aHead[1:36]
Radiola 10CMR2

As preceding, February 17, 1939

Every tub aBasie Head
Joyce 1152; *Radiola 10CMR2; Joyce C-679*

Sweet Georgia Brown aAndy Gibson
Joyce 1152; Radiola 10CMR2; Joyce C-679

The gal from Joe's (transcription of Duke Ellington arrangement)
Joyce 1152; Radiola 10CMR2

Echoes of Harlem aDuke Ellington
Joyce 1152; Radiola 10CMR2

Make believe ballroom (closing theme)
Radiola 10CMR2

The Barnet version of *Every tub* takes Basie's arrangement as its starting point and begins with the reeds playing an approximation of Lester Young's opening improvisation as recorded on Decca. Charlie played it in a different key.

As preceding, February 19, 1939

Make believe ballroom (Opening theme) aHorace Diaz, Jr.
Joyce 1152; Radiola 10CMR2

Jump session aBilly May
Joyce 1152; Radiola 10CMR2

Night and day aHead
Joyce 1152; Radiola 10CMR2

A prescient article in *Down beat*, Feb. 1939, declared: "When the events of 1939 have been compiled and filed into the annals of jazz, it is our guess that Charlie Barnett and his orchestra, which opened at the Famous Door Jan. 17, will hold a special place as one of the outstanding musical groups of the year. Barnett, whose frustrated barnstorming during the past six years made his potentialities an unknown quantity, has finally corralled himself a herd of musikers equal to the immense library of arrangements in his possession and settled himself in Swing Lane ... After a rugged tour in the hinterlands, selecting new men here and there, Barnett turned up in New York with an orchestra that not only surprised his first patrons, but delighted them with some of the most exciting music—instrumental and orchestrated—heard in a long time ... Instrumentalists who share the solo spotlight are Nat Jaffee ... Bob Burnett ... Johnny Mendell ... and Busse Etri ..."

NYC, RCA Victor recording session, February 24, 1939

33901-1 **The gal from Joe's** (transcription of Duke Ellington arrangement)
BB B10153°; BB AXM2 5577; *Vi LPT-3062°, LPV-567°; RCA (Fr) PM 42041, PM 45689; RCA (Ger) LPM 567; RCA (Ja) RA 60-68; RCA Vi (E) RD 8088; RCA Vi (Arg) AVLT-7; RCA (It?) 34048*; ***RCA Vi***

EPBT 3062; BB AXK2 5577; **BB 6273-2RB; RCA 2135554-2; ARISTA 886281; JAZZ ARCHIVES (FR) 30; GIANTS OF JAZZ (IT) CD 53274; KAZ (E) CD 311; TOPAZ JAZZ (E) TPZ 1041; RCA (E) 86273; ZETA (GER) ZET 749; JAZZ GREATS (E) CD 071; RCA (FR) 74321355542**

33901-2 **The gal from Joe's** (transcription of Duke Ellington arrangement)
Unissued

33902-1 **Where can she be?** aBilly May; vJudy Ellington
BB B10162°; *BB AXM2 5577*; BB AXK2 5577

33903-1 **Jump session** aBilly May
BB B10172°; *BB AXM2 5577*; *RCA (Fr) PM 45689*; *Sounds of Swing LP 103*; BB AXK2 5577; **RCA 2135554-2; GIANTS OF JAZZ (IT) CD 53274; RCA (FR) 74321355542**

33904-1 **I wouldn't give that for love** aBilly May; vJudy Ellington
BB B10162°; *BB AXM2 5577*; BB AXK2 5577

33904-2 **I wouldn't give that for love** a Billy May; vJudy Ellington
Unissued

33905-1 **A new moon and an old serenade** vJudy Ellington
BB B10153°; Regal Zonophone (E) MR-3079; *BB AXM2 5577*; BB AXK2 5577

33905-2 **A new moon and an old serenade** vJudy Ellington
Unissued

33906-1 **Swing Street strut** aRoscoe Fritz
BB B10172°; *BB AXM2 5577*; *RCA (Fr) PM 42401*; *PM 45689*; *Sounds of Swing LP 103*; BB AXK2 5577; **RCA 2135554-2; JAZZ ARCHIVES (FR) 30; GIANTS OF JAZZ (IT) CD 53277; ZETA (GER) ZET 749; RCA (FR) 74321355542**

Charlie Barnet orchestra

NYC, RCA Thesaurus recording session, ca February 1939

33791-1 **I cried for you** aBenny Carter
THESAURUS 640, 1184°; Ajax C-679

33791-1 **I'm prayin' humble** aBenny Carter
THESAURUS 640

33791-1 **The gal from Joe's** (transcription of Duke Ellington arrangement)
THESAURUS 640

33791-1 **Gotta get some shut-eye** vJudy Ellington
THESAURUS 640; Ajax C-679

33793-1 **Where can she be** aBilly May; vJudy Ellington
THESAURUS 636 [as *Where can he be*]

33793-1 **Blame it on my last affair** aBilly May; vJudy Ellington
THESAURUS 636, 1154; Ajax C-671

33793-1 **I'm happy about the whole thing** vJudy Ellington
THESAURUS 636; Ajax C-679

33793-1 **It's easy to blame the weather** vJudy Ellington
THESAURUS 636, 1176°

33799-1 **This night** vJudy Ellington
THESAURUS 635; Ajax C-671

33799-1 **A new moon and an old serenade** vJudy Ellington
THESAURUS 635

33799-1 **I want my share of love** aBilly May; vJudy Ellington
THESAURUS 635; Ajax C-671

33799-1 **Undecided** aHead
THESAURUS 635; *Jazz Band (Fr) 8008*; *Cicala (IT) BLJ 8008*; *First Time 1504*; *Onward to Yesterday OTY 1504*; *IAJRC 8*; *Joyce 2017*; Ajax C-671; **GIANTS OF JAZZ (IT) CD 53274**

March 1939: Boston, Raymor Ballroom (brief engagement, perhaps on night off from Famous Door or between Door and Paramount Theater engagements)

NYC, "Magic Key of RCA," March 3, 1939

Songs performed unknown (Transcription of program may be in NBC collection at the Library of Congress)

March 10, 1939: Jamaica, NY, Loew's Theater

NYC, Famous Door, NBC b'cast, March 12, 1939

Good for nothin' but love aBilly May; vJudy Ellington
Joyce 1152; Radiola 10CMR2

Deep purple aBilly May
Joyce 1152; Radiola 10CMR2

Judy Ellington signed a one-year contract at $40/week.

NYC, RCA Victor recording session, March 17, 1939

35051-1 **In a mizz** aBilly May; vJudy Ellington

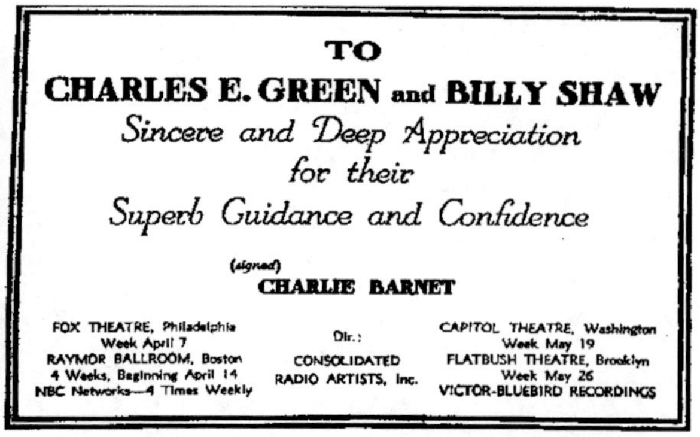

BB B10191°; *BB AXM2 5577; Sounds of Swing LP 103*; BB AXK2 5577; **BEST OF JAZZ (FR) 4039**

35052-1 **Night song** aJimmy Mundy or Billy May
BB B10191°; *BB AXM2 5577; RCA (Fr) PM 45689; Swing Era LP 1002, LPS 5001*; BB AXK2 5577; **RCA 2135554-2; TOPAZ JAZZ (E) TPZ 1041; RCA (FR) 74321355542**

35053-1 **Class will tell** aBilly May; vJudy Ellington
BB B10182°; *BB AXM2 5577*; BB AXK2 5577

35054-1 **Some like it hot** aBilly May; vJudy Ellington
BB B10182°; *BB AXM2 5577*; *RCA (Fr) PM 45689*; *Swing Era LP 1002, LPS 5001*; BB AXK2 5577; **RCA 2135554-2; JAZZ ARCHIVES (FR) 30; ZETA (GER) ZET 749; RCA (FR) 74321355542**

35054-2 **Some like it hot** aBilly May; vJudy Ellington
Unissued

March 22–April 4, 1939: NYC, Paramount Theater (also on bill: Mischa Auer, Dorothy Lamour)

Bob Burnet, John Mendell, Charles Huffine, Charlie Shavers, tpts; Ben Hall, Don Ruppersberg, Bill Robertson, tbns; Gene Kinsey, Donald McCook, as; Kurt Bloom, ts; James Lamare, ts & bar; Bill Miller, p; Bus Etri, g; Phil Stephens, b; Wesley Dean, d (ViSS)

NYC, RCA Victor recording session, April 5, 1939

35559-1 **Strange enchantment** aBilly May; vJudy Ellington
BB B10227°; *BB AXM2 5577*; *Big Band Archives BBA 1209*; BB AXK2 5577

35560-1 **Asleep or awake** aBilly May; vJudy Ellington
BB B10206; *BB AXM2 5577*; BB AXK2 5577

35560-2 **Asleep or awake** aBilly May; vJudy Ellington
Unissued

35561-1 **Only a rose** aBilly May
Unissued

35561-2 **Only a rose** aBilly May
BB B10227°; *BB AXM2 5577*; *RCA (Fr) PM 45689*; *Big Band Archives BBA 1209*; BB AXK2 5577; **RCA 2135554-2; GIANTS OF JAZZ (CZ) CD 53277; RCA (FR) 74321355542**

35562-1 **S'posin'** aBilly May
BB 10206; *BB AXM2 5577*; BB AXK2 5577

35563-1 **Echoes of Harlem** (transcription of Duke Ellington arrangement)
BB B10210°; Montgomery Ward M-7966; Vi (Ja) A-1093; *BB AXM2 5577; Vi LPV 567°; RCA (Fr) PM 42041, PM 45689; RCA (Ger) LPM 567; RCA (Ja) RA 60-68; RCA Vi (E) RD 8088; RCA (It?) 34048*; BB AXK2 5577; **RCA 2135554-2; BEST**

OF JAZZ (FR) 4039; DUET (E) DCD CD212; JAZZ ARCHIVES (FR) 30; GI-ANTS OF JAZZ (IT) CD 53277; KAZ (E) CD 311; TOPAZ JAZZ (E) TPZ 1041; ZETA (GER) ZET 749; RCA (FR) 74321355542

35564-1 **Scotch and soda** aRoscoe Fritz
BB B10210°; Montgomery Ward M-7966; Vi (Ja) A-1093; *BB AXM2 5577; RCA (Fr) PM 45689; Sounds of Swing LP 103*; BB AXK2 5577; RCA 2135554-2; **JAZZ ARCHIVES (FR) 30; GIANTS OF JAZZ (CZ) CD 53277; ZETA (GER) ZET 749; RCA (FR) 74321355542**

35564-2 **Scotch and soda** aRoscoe Fritz
Unissued

April 8, 1939: Atlantic City, Hamid's Pier
April 17–23, 1939: Philadelphia, Fox Theatre
April 24–??, 1939: Boston, Raymor Ballroom

Bob Burnet, John Mendell, John Owens, tpts; Ben Hall, Don Ruppersberg, Bill Robertson, tbns; Gene Kinsey, Donald McCook, as; Kurt Bloom, ts; James Lamare, ts & bar; Bill Miller, p; Bus Etri, g; Phil Stephens, b; Wesley Dean, d (ViSS)

NYC, RCA Victor recording session, May 8, 1939

36919-1 **Miss Annabelle Lee** aBilly May
BB B10294°; *BB AXM2 5577; RCA (Fr) PM 45689; Big Band Archives BBA 1209*; BB AXK2 5577; **RCA 2135554-2; BEST OF JAZZ (FR) 4039; GIANTS OF JAZZ (IT) CD 53277; RCA (FR) 74321355542**

36920-1 **Lazy bug** aCharlie Barnet
BB B10294°; *BB AXM2 5577; RCA (Fr) PM 45689; Sounds of Swing LP 103*; BB AXK2 5577; **RCA 2135554-2; JAZZ ARCHIVES (FR) 30; GIANTS OF JAZZ (IT) CD 53277; TOPAZ JAZZ (E) TPZ 1041; ZETA (GER) ZET 749; RCA (FR) 74321355542**

36921-1 **This is no dream** aBilly May; vJudy Ellington
Unissued

36921-2 **This is no dream** aBilly May; vJudy Ellington
BB B10273°; *BB AXM2 5577*; BB AXK2 5577

36922-1 **That's right—I'm wrong** aBilly May; vJudy Ellington
BB B10273°; *BB AXM2 5577*; BB AXK2 5577

36923-1 **Midweek function** aCharlie Barnet
BB B10285°; *BB AXM2 5577*; *RCA (Fr) PM 42041, PM 45689*; *Sounds of Swing LP 103*; BB AXK2 5577; **RCA 2135554-2; JAZZ ARCHIVES (FR) 30; KAZ (E) CD 311; TOPAZ JAZZ (E) TPZ 1041; ZETA (GER) ZET 749; RCA (FR) 74321355542**

36924-1 **I never knew** aBilly May
BB B10285°; *BB BAXM2 5577; RCA (Fr) PM 45689; Swing Era LP 1002, LPS 5001*; BB AXK2 5577; **GIANTS OF JAZZ (IT) CD 53277; RCA 2135554-2; JAZZ ARCHIVES (FR) 30; ZETA (GER) ZET 749; RCA (FR) 74321355542**

May 12, 1939: Schenectady, NY, Union College
May 13, 1939: NYC, Manhattan Center
(May 14, 1939: NYC, Savoy Ballroom?)
May 15, 1939: NYC, Famous Door
May 17, 1939: Berwick, PA, West Side Park
May 19–25, 1939: Washington, DC, Capitol Theatre
May 26–June 1, 1939: Brooklyn, Flatbush Theater

Charlie took part in the National Swing Club of America concert at the New York Hippodrome on May 29. He was part of the accompaniment for Billie Holiday; others were Duke Ellington, Frankie Newton, Sandy Block (b)

LAMOUR'S BOY FRIEND CRASHES INTO TRUCK; GREENWICH GIRL HURT

Orchestra Leader Charles Barnet, Who Is Expected To Wed Film Star Soon, And Miss Kay Wiles, 17, Escape Serious Injury In Smashup

Miss Kay Wiles, 17-year-old Greenwich High School graduate, and Charlie Barnet, popular dance orchestra lead-

Barnet Lends His Car to Pal; Pal, Gal Both in Bad Crash

and Henry Adler (d) (*Down beat* July 1939).

June 9, 1939: Woodbury Forest, VA, College
June 10–15, 1939: Brooklyn, Hi-Ho (Heigh Ho?) Casino
June 16–ca. July 17, 1939: Rye, NY, Playland

Personnel at Playland included Billy May (tpt) in place of Huffine, Ray Michaels, d, and Larry Taylor (vocal).

During an early morning rehearsal "a fellow brought in an arrangement for us to try. I stopped the band at the end of the first chorus. 'Sorry,' I said, 'I can't use this. Why don't you take it down to Glenn Miller?' Well, he did and that's how Glenn came up with *In the mood*. I still don't like it but it turned out to be his biggest hit." (*MS*)

The musical press carried a story about a proposed recording session involving Charlie and Dorothy Lamour (his current girl friend) but this was scotched by Lamour's film bosses.

Barnet Not Driver Of Auto In Crash

Orrhestra Leader Was Not Involved In Accident Yesterday Morning

Donald E. McCook, of Rye, N. Y. was the operator of an automobile in which he and Miss Kay Wiles 17, of 274½ Greenwich

Charlie Barnet and his orchestra

Bob Burnet, John Mendell, John Owens, tpts; Ben Hall, Don Ruppersberg, Bill Robertson, tbns; Gene Kinsey, Donald McCook, as; Kurt Bloom, ts; James Lamare, ts & bar; Bill Miller, p; Bus Etri, g; Phil Stephens, b; Ray Michaels, d

<u>NYC, RCA Victor recording session, June 26, 1939</u>

37687-1 **Danger in the dark** aBilly May; vLarry Taylor
BB B10336°; *BB AXM2 5577*; <u>BB</u> <u>AXK2</u> <u>5577</u>

37688-1 **An apple for the teacher** aBilly May; vLarry Taylor
BB B10349°; Montgomery Ward M-8323; *BB AXM2 5577*; <u>BB</u> <u>AXK2</u> <u>5577</u>

37689-1 **It must have been two other people** aBilly May; vLarry Taylor
BB B10336°; *BB AXM2 5577*; <u>BB</u> <u>AXK2</u> <u>5577</u>

37690-1 **Still the bluebird sings** aBilly May; vLarry Taylor
BB B10349°; Montgomery Ward M-8323; *BB AXM2 5577*; <u>BB</u> <u>AXK2</u> <u>5577</u>

37691-1 **Ebony rhapsody** (transcription of Duke Ellington arrangement)
BB B10341°; HMV (E) B-9461; HMV (India) B-9461; HMV (It) HN 2255; HMV (Switz) JK 2409; *BB AXM2 5577; RCA (Fr) PM 42041, PM 45689; Swing Era LP 1002, LPS 5001*; <u>BB</u> <u>AXK2</u> <u>5577</u>; **RCA 2135554; JAZZ ARCHIVES (FR) 30; GIANTS OF JAZZ (IT) CD53277; KAZ (E) CD 311; ZETA (GER) ZET 749; RCA (FR) 74321355542**

37692-1 **Lament for a lost love** aCharlie Barnet
BB B10341°; *BB AXM2 5577; RCA Vi LPT 3062°; Vi LPV 567°; RCA (Fr) PM 42041, PM 45689; RCA (Ger) LPM 567; RCA (E) RD 8088; RCA (It?) LPM 34048; RCA Vi*

(Arg) AVLT-7; *RCA Vi EPBT 3062*; BB AXK2 5577; **RCA 2135554-2; JAZZ ARCHIVES (FR) 30; GIANTS OF JAZZ (CZ) CD 53277; KAZ (E)CD 311; TOPAZ JAZZ (E) TPZ 1041; RCA (FR) 74321355542**

NYC, Magic Key of RCA, NBC b'cast, July 3, 1939

That's right, I'm wrong aBilly May; vJudy Ellington
Echoes of Harlem aDuke Ellington
I've got to be a rug cutter aAndy Gibson; vJudy Ellington and trio (probably Etri, Burnet and Lamare)
Danger in the dark aBilly May; vLarry Taylor
Ebony rhapsody aAndy Gibson?

July 5?–17?, 1939: Rye, NY, Playland
(engagement cut short due to the powerful draw of the Glenn Miller band just down the road at Glen Island Casino.)

Billy May notes that the band was scheduled to record at 3PM. "[*Cherokee*] was about the last thing to be recorded. I had the idea for the beginning of it and I wrote that out but that Sunday I remembered that I didn't have an out chorus—the ensemble chorus—so I wrote that in the car riding down—somebody was driving—when we got down there, it wasn't really a strip of paper. Each guy had like 3 staffs which I wrote out (there was no copyist), about 24 bars. It was a continuation of the previous stuff I'd given them the day before, so we tried it down, and it was easy to play, and we made it. I think it was like sight reading the thing." (*Cecil*)

Charlie Barnet orchestra

NYC, RCA Thesaurus recording session, possibly July 16, 1939

38288-1 **In a mizz** aBilly May; vJudy Ellington
THESAURUS 680, 1175 (as The Rhythm Makers)
38288-1 **It must have been two other people** aBilly May; vJudy Ellington
THESAURUS 680
38288-1 **Cherokee** aBilly May
THESAURUS 680, 1171° (as The Rhythm Makers)
38288-1 **I'll remember** vLarry Taylor
THESAURUS 680, 1175 (as The Rhythm Makers); Ajax C-679
38289-1 **Ain'tcha comin' out** vJudy Ellington
THESAURUS 680; Ajax C-679
38289-1 **A man and his dream** vLarry Taylor
THESAURUS 680; Ajax C-679
38289-1 **Still the bluebird sings** aBilly May; vLarry Taylor
THESAURUS 680 [as *Still the bluebirds sing*]
38289-1 **I've got to be a rug cutter** aAndy Gibson; vJudy Ellington and trio (possibly Etri, Burnet and Lamare)
THESAURUS 680; *IAJRC 8*; Ajax C-679
38290-1 **An apple for the teacher** aBilly May; vLarry Taylor
THESAURUS 681
38290-1 **Oh, you crazy moon** aBilly May; vLarry Taylor
THESAURUS 681; Ajax C-679
38290-1 **Danger in the dark** aBilly May; vLarry Taylor
THESAURUS 681
38290-1 **My heart has wings** aBilly May; vLarry Taylor
THESAURUS 681; Ajax C-679
38290-1 **Make believe ballroom** aHorace Diaz, Jr.
THESAURUS 681; *Jazz Band (Fr) 8008*; *Cicala (It) BLJ 8008*; *First Time FTR 2501*; **GIANTS OF JAZZ (IT) CD 53274**

Charlie Barnet and his orchestra

NYC, RCA Victor recording session, July 17, 1939

38276-1 **Cherokee** aBilly May
BB B10373°; Vi 20-1756; 420-0071; Vi (Brazil) [number??]; HMV (E) B-9410; HMV (India) B-9410; HMV (Fr) SG-31; HMV (Finland) TG-166; ***Vi 447-0071, 447-0872***; *BB AXM2 5577*; *Vi LPT-1°, LPV-551°*; *Franklin Mint 33*; *Franklin Mint record no. 19*; *RCA PRM/PRS-401*; *Reader's Digest RD4-21, RD4-44, RD4-113, RB4-136*; *Reader's Digest (E) RDM-2173*; *Smithsonian DMM 60610 44R030*; *Big Bands (Time-Life) STBB0-07*; *Camden CCL2 0619*; *RCA PRS 356*; *RCA VPM-6043°*; *RCA Special Products DMM1-0698*; *Vi LPM-2081*; *RCA Special Products DPL1-0013; Vi PR 111*; *Vi PR 125*; *MP Records (Ger) 33013*; *RCA (It) EDP-1004*; *RCA (E) RD-7965*; *RCA (Fr) PM 42401,*

PM 45689; *RCA (Ger) LPM-551*; *RCA (It?) LPM 34022*; *RCA (Ja) RA 60-68, RJL 2019-20*; *RCA Special Prod-ucts (C) DPM2-0813*; ***Vi EPA-5001, WPT-1, EPAT-1, EPAT-404***; ***RCA (E) RCX-1008***; ***RCA (N) 21-016***; RCA 68507, RCA 1055-4, PK 5099; BB 61059-4, 61109-4; Intersound PCD-1014; ESX JCT-7006; Franklin Mint Tape no.19; Big Bands America 129312; Smithsonian DMK-3 0610 C/D RC030; Big Bands (Time-Life) 4TL-0011-R959-11, 4TBB-07 [CrO2 release]; Castle (E) MAC MC 358; Razor and Tie 89023-4, tape 1; **BMG JCD 7006; BB 61109-2; RCA 9972-2-R; BB 6273-2-RB; ESX JCD-7006; BIG BANDS AMERICA 129320; RCA 2135554-2; 63119, 68502-2, 68507, 68987, 09026-63119-2, RCA 09026-68778-2, 68735; SMITHSONIAN DMC-40610-4RD-030; BIG BANDS (TIME-LIFE) TCD-011-R690-11; BB 61059-2; RCA 1055-2; BEST OF JAZZ (FR) 4039; CASTLE (E) MAC MC 358; JAZZ ARCHIVES (FR) 30; GIANTS OF JAZZ (IT) CD 53277; SECOND STREET SSP 1204; TOPAZ JAZZ (E) TPZ-1041; RCA (E) 86273; READER'S DIGEST (E) RDCD-123; ZETA (GER) ZET 749; QUALITONE JTD 102-401; AFFINITY (E) CDAFS-1036-4; ARISTA 886281; INTERSOUND CDC-1014,CDC 1041; LIVING ERA CD AJA 5141, 5288;JAZZ GREATS (E) CD 071; EMPRESS (E) RAJCD 898; RCA (FR) 74321355542**; AFRS BML P-562; AFRS DOWNBEAT 30; AFRS G.I. JIVE 1451, (859?), (893?), 998; AFRS JATJB 10; AFRS MUSIC TRANSCRIPTION LIBRARY P-S 16; USIA-VOA WORLD OF JAZZ 63; AFRS SWINGTIME (no. unknown)

38277-1 **For tonight** aBilly May; vLarry Taylor
BB B10361°; Montgomery Ward M-8651; *BB AXM2 5577*

38278-1 **What's new** aBilly May; vLarry Taylor
BB B10361°; Montgomery Ward M-8651; *BB AXM2 5581*; *Bandstand 7123*; **AERO SPACE RACD 7123; EMPRESS (E) RAJCD 898**

38279-1 **Love grows on the white oak tree** aBilly May; vJudy Ellington
BB B10389°; Montgomery Ward M-8322; Vi 20-2627; *BB AXM2 5581*; *Bandstand 7123*; **AERO SPACE RACD 7123**

38279-2 **Love grows on the white oak tree** aBilly May; vJudy Ellington
Unissued

38280-1 **(Stay up "Stan") The all night record man** aBilly May; vJudy Ellington, Charlie Barnet and trio (probably Etri, Burnet, Lamare) [dedicated to disc jockey Stan Shaw]
BB B10373°; *BB AXM2 5581*; *Big Bands (Time-Life) STBB-07; RCA (Fr) PM 45689*; Big Bands (Time-Life) 4TL-0011-R959-11, 4TBB-07 (CrO2 issue); **RCA 2135554-2; BIG BANDS (TIME-LIFE) TCD-0011-R690-11; GIANTS OF JAZZ (CZ) CD 53277; TOPAZ JAZZ (E) TPZ-1041; RCA (FR) 74321355542**; AFRS SWINGTIME (no.??)

38281-1 **The last jump (A jump to end all jumps)** aRoscoe Fritz
BB B10389°; Montgomery Ward M-8322; Vi 20-2627; HMV (E) B-9638; *BB AXM2 5581*; *RCA (Fr) PM 45689*;*Swing Era LP-1002, LPS 5001*; **RCA 2135554-2; GIANTS OF JAZZ (CZ) CD 53277; TOPAZ JAZZ (E) TPZ-1041; EMPRESS (E) RAJCD 898; RCA (FR) 74321355542**

About *Cherokee* Charlie remembered, "When we had gotten our best take, the guy in charge of the date in the control room ... Leonard Joy called to me through the playback system. 'When's your birthday, Charlie? You can have that last one.' He didn't think much of it but I can truthfully say it was the nicest birthday present I ever received ... The record started to break real big during our engagement at the Palomar. We were booked to appear in a picture at Univeral Studios and the studio wanted us to do *Cherokee* in the picture. At a studio conference I was asked how long the arrangement ran, and I replied, 'Three minutes.' The director's next question floored me. 'How can we get it down to one minute and a half?' After spending all the money they were paying us in order to incorporate a hit record in the picture, they proposed to butcher it completely but that is Hollywood for you." (*MS*)

July 23, 1939: Bridgeport, CT, Pleasant Beach Ballroom

July 25–Aug. (11?), 1939: Cedar Grove, NJ, Meadowbrook Ballroom

Aug. 12, 1939: Pottstown, PA, Sunnybrook Ballroom

Aug. 14, 1939: New Castle, PA, Cathedral Theater
Aug. 15, 1939: Columbus, Centennial Terrace
Aug. 23–Oct. 2, 1939: Hollywood, Palomar Ballroom

Band members had leased accommodations in Rye and continued to live there after the job was terminated, commuting to the Meadowbrook.

"Coming into the Palomar when business was at low ebb, Barnet, on his first visit to the Coast with his band, drew over 6,000 admissions on his opening night ... With its seven brass, six saxes (with Barnet) this band is loud and lusty, but it swings." (*Tempo,* September 1939)

Bob Burnet, John Owens, Lyman Vunk, Billy May, tpts; Don Ruppersberg, Bill Robertson, Ben Hall, tbns; Gene Kinsey, Don McCook, as; Kurt Bloom, Skippy Martin, ts; Bill Miller, p; Phil Stephens, b; Bus Etri, g; Ray Michaels, d

Hollywood, Palomar Ballroom, (KHJ?) b'cast, Aug. 31, 1939.

Make believe ballroom# (opening theme) [fragment: 0:25]

As preceding, ca Aug. 31, 1939

Melancholy mood# aBilly May [1:17]
Redmond Nostalgia Co. CO-4391

World War II started with Germany's attack on Poland, followed a few days later by the U.S.S.R.'s attack on the same country.

As preceding, Sept. 3, 1939

Love grows on the white oak tree aBilly May; vJudy Ellington
Redmond Nostalgia Co. CO-4391
The Sheik of Araby
IAJRC 14; *Joyce 1152*; Redmond Nostalgia Co. CO-4391
New York nocturne (closing theme)
IAJRC 14; *Joyce 1152*; Redmond Nostalgia Co. CO-4391

Hollywood, RCA Victor recording session, Sept. 10, 1939

36482-2 **The Duke's idea** aHead
Unissued
36482-4 **The Duke's idea** aHead
BB B10453°; HMV (E) B-9410; HMV (India) B-9410; HMV (Fr) SG-24; HMV (Finland) TG-166; *BB AXM2 5581; Vi LPT-3062°, LPV-551°; Franklin Mint 33, record no.19; Big Bands (Time-Life) STBB-07; Vi LPM-2081; RCA (E) RD-7965; RCA (Fr) PM-42041, PM 45689; RCA (Ger) LPM-551; RCA (It?) LPM 34022; RCA (Ja) RA-60-68; RCA (Argentina) AVLT-7; RCA EPBT-3062; Vi EPAT-433°;* Franklin Mint tape no.19; Big Bands (Time-Life) 4TL-0011 59-11, 4TBB-07 (CrO2 release); **BB 6273-2-RB; RCA 2128562-2, 2135554-2; Big Bands (Time-Life) TCD-011 R960-11; Arista 886281; Best of Jazz (Fr) 4039; Jazz Archives (Fr) 30; Giants of Jazz (Cz) CD 53277; Kaz (E) CD-311; Topaz Jazz (E) TPZ 1041; RCA (E) 86273; Zeta (Ger) ZET-749; Jazz Greats (E) CD 071; RCA (Fr) 74321355542; Living Era (E) CD AJA 5288;** USIA-VOA WORLD OF JAZZ 63
36483-2 **My heart keeps crying** aBilly May; vJudy Ellington
Unissued
36483-4 **My heart keeps crying** aBilly May; vJudy Ellington
BB B10426°; *BB AXM2 5581*; **Empress (E) RAJCD 898**
36484-2 **Lilacs in the rain** aBilly May; vDel Casino
Unissued
36484-5 **Lilacs in the rain** aBilly May; vDel Casino
BB B10439°; Montgomery Ward M-8350; HMV (India) NE-777; *BB AXM2 5581*
36485-3 **Take a tip from the whip-poor-will** aBilly May; vJudy Ellington
Unissued
36485-6 **Take a tip from the whip-poor-will** aBilly May; vJudy Ellington
BB B10426°; *BB AXM2 5581*
36486-6 **The Count's idea** aHead
Unissued
36486-8 **The Count's idea** aHead
BB B10453°; *BB AXM2 5581*; *Vi LPV-551°*; *Big Bands (Time-Life) STBB-07*; *Vi LPM-2081*; *RCA (Fr) PM-42401, PM-45689*; *RCA (E) RD-7965*; *RCA (Ger) LPM-551*; *RCA (It?) LPM 34022*; *RCA (Ja) RA-60-68*; *Vi EPAT-433°*; Big Bands

Fire Razes Palomar; Loss Heavy

More Than 2000 Leave Ballroom Safely After Flames Start on Stage

Fire which broke out on the stage at the Palomar Ballroom, Second St. and Vermont Ave., early today during the floor show, endangered the lives of more than 2000 patrons and destroyed the huge dance place with an estimated loss of $500,000.

(Time-Life) 4TL-0011 59-11, 4TBB-07 (CrO2 release); BB 61059-4; **BB 6273-2-RB; RCA 2135554-2; Big Bands (Time-Life) TCD-011 R960-11; BB 61059-2; Arista 886281; Best of Jazz (Fr) 4039; Jazz Archives (Fr) 30; Giants of Jazz (It) CD 53277; Topaz Jazz (E) TPZ-1041; RCA (E) 86273; Zeta (Ger) ZET-749; Jazz Greats (E) CD 071; RCA (Fr) 74321355542; Living Era (E) CD AJA 5288**

36487-2 **The girl with the pigtails in her hair** aBilly May; vJudy Ellington
Unissued

36487-3 **The girl with the pigtails in her hair** aBilly May; vJudy Ellington
BB B10439°; Montgomery Ward M-8350; HMV (India) NE-777; *BB AXM2 5581*

On October 2, the next-to-last day of the engagement, the Palomar burned to the ground, along with the band's instruments and library. "Hell, it's better than being in Poland with bombs dropping on your head." (Charlie quoted by Billy May)

ca. early Oct. 1939: Los Angeles, CA, Domar Ballroom (*Sm*)

Basie gave him a few arrangements including *Moonlight serenade* and other pop tunes, some of which had been arranged by Skippy Martin. (Contrary to reports, Duke did not give him any arrangements.) (*Sm*)

Personnel as preceding except Phil Stephens played brass bass on *The wrong idea* and Phil Moore replaced Bill Miller on *Ogoun badagris.*

Hollywood, RCA Victor recording session, Oct. 9, 1939

42174-4 **Ogoun badagris** aPhil Moore ["Phallus of the Haitian voodoo war god"]
Unissued

42174-5 **Ogoun badagris** aPhil Moore
BB B10530°; *BB AXM2 5581; RCA (Fr) PM 45689; Sounds of Swing LP-103*; **RCA 2135554-2; Jazz Archives (Fr) 30; Giants of Jazz (Cz) CD 53277; Zeta (Ger) ZET-749; RCA (Fr) 74321355542**; AFRS DOWNBEAT 298

42175-1 **Cuban boogie woogie** aBilly May; vJudy Ellington
Unissued

42175-2 **Cuban boogie woogie** aBilly May; vJudy Ellington
BB B10479; *BB AXM2 5581; Big Bands (Time-Life) STBB-07; Swing Era LP-1002, LPS-5001*; Big Bands (Time-Life) 4TL-0011 59-11, 4TBB-07 (CrO2 release); **Big Bands (Time-Life) TCD-011 R960-11**

42176-6 **Are we burnt up** aBilly May and Skippy Martin; vBand
[When this was issued in 1981 the title was changed to *Oh what you said (Are we burnt up)*. This song and *Leapin' at the Lincoln* are based on *Oh! lady be good* and are basically the same arrangement; the recorded versions differ in that this one has a vocal and is 32 bars longer than the later *Leapin'* recording.]
BB AXM2 5581; RCA (Fr) PM 45689; **RCA 2135554-2; Jazz Archives (Fr) 30; Giants of Jazz (Cz) CD 53277; Zeta (Ger) ZET-749; RCA (Fr) 74321355542**

42177-1 **A lover is blue** aSkippy Martin; vJudy Ellington
BB B10511°; *BB AXM2 5581; Sounds of Swing LP 103*

42178-1 **The wrong idea** aBilly May; vBilly May ("Slappy Habits") [Billy says the phrase "Swing and sweat…" may have originated with Lyman Vunk.]

BB B10804°; VeeJay 8007 [title as *Swing and sweat (Or Mr. K. has the wrong idea)*]; *Vi LPV-567°, LPM-2081; BB AXM2 5581; RCA (Ger) LPM-567; RCA (E) RD-8088; RCA (Fr) PM 45689; RCA (It?) LPM 34048; RCA (Ja) RA 60-68; Bandstand 7118; Vi EPAT-433°*; RCA 2135554-2; **Giants of Jazz (Cz) CD 53277; Topaz Jazz (E) TPZ-1041; RCA (Fr) 74321355542**

42179-1 **The right idea** aSkippy Martin
Unissued

42179-4 **The right idea** aSkippy Martin
BB B10530°; *BB AXM2 5581; Vi LPV-551°; RCA (E) RD-7965; RCA (Fr) PM-42401, PM-45689; RCA (Ger) LPM-551; RCA (It?) LPM 34022; RCA (Ja) RA 60-68; Big Bands (Time-Life) STBB-07; Vi EPAT-433°*; Big Bands (Time-Life) 4TL-0011 R059-11, 4TBB-07 (CrO2 release); BB 61059-4; **BB 6273-2-RB, 61059-2;RCA 2135554-2; RCA 63446; Big Bands (Time-Life)TCD-0011 RB60-11; Best of Jazz (Fr) 4039; Jazz Archives (Fr) 30; Giants of Jazz (It) CD 53277; Topaz Jazz (E) TPZ-1041; RCA (E) 86273; Zeta (Ger) ZET-749; Arista 886281; RCA (Fr) 74321355542; Living Era (E) CD AJA 5288**

42180-4 **Night glow** aBilly May
Unissued

42180-7 **Night glow** aBilly May
BB B10511°; *BB AXM2 5581; RCA (Fr) PM 45689; Sounds of Swing LP-103*; **RCA 2135554-2; Jazz Archives (Fr) 30; Giants of Jazz (Cz) CD 53277; Zeta (Ger) 749; RCA (Fr) 74321355542**

42181-3 **Two hearts are better than one** aBilly May; vJudy Ellington
BB B10479; HMV (Australia) EA-2682; *BB AXM2 5581* (an early example of Charlie playing soprano)

42181-6 **Two hearts are better than one** aBilly May; vJudy Ellington
Unissued

The band headed east with jobs to go to "but no music or instruments and, I might add, no insurance." With newly purchased instruments "plus what we could remember of our own arrangements we were able to struggle out of town. In the meantime my arrangers were busy recreating the most important tunes of our repertoire plus new ones." (*MS*)

Claude M. "Spud" Murphy—not to be confused with the "real" Spud Murphy (the arranger and woodwind player Lyle M. Murphy)—replaced Ben Hall at about this time. (Lyle Murphy says it was Charlie who gave Claude Murphy the nickname "Spud.")

October 1939: Tucson, unidentified location
October 1939: Lexington, unidentified location
October 26, 1939:Toledo, unidentified location
October 1939: Toronto, Old Mill Ballroom
Oct. or Nov. 1939: Cincinnati, unidentified location
Nov. 6–19, 1939: Boston, Southland Cafe
Nov. 21, 1939: Washington, Colonnade Ballroom
Nov. 23?, 1939: Baltimore, Strand Ballroom
Nov. 26, 1939: White Plains, NY, County Center [with Hal Kemp]
Nov. 27, 1939: NYC, Local 802 Medical Fund, Madison Sq. Garden

Judy Ellington left Charlie probably in late November and joined Tommy Reynolds. Mary Ann McCall was her replacement and appeared at the Apollo on December 1. It was probably this early December engagement which Charlie reminisced about many years later: "The worst week in show business is just before Christmas. We had a problem with a couple of dates that fell out, so I got hold of Frank Schiffman at the Apollo theatre in Harlem and I said, 'Frank, who have you got booked pre-Christmas?' He said, 'Nobody.' So I said, 'How would about 50-50 for the first (night) and you're off the hook with a guarantee and everything?' He thought he had a hell of a deal. The bottom line: It took mounted police out on the sidewalk in front of the theater to hold the people back. We wound up doing six days, seven shows a day. It was a hit all right, because when the people from Harlem put their stamp of approval on it, you had it."

Dec. 1–7, 1939: NYC, Apollo Theater

NYC, Apollo Theater, stage performance, Dec. 1, 1939

Trumpet in spades aBob Burnet, Andy Gibson
Echoes of Harlem aDuke Ellington
Cherokee aBilly May
South of the border aHead; vMary Ann McCall
My blue heaven aMary Ann McCall

"I came within 200 votes of being elected honorary mayor of Harlem ... Willie Bryant beat me out by about 214 votes." (*Sm*)

Dec. 8, 1939: Newark, NJ, Kruger's Auditorium
Dec. 9, 1939: Durham, NC, Duke University

Bob Burnet, Billy May, Johnny Owens, Lyman Vunk, tpts; Claude M. "Spud" Murphy (lead), Don Ruppersburg, Bill Robertson, tbns; Gene Kinsey, Skippy Martin, as; Kurt Bloom, ts, Jim Lamare, ts & bar; Bill Miller, p; Bus Etri, g; Phil Stephens, b; Cliff Leeman, d (ViSS)

NYC, RCA Victor recording session, December 11, 1939

43989-1 **Now you know** vMary Ann McCall
BB B10549°; *BB AXM2 5581*; **EMPRESS (E) RAJCD 898**
43990-1 **I kinda like you** aBilly May; vMary Ann McCall
BB B10568; *BB AXM2 5581*
43991-1 **Night after night after you** aBilly May; vMary Ann McCall
BB B10549°; *BB AXM2 5581*
43992-1 **Between 18th and 19th on Chestnut Street** aBilly May; vMary Ann McCall
BB B10543°; *BB AXM2 5581*; *Vi LEJ-1*; *RCA (Fr) PM 45689*; *Bandstand 7123*; *Vi WEJ-1*; **BB 6273 2-RB; AERO SPACE RACD 7123; RCA 2135554-2; ARISTA 886281; GIANTS OF JAZZ (CZ) CD 53277; RCA (E) 86273; EMPRESS (E) RAJCD 898; RCA (FR) 74321355542**
43993-1 **Somebody told me** aBilly May; vMary Ann McCall
BB B10543°; *BB AXM2 5581*
43994-1 **Clap hands! here comes Charley!** aSkippy Martin
BB AXM2 5590; *RCA (Fr) PM 42401, PM 45689*
43994-2 **Clap hands! here comes Charley!** aSkippy Martin
BB B10602°; *BB AXM2 5581*; *Franklin Mint 33, Record no.19*; *Big Bands (Time-Life) STBB-07*; *Camden CAL 389*; *Bandstand 7123*; **Camden CAE-432**; Franklin Mint Tape no.19; Big Bands (Time-Life) 4TL-0011 R059-11, 4TBB-07 (CrO2 release); **BB 6273 2-RB; BIG BANDS (TIME-LIFE) TCD-011R960-11; ARISTA 886281; BEST OF JAZZ (FR) 4039; GIANTS OF JAZZ (IT) CD 53277; RCA (E) 86273; JAZZ GREATS (E) CD 071; EMPRESS (E) RAJCD 898; RCA (FR) 74321355542;**
LIVING ERA (E) CD AJA 5288

Dec. 14, 1939: NYC, Golden Gate Ballroom
Dec. 16, 1939: Providence, RI, Arcadia Ballroom
Dec. 17, 1939: Worcester, MA, Auditorium
Dec. 19, 1939: Brunswick, ME, Bowdoin College
Dec. (20?), 1939: Boston, unidentified location
Dec. 25, 1939: NYC, Manhattan Center
Dec. 26, 1939: Philadelphia, Club Morocco
Dec. 27, 1939: Baltimore, Keith's Roof
Dec. (29-30?), 1939: Hartford, State Theater
Dec. 31, 1939: NYC, Savoy Ballroom
December 1939: Tiverton, RI, unidentified location

Bob Burnet, Billy May, John Owens, Lyman Vunk, tpts; Spud Murphy (lead), Don Ruppersburg, Bill Robertson, tbns; Gene Kinsey, Noni Bernardi (substituting for Skippy Martin who was ill), as; Kurt Bloom, ts; James Lamare, ts & bar; Bill Miller, p; Bus Etri, g; Phil Stephens, b; Cliff Leeman, d. (Vi SS) (Etri's name omitted from Vi SS but he's audible.)

NYC, RCA Victor recording session, January 3, 1940

46056-1 **Thank your stars** aBilly May; vMary Ann McCall
BB B10568; *BB AXM2 5581*
46057-1 **Tappin' at the Tappa** aHead
BB B10584°; *BB AXM2 5581*; *RCA (Fr) NL 89483-2*; *Sounds of Swing LP-103*; **RHINO R2-70722; RCA (FR) 74321355532**

(The Tappa was a bar across the street from the Apollo Theater. This music was put together a few weeks earlier for a dancing act at the Apollo, whose written music "was really shitty" [Billy May].)

46058-1 **Comanche war dance** aBilly May
BB B10584°; HMV (E) B-9553; HMV (Fr) SG-42; *BB AXM2 5581*; *Vi LJM 1008*; *Big Band Archives BBA-1209*; *Vi (Australia) L-10051*; *RCA (Fr) NL-89483-2*; *Vi EJC-1008*; **Avid (E) AMSC 676; RCA (Fr) 74321355532;Living Era (E) CD AJA 5288**

46058-2 **Comanche war dance** aBilly May
Unissued

46059-1 **Southland shuffle** aBilly Gray
BB B10602°; *BB AXM2 5581*; *RCA (Fr) NL-89483-2*; *Big Band Archives BBA-1209*; **RCA (Fr) 74321355532; Living Era (E) CD AJA 5288**

46059-? **In-a-jam** aBob Burnet
Unissued
[Session sheet indicates that one take of this song was attempted to which mx 46059 was initially assigned.]

Bluebird 10602 was the subject of a *Down beat* review: "Outright Basie apings, but good nevertheless because of Charlie's alto (on *Southland*) and tenor. The leader is full of tricks when he solos and his performances invariably sound a lot more difficult than they really are…" (Mar. 15, 1940)

Jan. 5–11, 1940: Washington, DC, Howard Theater ("Charlie Barnet stopped every show") (*Down beat, Feb. 1, 1940*)

Jan. 14, 1940: NYC, Savoy Ballroom

Jan. 17, 1940: Youngstown, Nu Elms Ballroom [It may have been on this occasion that Charlie inquired as to where was the best whorehouse, "and the bell hop told me where to go, and I got in a cab and I went out there, and as I drove up, here's a great big Greyhound bus out in front of it with an electric sign on it that says 'Charlie Barnet and his Orchestra,' and the whole band is inside there, they had taken over the joint." (*Sm*)]

Jan. 23, 1940: Toronto, Palais Royale

Feb. 1, 1940: Brooklyn, Flatbush Theater

Feb. 3, 1940: Syracuse, Snell's Dancing Academy

Metronome All Star Band

Charlie Spivak, Harry James, Ziggy Elman, tpts; Jack Teagarden, Jack Jenney, tbns; Benny Goodman, cl; Toots Mondello, Benny Carter, as; Eddie Miller, ***Charlie Barnet****, ts; Jess Stacy, p; Charlie Christian, g; Bob Haggart, b; Gene Krupa, d*

NYC, Columbia recording session, February 7, 1940

26489-X **King Porter stomp** aFletcher Henderson (Breakdown)
Blu-disc T-1012

26489-A **King Porter stomp** aFletcher Henderson
Col 35389; V-Disc 894; Col (Arg) 291180; Col (Australia) DO-2107; Col (Ja) M-233; Parlophone (E) R-2746; Parlophone (It) B-71082; Parlophone (Switz) PZ-11172; *Col CL-2528*; *Harmony HL-7044*; *CBS-Sony (Ja) SOPM-188*

26489-B **King Porter stomp** aFletcher Henderson
Phontastic (Swed) NOST-7610; **Phontastic CD-7668**

Charlie Barnet and his orchestra

Personnel as for Jan. 3, 1940 except Noni Bernardi was replaced by Skippy Martin. (*ViSS*)

NYC, RCA Victor recording session, February 7, 1940

47015-1 **It's a wonderful world** aBilly May; vMary Ann McCall
BB B10610°; Vi (Arg) 83111; *BB AXM2 5581*; *Camden CAL-389*; *RCA (Fr) PM 42041*; BB AXK2-5585

47016-1 **720 in the books** aBilly May; vMary Ann McCall
BB B10618°; Vi (Arg) 26989 [Reverse is *Russian rag* by Curly Hicks y sus muchachos]; *BB AXM2 5581*; *Bandstand 7123*; BB AXK2 5585; AFRS JATJB 14; **Aero Space RACD-7123**

47017-1 **Busy as a bee (I'm buzz, buzz, buzzin')** aSkippy Martin; vMary Ann McCall
BB B10610°; Vi (Arg) 83111; *BB AXM2 5581*; BB AXK2 5585

47018-1 **So far, so good** aSkippy Martin; vMary Ann McCall
BB B10618°; *BB AXM2 5581*; Big Bands (Time-Life) 4TL-0011 R059-11, 4TBB-07 (CrO2 release); BB AXK2 5585; **BIG BANDS (TIME-LIFE) TCD-011 R960-11**

Feb. 8, 1940: Bronx, Windsor Theater (reported as playing week of Feb. 8)
Feb. 9–ca Mar. 22, 1940: NYC, Hotel Lincoln

Variety's reviewer was on hand for Charlie's Lincoln opening, noting that "Barnet keeps his powerful seven brass, four sax, four rhythm neatly under wraps during dinner here, but once the á la carte is disposed of it's a case of hang onto your hat, a good band's going riding ... a band much improved since his last catching. It has punch in its playing and in its arrangements. One of his best is his click arrangement of *Cherokee*."

At about this time he began using (what came to be called) *Redskin rhumba* as his opening theme, continuing to close with *Make believe ballroom*. (*Variety*, Feb. 14, 1940). The band was carried by WEAF, WJZ, WOR and WHN from February through July 27.

NYC, Hotel Lincoln, NBC b'cast, probably between Feb. 9 and March 22, 1940

Wanderin' blues aCharlie Barnet; vMary Ann McCall
Redmond Nostalgia Co. CO 4391
Make believe ballroom (closing theme) aHorace Diaz, Jr.
Redmond Nostalgia Co. CO 4391

As preceding

Cherokee# aBilly May [0:20]

As preceding

#The Count's idea aHead [1:38]

As preceding

#What's the matter with me# vMary Ann McCall [0:46]

As preceding

#Ev'ry Sunday afternoon aBilly May [0:46]

NYC, William Hillman News Commentary (NBC-Blue), Feb. 11, 1940

(Band was scheduled to be heard for five minutes at conclusion of program)

NYC, Hotel Lincoln, NBC b'cast, Feb. 20, 1940

Make believe ballroom (opening? theme) [10 second fragment]

Feb. 26, 1940: Pittsburgh, Syria Mosque
ca. late Feb., early March: NYC, Paramount Theater (was one of several leaders who fronted Miller band while Glenn was ill)

Charlie Barnet orchestra

Personnel as for Feb. 7, 1940.

NYC, RCA Thesaurus recording session, possibly late February, 1940

47449-1 **Ooh! what you said** aBilly May; vMary Ann McCall
THESAURUS 755, 1183
47449-1 **A lover is blue** aSkippy Martin; vMary Ann McCall
THESAURUS 755, 1183; *Joyce 2017*
47449-1 **You've got me out on a limb** vMary Ann McCall
THESAURUS 755, 1176°, 1183; Joyce JRC C1521
47449-1 **You, you darlin'** vMary Ann McCall
THESAURUS 755, 1183; Joyce JRC C1521
47449-1 **The Count's idea** aHead
THESAURUS 755, 1176°, 1183; Joyce JRC C1521
47450-1 **Castle of dreams** aBilly May; vMary Ann McCall
THESAURUS 756, 1183; *Trip TLP-5804*; *DJM (E) DJML-061*; *Jazz Bird JAZ 2016*; *Parnaso (Arg) 13032*; Joyce JRC C1521; **B&C RECORDS 74081-2; PILZ (GER) 44-2042-4**
47450-1 **Busy as a bee (I'm buzz, buzz, buzzin')** aSkippy Martin; vMary Ann McCall
THESAURUS 756, 1183; *Trip TL-5804*; *DJM (E) DJML-061*; *Jazz Bird JAZ 2016*; *Parnaso (Arg) 13032*; Joyce JRC C1521; **B&C RECORDS 74081-2; PILZ (GER) 44-2042-4**
47450-1 **It's a wonderful world** aBilly May; vMary Ann McCall

THESAURUS 756, 1183; Joyce JRC C1521

47450-1 **So far, so good** aSkippy Martin; vMary Ann McCall

THESAURUS 756, 1183; *Trip TLP 5804*; *DJM (E) DJML-061*; *Jazz Bird JAZ 2016*; *Parnaso (Arg) 13032*; Joyce JRC C1521

47450-1 **The Duke's idea** aHead

THESAURUS 756, 1183; *Trip TLP 5804*; *DJM (E) DJML-061*; *Jazz Bird JAZ 2016*; *Limited Editions LP-101*; *Parnaso (Arg) 13032*; Joyce JRC C1521

PLACES TO DINE

CAFE LOYALE 5TH AVE. AT E. 43 ST. Whole Lobster, Fried Clams, Soft Shell Crabs Luncheon 75c, Whole Lobster, Prime Ribs of Beef, Spring Chicken Dinner $1.00. Dancing.

CAVANAGH'S 258-260 WEST 23rd. Since 1876. Sea Food, Steaks, Chops. Banquet Rooms. Beefsteak Parties. AIR-CONDITIONED

CHARLIE BARNET Blue Room — Hotel Lincoln 44th-45th at 8th Dinner $1.50. Cover after 10:30 P.M., Weekday 50c; Sat. & Holiday Eves. $1.00

Charlie Barnet and his orchestra

Personnel as preceding. (*ViSS*)

NYC, RCA Victor recording session, February 27, 1940

47709-1 **Ev'ry Sunday afternoon** aBilly May; vMary Ann McCall

BB B10637°; *BB AXM2 5581*; BB AXK2 5585

47710-1 **From another world** vMary Ann McCall

BB B10637°; *BB AXM2 5581*; BB AXK2 5585

47711-1 **You've got me out on a limb** vMary Ann McCall

BB B10644; HMV (Australia) EA 2498; *BB AXM2 5585*; BB AXK2 5585; **EMPRESS (E) RAJCD 898**

47712-1 **Castle of dreams** aBilly May; vMary Ann McCall

BB B10644; *BB AXM2 5585*; BB AXK2 5585

47712-2 **Castle of dreams** aBilly May; vMary Ann McCall

Unissued

A news item in *Down beat* noted that he recently "showed up with a soprano and since that time has been getting his kicks on the 'short' horn." (Apr. 1, 1940).

As preceding, March 21, 1940

47985-1 **A lover's lullaby** aSkippy Martin

BB B10662°; HMV (Australia) EA 2613; *BB AXM2 5585*; *RCA (Fr) NL 89483-2*; *Sounds of Swing LP-103*;BB AXK2 5585; **EMPRESS (E) RAJCD 898; RCA (FR) 74321355532**

47986-1 **Where was I?** aBilly May; vMary Ann McCall

BB B10669°; HMV (Australia) EA 2525; *BB AXM2 5585*; *Reader's Digest RB4-084, RD4-078-1*; *The Music Makers, pgm 334*; BB AXK2 5585; Reader's Digest RD2 078; Reader's Digest RD5-078 (8-track); **RCA 63116, 44546; AFFINITY (E) CDAFS-036-4; BEST OF JAZZ (FR) 4039; LIVING ERA (E) CD AJA 5288**

47987-1 **'Deed I do** aBilly May; vMary Ann McCall

BB B10669°; HMV (Intl) J-068; *BB AXM2 5585*; *Big Bands (Time-Life) STBB-07*; BB AXK2-5585; Big Bands (Time-Life) 4TBB-07 (CrO2 release); Big Bands (Time-Life) 4TL-0011 R959-11; **BIG BANDS (TIME-LIFE) TCD-0011 R960-11; EMPORIO (E) DEMPCD-011; EMPRESS (E) RAJCD 898**

47988-1 **You've got me voodoo'd** aBilly May; vMary Ann McCall

BB B10662°; HMV (Australia) EA-2772; *BB AXM2 5585*; *Swing Era LP-1019*; BB AXK2 5585

47989-1 **Wanderin' blues** aCharlie Barnet; vMary Ann McCall

BB B10721°; HMV (Australia) EA-2707; HMV (E) B-9156; *AXM2 5585*; *Vi LPV 551°*; *RCA (E) RD 7965*; *RCA (Fr) NL 89483-2*; *RCA (Ger) LPM 551*; *RCA (It?) LPM 34022;* BB AXK2-5585; **RCA (FR) 74321355532; LIVING ERA (E) CD AJA 5288**

47990-1 **Leapin' at the Lincoln** aBilly May and Skippy Martin

BB B10774°; RCA Vi 420-0002, 20-2540; Vi (Arg) 29851; HMV (Australia) EA-3195; HMV (E) B-9156; ***Vi 447-0002***; ***Vi 447-0072***; ***RCA (N) 11-016***; *BB AXM2 5585*; *Vi LPV 567°*; *Big Bands (Time-Life)*

> **. . . Charlie Barnett has a hit record in the eyes of swing fans with his "Leapin' At The Lincoln" and it is due to his trumpet man's sensational job. The man has an amazing tone and attack that reminds you of the immortal "Bix". . . Give him more to do, Charlie, and you can never miss . . . Backing is "Dark Avenue", a slow blues that has a certain charm . . .**

Song Hits, October 1940

STBB-07; *RCA (E) RD 8088*; *RCA (Fr) NL 89483-2*; *RCA (Ger) LPM 567*; *RCA (It?) LPM 34048*; *RCA (Ja) RA 60-68*; ***RCA Vi EPA 5001***; ***RCA Vi EPAT 404***; ***RCA (E) RCX 1008***; Big Bands (Time-Life) 4TBB-07 (CrO2 release); Big Bands (Time-Life) 4TL-0011 R959-11; BB 61059-4; BB AXK2 5585; **BB 61059-2; BB 6273 2-RB; Big Bands (Time-Life) TCD-0011 R960-11; Arista 886281; Kaz (E) CD-311; RCA (E) 86273; Best of Jazz (Fr) 4039; Giants of Jazz (Cz) CD 53277; Jazz Greats (E) CD 071; Empress (E) RAJCD 898; RCA (Fr) 74321355532; Living Era (E) CD AJA 5288**

March 25, 1940: Pittsburgh, Harry Hendel's ballroom ("...a 2,000 draw was the season's top. It was black and tan stomp" [*Down beat* Apr. 15, 1940])
March 28–(April 3?), 1940: Brooklyn, Flatbush Theater
April 3–9, 1940: NYC, Windsor Theater
April 10–16, 1940: NYC, Carlton Theater

At the Flatbush Theater there was a magician on the bill whose music was performed by the Barnet band. On several occasions the accompaniment became a little raucous and out of keeping with the mood that the magician, Paul Duke, was trying to establish. "Instead of playing his music the way it was written it's claimed the band played it as they wanted to, interpolating their own breaks, etc. At one show Barnet is alleged to have turned over the baton to a sub conductor from the band [Bloom?] who in turn walked off the stage in the middle of Duke's act and left the band to its own devices because they didn't follow what was written." Charlie paid Duke off for the balance of the Brandt circuit tour. *Variety's* reviewer had noted earlier that "a trumpet member of the band stood up and took a hot solo behind the tap act of the Four Step Bros." (*Variety* Apr. 10, 1940)

NYC, RCA Victor recording session, April 16, 1940

48791-1 **You're lonely and I'm lonely** aBilly May; vMary Ann McCall
BB B10691º; *BB AXM2 5585*; BB AXK2 5585

48792-1 **Fools fall in love** aSkippy Martin; vMary Ann McCall
BB B10691º; *BB AXM2 5585*; BB AXK2 5585; **Empress (E) RAJCD 898**

48909-1 **Dark avenue** aBilly May; vMary Ann McCall
BB B10774º; HMV (E) B-9513; HMV (India) B-9513; HMV (It) HN-2156; *BB AXM2 5585*; BB AXK2 5585

48910-1 **The breeze and I** aBilly May; vMary Ann McCall
BB B10696º; HMV (Australia) EA 2653; *BB AXM2 5585*; BB AXK2 5585; **Empress (E) RAJCD 898**

48911-1 **Afternoon of a moax (Shake, rattle 'n' roll)** aCharlie Barnet
BB B10721º; HMV (Australia) EA 2707; *BB AXM2 5585; Vi LPV 567º, LPM 2081; RCA Vi (E) RD 8088; RCA (Fr) NL 89483; RCA (Ger) LPM 567; RCA (It?) LPM 34048*; BB AXK2 5585; BB 61059-4; **BB 6273 2-RB; BB 61059-2; Arista 886281; Kaz (E) CD-311; RCA (E) 86273; Giants of Jazz (Cz) CD 53277; RCA (Fr) 74321355532; Jazz Band (Cz) SDCD 2261-2;** AFRS DOWNBEAT 277

48912-1 **The fable of the rose** aSkippy Martin; vMary Ann McCall
BB B10696º; *BB AXM2 5585*; BB AXK2 5585

48912-2 **The fable of the rose** aSkippy Martin; vMary Ann McCall
Unissued

NYC, RCA Victor recording session, May 8, 1940

50617-1 **When the spirit moves me** aBilly May; vMary Ann McCall
BB B10734º; *BB AXM2 5585*; BB AXK2 5585; **Empress (E) RAJCD 898**

Songs and Songsters

CHARLIE "CHEROKEE" BARNET has just recovered "Shake, Rattle'n Roll" for Bluebird. He thought up that title after watching a negro porter who had a way with the spotted cubes. Later, however, the name of this release was changed to "Afternoon of a Moax", since the first title had to be explained. In case you don't understand the second version, a "moax" is a "gleep", or in collegiate circles, a "weemus" or even a "weir".

International Musician, June 1940

50618-1 **Reminiscing** aOtto Cesana; vMary Ann McCall
BB B10846°; *BB AXM2 5585*; *Swing Era LP 1002, LPS 5001*; BB AXK2 5585

50619-1 **You and who else** aBilly May; vLarry Taylor
BB B10734°; *BB AXM2 5585*; AXK2 5585

50620-1 **Flying home** aSkippy Martin
BB B10794°; HMV (E) B 9461; HMV (India) B 9461; HMV (It) HN2255; HMV (Switz) JK 2409; *BB AXM2 5585*; *Vi LPM 2081*; *RCA (Fr) NL 89483-2*; *RCA (It) EDP 1004*; *Bandstand 7123*; BB 61059-4; BB AXK2 5585; **BB 6273 2-RB; BB 61059-2; RCA (E) 86273; Giants of Jazz (Cz) CD 53280; Aero Space RACD 7123; Empress (E) RAJCD 898; Avid (E) AMSC 676; RCA 09026-63342-2; RCA (Fr) 74321355532**

56020-2 **Flying home** aSkippy Martin
Unissued

50621-1 **Lament for May** aCharlie Barnet
BB B10743°; *BB AXM2 5585*; *Vi LPV 551°*; *Vi LPM 2081*; *RCA (E) RD 7965*; *RCA (Fr) NL 89483-2*; *RCA (Ger) LPM 551*; *RCA (It?) LPM 34022*; BB AXK2 5585; **Best of Jazz (Fr) 4039; Jazz Greats (E) CD 071; RCA (Fr) 74321355532**

50622-1 **Six lessons from Madame La Zonga** aBilly May; vMary Ann McCall
BB B10743°; *BB AXM2 5585*; *Vi LPM 2081*; BB AXK2 5585; **BB 6273 2-RB; RCA (E) 86273; Arista 886281; Empress (E) RAJCD 898**

Charlie Barnet and his orchestra

Personnel as preceding.

As preceding, May 16, 1940

50586-1 **Where do you keep your heart?** aBilly May; vLarry Taylor
BB B10751°; *BB AXM2 5585*; BB AXK2 5585

50586-2 **Where do you keep your heart?** aBilly May; vLarry Taylor
Unissued

50587-1 **No name jive, pt. 1** aSkippy Martin
BB B10737°; HMV (Intl) J 067; HMV (Switz) JK 2514; *BB AXM2 5585*; *Reader's Digest RD4-45*; *Reader's Digest (Can) 627*; *Reader's Digest (UK) RDM 265*; *RCA (Fr) NL 89483-2*; *Bandstand 7123*; *Swing Era LP 1002, LPS 5001*; BB AXK2 5585; **Aero Space RACD 7123; RCA (Fr) 74321355532**

50588-1 **No name jive, pt. 2** aSkippy Martin
Issues as for pt.1

50589-1 **All this and heaven too** aBilly May; vLarry Taylor
BB B10751°; *BB AXM2 5585*; *Reader's Digest RD4-25*; *Reader's Digest (Ja) 9S*; BB AXK2 5585; Reader's Digest RD-3; READER'S DIGEST RD-8 5386, RD-5 025-1/2 (8-track); **Reader's Digest RDD25/CD11**

50622-2 **Six lessons from Madame La Zonga** aBilly May; vMary Ann McCall
Unissued

May 22–June 4, 1940: NYC, Paramount Theater (doubling from Lincoln)

NYC, Hotel Lincoln, NBC b'cast, between May 1 and July 28, 1940

#Begin the beguine# (1:36)
#My old Kentucky home (3:15)

As preceding

#Flying home (2:57) aSkippy Martin
#Lament for May (2:43) aCharlie Barnet

As preceding

#It's the last time I'll fall in love (2:46) aBilly May; vMary Ann McCall
#Afternoon of a moax (3:23)

<u>*As preceding*</u>

Dardanella (2:43)
Leapin' at the Lincoln (2:38) aBilly May
Make believe ballroom# aHorace Diaz, Jr.

<u>*As preceding*</u>

#Rockin' in rhythm# (2:56) aBilly May
Afternoon of a moax# (3:01) aCharlie Barnet
#Flying home (3:02) aSkippy Martin

<u>*As preceding*</u>

 # When you wish upon a star (0:10)

Approximately at this time, Billy Moore is reported to have composed a song for the Barnet band entitled *Ode to a horsefly*. (*Down beat*, June 1, 1940)

<u>*NYC, Paramount Theater, stage performance, ca. May 25, 1940*</u>

Comanche war dance aBilly May
Cherokee aBilly May
Tappin' at the Tappa aHead
720 in the books aBilly May; vMary Ann McCall
My blue heaven vMary Ann McCall
Wanderin' blues aCharlie Barnet; vMary Ann McCall

<u>*NYC, Apollo Theater, stage performance, May 29, 1940*</u>

The Barnet band was among several performers taking part in a midnight benefit concert in aid of the Harlem Children's Center. Others appearing were Billie Holiday, Abbott and Costello, Danny Kaye, Count Basie and Andy Kirk. (*Lady Day's diary*)

During one of his New York sojourns, Charlie rented an apartment at the Beaux Arts Apartments (there were several such places which catered to longish stays) where band members would gather to smoke pot using a "coconut rig" (a coconut shell filled with wine and fitted out as a hookah). During these times the Ferguson Sisters are said to have paid visits. The sisters were two "super-annuated hookers" who specialized in "doing bands," which involved the two ladies ministering simultaneously to each client. It is also said that they would only handle a band and not individual customers; at least one observer had respect for their *modus operandi*, taking into account their ages and their ingenious and possibly unique way of staying in business. (*Atwood*)

<u>*NYC, Apollo Theater, June 14, 1940*</u>

Charlie jammed with Coleman Hawkins, Count Basie, Lester Young, Teddy Wilson (and possibly Gene Krupa). (*Down beat* July 1, 1940)

Bob Burnet, Billy May, John Owens, Lyman Vunk, tpts; Spud Murphy,

Don Ruppersburg, Bill Robertson, tbns; Gene Kinsey, Leo White, as; Kurt Bloom, James Lamare, ts & bar; Bill Miller, p; Bus Etri, g; Phil Stephens, b; Cliff Leeman, d (ViSS)

NYC, RCA Victor recording session, June 19, 1940

51528-1 **And so do I** aBilly May; vLarry Taylor
BB B10778°; *BB AXM2 5585*; BB AXK2 5585; **EMPRESS (E) RAJCD 898**

51529-1 **It's the last time I'll fall in love** aBilly May; vMary Ann McCall
BB B10778°; Vi (Arg) 29851; *BB AXM2 5585*; *RCA (Fr) NL 89483-2*; *Sounds of Swing LP 103*; BB AXK2 5585; **RCA (FR) 74321355532**

51530-1 **The reverie of a moax (Oh Claire the Goon)** [2:50] aCharlie Barnet
BB B10785°; *BB AXM2 5585*; *Vi LPV 567°*; *RCA (E) RD 8088*; *RCA (Fr) NL 89483-2*; *RCA (Ger) LPM 567*; *RCA (It?) LPM 34048*; BB AXK2 5587; **RCA (FR) 74321355532**

51530-2 **The reverie of a moax (Oh Claire the Goon)** [2:48] aCharlie Barnet
BB B10785

51531-1 **Tangleweed 'round my heart** aBilly May; vLarry Taylor
BB B10794°; *BB AXM2 5585*; BB AXK2 5587

51532-1 **Rockin' in rhythm** aBilly May
BB B10785°; HMV (Australia) EA 3195; *AXM2 5585*; *Vi LPT 3062°*, *LPV 551°*; *RCA (Argentina) AVLT 7*; *RCA (E) RD 7965*; *RCA (Fr) NL 89483-2, PM 42041*; *RCA (Ger) LPM 551*; *RCA (It?) LPM 34022*; *RCA (Ja) RA 60-68*; *Vi EPBT 3062*; BB 61059-4; BB AXK2 5587; **BB 6273 2-RB; BB 61059-2; GIANTS OF JAZZ (CZ) CD 53280; KAZ (E) CD 311; RCA (E) 86273; JAZZ ARCHIVES (FR) 158532; ARISTA 886281; RCA (FR) 74321355532; LIVING ERA (E) CD AJA 5288**; AFRS DOWN BEAT 30.

51533-1 **Peaceful valley** aBilly May
BB B10846°; *AXM2 5585*; *Big Bands (Time-Life) STBB-07*; *Big Band Archives LP 2204*; BB AXK2 5587; Big Bands (Time-Life) 4TBB-07 (CrO2 release); Big Bands (Time-Life) 4TL-0011 R959-11; **BIG BANDS (TIME-LIFE) TCD-0011 R960-11**

51533-2 **Peaceful valley** aBilly May
BB B10846

Charlie Barnet is a disciple of the great Duke Ellington and loves to play his music. Charlie manages to inject a bit of musical humor into his arrangement of his "Rockin' In Rhythm" and "The Reverie of a Moax" (No. B-10785) . . .

Skippy Martin was reported to have joined Jan Savitt. (*Billboard* June 15, 1940)

NYC, Show of the Week (MBS), June 27, 1940

Make believe ballroom aHorace Diaz, Jr.
Flying home aSkippy Martin
Rockin' in rhythm aBilly May
You're lonely and I'm lonely aBilly May [Bus Etri solos where a vocal would be expected]
All this and heaven too aBilly May; vLarry Taylor
Hear my song, Violetta vJack Parson and audience
Afternoon of a moax aCharlie Barnet
Devil may care
Avalon aSkippy Martin
Cherokee aBilly May

At about this time Harriet Clarke replaced Mary Ann McCall. *Down beat* carried a report that Roy Eldridge was joining the Barnet band but the deal fell through. Another news item in the musical press noted that Charlie was slated to record a long work by Otto Cesana—*Symphony in swing*—on six 12" sides, but this also came to naught.

July 8, 1940: Brooklyn, Manhattan Beach

Charlie Barnet and his orchestra

Bernie Privin, Billy May, Sam Skolnick, Lyman Vunk, tpts; T.C. Murphy [sic], Don Ruppersberg, Bill Robertson, tbns; Gene Kinsey, Leo White, as; Kurt Bloom, ts; Jim Lamare, ts & bar; Bill Miller, p; Bus Etri, g; Phil Stephens, b; Cliff Leeman, d (ViSS)

NYC, RCA Victor recording session, July 19, 1940

54600-1 **I don't want to cry anymore** aBilly May; vLarry Taylor

BB B10825°; Regal Zonophone (E) MR 3422; *BB AXM2 5587; Swing Era LP 1019*; BB AXK2 5587; **FLAPPER (E) PAST CD9787**

54601-1 **Pompton Turnpike** aBilly May [3:03]
BB B10825°

54601-1R **Pompton Turnpike** aBilly May [2:58]
BB B10825°; Vi 420-0002; Vi 20-2540; HMV (E) B9498; HMV (India) B 9498; HMV (It) HN 2183; ***Vi 447-0002; Vi 447-0072; Vi 447-0872; RCA (N) 11-016***; *AXM2 5587; Vi LPV 551°; Franklin Mint 33; Franklin Mint record no.19; Reader's Digest RD4-21, RD4A-078, RD4A-113; Big Bands (Time-Life) STBB-07; Camden CCL2-0619; Vi LPM 2081, VPM/VPS 6043; RCA (E) RD 7965; RCA (Fr) NL 89483-2; RCA (Fr) PM 42041; RCA (Ger) LPM 551; RCA (It?) LPM 34022; RCA (Ja) RA 60-68*; ***Vi EPAT 404; RCA (E) RCX 1008***; Franklin Mint Tape no.19; Reader's Digest RD-078; Big Bands (Time-Life) 4TBB-07 (CrO2 release); Big Bands (Time-Life) 4TL-0011 R959-11; BB AXK2 5587; RCA PK 5099; **RCA 9855-2R; BB 6273-2RB; COLLECTABLES COL CD 6097; BIG BANDS (TIME-LIFE) TCD-0011 R960-11; GIANTS OF JAZZ (CZ) CD 53280; LIVING ERA (E) CD AJA 5247; AFFINITY (E) CD AFS 1036-4; LIVING ERA (E) CD AJA 5247, 5288; KAZ (E) CD 311; RCA (E) 86273; 4039; BEST OF JAZZ (FR) JAZZ ARCHIVES (FR) 158532ARISTA 886281; JAZZ GREATS (E) CD 071; RCA (FR) 74321355532**; AFRS G.I.JIVE 896, 986, 1012, 1142, 1143; AFRS JATJB 17; AFRS MUSIC TRANSCRIPTION LIBRARY P-S 16; AFRS REMEMBER 951; THE MUSICMAKERS 334; AFRS SWINGTIME (no. unknown)

54602-1 **At a Dixie roadside diner** aBilly May; vHarriet Clarke
BB B10817°; *BB AXM2 5587*; BB AXK2 5587

54602-2 **At a Dixie roadside diner** aBilly May; vHarriet Clarke
BB B10817

54603-1 **That's for me** aBilly May; vLarry Taylor
BB B10817°; Vi (Brazil) 27176 [Reverse side by Abe Lyman]; Regal Zonophone (E)MR 3422; Twin (India) FT 8968 [Reverse side is Wingy Manone: *Ain't it a shame about Mame*]; *BB AXM2 5587*; BB AXK2 5587; **FLAPPER (E) PAST CD 9787**

54604-1 **The sergeant was shy** aBilly May
BB 10862°; *BB AXM2 5587; Vi LPT 3062°, VPM/VPS 6043°; RCA (Arg) AVLT 7; RCA (Fr) NL 89483-2; RCA (Fr) PM 42041; Bandstand 7123*; ***Vi EPBT 3062***; BB AXK2 5587; **AERO SPACE RACD 7123 ; KAZ (E) CD 311; BEST OF JAZZ (FR) 6039; JAZZ ARCHIVES (FR) 158532; RCA (FR) 74321355532**; AFRS DOWN BEAT 30; AFRS G.I. JIVE 414, 2225; AFRS SOUND OFF 18, 242;AFRS YANK SWING SESSION 73

54605-1 **Ring dem bells** aBilly May
BB B10862°; HMV (E) B 9469; HMV (India) B 9469; HMV (It) HN 2237; *BB AXM2 5587; Vi LPT 3062°; RCA (Argentina) AVLT 7; RCA (Fr) NL 89483; RCA (Fr) PM 42041; Bandstand 7123*; ***Vi EPBT 3062***; *BB AXK2 5587*; **AERO SPACE RACD 7123; KAZ (E) CD 311; JAZZ ARCHIVES (FR) 158532; RCA (FR) 74321355532**

Subsequent to the first release of *Pompton Turnpike* Victor engineers discovered a fault in the master which had been passed for issue: the last 5-6 seconds of the music included a fairly loud electronic hum. The side was remastered—that is, dubbed—eliminating the 4-bar tag (resulting in the abrupt ending) and this revised master, -1R, has been used for all issues over the years. Some 78 issues show "1R" at the 9 o'clock position.

NYC, World's Fair, stage performance, July 25, 1940?

The Barnet and Ellington bands performed part of Otto Cesana's *Symphony in swing*. (Note that Stratemann dates this as August 1, 1940.)

NYC, Hotel Lincoln, b'cast, July 26, 1940

Fools rush in vLarry Taylor
Redmond Nostalgia CO 4391; J.C.Entertainment JCS 110; **J.C.Entertainment JCD 110**

Where do you keep your heart aBilly May; vLarry Taylor
Redmond Nostalgia CO 4391

Aviation suite aBilly May
Redmond Nostalgia CO 4391

#Pavanne (M.Gould) a(Bud Estes?) [1:12]

July 28-31, 1940: Atlantic City, Steel Pier
Aug. 1, 1940: Vermillion, OH, Crystal Beach Park
Aug. 2–8, 1940: Sandusky, Cedar Point Ballroom

<u>*Sandusky, Ohio, Cedar Point Ballroom, b'cast, Aug. 2, 1940*</u>

The right idea aSkippy Martin
<u>Redmond</u> <u>Nostalgia</u> <u>CO</u> <u>4390</u>
Ring dem bells aBilly May
Limited Edition LP 101; Aircheck 5
Orchids for remembrance# vLarry Taylor [1:30]
Flying home aSkippy Martin
Aircheck 5; Joyce 1152
And so do I# aBilly May; vLarry Taylor [0:43]
Rockin' in rhythm aBilly May

The dunking incident that was memorialized in *Wild mab of the fish pond* took place during this engagement: "We got back late and had a few. We were feeling no pain. Somebody picked up Bus Etri and dunked him into the hotel's fountain." (Jimmy Lamare in *Bluebird v.5*)

BEGINNING TONIGHT AND continuing for two weeks the western border drama, "Wild Mab" will be given by the Gay Nineties Theater at Cedar Point.

"While Barnet was playing Cedar Point, a local melodrama theater circulated yellow handbills for advertising on which was written 'Where is the wild mab?' The boys in the band promptly advised the acting company that the wild mab was leading the band and ever since Charlie has been known to musicians as The Mab." (*Down beat* Aug. 1, 1943)

According to the *Sandusky Register* a song entitled *Corporal Moax* (arranged by Charlie Barnet and Bud Estes) was performed during their stay.

Aug. 9–15, 1940: Detroit, Eastwood Gardens

<u>*Detroit, Eastwood Ballroom/ Gardens, b'cast, Aug. 12, 1940*</u>

You're lonely and I'm lonely aBilly May; vHarriet Clarke
Joyce 1152
All this and heaven too aBilly May; vLarry Taylor
Joyce 1152
Begin the beguine
<u>Redmond</u> <u>Nostalgia</u> <u>CO</u> <u>4390</u>

Aug. 17, 1940: Celoron, NY, Pier Ballroom
Aug. 18, 1940: Columbus, Valley Dale
Aug. 19, 1940: Youngstown, The Mansions
Aug. 21, 1940: Hershey, PA, Hershey Park
Aug. 23–28?, 1940: Dayton, Colonial Theater
Aug. 30–Sept. 5, 1940: Cleveland, Palace Theater
ca late Aug., 1940: Buffalo [battle of music with Andy Kirk]
ca late Aug., 1940: Erie, PA
ca late Aug., 1940: Johnstown, PA
ca late Aug., 1940: Middleport, PA
Sept. 6–12, 1940: Detroit, Michigan Theater
Sept. 13–28?, 1940: NYC, Fiesta Danceteria

<u>*NYC, Fiesta Danceteria, (NBC?) b'cast, Sept. 13, 1940*</u>

#Afternoon of a moax aCharlie Barnet
Joyce JRC 1214; Redmond Nostalgia CO 4390
Begin the beguine
Joyce JRC 1214
Whispering grass# aBud Estes; vLarry Taylor
Redmond Nostalgia CO 4390

Bernie Privin, Bill May, John Owens, Lyman Vunk, tpts; Spud Murphy, Don Ruppersburg, Bill Robertson, tbns; Gene Kinsey, Leo White, as; Kurt Bloom, ts; James Lamare, ts & bar; Bill Miller, p; Bus Etri, g; Phil Stephens, b; Cliff Leeman, d (ViSS)

NYC, RCA Victor recording session, Sept. 17, 1940

56124-1 **The moon is cryin' for me** aBilly May; vLarry Taylor
BB B10934°; *BB AXM2 5587*; BB AXK2 5587

56125-1 **Wild mab of the fish pond** aBud Estes
BB B10888°; Jay 8 [as "The All Stars"]; *BB AXM2 5587*; *Vi LPV 567°*; *Franklin Mint 33*; *Franklin Mint Record 19*; *Big Bands (Time-Life) STBB 07*; *Camden CAL 389*; *RCA (E) RD 8088*; *RCA (Fr) NL 89483-2*; *RCA (Ger) LPM 567*; *RCA (It?) LPM 34048*; ***Camden CAE 432***; BB AXK2 5587; Franklin Mint Tape no.19; Big Bands (Time-Life) 4TBB 07 (CrO2 release); Big Bands (Time-Life) 4TL-0011 R959-11; **BB 6273 2-RB; BIG BANDS (TIME-LIFE) TCD-0011R960-11; ARISTA 886281; GIANTS OF JAZZ (CZ) CD53280; KAZ (E) CD 311; RCA (E) 86273; RCA (FR) 74321355532**

56126-1 **Wings over Manhattan, pt. 1** aBilly May
BB B10885°; *BB AXM2 5587*; *Camden CAL 389*; *Vi LPV 567°*; *Franklin Mint 33*; *Franklin Mint Record no.19*; *Big Bands (Time-Life) STBB 07*; *RCA (E) RD 8088*; *RCA (Ger) LPM 567*; *RCA (It?) LPM 34048*; *RCA (Ja) RA 60-68*; BB AXK2 5587; Franklin Mint Tape no.19; Big Bands (Time-Life) 4TBB 07 (CrO2 release); Big Bands (Time-Life) 4TL-0011 R959-11; **BIG BANDS(TIME-LIFE) TCD-0011 R960-11; KAZ (E) CD 311; JAZZ GREATS (E) CD 071**

56127-1 **Wings over Manhattan, pt. 2** aBilly May
Issues as for pt. 1

56128-1 **Night and day** aHead
BB B10888°; Jay 8 [as "The All Stars"]; *BB AXM2 5587*; *Vi LPV 551°*; *Vi LPM 2081*; *RCA (E) RD 7965*; *Reader's Digest 2-776, 4-45* (stereo, mono); *Reader's Digest (C) 2-776*; *Reader's Digest (E) RDM 265*; *RCA (Fr) NL 89483-2*; *RCA (Ger) LPM 551*; *RCA (It?) LPM 34022*; BB AXK2 5587; **READER'S DIGEST RBD 114/CDI; RCA (FR) 74321355532**

56129-? **Avalon** aSkippy Martin
Unissued (mx 56129 subsequently assigned to *Southern fried*)

56129-1 **Southern fried** aBill Miller
BB B10944°; HMV (Australia) EA 3599; *BB AXM2 5587*; *Big Bands (Time-Life) STBB 07*; *Bandstand 7123*; BB AXK2 5587; Big Bands (Time-Life) 4TL-0011 R959-11; *Big* Bands (Time-Life) 4TBB 07 (CrO2 release); **BB 6273 2-RB; RCA (E) 86273; BIG BANDS (TIME-LIFE) TCD-0011 R960-11;ARISTA 886281; AERO SPACE RACD 7123; GIANTS OF JAZZ (CZ) CD 53280**; THE MUSIC MAKERS 334

Consolidated Radio Artists had been handling Charlie's bookings for a time, and especially since about March of 1939 when a new contract had been signed, but trouble between the two began to brew in 1940. Just what it was that caused Charlie to be unhappy with the arrangement is not precisely known, but it was enough to make him try to sever the relationship. In September he wrote to CRA telling them that he no longer required their services, having self-booked a two-and-a-half week engagement at Fiesta Danceteria commencing Sept. 13. CRA had already booked the band for several one nighters for this period (Canton, Cumberland, etc.) but Charlie countered by sending out the word that he would not be able to honor these engagements. Early on in the proceedings James Petrillo got involved, along with several lawyers. Following lengthy negotiations, Petrillo lifted Charlie's union card, but allowed the band to fulfill some engagements, so long as the now non-union Charlie was not on hand. Late in the year Charlie was able to break with CRA by buying up the balance of his contract, "for an undisclosed sum"; Petrillo restored Charlie's card. The dispute made headlines in all the popular music press.

Another affair centered around Maria Kramer, owner of the Lincoln and Edison hotels. Charlie entered into an agreement with her that guaranteed him a home base in NYC, with plenty of coast-to-coast air time, in return for which she (through an intermediary) shared in the band's earnings. The Mab's lawyer and his then-manager, Charlie Weintraub, advised against this, warning that he was going to be soon operating in the red. "As it turned out, Weintraub was right." (*MS*)

Larry Taylor left the band late in September to take a job with the Carnation Contented Hour; he was tired of traveling. He is believed to have briefly rejoined the band sometime later. Bob Carroll was his replacement. Early in October Charlie hired Ford Leary, trombonist and vocalist, from Larry Clinton's band. This made a four-man trombone section, quite unusual for the time.

Sept. 29, 1940: NYC World's Fair, Dancing Campus [with John Kirby]
Oct. 3–(9?), 1940: NYC World's Fair, Dancing Campus

Personnel as preceding with the addition of Ford Leary, tbn, vocal.

NYC, RCA Victor recording session, October 14, 1940

56483-1 **I hear a rhapsody** aConn Humphries; vBob Carroll
BB B10934°; *BB AXM2 5587*; *Camden CAL 389*; *Reader's Digest RD4-25* (mono and stereo issues); *Reader's Digest (Ja) 9S*; ESX JCT 7004; Time-Life 164; Good Music 143818-2; BB AXK2 5587; Reader's Digest RD 3; READER'S DIGEST RD-8 5386, RD-5 025-1/3 (8-track); **JCI 42446; GOOD MUSIC 143826; RCA 44547; RCA 9855 2-R; ESX JCD 7004; TIME-LIFE 162; READER'S DIGEST RDD 25/C11; HOMECOMING 1945 GMCD80037-1** [Columbia Special Prod.]; **LIVING ERA (E) CD AJA 5288**; THE MUSIC MAKERS 334

56484-1 **Whatcha know Joe** aBud Estes; vFord Leary & the Three Moaxes (Barnet; May; [Etri?])
BB B10918; *BB AXM2 5587*; BB AXK2 5587

56485-1 **Isola bella** aBilly May; vBob Carroll
BB B10918; HMV (Australia) EA 2886; *BB AXM2 5587*; BB AXK2 5587

56486-1 **Redskin rhumba** aHead
BB B10944°; Vi 20-1756; Vi (Brazil) [number ???]; HMV (E) B 9442; HMV (India) B 9442; ***Vi 420-0071***; ***Vi 447-0071***; *BB AXM2 5587*; *Vi LPV 551°*, *LPM 2081*; *Big Bands (Time-Life) STBB 07*; *Reader's Digest RD4-45*; *RCA (E) RD 7965*; *Reader's Digest (E) RDM 265*; *RCA (Fr) NL 89483-2*; *RCA (Fr) PM 42401*; *RCA (Ger) LPM 551*; *RCA (It) EDP 1004*; *RCA (It?) LPM 34022*; *RCA (Ja) RA 60-68*; ***Vi EPA 5001***; ***Vi EPAT 404***; ***Vi (E) RCX 1008***; BB AXK2 5587; BB 61059-4; Big Bands (Time-Life) 4TBB 07 (CrO2 release); Big Bands (Time-Life) 4TL-0011 R959-11; **BB 61059-2; BB 6273 2-RB; BIG BANDS (TIME-LIFE) TCD-0011 R960-11; ARISTA 886281; RCA (E) 86273; ALLEGRO (FR) 151832; BEST OF JAZZ (FR) 4039; GIANTS OF JAZZ (CZ) CD 53280; AVID (E) AMSC 676; RCA (FR) 74321355532; LIVING ERA (E) CD AJA 5288**; AFRS DOWNBEAT 30; AFRTS MISCELLANEOUS MISC S 8; THE MUSIC MAKERS 334

56487-1 **Buffy boy** aBud Estes
BB B11093°; HMV (E) B 9394; HMV (India) B 9394; *BB AXM2 5587*; *Swing Era LP 1002, LPS 5001*; BB AXK2 5587

56488-1 **Lumby** aBilly May
BB B11014°; HMV (E) B 9405; BB AXM2 5587; *Vi LPM 2081; RCA (Fr) NL 89483-2*; BB AXK2 5587; BB 61059-4; **BB 6273 2-RB; BB 61059-2; ARISTA 886281; RCA (E) 86273; GIANTS OF JAZZ (CZ) CD 53280; RCA (FR) 74321355532; JAZZ BAND 2260**

Oct. 14–(19?), 1940: Boston, Brunswick Hotel
Oct. 20–(26?), 1940: NYC, World's Fair Dancing Campus
Oct. 27, 1940: Bridgeport, Ritz Ballroom

It was at approximately this time that the incident of the deck chairs into Lake Erie took place (*TSY*, p. 97).

Billy May left Charlie about October 31, joining Miller on November 3.

Charlie was one of several leaders

who filled in for an ailing Bobby Byrne at the Strand Theater, NYC.

Martin Block ceased using Charlie's *Make believe ballroom* for a theme and adopted the specially commissioned *It's make believe ballroom time* by Glenn Miller.

Nov. 1-7, 1940: Buffalo, Buffalo (Shea's) Theater

A Buffalo performance review averred, "If you like your music hot, loud and brassy, Charlie Barnett's combination is made to order. Outfit is currently handing out an over-load of jittermania and its reception by the early-bird jivers was plenty boisterous..." (*Variety* Nov. 6, 1940)

Buffalo, NY, Shea's Theater, stage performance, Nov. 1, 1940

Pompton Turnpike aBilly May
Only forever vBob Carroll
Summertime vBob Carroll
That's for me aBilly May; vBob Carroll
Whispering grass aBud Estes; vBob Carroll
Indian suite (Cherokee/Comanche war dance) aBilly May
Rhumboogie aSkippy Martin; vFord Leary
Inspiration
Shadrack vFord Leary

Nov. 8–14, 1940: Chicago, State-Lake Theater

Petrillo took Charlie's union card during the State-Lake Theater engagement so the following one-nighters were performed without his presence.

Nov. 15, 1940: Purdue, IN Purdue University
Nov. 16, 1940: Flint, unnamed venue
Nov. 17, 1940: NYC, Savoy Ballroom

Charlie married Harriet Clarke in Miami on November 27. His union card was restored about December 1, 1940.

Dec. 2, 1940: NYC, Famous Door

Charlie Barnet and his orchestra

Bernie Privin, Bob Burnet, George Esposito, Lyman Vunk, tpts; Spud Murphy, Bill Robertson, Don Ruppersburg, Ford Leary, tbns; Conn Humphreys, Leo White, as; Kurt Bloom, ts; Jim Lamare, ts & bar; Bill Miller, p; Bus Etri, g; Phil Stephens, b; Cliff Leeman, d

NYC, RCA Victor recording session, Dec. 3, 1940

58210-1 **Scrub me mama with a boogie beat** aBud Estes; vFord Leary
BB B10975°; HMV (Australia) EA 2793; *BB AXM2 5587; Big Bands (Time-Life) STBB-07*; Big Bands (Time-Life) 4TBB-07 (CrO2); Big Bands (Time-Life) 4TL-0011 R959-11; BB AXK2 5587; **BIG BANDS (TIME-LIFE) TCD-0011 R960-11; JASMINE (E) JASMCD 2540**

58211-1 **Nowhere** aCharlie Barnet
BB B11141°; HMV (Australia) EA 3599; *BB AXM2 5587; Bandstand 7123*; BB AXK2 5587; Aero SpaceRACD 7123

58212-1 **I can't remember to forget** aBilly May; vBob Carroll
BB 10975°; Vi 20-2632; *BB AXM2 5587*; BB AXK2 5587

58213-1 **He's a Latin from Staten Island** aBilly May; vFord Leary
BB B11004; *BB AXM2 5587; Bandstand 7123*; BB AXK2 5587; **AERO SPACE RACD 7123**

58214-1 **These things you left me** aBilly May; vBob Carroll
BB B11004; *BB AXM2 5587*; BB AXK2 5587

58215-1 **Phyllysse** aCharlie Barnet
BB B11014°; HMV (E) B 9553; HMV (Fr) SG 42; *BB AXM2 5587; Vi LPV 567°; RCA (E) RD 8088; RCA (Fr) NL 89483-2, PM 42041; RCA (Ger) LPM 567;RCA (It?) LPM 34048*; BB AXK2 5587; **RCA (FR) 74321355532; LIVING ERA (E) CD AJA 5288**

Lena Horne joined the band in December. (Her contract with Charlie is dated December 24.) Charlie hired her for a short stand in December at the Casino Theater (Lena says it was the Windsor) in the Bronx.

Dec. 6–12, 1940: NYC, Apollo Theater
Dec., 1940: Bronx, Windsor or Casino Theater
Dec. 13, 1940: Baltimore, University of Maryland

Dec. 16, 1940: Washington, DC, The Colonnades (Lena's father in audience?)

At about this time Cliff Leeman left the band, due, it is said, to an argument with Charlie. He was replaced by Harry (Wally) Gordon.

Lips Page, tpt; Coleman Hawkins, Lester Young, ***Charlie Barnet****, ts; Teddy Wilson, p; unknown g, b, d; there may be a second trumpet and a clarinet.*

NYC, WNEW b'cast, December 19, 1940

The man I love vBillie Holiday
Boulevard (E) 4113; Roy (E) Br C-2; Roy (E) LP-1; Saga (E) ERO/EROS 8014; Saga (E) PAN 6918; **Masters of Jazz MJCD 90**
Wham
Oh! lady be good

MCA became Charlie's booking agent late in December.

Dec. 23, 1940: Paramount Theater (subbed for Tommy Dorsey who played a private party)
Dec. 24–(30?), 1940: Newark, Adams Theater

Newark, NJ, Adams Theater, stage performance, Dec.28, 1940

Only forever vBob Carroll
That's for me aBilly May; vBob Carroll
Whispering grass aBud Estes; vBob Carroll
Down Argentina way a Billy May; vLena Horne
Good-for-nothin' Joe aBud Estes; vLena Horne
Exactly like you aSkippy Martin; vLena Horne
I can't get started with you vLena Horne

Charlie shared the bill at the Adams with several vaudeville acts and the film, "The Bowery boys." "Setting pace is Charlie Barnet's brass-heavy crew. Sound and fury characterize arrangements for most part, and Barnet does full share of horn-tooting. Leader makes okay appearance, but seemed uncertain of lines as m.c. when caught [was this a Dewar's moment?] ... Lena Horn ... is exotic looker, enhances effect with flamboyant costume, and clicks pronto." (*Variety* Jan. 1, 1941)

Charlie Barnet "King of the Saxophone" and his orchestra

Personnel as for December 3, 1940.

NYC, Lang-Worth recording session, probably between Dec. 20, 1940 and Jan. 20, 1941

357a **Wings over Manhattan, pt. 1** aBilly May
LANG-WORTH 619, 623, CI 56A1, DL 59B1; *Blue Heaven BH-1 106; Circle CLP 65;* **CIRCLE CCD 65**; AFRS BML P-3206
357b **Wings over Manhattan, pt. 2** aBilly May
LANG-WORTH 619, 623, CI 56A1, DL 59B2, ART 117-B; *Blue Heaven BH-1 106; Circle CLP 65* **CIRCLE CCD 65**; AFRS BML P-3206
357c **Nowhere** aCharlie Barnet
LANG-WORTH 619, 623, DL 59A2; *Blue Heaven BH-1 106; Ajax 147; Swing Era LP 1019;* Ajax C-679; Radio Classics AFP 7141 AC; **CIRCLE CCD 112**; AFRS BML P-3205
357d **Fantasia** aBud Estes
LANG-WORTH 619, 623, DL 18A1; *Blue Heaven BH-6 604; Circle CLP 65;* **CIRCLE CCD 65**; AFRS BML P-3205
358a **All I desire** aBud Estes; vLena Horne
LANG-WORTH 620, 624, CI 57A2; DL 214A2; *Blue Heaven BH-1 106; Circle CLP 65; Trip TLP 5804; DJM (E) DJML 061; Jazz Bird JAZ 2016; Parnaso (Arg) 13032;* Ajax C-679; CHG 0155 32789-1; Radio Classics AFP 7140-AC; **CIRCLE CCD 65; LIVING ERA (E) CD AJA 5238; B&C RECORDS 74081-2; PILZ (GER) 44 2042-2**
358b **Blue juice** aCharlie Barnet [Named for Charlie's Lincoln Continental]
LANG-WORTH 620, 624, DL 30B1; *Blue Heaven BH-7 702; Circle CLP 65; Trip TLP 5804; DJM (E) DJML 061; Jazz Bird JAZ 2016; Parnaso (Argentina) 13032;* **CIRCLE CCD 65**
358c **Charleston alley** aHorace Henderson
LANG-WORTH 620; 624; CI 56B2; DL 30A2; V-Disc (Army) 266, (Navy) 46; *Blue Heaven BH-1 106; Trip TLP 5804; DJM (E) DJML 061; Jazz Bird JAZ 2016;*

Parnaso (Argentina) 13032; *First Heard (E) FH-44*; First Heard CFH-44; **CIRCLE CCD 112**

358d **I can't remember to forget** aBilly May; vBob Carroll
LANG-WORTH 620, 624; *Blue Heaven BH-7 702; Trip TLP 5804; DJM (E) DJML 061; Jazz Bird JAZ 2016; Parnaso (Argentina) 13032*; **CIRCLE CCD 65; PILZ (GER) 44 2042-2; B&C RECORDS 74081-2**

358e **Uptown blues** aBud Estes
LANG-WORTH 620, 624, CI 56B3, DL 30A1; V-disc (Army) 294, (Navy) 74; *Blue Heaven BH-6 604*; *Trip TLP 5804*; *DJM (E) DJML 061*; *Big Band Archives BBA 1209*; *Jazz Bird JAZ 2016*; *Joyce LP 2012*; *Parnaso (Argentina) 13032*; **CIRCLE CCD 65; PILZ (GER) 44 2042-2; B&C RECORDS 74081-2**

Due to a dispute between ASCAP and the networks over royalties, no ASCAP songs were played on the air after December 31, 1940. Only those songs licensed by BMI or in the public domain (e.g., *Jeannie with the light brown hair*) were played. This caused some band leaders to change their themes at this time: Glenn Miller used *Slumber song* and Tommy Dorsey used one called *Anything*. (Mutual signed with ASCAP on May 14; NBC & CBS signed in September, having won the battle.)

Jan. 2–5, 1941: Hartford, State Theater

Charlie Barnet and his orchestra

Bernie Privin, Bob Burnet, George Esposito, Lyman Vunk, tpts; Spud Murphy, Don Ruppersburg, Bill Robertson, Ford Leary, tbns; Leo White, Conn Humphreys, as; Kurt Bloom, ts; James Lamare, ts & bar; Bill Miller, p; Bus Etri, g; Phil Stephens, b; Cliff Leeman, d (Vi SS)

NYC, RCA Victor recording session, January 7, 1941

58767-1 **Blue juice** aCharlie Barnet
BB B11111°; HMV (E) B9394; HMV (Australia) EA 3742; HMV (India) B 9394; *BB AXM2 5587*; *Camden CAL 389*; *RCA (Fr)NL 89483-2*; *RCA (Fr) PM 42401*; ***Camden CAE 432***; BB AXK2 5587; CDE (E) RPMC611; **CDS (E) 541, RPCD611, RPCD 641; JAZZ ARCHIVES (FR) 158432; RCA (FR) 74321355532**

58768-1 **Good-for-nothin' Joe** aBud Estes; vLena Horne
BB 11037°; BB 30-0823; *BB AXM2 5587; Camden CAL 389; Vi LPV 567°; Franklin Mint 33; Franklin Mint Record no. 19; Big Bands (Time-Life) STBB-07; RCA (E) RD 8088; RCA (Fr) PM 42401; RCA (Ger) LPM 567*; Franklin Mint Tape no.19; Big Bands (Time-Life) 4TBB-07 (CrO2); Big Bands (Time-Life) 4TL-0011 R959-11; BB AXK2 5590; **BIG BANDS (TIME-LIFE)TCD-0011 R960-11; LIVING ERA (E) CD AJA 5238; RCA (E) ND90441; BEST OF JAZZ (FR) 4039;FLAPPER (E) 7091; L'ART VOCAL (FR) 11; PILZ(GER) 44 2042-2; B&C RECORDS 74081-2;** AFRS DOWNBEAT 30

58769-1 **Harmony haven** vBob Carroll and Glee Club [Miller also plays celesta]
BB B11111°; *BB AXM2 5587*; BB AXK2 5590

58770-1 **The captain and his men** aBud Estes; vLena Horne
BB B11081°; *BB AXM2 5587*; *Bandstand 7123*; BB AXK2 5590; **L'ART VOCAL (FR) 11; AERO SPACE RACD 7123; FLAPPER (E) 7091**

58771-1 **You're my thrill** aBud Estes; vLena Horne
BB B11141°; *BB AXM2 5587*; *Camden CAL 389, 811°, CAS 811*; *Vi LPV 551°*; *Reader's Digest RD 184-2*; *Reader's Digest (C) RD2 710*; *Smithsonian R-035*; *Big Bands (Time-Life) STBB-07*; *RCA (E) RD 7965*; *RCA (Fr) PM 42401*; *RCA (Ger) LPM 551*; BB AXK2 5590; Vi CAK 811; Smithsonian RC-035; Smithsonian RC-102; Big Bands (Time-Life) 4TBB-07 (CrO2); Big Bands (Time-Life) STL-0011 R959-11; **BB 6273 2-RB; RCA 63115; SMITHSONIAN RD 102; BIG BANDS (TIME-LIFE) TCD-0011 R960-11; ARISTA 886281;RCA (E) 86273; READER'S DIGEST (E) ND 90441; BEST OF JAZZ (FR) 4039; L'ART VOCAL (FR) 11; GIANTS OF JAZZ (CZ) CD 53280; FLAPPER (E) 7091; LIVING ERA (E) CD AJA 5238, 5288;** THE MUSIC MAKERS 334

58772-1 **Charleston alley** aHorace Henderson [1st tpt solo Privin; 2d Burnet]
BB B11037°; HMV (E) B 9442; HMV (India) B 9442; *BB AXM2 5587*; *Vi LPV*

551°; Franklin Mint record no.19; Big Bands (Time-Life) STBB 07; RCA (E) RD 7965; RCA (Fr) NL 89483-2; RCA (Fr) PM 42401; RCA (Ger) LPM 551; BB AXK2 5590, 61059-2; Franklin Mint tape no.19; Big Bands 4TBB 07 (CrO2); Big Bands (Time-Life) 4TL-0011 R959-11; **BB 61059-2; RCA 63445; ARISTA 886281; RCA (E) 86273; BEST OF JAZZ (FR) 4039; JAZZ ARCHIVES (FR) 158532; GIANTS OF JAZZ (CZ) CD53280; AVID (E) AVC 540; JAZZ GREATS (E) CD 071; RCA (FR) 74321355532; LIVING ERA (E) CD AJA 5288** [May have also appeared on AFRS Remember 951]

In an uncited interview in the notes for Hep CD 53, Charlie says some of the band hit the red light district of Charleston, SC, "so I called one of our numbers *Charleston alley* to remind them of their transgressions."

Jan. 10–13, 1941: Providence, Metropolitan Theater

Charlie Barnet orchestra

Personnel probably as preceding

NYC, RCA Thesaurus recording session, ca January 15, 1941

57971-1 **Charleston alley** aHorace Henderson
THESAURUS 930; Joyce JRC C1521; **HEP (E) CD 53**; AFRS DOWNBEAT 91

57971-1 **Conga del moaxo** aBud Estes
THESAURUS 930; *Joyce 2017*; Joyce JRC C-1523; **HEP (E) CD 53**; AFRS DOWNBEAT 91

57971-1 **Lumby** aBilly May
THESAURUS 930; *Joyce 2017*; Joyce JRC C-1521; Big Band Era (N) 40180; **HEP (E) CD 53**; AFRS DOWNBEAT 93, 140

57971-1 **The moon is crying for me** aBilly May; vBob Carroll
THESAURUS 930; Joyce JRC C-1521

57971-1 **Redskin rhumba** aHead
THESAURUS 930; Joyce JRC C-1523; **HEP (E) CD 53**; AFRS DOWNBEAT 91, 140

57972-6 **Afraid to say hello** aBob Burnet; vBob Carroll
THESAURUS 929; Joyce JRC C-1521; **VIPER'S NEST VN 1002**

57972-6 **Harmony haven** vBob Carroll and chorus
THESAURUS 929; Joyce JRC C-1521; **VIPER'S NEST VN 1002**

57972-6 **Haunted town** aBud Estes; vLena Horne
THESAURUS 929; Joyce JRC C1521; **HEP (E) CD 53; VIPER'S NEST VN 1002**

57972-6 **Somewhere** aCharlie Barnet
THESAURUS 929; Joyce JRC C1521; **VIPER'S NEST VN 1002**

57972-6 **Swing low, sweet chariot** aHorace Henderson
THESAURUS 929; Ajax C 679; Joyce JRC C1521; **HEP (E) CD 53; VIPER'S NEST VN 1002**; AFRS DOWNBEAT 91

Jan. 19, 1941: Bridgeport, Lyric Theater
(January?) 1941: Pottstown, PA, Sunnybrook Ballroom

Charlie Barnet and his orchestra

Personnel as for Jan. 7 (*ViSS*)

NYC, RCA Victor recording session, January 23, 1941

60361-1 **Little John ordinary** aHorace Henderson
BB B11165°; HMV (E) B 9469; HMV (India) B 9469; HMV (It) HN 2237; *BB AXM2 5587; RCA (Fr) NL 89483-2, PM 42401; Sounds of Swing LP 103*; BB AXK2 5590; **JAZZ ARCHIVES (FR) 158532; RCA (FR) 74321355532; EMPRESS (E) RAJCD 888**

60362-1 **Haunted town** aBud Estes; vLena Horne
BB B11093°; BB 30-0823; *BB AXM2 5587; Camden CAL 389; Vi LPV 567°; RCA (E) RD 8088; RCA (Fr) NL 89483-2; RCA (Ger) LPM 567*; BB AXK2 5590; **L'ART VOCAL (FR) 11; RCA (FR) 74321355532**

60363-1 **Afraid to say hello** aBob Burnet; vBob Carroll
BB B11051°; *BB AXM2 5590*; BB AXK2 5590

60364-1 **Merry-go-round** aBilly May
BB B11153°; HMV (Australia) EA 3635; Vi (Brazil) 28378; *BB AXM2 5590; RCA (Fr) NL 89483-2; RCA (Fr) PM 42041; Swing Era LP 1002, LPS 5001*; BB AXK2 5590; **KAZ (E) CD 311; JAZZ ARCHIVES (FR) 158532; RCA (FR) 74321355532**

60365-1 **Conga del moaxo** aBud Estes; vTrio (prob. Etri, Lamare, Leary) & Band
BB B11051°; *BB AXM2 5590; Sounds of Swing LP 103*; BB AXK2 5590

60366-1 **Birmingham breakdown** aBilly Gray
BB B11081°; *BB AXM2 5590*; *Vi LPT 3062°*; *RCA (Argentina) AVLT 7*; *RCA (Fr) NL 89483-2, PM 42041; Bandstand 7123*; *RCA EPBT 3062*; BB AXK2 5590; JAZZ ARCHIVES (FR) 158532; AERO SPACE RACD 7123; RCA (FR) 74321355532

NYC, Fitch Bandwagon, January 26, 1941

Program content unknown

Charlie Barnet "King of the Saxophone" and his orchestra

NYC, Lang-Worth recording session, January 27, 1941

375-a **Para vigo me voy (Say si si)** aAndy Gibson
LANG-WORTH 621, DL 18B3; V-disc (Army) 266, (Navy) 46; *Blue Heaven BH-6 604*; Ajax C 683; CIRCLE **CCD 65**

375-b **Haunted town** aBud Estes; vLena Horne
LANG-WORTH 621, CI 57A1, DL214A1; V-Disc (Army) 294, (Navy) 74; *Blue Heaven BH-6 604; Circle CLP 65*; CIRCLE **CCD 65**

375-c **Little John ordinary** aHorace Henderson
LANG-WORTH 621, DL 30A3; *Blue Heaven BH-7 702*; *Circle CLP 65*; CIRCLE **CCD 65**

375-d **You walk by** vBob Carroll
LANG-WORTH 621, DL234A1; *Circle CLP 65*; CIRCLE **CCD 65**; AFRS BML P-3206

375-e **Redskin rhumba** aHead [0:54]
LANG-WORTH 621; (LANG-WORTH CI 56B1?);

376-a **Afraid to say hello** aBob Burnet; vBob Carroll
LANG-WORTH 622, DL214B1; *Blue Heaven BH-6 604*; CIRCLE **CCD 65**

376-b **Phyllysse** aCharlie Barnet
LANG-WORTH 622 [*As Phylisse*]; *Blue Heaven BH-7 702; Circle CLP 65*; CHG 0155 32789-1; CIRCLE **CCD 65**

376-c **Lumby** aBilly May
LANG-WORTH 622; *Blue Heaven BH-1 106; Circle CLP 65*; Radio Classics AFP 7141 [as *Lumpy*; lacks first 27 seconds]; CIRCLE **CCD 65**

376-d **I hear a rhapsody** aConn Humphreys; vBob Carroll
LANG-WORTH 622, DL214B2; *Blue Heaven BH-1 106; Circle CLP 65*; Radio Classics AFP 7141-AC; CIRCLE **CCD 65**

376-e **Swing low, sweet chariot** aHorace Henderson
LANG-WORTH 622; *Blue Heaven BH-6 604*; CIRCLE **CCD 65**

Feb. 2, 1941: Canton, OH, Moonlight Ballroom, Meyers Lake Park

"We used to have a gag we'd pull. The manager of the band would come in, and he'd say, 'That'll be so many doubles' and he'd say, 'And we want a single room for our Cuban vocalist.' And he'd reel off a bunch of Spanish sounding words ... and [Lena would] say 'Si' ... of course when we went into the deep south one time, we were down at the University of Alabama, I said, 'Lena, I don't think you'd better make this trip because we've got to play some funny places ... we'll pick you up in two weeks. You're still on salary' ... and of course I got to the University of Alabama and that dean ate my butt out for not bringing her. I said, 'Well, I hope you can understand. I can realize that probably here everything would have been fine' ... and he was a very astute gentleman, and he said, 'Well, I guess we'll just have to forego the pleasure of hearing Miss Horne.'" (*Sm*)

Feb. 6, 1941: University, AL, University of Alabama

Feb. 7-8, 1941: Clemson, SC, Clemson University

Feb. 14-15, 1941: Charleston, SC, The Citadel

(Mar. 1, 1941?): Washington, DC, Lincoln Colonnades

Metronome reported that this was Charlie's fifth appearance here (Colonnades) in less than a year. Fights broke out and Charlie ordered the band to pack up and leave two hours ahead of schedule. (This may have been the time that Lena's father was in the audience.)

(March 1941?): Cleveland, Palace Theater

(March 1941?): Youngstown, site unknown

Mar. 2, 1941: White Plains, NY, Westchester County Center
Mar. 23, 1941: Bridgeport, Ritz Ballroom
Mar. 26–Apr. 8, 1941: NYC, Paramount Theater

Dinah Shore was also on the bill at the Paramount and it was during this engagement that Shore objected to Lena's presence—not because of her race but because she was such a powerful and dominating competitor: "Let's put it this way, Lena was murdering her," Charlie remarked. (*Sm*) By the terms of his contract, Charlie was compelled to agree to drop Lena from the bill. "And I said, 'Lena, all I can say is your contract with me is yours if you want it. I can't protect you … They're not going to let you go on any more … don't worry about any contract you have with me, because if I can't protect you I don't deserve to have you.'" (*Sm*)

Charlie Barnet orchestra

Personnel probably as preceding

NYC, RCA Thesaurus, recording session, ca early April, 1941

63182-1 **Blue juice** aCharlie Barnet
THESAURUS 945; Joyce JRC C-1523; **Hep (E) CD 53; Viper's Nest VN 1002**; AFRS DOWNBEAT 91
63182-1 **Buffy boy** aBud Estes
Issues as for *Blue juice*
63182-1 **Fantasia** aBud Estes
THESAURUS 945; *Golden Era 15015*; *Joyce 2017*; Ajax C-679; Joyce JRC C-1523; Big Band Era (N) 40180; **Hep (E) CD 53; Viper's Nest VN 1002**; AFRS DOWNBEAT 93, 140
63182-1 **Phyllysse** aCharlie Barnet
THESAURUS 945; Joyce JRC C-1523; **Hep (E) CD 53; Viper's Nest VN 1002**
63182-1 **Wings over Manhattan, pt. 1** aBilly May
THESAURUS 945; Joyce JRC C-1523; Big Band Era (N) 40180; **Hep (E) CD 53; Viper's Nest VN 1002**; AFRS DOWNBEAT 93, 140
63183-1 **Little Dip** aHorace Henderson
THESAURUS 946; Joyce JRC C-1523; **Viper's Nest VN 1002**; AFRS DOWNBEAT 91
63183-1 **Little John ordinary** aHorace Henderson
THESAURUS 946; Joyce JRC C-1523; **Hep (E) CD 53; Viper's Nest VN 1002** [This song appears twice on this CD]; AFRS DOWNBEAT 91
63183-1 **Why** vBob Carroll
THESAURUS 946; Ajax C 683; Joyce JRC C-1523; **Viper's Nest VN 1002**
63183-1 **Wild mab of the fish pond** aBud Estes
THESAURUS 946; *Joyce 2017*; Joyce JRC C-1523; Big Band Era (N) 40180 [as *Wild man…*]; **Hep (E) CD 53; Viper's Nest VN 1002**; AFRS DOWNBEAT 93, 140
63183-1 **Wings over Manhattan, pt. 2** aBilly May
THESAURUS 946; *Joyce 2017*; Joyce JRC C-1523; Big Band Era (N) 40180; **Hep (E) CD 53**; AFRS DOWNBEAT 93, 140

In early April—probably on the 9th—Bob Price (tpt) replaced George Esposito. The contemporary popular music press reported on several proposed arrangements to replace Lena Horne. Mary Ann McCall was mentioned as was a vocal quartet named "The Airliners" (Phyllis Kenny, Pat Haywood, Jimmy Engler, Web Tilton). A female quartet which included Mary Ann McCall was also said to have been hired by Charlie; it was made up of Marie McDonald, Toni Traub and Vivian Blaine. If any of these reports is correct, the arrangements did not last long. The Quintones (Patti Morgan, Al Lane, Murray Deutsch, Irving Deutsch and Lloyd Hundling) became part of the Barnet family on about April 25 and together with Bob Carroll and Ford Leary took care of the vocal chores for the ensuing weeks.

April 10, 1941: Brooklyn, Flatbush Theater
April 17, 1941: Bronx, Windsor Theater
April 24, 1941: Philadelphia, Swing Club
April 25, 1941: Lancaster, PA, Franklin and Marshall College
April 26, 1941: Lawrenceville, NJ, Lawrenceville School
April 27, 1941: NYC, Savoy Ballroom

Charlie Barnet and his orchestra

Bernie Privin, Charles Zimmerman, Walter Price, Lyman Vunk, tpts; Spud Murphy, Tommy Reo, Bill Robertson, Ford Leary, tbns; Leo White, Conn Humphreys, as; Kurt Bloom, ts; James Lamare, ts & bar; Bill Miller, p; Bus Etri, g; Phil Stephens, b; Cliff Leeman, d (ViSS)

NYC, RCA Victor recording session, April 29, 1941

63831-1 **Consider yourself kissed** aFranklyn Marks; vBob Carroll
BB B11165°; *BB AXM2 5590*; BB AXK2 5590

63832-1 **You talk too much** aFranklyn Marks; vFord Leary
Unissued

63832-2 **You talk too much** aFranklyn Marks; vFord Leary
BB B11153°; *BB AXM2 5590*; BB AXK2 5590

63833-1 **Ponce de Leon** aHorace Henderson
BB B11194°; HMV (Australia) EA 3257; HMV (Intl) J 146; *BB AXM2 5590*; *RCA (Fr) NL 89483-2*; *Swing Era LP 1002, LPS 5001*; *Big Bands (Time-Life) STBB 07*; BB AXK2 5590; Big Bands (Time-Life) 4TBB-07 (Cr02 release); Big Bands (Time-Life) 4TL-0011 R959-11; **Big Bands (Time-Life) TCD-0011 R960-11; RCA (Fr) 74321355532**

63834-1 **Little Dip** aHorace Henderson [named for a pickpocket]
BB B11194°; HMV (Australia) EA 3257; HMV (E) B 9390; HMV (India) B 9390; *BB AXM2 5590*; *RCA (Fr) NL 89483-2*; *Swing Era LP 1002, LPS 5001*; BB AXK2 5590; **RCA (Fr) 74321355532**

April 30, 1941: Pittsburgh, Hill City Ballroom
May 2–13, 1941: Chicago, Sherman Hotel (Panther Room)

From a review of an evening in the Panther Room: "Currently the Charlie Barnet orchestra is the magnet which is corralling the swingers. They were jampacked in here on the opening night and an indication of the power of the Barnet band with this gang was the large number of listeners. When they jam up against the bandstand and lend an ear instead of concentrating on the body-holds, then the band must have something. And the Barnet orchestra does have something ... The Quintones attempt to be the string section of the orchestra, operating strictly with their vocal chords..." (*Variety* May 2, 1941)

Lillian Roth was appearing in Chicago at the High Hat, and one wonders if Charlie and his old flame got together.

May 30–(June 12?), 1941: NYC, Madison Square Garden, Monte Proser Dance Carnival

"Monte Proser had leased NY's Madison Square Garden and was turning it into a huge ballroom for the summer. He spent a fortune having a suspended ceiling, depicting a starry night, installed ... He installed bars, restaurants, every possible convenience except one thing ... not one stinking bandstand. We had to set up on the floor and all night long 24,000 people kept falling over the music racks into our laps. This was finally rectified the next night by setting up three regulation boxing rings, one for each band ... I wound up holding the bag for a nice bundle when Monte Proser folded his carnival..." (*MS*)

The Mutual Broadcasting System signed with ASCAP and began carrying their songs once again. NBC and CBS continued to reject the Academy's terms and confined their programming to public domain tunes and the growing BMI catalog.

NYC, Madison Square Garden, Monte Proser Dance Carnival, b'cast, June 9, 1941

Merry-go-round aBilly May
Joyce JRC 1214; Redmond Nostalgia CO 4390
#Nowhere aCharlie Barnet [1:05]
Redmond Nostalgia CO 4390
Spanish kick aBilly Moore
Joyce JRC 1214; Redmond Nostalgia CO 4390
The great lie# aAndy Gibson [1:08]
Redmond Nostalgia CO 4390

NYC, RCA Victor recording session, June 11, 1941

65699-1 **When the sun comes out** aBilly Moore; vBob Carroll
BB B11202; *BB AXM2 5590*; *Big Band Archives BBA 1209*; BB AXK2 5590
66100-1 **I'll never let a day pass by** (aBilly Moore?); vBob Carroll and Quintones
BB 11202; *BB AXM2 5590*; BB AXK2 5590;
66101-1 **Lois** aCharlie Barnet; vocal effects Quintones
BB B11265°; *Camden CAL 389*; *BB AXM2 5590*; *Vi LPV 567°*; *RCA (E)RD 8088*; *RCA (Ger) LPM 567*; BB AXK2 5590
66102-1 **Be fair** aBilly Moore; vBob Carroll
BB B11223; *BB AXM2 5590*; BB AXK2 5590
66103-1 **Spanish kick** aBilly Moore
BB B11265°; Vi (Brazil) 28378; *Camden CAL 389; BB AXM2 5590; Vi LPV 567°; RCA (E) RD 8088; RCA (Ger) LPM 567*; BB AXK2 5590; **KAZ (E) CD 311**
66104-1 **Wasn't it you** aBilly Moore; vBob Carroll and Quintones
BB B11223; *BB AXM2 5590*; BB AXK2 5590

June 15, 1941: Lincoln, Neb., Turnpike Casino ["...so-so $612 from approximately same number stubs" (*Variety* July 23, 1941)]

Leo White was replaced by Ray Hopfner. Bob Burnet rejoined at about this time, leading to the formation of a small group variously called "The Barnet Heptet" and "The Cherokees." Members of the group were Burnet, Hopfner, Bill Miller, Phil Stephens, Bus Etri and Cliff Leeman. Tony Faso may have briefly replaced Charles Zimmerman, in turn replaced by Burnet.

June 29, 1941 (afternoon)**: Annapolis, MD, Carr's Beach** ["race resort ... 3 to 7PM ... 7,005 customers..." (*Billboard* July 19, 1941)]
June 29, 1941 (evening)**: Washington, DC, Turner's Hall** ["race spot ... drew about 1,000" (*Billboard* July 19, 1941)]
July 3, 1941: Rochester, NY (site unidentified)
July 4, 1941: Carrolltown, PA (site?)
July 5, 1941: Allentown, PA (site?)
July 6, 1941: Bristol, CT (site?)
July 7–11, 1941: Atlantic City, Steel Pier
July 13, 1941: Canton, OH, Moonlight Ballroom, Meyers Lake Park
July 15, 1941: Cheyenne, WY (site?)

Charlie Barnet orchestra

Personnel approximately as for April 29, 1941.

NYC, RCA Thesaurus recording session, ca mid-July, 1941

66505- **Consider yourself kissed** aFranklyn Marks; vBob Carroll
THESAURUS 961; **HEP (E) CD 53; VIPER'S NEST VN 1002**
66505- **Dutch kitchen stomp** aBud Estes
THESAURUS 961; *IAJRC 8*; Ajax C 708; Joyce JRC C 1523; **HEP (E) CD 53; VIPER'S NEST VN 1002**
66505- **Plowin'** aHorace Henderson
As preceding
66505- **Spanish kick** aBilly Moore;
THESAURUS 961; **HEP (E) CD 53; VIPER'S NEST VN 1002, VN 1010**; AFRS DOWNBEAT 91
66505- **The heart you stole from me** aBilly Moore; vBob Carroll
THESAURUS 961; **VIPER'S NEST VN 1002**

66506-1 **The bar is now open** aHorace Henderson
THESAURUS 962; *Trip TLP 5804*; *DJM (E) DJML 061*; *IAJRC 8*; *Jazz Bird JAZ 2016*; *Parnaso (Argentina) 13032*; Ajax C 683; **HEP (E) CD 53; VIPER'S NEST VN 1002**

66506-1 **Barcarolle** aBilly Moore
THESAURUS 962; *Trip TLP 5804; DJM (E) DJML 061; IAJRC 8; Jazz Bird JAZ 2016; Joyce 2017; Parnaso (Argentina) 13032*; Ajax C 683; Big Band Era (N) 40180; **HEP (E) CD 53; VIPER'S NEST VN 1002, VN 1010; PILZ (GER) 44 2042-2; B&C RECORDS 74081-2**; AFRS DOWNBEAT 93, 140

66506-1 **Ponce de Leon** aHorace Henderson
THESAURUS 962; *Trip TLP 5804*; *IAJRC 8*; **HEP (E) CD 53; VIPER'S NEST VN 1002, VN 1010**; AFRS DOWNBEAT 91

66506-1 **Song of the Volga boatmen** aHorace Henderson
THESAURUS 962; *Trip TLP 5804*; *DJM (E) DJML 061*; *Big Band Archives BBA 1209*; *IAJRC 8*; *Jazz Bird JAZ 2016*; *Joyce 2017*; *Parnaso (Argentina) 13032*; Ajax C 683; **HEP (E) CD 53; VIPER'S NEST VN 1002; PILZ (GER) 44 2042-2; B&C RECORDS 74081-2**; AFRS DOWNBEAT 93, 140

66506-1 **Reflections** a(Charlie Barnet?)
THESAURUS 962; *Golden Era 15015*; *IAJRC 8*; *Joyce 2017*; Ajax C 683; **HEP (E) CD 53; VIPER'S NEST VN 1002**; AFRS DOWNBEAT 93, 140

July 17, 1941: Salt Lake City, (Rendezvous?)
July 18, 1941: Reno, El Patio Ballroom
July 19, 1941: Sacramento, Sweet's Ballroom
July 20, 1941: Oakland, Sweet's Ballroom

A review of the Oakland performance noted that "the glamour boy of the evening with his impossibly weird chords and progressions..." was Bus Etri. (*Down beat* Aug. 15, 1941)

July 22–Aug. (20?),1941: Culver City, Calif., Casa Mañana

"I used to like the Casa Mañana better than any place to play. It was such a warm room and good feeling bandstand to play on and the crowd was great." (*Sm*)

Culver City, Casa Mañana, b'cast July 29, 1941

#You can depend on me

Bob Burnet, Bob Price, Cy Baker, Mickey Bloom, tpts; Spud Murphy, Tommy Reo, Bill Robertson, Ford Leary, tbns; Ray Hopfner, Conn Humphreys, as; Kurt Bloom, ts; James Lamare, ts & bar; Bill Miller, p; Bus Etri, g; Phil Stephens, b; Cliff Leeman, d (ViSS)

Hollywood, Calif., RCA Victor recording session, August 14, 1941

61531-1 **Harlem speaks** aAndy Gibson
BB B11281°; HMV (Australia) EA 3635; HMV (E) B 9513; HMV (India) B 9513; HMV (It) HN 2156; *BB AXM2 5590*; *Vi LPT 3062°*; *Vi LPV 567°*; *RCA (Arg) AVLT 7*; *RCA (E) RD 8088*; *RCA (Fr) NL 89483-2, PM 42041*; *RCA (Ger) LPM 567*; ***RCA EPBT 3062***; BB AXK2 5590; **KAZ (E) CD 311; JAZZ ARCHIVES (FR) 158532; RCA (FR) 74321355532**

61532-1 **Swingin' on nothin'** aBilly Moore; vFord Leary
BB B11281°; Vi 20-2632; HMV (E) B 9498; HMV (India) B 9498; HMV (It) HN 2183; *BB AXM2 5590*; *Big Band Archives BBA 1209*; BB AXK2 5590; **LIVING ERA (E) CD AJA 5288**; AFRTS GOLD LABEL LIBRARY P-GL 35

61533-1 **The heart you stole from me** aBilly Moore; vBob Carroll
BB B11292°; *BB AXM2 5590*; *Vi LPV 551°*; *RCA (E) RD 7965*; *RCA (Ger) LPM 551*; BB AXK2 5590

61534-1 **Murder at Peyton Hall** aAndy Gibson [Named for an apartment house used by the band while on the Coast]
BB B11292°; HMV (Australia) EA 3742; HMV (E) B 9390; HMV (India) B 9390; *Camden CAL 389*; *BB AXM2 5590*; *Vi LPV 551°*; *RCA (E) RD 7965*; *RCA (Ger) LPM 551*; *RCA (Ja) RA 60-68*; *Camden CAE 432*; BB AXK2 5590; **BB 6273 2-RB; ARISTA 886281; RCA (E) 86273**

Charlie and the band took part in a "battle of music" with the Duke Ellington band on August 20. The next day Charlie threw a party for Ellington and his men. (*Stratemann, p.171*)

Barnet Musician Killed, Singer Hurt In L.A. Car Crash, Marijuana Found

(Variety Aug. 27, 1941)

Bus Etri died in a car accident early in the morning of August 21.

Mickey Bloom and Manny Klein filled in for Lloyd Hundling in the brass section. Hundling died Aug. 29.

A *Down beat* story asserted that Etri would not be replaced and further that Billy Moore was to compose a song that would include some of Etri's solos to be played by Charlie.

ca. late Aug., early Sept., 1941: Sacramento, State Fair
Sept. 7, 1941: Oakland, Sweet's Ballroom

Personnel as preceding except that Etri was replaced by Jack LeMaire.

Hollywood, RCA Victor recording session, September 11, 1941

61630-1 **You were there** vBob Carroll
BB B11321°; HMV (India) NE 613 [Reverse is Teddy Pow-ell's *Birth of the blues*]; *BB AXM2 5590*; BB AXK2 5590
61631-1 **Blues in the night** aAndy Gibson; vBobbie Canvin and Ford Leary
Unissued
61632-1 **I'm coming Virginia** aBilly Moore; vFord Leary & 4 members of Quintones
BB B11417; *BB AXM2 5590*; BB AXK2 5590
61633-1 **Mother fuzzy** aAndy Gibson ("as close as we could get to 'Mother f____'" [Billy May])
BB 11321°; HMV (E) B 9405; *BB AXM2 5590*; *Vi LPV 551°*; *RCA (E) RD 7965*; *RCA (Fr) PM 42041*; *RCA (Ger) LPM 551*; BB AXK2 5590; **BMG 09026 653345-2; Jazz Archives (Fr) 158532; RCA 7863 66746 2**

Sept. 17–23, 1941: LA, Orpheum Theater

Los Angeles, Orpheum Theater, stage performance, Sept. 17, 1941

Pompton Turnpike aBilly May
It's so peaceful in the counry aConn Humphreys; vBob Carroll
Just what we're doin' tonight vBob Carroll
Honeysuckle rose (aHorace Henderson?) (feat. Si Baker "on his tricky trumpet")
Baa baa black sheep vQuintones [four members thereof]
Star dust vQuintones
Indian medley (Cherokee/Comanche war dance) aBilly May
Solitude
Shadrach (aAndy Gibson?) vFord Leary
Ol' Man River vFord Leary
Scotch and soda aRoscoe Fritz

An agreement was reached between ASCAP and the two major networks and on September 28 ASCAP songs were once again heard on all the networks.

Charlie Barnet and his orchestra

Bernie Privin, Paul McCoy, Cy Baker, Bob Burnet, tpts; Spud Murphy, Tommy Reo, Bill Robertson, Ford Leary, tbns; Ray Hopfner, Conn Humphreys, as; Kurt Bloom, ts; James Lamare, ts & bar; Bill Miller, p; Jack LeMaire, g; Phil Stephens, b; Cliff Leeman, d; Harry Bluestone, Mischa Russell, Nick Pisane, James Cathcart, vns; Norman Botnick, vla; Cy Bernard, cello (ViSS)

Hollywood, RCA Victor recording session, October 5, 1941

61631-2 **Blues in the night** aAndy Gibson; vBobbie Canvin & Ford Leary. (no strings)
BB B11327°; *BB AXM2 5590*; BB AXK2 5590
61712-1 **I'll remember April** aConn Humphreys; vBob Carroll
BB 11417; BB 30-0826°; HMV (India) NE 820; *BB AXM2 5590*; **Reader's Digest RBD 114/CDI**; AFRS DOWNBEAT 30
61713-1 **Isle of pines** aConn Humphreys; vBob Carroll
BB 11327°; *BB AXM2 5590*
61714-1 **Macumba** aConn Humphreys
BB 11396°; HMV (E) B 9638; *BB AXM2 5590*
61715-1 **Fifty million nickels** vFord Leary and female trio (no strings)
BB 11396°; *BB AXM2 5590*

Hollywood, Universal Studios, Oct. 6–12, 1941

"*JUKE BOX JENNY*" (preliminary title "Fifty million nickels")

A feature film starring Harriet Hilliard and Ken Murray with Charlie Barnet and his orchestra, Milt Herth, Wingy Manone and The King's Men. 65m. Released about April 1942

Fifty million nickels vFord Leary and female trio (1:46)
Audio: Universal UPC 297 (2:39)
Unidentified rhumba (3:06)
Then you'll remember me vHarriet Hilliard and The King's Men (2:10)
Swing it, Mother Goose vIris Adrian and The King's Men (1:22)
Then you'll remember me# vIris Adrian (0:15)
Then you'll remember me# vHarriet Hilliard (0:15)
Sweet Genevieve vHarriet Hilliard and the King's Men (1:10)
Sweet Genevieve vHarriet Hilliard (0:10)
#Fifty million nickels (1:05)
Sweet Genevieve vHarriet Hilliard, The King's Men (1:08)
Give out vHarriet Hilliard, The King's Men (3:45)

Other non-Barnet musical numbers include *Tiger rag* by Wingy Manone, *Carry me back to old Virginny* by The King's Men, accompanied by Phil Stephens, Cliff Leeman and Jack LeMaire, The Milt Herth Trio doing *Dark eyes* and *The whistler and his dog*, and another brief version of *Sweet Genevieve* by Harriet Hilliard with guitar (LeMaire?) accompaniment. *Macumba* is credited to the film on the Bluebird record label but is not heard in the version of the film as shown on TV.

(The music behind the opening credits is by a big band, with trumpet and clarinet solos. The compiler thinks it is not by Charlie—surely we would have heard a Barnet solo if it was. Compiler hasn't been able to identify the song played by this group.)

The press reported that Bob Carroll left the band to go with NBC (*Down beat*, Nov. 1, 1941). Alan Lane from the Quintones became Charlie's boy singer and Hazel Bruce was the chirp. (*Billboard* Nov. 1, 1941)

Late in the year the popular music press carried a number of stories having to do with personnel changes, Charlie firing Charlie Weintraub, experimenting with strings, "revamping" the band and the like. There was a report that he was going to put the band on notice, take a two-week vacation, and reform the band. Clearly changes were taking place. Dizzy Gillespie was with the band for a short time—probably in December: "Well, I had a job to go on the road and I didn't have a trumpet section. You know, it was scuffling time and we were going to play at some hotel … in Cincinnati. So I got ahold of Dizzy, I said, 'Hey, you want to make this trip?' He said, 'Yeah, sure.' I said, 'Well, John, we need another trumpet player, too. You got anybody in mind?' He said, 'How about Joe Guy?' I said, 'Okay. I don't know him, but if you…,' He said, 'Yeah, he'll be fine.' I said, 'There's only one thing, John, you've got to play first trumpet.' He said, 'I'll play it.' And he did. He did a heck of a job." (*Sm*)

Oct. 17–23, 1941: Philadelphia, Earle Theater
Oct. 24–26, 1941: Newark, Adams Theater
Oct. 27, 1941: Bridgeport, Ritz Ballroom ("drew 2,348")
Oct. 31–??, 1941: Worcester, Providence Theater
Nov. 4?, 1941: Providence, Metropolitan Theater
Nov. 6–12, 1941: Passaic, Central Theater (Charlie was down with a cold and during his absence the band was led by Teddy Powell, Michael Loring, Ray Heatherton, Tommy Tucker [!] and Harry James.)
Nov. 13–19, 1941: Baltimore, Hippodrome Theater (he missed 2½ days of this engagement also)

Nov. 21–27, 1941: NYC, Apollo Theater
Nov. 29, 1941: Philadelphia, Brookline Country Club
Nov. 30, 1941: Bridgeport, Ritz Ballroom

(NYC?), WOR, 10:15PM, Spotlight Bands b'cast, Dec. 1, 1941

Program content unknown

The Japanese bombed Pearl Harbor on December 7.

Dec. 4–10, 1941: Brooklyn, Flatbush Theater
Dec. 12–(18?), 1941: Bronx, Windsor Theater
(Dec. 1941?: Cincinnati, Netherlands Plaza?)

Charlie has been suggested as the tenor sax soloist on Jimmy Dorsey's *Murderistic*, recorded on December 22. (Compiler cannot hear any important resemblance to Charlie's playing.)

On December 27, Charles Daly Barnet, Jr., was born to Harriet (Clarke) Barnet. "The father flew in from Ohio when informed of his son's arrival." (*Down beat,* Jan. 15, 1942)

A possibility exists that Charlie again played a Spotlight Bands program, this time on December 30.

Dec. 31, 1941: Toronto, Mutual Arena
Jan. 1, 1942: Bradford, PA, Bradford Theater

This January 1 date is reported to have been the last for this particular band. Charlie was to take a vacation and resume activities later on, according to the press.

Chapter 4

Skyliner— The Andy Gibson Band 1942–1945

Metronome All Star Leaders

Cootie Williams, tpt; J. C. Higginbotham, tbn; Benny Goodman, cl; Benny Carter, as; ***Charlie Barnet****, ts; Count Basie, p; Alvino Rey, g; John Kirby, b; Gene Krupa, d*

NYC, Columbia recording session, January 16, 1942

32261-1 **I got rhythm**
Col (Australia) DO 2107; *CBS-Sony (Ja) SOPM 188*; *Sony (Ja) NP 50419*; *Tax 8039*

32261-2 **I got rhythm**
Col 36499; Col (C) C 601; Parlophone (E) R 2967; Parlophone (UK-export) DP 253; Parlophone (It) B 71103; Parlophone (Switz) PZ 11210; *CBS-Sony (Ja) SOPM 188*; *Sony (Ja) NP 50419*; *Tax 8039*

32261-3 **I got rhythm**
Col (Australia) DO 2481; *Col CL 2528*; *Harmony HL 7044*; *Sony (Ja) NP 50419*; *Tax 8039*

Charlie Barnet and his orchestra

Neal Hefti, Joseph Ferrante, Henry McQuiness, Robert Burnet, tpts; Spud Murphy, Kahn Keene, Wallace Barron, Bill Robertson, tbns; George E. Bone, Conn Humphreys, as; Kurt Bloom, ts; James Lamare, ts & bar; Bill Miller, p; Edward Scala, g; Phil Stephens, b; Jack Mills, d (ViSS)

NYC, RCA Victor recording session, January 20, 1942

71651-1 **Ya lu-blu** vAlan Lane
BB B11446°; *BB AXM2 5590*

71652-1 **Night of nights** vAlan Lane
BB B11446°; *BB AXM2 5590*

71653-1 **Do you know (well I do)** vAlan Lane
BB AXM2 5590

71654-1 **I can't get started** aAndy Gibson
Vi LPV 551°; *BB AXM2 5590*; *RCA (Ja) RA 60-68*; *RCA (E) RD 7965*; *RCA (Fr) PM 42401, NL 89483-2*; *RCA (Ger) LPM 551*; *RCA (It) LPM 34022*; **RCA (Fr) 74321355532**; THE MUSIC MAKERS 334

There is a remote possibility that the piece honoring the memory of Bus Etri (*In memory of*) was recorded. However, no evidence of this has come to light.

Hamilton, NY, Colgate University, Spotlight Bands b'cast, Jan. 30, 1942

Program content unknown

Jan. 30-31, 1942: Hamilton, NY, Colgate University

NYC, Fox Movietone Studios, ca early February, 1942

"Syncopation" (RKO)

An RKO feature film starring Bonita Granville and Jackie Cooper with an all-star band. 88m.

The Saturday Evening Post All-American Jazz Band

Harry James, tpt; Jack Jenney, tbn; Benny Goodman, cl; ***Charlie Barnet,*** *ts; Joe Venuti, vn; Howard Smith, p; Alvino Rey, g; Bob Haggart, b; Gene Krupa, d*

(Connor and Hicks note, in "BG on the record" [1969], that Benny is heard but not seen, having recorded his solo separately. An actor with his back to the camera substituted for the King of Swing on screen. Eddy Duchin won the piano spot but Howard Smith performed in his place.)

Untitled blues

Feb. 1, 1942: New Haven, Shubert Theater
(Feb. 1942?): Manchester, NH, Ritz Ballroom
Feb. (10?), 1942: Baltimore, Regal [Royal?] Theater
Feb. 14, 1942: Philadelphia, Brookline Country Club

Band personnel on February 16, 1942:

*Sidney DeParis, Joe Ferrante, Buddy McQuinness, Neal Hefti, tpts; Russell Brown, Wally Barron, Kahn Keene, Bill Robertson, tbns; George Bone, Conn Humphreys, as; Kurt Bloom, ts; Jimmy Lamare, ts & bar; Bill Miller, p; Tom Moore, g; Olin Anderhold, b; Jack Mills, d. Singers were Hazel Bruce and Alan Lane. (*Down beat *Feb. 15, 1942)*

Feb. 16–March 15, 1942: Boston, Brunswick Hotel

Boston, Brunswick Hotel, WBZ b'cast, Feb. 17, 1942

Redskin rhumba (opening theme)
He's 1-A in the Army vHazel Bruce
This is no laughing matter vAlan Lane
The story of a starry night [gap in recording]
The right idea# aSkippy Martin

Feb. 23, 1942: Philadelphia, Strand Ballroom

Peanuts Holland was a member of the trumpet section on Feb. 23.

Cliff Leeman, free of legal entanglements in Los Angeles, replaced Jackie Mills on about February 28. At about the same time there were changes in the trumpet section: Irving Berger replaced Buddy McQuinness and Johnny Carroll took the place of Neal Hefti (who went to full time arranging, along with Bob Burnet).

Mar. 1, 1942: Bridgeport, Ritz Ballroom

Boston, Brunswick Hotel, WBZ b'cast, March 5, 1942

Redskin rhumba (opening theme)
Ev'rything I love vAlan Lane
Honeysuckle rose (performed by "The Cherokees")
Flying home# aSkippy Martin
I don't want to walk without you vHazel Bruce

Mar. 15, 1942: NYC, Savoy Ballroom
Mar. 17, 1942: Philadelphia, Town Hall
Mar. 19–25, 1942: Newark, Adams Theater
Mar. 28, 1942: Pottstown, Sunnybrook Ballroom

Alan Lane joined the Army at about this time; his replacement was Larry Taylor. Jack Jarvis joined on bass.

(April 1, 1942?): Springfield, Loew's Court Square Theater
April 8, 1942: Lowell, Commodore Ballroom
April 9, 1942: Taunton, MA, Roseland Ballroom
April 10, 1942: Durham, NH, Univ. of NH
April 11, 1942: Boston, Rosalind State Ballroom
April 14–15, 1942: Montreal, Auditorium ("Barnet socko")

Variety noted (April 22) that Charlie had been ordered to report to his local draft board in NYC for a physical.

April 19, 1942: Bristol, CT, Lake Compounce ballroom ("Stars of the evening were ... Peanuts Holland ... Cliff Leeman ... and Jack Jarvis, Negro bassist" [*Down beat* June 1, 1942])

April 20, 1942: Toronto, Palais Royale ballroom

Irving Berger, Joseph Ferrante, Charles Zimmerman, Peanuts Holland, tpts; Kahn Keene, Wally Barron, Bill Robertson, Russell Brown, tbns; George Bone, Conn Humphreys, as; Kurt Bloom, ts; James Lamare, ts & bar; Bill Miller, p; Tom Moore, g; Jack Jarvis, b; Cliff Leeman, d

NYC, Decca recording session, April 30, 1942

70700-A **That real romance** aBill Miller; vLarry Taylor
De 18363°; *Ajax 140*; Stack of 78s Stack 73; **STACK OF 78S STACK 73**

70701-A **I like to riff** aAndy Gibson; vPeanuts Holland
De 18378°; Odeon (Arg) 286333 (as *Me gusta frasear*); Brunswick (E) 0.3434; Brunswick (Ger) LPM 87096; Brunswick (India) 0.3434; *Ace of Hearts (E) AH 157*; *MCA (Ja) 3146*; *Ajax 140*; Stack of 78s Stack 73; **STACK OF 78S STACK 73; HINDSIGHT HCD 264**; AFRS DOWNBEAT 30

70702-A **Smiles** aAndy Gibson
De 18363°; Odeon (Brazil) 288.729; Brunswick (Ger) A 82584; Brunswick (Norway) A 82584; *Decca DL 8098*; *Franklin Mint Record 33*; *Franklin Mint Record no.19*; *MCA MCA2 4069°*; *Brunswick (E) LAT 8094*; *MCA (Ja) 3146*; *Ajax 140*; Franklin Mint Tape no.19; MCA (Sp) L 404302; Stack of 78s Stack 73; *MCA 4069* (8-track); **DE JAZZ GRD 612; JAZZ HERITAGE 514960-T; MCA (E) GRP 16122; BEST OF JAZZ (FR) 4039; JAZZ ARCHIVES (FR) 158532; DECCA JAZZ (JA) MVCR 20008; STACK OF 78S STACK 73; JAZZ GREATS (E) CD 071**; AFRS DOWNBEAT 30

70703-A **Shady lady** aAndy Gibson
De 18378°; Odeon (Brazil) 288.729; Brunswick (E) 03434; Brunswick (India) 0.3434; *De DL 8098; MCA MCA2 4069°; Brunswick (E) LAT 8094; Coral (Ger) 6 22182; Coral (Ger) PCO 7840, PCO 7995; MCA (Ja) 3146; Ajax 140*; De ED 725; Stack of 78s Stack 73; MCA 4069 (8-track); **DECCA JAZZ GRD 612; JAZZ HERITAGE 514960-T; MCA (E) GRP 16122; BEST OF JAZZ (FR) 4039; DECCA JAZZ (JA) MVCR 20008; STACK OF 78S STACK 73**

Huck Andrews replaced Larry Taylor and Frances Wayne replaced Hazel Bruce at about this time: "[Frances] was very much a lady ... She's the most lady-like singer I ever had in my life. Now I'm not saying that Lena Horne wasn't a lady, because she was. But you know, Lena could read somebody off if they came on too strong. But not Frances. Frances would just recoil in horror and gasp, you know, [but] she always took care of things." (*Sm*)

U.S. forces in the Philippines surrendered to the Japanese May 6.

May 15–21, 1942: Buffalo, (Twentieth Century Theater?)

May 23, 1942: Port Stanley, ON, Port Stanley Ballroom

May 29–June 11, 1942: Denver, Elitch's Gardens

June 13–19, 1942: Wichita, Blue Moon

Information at the Library of Congress indicates that Charlie was heard on an Office of War Information program, "Jazz in America, LWO 6087 GR 14 3A1, June 18, 1942, OWI Recording E17-35." (Probably it was one of the band's commercial releases.)

June 26–July 2, 1942: Detroit, Eastwood Park

July 6–(20?), 1942: Atlantic City, Steel Pier

Atlantic City, Steel Pier, between July 6 & 20,1942, (WOR?) b'cast

Washington whirligig aAndy Gibson
V-Disc (Army) 137; *Aircheck 30*; *Joyce LP 2012*; (AFRS MUSIC IN THE MODERN MANNER 268?)

Caravan aRalph Burns
V-Disc (Army) 137; *Joyce LP 2012*
Cotton tail aGeorge Siravo
V-Disc (Army) 137; *Aircheck 30*; *Joyce LP 2012*; Ajax C708

Personnel as preceding but Murray Williams (as) replaced Conn Humphreys and Bob Elden (b) replaced Jack Jarvis.

NYC, Decca recording session, July 17, 1942

71097-A **I don't want anybody at all** aAndy Gibson; vHuck Andrews
De 18541º; Odeon (Arg) 286304; Odeon (Brazil) 288.762; Bon Marché (Australia) 1173; Brunswick (E) 03391; *Ajax 140*; Stack of 78s Stack 73; **STACK OF 78S STACK 73**
71098-A **That old black magic** aAndy Gibson; vFrances Wayne
De 18541º; Bon Marché (Australia) 1173; Odeon (Brazil) 288.762; Brunswick (E) 03391; *MCA 2 4069º*; *Ajax 140*; Stack of 78s Stack 73; MCA (Sp) L 404302; MCA 4069 (8-track); **DECCA JAZZ GRD 612; JAZZ HERITAGE 514960-T; MCA (E) GRP 16122; DECCA JAZZ (JA) MVCR-20008; EMPRESS (E) 829; EMPRESS (E) RAJCD 898; STACK OF 78S STACK 73**
71099-A **Oh! Miss Jaxson** aAndy Gibson; vPeanuts Holland
De 18547º; Brunswick (E) 03421; Brunswick (India) 0.3421; *De DL 8098*; *MCA 2 4069º*; *Reader's Digest RD 184-2*; *Reader's Digest (C) RD2 710*; *Brunswick (E) LAT 8094*; *Ajax 140*; De ED 725; Stack of 78s Stack 73; MCA (Sp) L 404302; *MCA 4069* (8-track); **DECCA JAZZ GRD 612; JAZZ HERITAGE 514960-T; MCA (E) GRP 16122; JAZZ ARCHIVES (FR) 158532; DECCA JAZZ (JA) MVCR20008**; AFRS G.I. JIVE 484
71100-A **Things ain't what they used to be** aAndy Gibson
De 18507º; Brunswick (E) 03451; Brunswick (India) 0.3451; *De DL 8098; MCA 2 4069º; Affinity (E) AFS 1012; Ace of Hearts (E) AH 157; Brunswick (E) LAT 8094; Coral (E) CDLM 8046; MCA (Ja) 3146; Ajax 140*; *DE ED 725*; MCA (Sp) L 404302; Stack of 78s Stack 73; MCA 4069 (8-track); **DECCA JAZZ GRD 612; JAZZ HERITAGE 514960-T; KAZ (E) CD 311; MCA (E) GRP 16122; TOPAZ JAZZ (E) TPZ 1041; JAZZ ARCHIVES (FR) 158532; DECCA JAZZ (JA) MVCR20008; GIANTS OF JAZZ (CZ) CD 53280**
71101-A **Washington whirligig** aAndy Gibson
De 18547º; Brunswick (E) 03421; Brunswick (India) 0.3421; *Affinity (E) AFS 1012*; *Ace of Hearts (E) AH 157*; *Coral (E) CDL 8024*; *Coral (E) MCM 1001*; *Coral (Ger) 6 22182, PCO 7840, PCO 7995*; *MCA (Ja) 3146*; *Ajax 140*; Stack of 78s Stack 73; **CLASSIC JAZZ (E) CDCD1239; KAZ (E) CD 311; TOPAZ JAZZ (E) TPZ 1041; GIANTS OF JAZZ (CZ) CD 53280; STACK OF 78S STACK 73**
71102-A **The victory walk** aAndy Gibson
De 18507º; Brunswick (E) 03451; Brunswick (India) 0.3451; *Ajax 140*; Stack of 78s Stack 73; **STACK OF 78S STACK 73**

Atlantic City, NJ, Steel Pier, July 20,1942, (WOR?) b'cast

Keepin' out of mischief now
Oh! Miss Jaxson vPeanuts Holland
Keep the home fires burning

Writing for *Metronome* Barry Ulanov reviewed the July 20 broadcast where he knocked the band's lack of precision and the poor intonation of the vocalists. Peanuts Holland's singing and playing were much to his liking. (Aug. 1942)

July 22, 1942: Washington, DC, Griffith Stadium

The July 22 engagement was a joint appearance with the Louis Armstrong band, "a swing session combined with a jitterbug contest ... When the bands started to send, all hell broke loose." The affair had to be halted due to the riotous behavior of the audience. (*Billboard,* Aug. 1, 1942)

Charlie Barnet "King of the Saxophone and his orchestra"

NYC, Lang-Worth recording session, July 28, 1942

1273-a **The victory walk** aAndy Gibson
LANG-WORTH AS-7; *Blue Heaven BH-6 604; First Heard (E) FH 44*; First Heard (E) CFH 44; **CIRCLE CCD 112**
1273-b **That old black magic** aAndy Gibson; vFrances Wayne

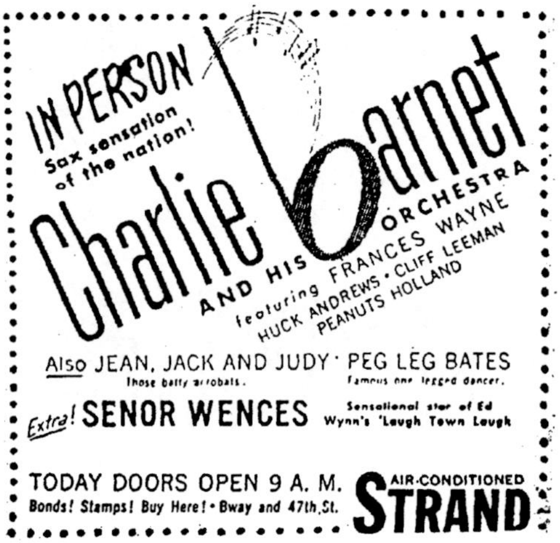

LANG-WORTH AS-7; LANG-WORTH DL 234B1; *Blue Heaven BH-7 702*; CIRCLE **CCD 112**

1273-c **I don't want anybody at all** aAndy Gibson; vHuck Andrews
LANG-WORTH AS-7; *Blue Heaven BH-7 702*; CIRCLE **CCD 112**

1273-d **Oh! Miss Jaxson** aAndy Gibson; vPeanuts Holland
LANG-WORTH AS-7, DL 234B2; *Blue Heaven BH-1 106*; CIRCLE **CCD 112**

1280-a **Wichita windstorm** aAndy Gibson
LANG-WORTH 820, CI 57B1; DL 59A1; *Blue Heaven BH-7 702*; *Swing Era LP 1019*; Ajax C 683; CIRCLE **CCD 112**; AFRS BML P-3205

1280-b **Washington whirligig** aAndy Gibson
LANG-WORTH 820, CI 57B2, DL 18A2; AFRS BML P-3205; CIRCLE **CCD 112**

1280-c **Shady lady** aAndy Gibson
LANG-WORTH 820, DL 30B2; *Blue Heaven BH-6 604*; CIRCLE **CCD 112**

1280-d **Plowin'** aHorace Henderson
LANG-WORTH 820; LANG-WORTH DL 18B; *Blue Heaven BH-7 702*; CIRCLE **CCD 112**; AFRS BML P-3206

1280-e **Redskin rhumba** aHead
LANG-WORTH 820, DL 18B, MP 17; *Blue Heaven BH-1 106, BH-6 604; Circle CLP 65*; CHG 0155 32789-1; Radio Classics AFP 7141 AC; CIRCLE **CCD 65**

1281-a **That real romance** aBill Miller; vHuck Andrews
LANG-WORTH 822; LANG-WORTH DL 234A; *Blue Heaven BH-1 106*; CIRCLE **CCD 112**; AFRS BML P-3206

1281-b **Things ain't what they used to be** aAndy Gibson
LANG-WORTH 822; CIRCLE **CCD 112**

1281-c **I like to riff** aAndy Gibson; vPeanuts Holland
LANG-WORTH 822; *Blue Heaven BH-6 604*; CIRCLE **CCD 112**

1281-d **Midsummer matinee** vHuck Andrews
LANG-WORTH 822; *Blue Heaven BH-7 702*; CIRCLE **CCD 112**

July 29, 1942: Hershey, PA, site unidentified
July 31–Aug. 13, 1942: NYC, Strand Theater

U.S. Marines landed on Guadalcanal on Aug. 7 in what would be the first taking of territory conquered by Japan.

The first American Federation of Musicians recording ban took effect on August 1. Except for V-Discs (and some non-union sessions marketed by Eli Oberstein on his Hit label and a few *a capella* vocals) no commercial recordings were made for over a year. On about October 6, 1943, Decca agreed to the AFM terms, signed and resumed recording. Capitol signed on about November 3. It was not until November 11, 1944, that Victor and Columbia were brought to heel.

The press noted that Charlie's draft classification remained 3-A (man with dependents but who is not engaged in an activity either essential to the war production program or essential to the support of the war effort).

NYC, Strand Theater,
stage performance, Aug. 13, 1942

Medley of Barnet hits aAndy Gibson
Just as though you were here vHuck Andrews
I like to riff aAndy Gibson; vPeanuts Holland
Keepin' out of mischief now
Solitude
All I need is you vFrances Wayne
Cheatin' on me vFrances Wayne
Rockin' in rhythm aBilly May
Cherokee aBilly May

Variety's correspondent reviewed the band during its Strand appearance and noted that, "Led by its leader's Negroid sax style and the penchant for a blazing groove, the outfit has never been 'commercial' which has kept it out of many a buildup location that often leads to bigger money. ... Frances Wayne...has exceptional control, good range..." (Aug. 5, 1942) George Simon in *Metronome* wrote of Frances Wayne, "She stopped it cold with her exotic versions of *All I need is you* and *Cheatin' on me* ... a really valuable lass." (Aug. 1942)

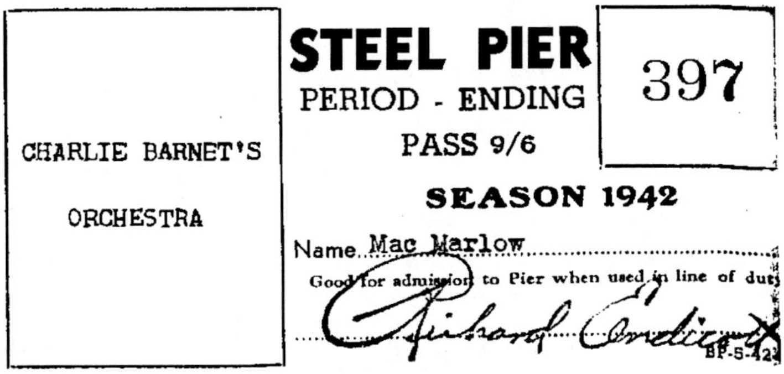
CHARLIE BARNET'S
ORCHESTRA
STEEL PIER
PERIOD - ENDING
PASS 9/6
397
SEASON 1942
Name Mac Marlow
Good for admission to Pier when used in line of duty
Richard Endicott
SP-5-42

Aug. 14–20, 1942: Boston, RKO Theater

<u>*Boston, RKO Theater, stage performance, Aug. 14, 1942*</u>

Medley of Barnet hits aAndy Gibson
Just as though you were here vHuck Andrews
Sleepy lagoon vHuck Andrews
Rockin' in rhythm aBilly May
All I need is you vFrances Wayne
Cheatin' on me vFrances Wayne
Cherokee aBilly May

Benny Lagasse, as, replaced George Bone. Mac Marlowe, tbn and vn, replaced Bill Robertson on September 6.

Aug. 22, 1942: Palisade, NJ, Palisades Park
Aug. 23, 1942: Bridgeport, Pleasure Beach Park
Aug. 24–Sept. 6, 1942: Atlantic City, Steel Pier (MBS wire)

Personnel lined up about as follows in the late summer:

Irv Berger, Max Gussak, Charlie Zimmerman, Peanuts Holland, tpts; Russ Brown, Kahn Keene, Walt McGuffin, Mac Marlow, tbns; Murray Williams, Benny Lagasse, as; Kurt Bloom, ts; James Lamare, ts & bar; Bill Miller, p; Tom Moore, g; Bob Elden, b; Cliff Leeman, d.

Howard McGhee left Andy Kirk to join Charlie at about this time. (He was present for the Earle Theater engagement Sept. 11.)

Early in September Nita (Leeman) Bradley replaced Frances Wayne. Sam Kublin and Tony Lala were reported to be in the trombone section. Charlie Zimmerman (tpt) returned. Rudy Novack (tpt) was reported to have been in and out, briefly. Steve Cole came in on tenor. Jimmy Lamare took over the managerial duties, replacing the drafted Mort Davis (whom Charlie kept on the payroll "for the duration").

Sept. 7, 1942: Baltimore, Dixie Ballroom at Gwynn Park
Sept. 11–17, 1942: Philadelphia, Earle Theater
Sept. 18–24, 1942: Cleveland, Palace Theater
Sept. 25–Oct. 1, 1942: Pittsburgh, Stanley Theater ["...biz ... very poor"]

The press mentioned singers Perry Russell and Dell Parker as appearing briefly with Charlie. Herb Reis took over management from James Lamare. Joe Ferrante (tpt) was inducted into the Army in October.

Oct. 2–4, 1942: Hartford, State Theater [When band did Kalamazoo it "nearly brought the house down"]
Oct. 5–7, 1942: Bridgeport, Lyric Theater
Oct. 8–14, 1942: Newark, Adams Theater
Oct. 15–21, 1942: Baltimore, Hippodrome Theater

Chubby Jackson was in the band for the Baltimore performance.

Oct. 24, 1942: Pottstown, [Sunnybrook Ballroom?]
Oct. 24, 1942: New Haven, [Shubert Theater?]

Oct. 29, 1942: Allentown, Empire Ballroom
Oct. 30–Nov. 2, 1942: Harrisburg, State Theater
Nov. 1, 1942: Cleveland, Aragon Ballroom
Nov. 2, 1942: Mansfield, OH [location not specified]
Nov. 3–5, 1942: Columbus, Palace Theater
Nov. 6–9, 1942: Akron, Palace Theater
Nov. 10–12, 1942: Youngstown, Palace Theater
Nov. 13, 1942: Buffalo, Memorial Hall
Nov. 14, 1942: Detroit, Masonic Temple
Nov. 15, 1942: Cleveland, Aragon Ballroom
Nov. 16–18, 1942: Canton, Palace Theater
Nov. 19, 1942: Toledo, Trianon Ballroom
Nov. 20–26, 1942: Chicago, Oriental Theater

Montgomery defeated Rommel at El Alamein on November 5. On the 8th British and U. S. forces landed in North Africa.

Huck Andrews, vocal, went into the Army and was replaced by George Tuttle, possibly during the Oriental Theater engagement.

Band personnel was about as follows as winter came on:

Irving Berger (lead), Peanuts Holland, Howard McGhee, Max Gussak, tpts; Sam Kublin, Mac Marlow, Tony Lala, Walter McGuffin, tbns; Steve Cole, Murray Williams, Kurt Bloom, Jimmy Lamare, reeds; Roger Ramirez, p; Chubby Jackson, b; Cliff Leeman, d

Nov. 27–Dec. 3, 1942: Milwaukee, Riverside
Dec. 5, 1942: Racine, WI, Memorial Hall
Dec. 6, 1942: Indianapolis, Sunset Terrace
Dec. 8, 1942: Warren, OH, Robbins Theater
Dec. 9, 1942: Sharon, PA, Columbia Theater
Dec. 11–13, 1942: Providence, Metropolitan Theater
Dec. 14–16, 1942: Worcester, Plymouth Theater
Dec. 18–24, 1942: NYC, Apollo Theater

NYC, Apollo Theater, stage performance, Dec. 23, 1942

Medley of Barnet hits aAndy Gibson
The victory walk aAndy Gibson
Mr. Five by Five vNita Bradley
This is the Army, Mr. Jones vNita Bradley
I like to riff aAndy Gibson (featuring Peanuts and Howard McGhee)
Trumpet typhoon (featuring Peanuts and Howard)
Cherokee aBilly May

Dec. 25, 1942: Manhattan Beach, NY, Coast Guard Station

Manhattan Beach, NY, "Uncle Sam's Christmas Tree of Spotlight Bands" b'cast on NBC-Blue, Dec. 25, 1942.

Four unknown songs

(The Barnet band was the 33rd of 43 to be broadcast.)

Dec. 26, 1942: Cleveland, private party
Dec. 27, 1942: Youngstown, Nu-Elms Ballroom
Dec. 28, 1942: Toronto, The Arena
Dec. 29, 1942: Saginaw, unspecified location
Dec. 30, 1942: Racine, unspecified location
Dec. 31–Jan. 7, 1942/3: Minneapolis, Orpheum Theater

It was about this time that some new faces [surprise!] appeared in the sections: Paul Cohen (tpt) joined about Dec. 20. Danny Bank, ts & bar, Ralph Burns, and Oscar Pettiford came in during the Orpheum date. James Lamare left because of the rigors of travel and Murray Williams joined the Army. Bob Swift (age 17), tbn, replaced Sam Kublin. Dean Sayres may have become the boy singer briefly.

Danny Bank remembered that he was set to room with Peanuts, "And he says to me, 'I'm going to tell you how it's going to be ... We come to a hotel, I can't check in ... but I got a plan: you check in with your chauffeur.' So it was Danny Bank and chauffeur with Charlie Barnet's band and we did that for months." (*DBank*)

Early in 1943 Lyman Vunk (tpt) replaced Irving Berger who joined the Army.

At some time during Mac Marlow's tenure, his violin playing talents were used in the Ellington item (*Mood indigo* and *Moon mist*) which was part of the band's theater appearances. Charlie had a special case made for Marlow's violin, trombone and mutes. Prior to violinist Marlow "coming out," Chubby Jackson had warned him that Charlie had a bad taste in his mouth when it came to strings, but after Charlie ventured that it would be great to have a violin so they could add *Moon mist* to the Ellington feature, Chubby broke the secret, leading to Marlow's participation.

Jan. 8, 1943: Omaha, Chermot Ballroom
Jan. 9, 1943: Des Moines, Tromak Ballroom
Jan. 12–13, 1943: Madison, Orpheum Theater (John Brechler went to one of these performance and remembers *Redskin rhumba* being played by the band behind a scrim, the band in a pyramid with drums at the apex, the brass section next, and the sax section forming the base, with a bass player—Chubby and Oscar—at each end.)
Jan. 14, 1943: South Bend, IN, Palace Theater
Jan. 15–21, 1943: Detroit, Paradise Theater
Jan. 22–28 1943: Chicago, Regal Theater ("The first white band to play the colored house" [*Variety*, Dec. 23, 1943])
Jan. 29–Feb. 4, 1943: Indianapolis, Circle Theater

Indianapolis, Circle Theater, stage performance, January 30, 1943

Medley of Barnet hits aAndy Gibson
Solitude
Dear old southland aAndy Gibson
I had the craziest dream vNita Bradley
Why don't you do right vNita Bradley
Tutti-frutti feat. Chubby Jackson
Trumpet typhoon feat. Peanuts and Howard McGhee
Cherokee aBilly May

The *Variety* writer noted in his review of the Jan. 30 performance that "The brassy jive of Charlie Barnet combines with the choice harmonizing of Marion Hutton and the Modernaires ... Barring a slowdown of Nita Bradley's vocals and a subdued arrangement of *Solitude* Barnet plays full blast throughout to the delight of the 'gators ... Barnet has an effective opening with shaded red lamps on the music stands and soft spots from overhead while the band plays a medley of its own music combined with *Smiles* to introduce most of the key men and vocalists on hot breaks." (*Variety* Feb. 3, 1943)

Field Marshal Paulus surrendered to the Russians at Stalingrad on January 31.

Feb. 5–7, 1943: Fort Wayne, Palace Theater

Camp Atterbury, Indiana, Coca Cola Spotlight Bands (no.122?), Feb. 9, 1943

Program contents unknown

After this performance Charlie started a doctor-ordered vacation of approximately a month. The band agreed to also lay off and re-form when Charlie was ready. He was in New Orleans for a short time, finding time to jam with some of the locals. However, most of his time was spent in Florida. In NYC on March 6 he substituted for Otto Hardwick for one set with the Ellington band at the Royal Windsor Ballroom. Others who appeared were Hazel Scott, Helen Ward and Hal McIntyre. (*Stratemann*, p. 241) Cliff Leeman joined Johnny Long's band while Mac Marlow worked for Clyde McCoy and Raymond Scott.

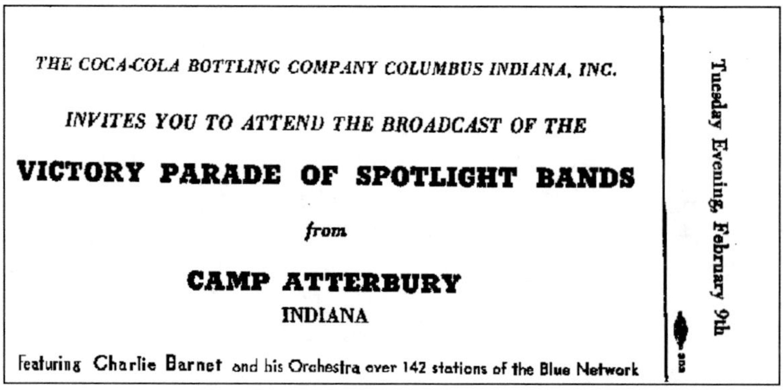

Turk van Lake, g, joined the band in early March. The reformed band opened in Philadelphia on March 11. Members included Peanuts Holland, Howard McGhee, Mary Ann McCall, Mike Goldberg, Jack Thompson, Chubby Jackson and Oscar Pettiford. Trummy Young joined about April 1.

Mar. 11–31, 1943: Philadelphia, Metropolitan Ballroom

Apr. 1–14, 1943: NYC, Capitol Theater (During this engagement, enthusiastic fans jumped over the railing and onto the descending pit elevator and had to be ejected using the stage door. A line of ushers took position to prevent a repetition during subsequent performances.)
Apr. (16?)–22, 1943: Baltimore, Regal Theater
Apr. 24, 1943: Worcester, MA, Mechanics Hall
Apr. 25, 1943: New Haven, Schubert Theater
Apr. 26, 1943: New Bedford, MA, Lincoln Park
Apr. 27, 1943: Lowell, Commodore Ballroom

Mac Marlow rejoined on May 1.

Apr. 30–May 6, 1943: NYC, Apollo Theater
May 7–13, 1943: Philadelphia, Earle Theater

May 13 was Marlow's last day. He was replaced by Eddie Bert on May 14. Oscar Pettiford's last day was May 16.

May 14–16, 1943: Hartford, State Theater
May 18–20, 1943: Utica, NY, Stanley Theater

The band which performed at the Howard Theater was composed of the following:

Dick Vance, Peanuts Holland, Howard McGhee, Paul Cohen, tpts; Bob Swift, Eddie Bert, Ed Fromm, Trummy Young, tbns; George Siravo, Steve Cole, as; Mike Goldberg, Kurt Bloom, ts; Danny Bank, bar; Ralph Burns, p; Turk Van Lake, g; Chubby Jackson, b; Lou Fromm, d (Bert)

On Turk van Lake's suggestion, Charlie hired Al Killian away from Count Basie. According to Turk, Al joined during the Howard Theater date.

May 21–27, 1943: Washington, Howard Theater (It was here that the notorious incident involving Trummy Young and the pursuing federal marshals took place.)
May 28, 1943: Princeton, NJ, Princeton University
May 29, 1943: NYC, Riverside Plaza
May 30, 1943: Holyoke, Valley Gardens Arena
May 31, 1943: West Point, NY, War Department Theater

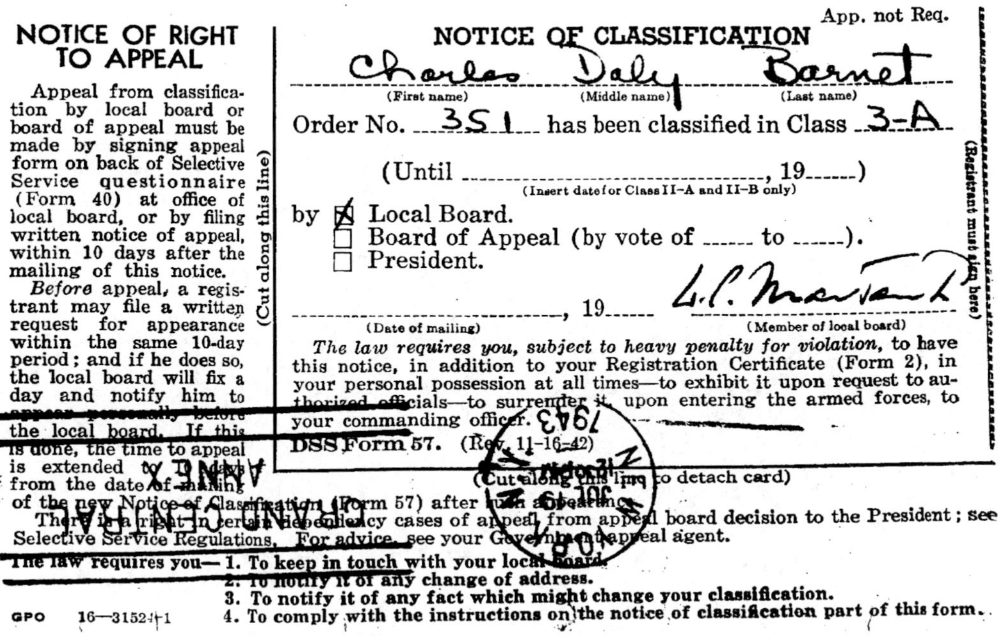

NOTICE OF RIGHT TO APPEAL

Appeal from classification by local board or board of appeal must be made by signing appeal form on back of Selective Service questionnaire (Form 40) at office of local board, or by filing written notice of appeal, within 10 days after the mailing of this notice. *Before* appeal, a registrant may file a written request for appearance within the same 10-day period; and if he does so, the local board will fix a day and notify him to appear personally before the local board. If this is done, the time to appeal is extended to 10 days from the date of mailing of the new Notice of Classification (Form 57) after such appearance.

There is a right in certain dependency cases of appeal from appeal board decision to the President; see Selective Service Regulations. For advice, see your Government appeal agent.

(Cut along this line)

App. not Req.

NOTICE OF CLASSIFICATION

Charles Daly Barnet
(First name) (Middle name) (Last name)

Order No. 351 has been classified in Class 3-A

(Until ______, 19____)
(Insert date for Class II-A and II-B only)

by ☒ Local Board.
☐ Board of Appeal (by vote of ____ to ____).
☐ President.

______, 19____ L. C. Martin
(Date of mailing) (Member of local board)

The law requires you, subject to heavy penalty for violation, to have this notice, in addition to your Registration Certificate (Form 2), in your personal possession at all times—to exhibit it upon request to authorized officials—to surrender it, upon entering the armed forces, to your commanding officer.

DSS Form 57. (Rev. 11-16-42)

(Registrant must sign here)

(Cut along this line to detach card)

The law requires you—1. To keep in touch with your local board.
2. To notify it of any change of address.
3. To notify it of any fact which might change your classification.
4. To comply with the instructions on the notice of classification part of this form.

GPO 16—31524-1

On the other side of the draft card Charlie had written Shorty Sherock's name and phone number.

June 1, 1943: Baltimore, Johns Hopkins University

The band had been scheduled to appear at the Steel Pier in Atlantic City but an agreement was reached cancelling the contract. This was due to the presence of black musicians in the band and the Pier management's fear that trouble might result from the many white southern Army recruits expected to attend the performances. In place of the Memorial Day weekend Steel Pier appearance, the band was booked for Riverside Plaza and Valley Gardens Arena.

<u>NYC (10th Ave. & 54th St.), June 1-2, 1943</u>

"JAM SESSION"

A Columbia feature film starring Ann Miller and including Charlie Barnet and his orchestra. 78m (Released ca. early May 1944)

Peanuts Holland, Howard McGhee, Al Killian, Paul Cohen,

tpts; Bob Swift, Eddie Bert, Trummy Young, Ed Fromm, tbns; Steve Cole, George Siravo, as; Kurt Bloom, Mike Goldberg, ts; Danny Bank, bar; Ralph Burns, p; Turk Van Lake, g; Chubby Jackson, b; Lou Fromm, d. (Holland, McGhee, Killian and Young are not seen; Paul Cohen acts out Killian's solo and the other three are portrayed by white actors.)

Cherokee/Redskin rhumba aBilly May
Audio: *Hollywood Sound Stage HS 5014*; HOLLYWOOD SOUND STAGE 4007

(Filming/recording commenced at 9AM, June 2, and ended at 3AM on the 3rd. Turk Van Lake states that Charlie was led to believe two versions of the song would be filmed: a northern [with the black musicians being seen on screen] and a southern showing an all-white aggregation. Van Lake remembers that the shooting took place on 8th Avenue and 150 something street. [*Bert*; *Van Lake*])

June 3–9, 1943: Boston, RKO Theater
June 12, 1943: (Boston?), Municipal Auditorium
June 13–15, 1943: Bridgeport, Lyric Theater
June16–17, 1943: Waterbury, CT, Poli Theater
June 18, 1943: Hartford, Foot Guard Ballroom
June 19, 1943: Old Orchard Beach, ME, Old Orchard Beach Pier
June 20, 1943: Bridgeport, Ritz Ballroom
June 24–July 3, July 5–6, 1943: Boston, Bradford Hotel
July 1, 1943: Boston, Boston Commons (bond drive)
July 4, 1943: Portland, ME, Exposition Hall
July 7, 1943: South Weymouth, MA, Naval Base

South Weymouth, MA, Naval Base, Coca Cola Spotlight Bands (249/93) July 7, 1943

Program contents unknown

July 10, 1943: Rochester, NY, Convention Hall
July 12, 1943: Lima, OH, Ohio Theater
July 13, 1943: Youngstown, Idora Park
July 14, 1943: Columbus, Columbus Auditorium
July 15, 1943: Akron, Summit beach Park
July 16–22, 1943: Chicago, Chicago Theater

Chicago, Chicago Theater, stage performance, July (16?), 1943

Medley of Barnet hits aAndy Gibson
Things ain't what they used to be vocal and featuring Peanuts Holland
Margie vocal and featuring Trummy Young
Mood indigo
You'll never know vMary Ann McCall
Happiness is a thing called Joe aRalph Burns; vMary Ann McCall
Tutti-frutti feat. Chubby Jackson

July 23–29, 1943: Buffalo, Shea's Theater
July 30–Aug. 5, 1943: Cleveland, Palace Theater

Cleveland, Palace Theater, stage performance, July 30, 1943

Mood indigo
Redskin rhumba aHead
Cherokee aBilly May
Dear old southland aAndy Gibson
You'll never know vMary Ann McCall
"*Piano concerto*" [aka *Dick Tracy liquidates 88 Keys*, probably this was *The Moose*] aRalph Burns, Turk Van Lake

Aug. 6–19, 1943: Detroit, Eastwood Gardens

There was concern about this last engagement because of the recent race riots in Detroit (June 19-20) and the fact that the band included African Americans but the gig proved uneventful.

Aug. 20, 1943: Buckeye Lake, OH, Buckeye Lake Park
Aug. 21, 1943: Parkersburg, WV, Coliseum
Aug. 22, 1943: Rehearsal
Aug. 23, 1943: Cambridge, OH, State Theater
Aug. 24–26, 1943: Columbus, Palace Theater
Aug. 27, 1943: Youngstown, The Mansion
Aug. 28, 1943: Dayton, Lakeside Park
Aug. 29, 1943: Canton, Meyers Lake Park
Aug. 30, 1943: Erie, PA, Columbia Theater

Aug. 31, 1943: Warren, OH, Robbins Theater

Mary Ann McCall was replaced by Virginia Maxey at about this time. Howard McGhee and Paul Cohen left and were replaced by Jimmy Pupa and Billy Robbins. Buddy DeFranco took Mike Goldberg's place and Steve Cole moved to a tenor chair.

Sept. 1, 1943: Greensburg, PA, Manos Theater
Sept. 2–8, 1943: Newark, NJ, Adams Theater
Sept. 9, 1943: Jamaica, NY, Jamaica Arena
Sept. 10–16, 1943: NYC, Apollo Theater

<u>*NYC, Apollo Theater, stage performance, September (10?), 1943*</u>

All or nothing at all vVirginia Maxey
People will say we're in love aGeorge Siravo; vVirginia Maxey
I like to riff aAndy Gibson; vPeanuts Holland
Cherokee aBilly May
Tutti-frutti feat. Chubby Jackson

Sept. 17–19, 1943: Springfield, MA Broadway Theater
Sept. 21–22, 1943: Rehearsals

Trummy Young left the band during the Park Central engagement. He was replaced by Spud Murphy. Ann Solloway, vocals, was reported to have been rehearsing with the band.

Sept. 23–Oct. 20, 1943: NYC, Park Central Hotel

Band personnel at this time:

Jimmy Pupa, Al Killian (lead), Lyman Vunk, Peanuts Holland, tpts; Spud Murphy (lead), Bob Swift, Eddie Bert, Ed Fromm, tbns; Rae de Geer, Buddy DeFranco, as; Mike Goldberg, Kurt Bloom, ts; Dodo Marmarosa, p; Turk van Lake, g; Russ Wagner, b; Harold Hahn, d; Virginia Maxey, vocals (Metronome *Nov. 1943; L. Feather*)

BARNET'S NEGRO-OFAY
BAND FOR PK. CENTRAL

Unusual aspect about the Charles Barnet booking into the Hotel Park Central, N.Y., Sept. 23, is that the band will play the hotel date using mixed Negro and white musicians. Barnet's band, which includes 'Peanuts" Holland, Al Killean and Trummy Young, all colored, goes into the hotel for four weeks. Mutual outlet (four wires per week) will be the first radio time Barnet has had around N. Y. for a long time.

Benny Goodman used a mixed band at the Waldorf-Astoria several seasons ago. (*Variety* Sept. 8, 1943)

<u>*NYC, Park Central Hotel, performance review, ca. September 23, 1943*</u>

Body and soul feat. Buddy DeFranco
People will say we're in love aGeorge Siravo; vVirginia Maxey
My ideal aGeorge Siravo

<u>***NYC, Park Central Hotel, MBS or CBS b'cast, between September 23 and October 20, 1943***</u>

My ideal aGeorge Siravo
AFRS YANK SWING SESSION 92
(Circumstantial evidence points to the Park Central engagement as the source for this recording, first reported by George Hall in his 1970 edition of the Barnet discography.)

Unidentified songs
AFRS NEWS FROM HOME

Leonard Feather, reviewing a Park Central performance for *Metronome*, declared: "I can predict confidently that if you catch this group during its current tour, you'll be hearing one of the greatest jump bands in the world. Charlie's alto work makes you realize what the word hot means in the term Hot Jazz." (November 1943)

NYC, Decca recording session, October 21, 1943

71460-A **Strollin'** aHoward McGhee
De 18585; De (C) 10159; Odeon (Arg) 286395; Odeon (Brazil) 288.841; De (Cz) 03601; Brunswick (E) 03527; *De DL 8098; MCA MCA2 4069°; Affinity (E) AFS 1012; Brunswick (E) LAT 8094; MCA (Ja) 3146; Ajax 140*; MCA (Sp) L 404302; Stack of 78s stack 73; MCA 4069 (8-track); **TOPAZ JAZZ (E) TPZ 1041; JAZZ ARCHIVES (FR) 158532; GIANTS OF JAZZ (CZ) CD 53280; STACK OF 78S STACK 73**

71461-A **The Moose** aRalph Burns and Turk Van Lake (*The Moose* is named for Dodo Marmarosa's profile. It was originally titled *Dick Tracy liquidates 88 Keys*)
Brunswick (E) 03601; De (E) 03601; Odeon(Arg) 286364; Odeon (Brazil) 288.841; Rhythm (Fi) BM 3601; *De DL 8098*; *Smithsonian RC 035*; *Ace of Hearts (E) AH 157*; *Brunswick (E) LAT 8094*; *Ajax 140*; *De ED 725*; Smithsonian RC *035*; Smithsonian RC 102; Stack of 78s stack 73; **DECCA GRD 639; DECCA JAZZ GRD 612; JAZZ HERITAGE 514150-X, 514960-T; SMITHSONIAN RD 102; DUET (E) DCD CD 212; KAZ (E) CD 311; DE (E) GRP 16122; JAZZ ARCHIVES (FR) 158532; DECCA JAZZ (JA) MVCR 20008; STACK OF 78S STACK 73; JAZZ GREATS (E) CD 071; EMPRESS (E) RACD 898; LIVING ERA (E) CD AJA 5288**

71461-alt **The Moose** aRalph Burns and Turk Van Lake
MCA 2 4069°; *Affinity (E) AFS 1012*; *MCA (Ja) 3146, 3043*; MCA 4069 (8-track); **TOPAZ JAZZ (E) TPZ 1028, 1041, 1058; GIANTS OF JAZZ (CZ) CD 53280**

71462-A **Pow-wow** aHead (The opening notes of Charlie's solo are the same as *Uptown rhapsody*, Teddy Hill's theme song.)
Coral 60029; Brunswick (E) 03527; *De DL 8098*; *MCA 1927*; *MCA MCA2 4069°*; *Affinity (E) AFS 1012*; *Ace of Hearts (E) AH 157*; *Brunswick (E) LAT 8094*; *Coral (Ger) 6 22182, PCO 7840, PCO 7995*; *MCA (Ja) 3146*; *Ajax 140*; *De ED 725*; MCA (Sp) L 404302; Stack of 78s stack 73; MCA 4069 (8-track); **DECCA JAZZ GRD 612; JAZZ HERITAGE 514960-T; KAZ (E) CD 311; DECCA(E) GRP 16122; TOPAZ JAZZ (E) TPZ 1041; JAZZARCHIVES (FR) 158532; DECCA JAZZ (JA) MVCR20008; GIANTS OF JAZZ (CZ) CD 53280; STACK OF 78S STACK 73**

71463-A **Sittin' home waitin' for you** aBilly Moore; vVirginia Maxey
De 18585; De (C) 10159; *Ajax 140*; Stack of 78s stack 73; **STACK OF 78S STACK 73**

Oct. 22–28, 1943: Baltimore, Royal Theater

October 28 was Eddie Bert's last day with Charlie. On the 29th he was sitting in the Woody Herman trombone section. At some point in this period, Virginia Maxey was temporarily replaced by Mary Ann McCall, making this at least her third hitch with Charlie.

Capitol Records signed with the AFM early in November.

Nov. 5–8, 1943: Akron, Palace Theater
Nov. 9–11, 1943: Youngstown, Palace Theater
Nov. 12–18, 1943: Chicago, Oriental Theater
Nov. 19–(24?), 1943: Omaha, Orpheum Theater
Nov. 25–28, 1943: Des Moines, Paramount Theater
Nov. 30–Dec. 2, 1943: Rock Island, IL, Joliet Theater
Dec. 3–5, 1943: Fort Wayne, Palace Theater

Harriet Clarke returned as the band's girl singer on about December 10, having signed a contract with Charlie on the 6th.

Dec. 10–16, 1943: Milwaukee, Riverside Theater
Dec. 17–23, 1943: Pittsburgh, Stanley Theater

Pittsburgh, Stanley Theater, stage performance, December 17, 1943

Caravan aRalph Burns
The man I love feat. Buddy DeFranco
Shoo, shoo baby vHarriet Clarke
They're either too young or too old vHarriet Clarke
Pistol packin' mama

"It's a big laugh when Barnet announces the band, like all others, is going to dip into the classics 'according to government order' with a Spanish sinfonietta by 'Alonzo Dextair' whereupon the boys come through with a pretentious introduction which leads into, naturally, *Pistol-packin' mama*." (*Variety* Dec. 22, 1943)

<u>*NYC, Strand Theater, stage performance, Dec. 31, 1943*</u>

Medley of Barnet hits aAndy Gibson
Things ain't what they used to be aAndy Gibson; vPeanuts Holland
I like to riff aAndy Gibson; vPeanuts Holland
I've had this feeling before vHarriet Clarke
I don't want to be alone vHarriet Clarke
Medley of band theme songs

<u>*As preceding, Jan. 5, 1944*</u>

Smiles aAndy Gibson
I've had this feeling before vHarriet Clarke
I don't want to be alone vHarriet Clarke
I like to riff aAndy Gibson; vPeanuts Holland

Things ain't what they used to be aAndy Gibson; vPeanuts Holland
The man I love (featuring Buddy DeFranco)
Medley of band theme songs

Buddy DeFranco signed a one-year contract on Jan. 21 for $200/week.

NYC, Strand Theater, Fitch Bandwagon, Jan. 23, 1944

Program content unknown

(The Golden Gate Quartet also appeared. The NBC file card indicates there was a guest conductor on this program; presumably it was Auld.)

On February 4, George Auld filled in for an ailing Charlie Barnet for two shows, then on the 5th he led the band while CB took an Army physical examination. When Charlie reported for a second exam on the 13th, Auld again took over.

Feb. 11–17, 1944: NYC, Apollo Theater

At some time after Feb. 15, Harriet Clarke was replaced by Gwen Tynes.

Feb. 22, 1944: (NYC?), Mecca Temple

Roy Eldridge, Art House, Jimmy Pupa, Lyman Vunk, Charles Zimmerman, tpts; Porky Cohen, Ed Fromm, Tommy Pederson, Ben Pickering, tbns; Rae De Geer, as; Buddy DeFranco, cl, as; Kurt Bloom, Andy Pino, ts; Danny Bank, bar; Dodo Marmarosa, p; Turk Van Lake, g; Andy Riccardi, b; Harold Hahn, d

NYC, Decca/World recording session, February 23/24, 1944

N-1748 **Bakiff** aAndy Gibson
WORLD 6289/6293, LP-R 640; *Fanfare LP38-138*; *Swing Era LP 1019*; Hindsight HCS 264; **HINDSIGHT HCD 264**; AFRS DOWNBEAT 128

(71792?) **West End blues** aAndy Gibson
Big Band Archives BBA 1209; *Fanfare LP38 138*; AFRS BML-P 562; AFRS DOWNBEAT 128

71794-A **In there**
WORLD 6289/6293, LP-R 613; *Queen (It) Q 066*; *Fan-fare LP38 138*; *Ajax 147*; *Swing Era LP 1019*; Hindsight HCS 264; **HINDSIGHT HCD 264**; AFRS DOWNBEAT 128

71795-A **Saltin' away my sweet dreams** aGeorge Siravo; vGwen Tynes
De 18601; De (C) 10177; Brunswick (E) 03645; WORLD 6279/6283, LP-R 689; *Ajax 147*; AFRS DOWNBEAT 128

71796-A **Baby, won't you please come home** aGeorge Siravo; vGwen Tynes
Coral 60029; WORLD 6289/6293, LP-R 613; *Ace of Hearts (E) AH 157*; *Ajax 147*; AFRS DOWNBEAT 128; AFRS OUTPOST CONCERT SERIES 19

71797-A **The great lie** aAndy Gibson
Odeon (Brazil) 288.182; WORLD 7109/7118, LP-R 640; *De DL 8098*; *MCA MCA2 4069°*; *Affinity (E) AFS 1012*; *Brunswick (E) LAT 8094*; *MCA (Ja) MCA 3043, 3146*; *Ajax 147*; Hindsight HCS 264; MCA (Sp) L 404302; MCA 4069 (8-track); **DECCA JAZZ GRD 612;HINDSIGHT HCD 264; JAZZ HERITAGE 514960-T;MCA (E) GRP16122; TOPAZ JAZZ (E) TPZ 1041;JAZZ ARCHIVES (FR) 158362; JAZZ ARCHIVES (FR) 158532; DECCA JAZZ (JA) MVCR 20008; GIANTS OF JAZZ (CZ) CD 53280**

?? **The Jeep is jumpin'** aAndy Gibson
WORLD 7109/7118; *Ajaz 201*; *Big Band Archives BBA 1209*; Hindsight HCS 264; **HINDSIGHT HCD 264**

N-1754 **Blue moon** aBill Miller
WORLD 6289/6293, LP-R 689; *Queen (It) Q 066; Ajax 147; Fanfare LP38 138; Swing Era LP 1019*; Hindsight HCS 264; Stack of 78s Stack 73; **HINDSIGHT HCD 264; STACK OF 78S STACK 73**; AFRS DOWNBEAT 128

N-1755 **In a mellow tone** aAndy Gibson
WORLD 6279/6283, LP-R 689; *Queen (It) Q 066*; *Fan-fare LP38 138*; *Limited Editions LP 101*; *Swing Era LP 1019*; Hindsight HCS 264; **HINDSIGHT HCD 264**; AFRS DOWNBEAT 128

71798-A (N-1750) **My heart isn't in it** aGeorge Siravo; vGwen Tynes
De 18601; De (C) 10177; Brunswick (E) 03645; WORLD 6279/6283, LP-R 613; *Ajax 147*

71799-A **Drop me off in Harlem** aRalph Burns
De 18810°; Odeon (Br) 288061; Brunswick (E) 03568; WORLD 7109/7118, LP-R 613; *De DL 8098*; *MCA2 4069°*; *Affinity (E) AFS 1012*; *Ace of Hearts (E) AH 157*; *Brunswick (E) LAT 8094*; *Coral (Ger)*

6-22182, PCO 7840, PCO 7995; MCA (Ja) MCA 3043, 3146; Ajax 147; De ED 725; Hindsight HCS 264; MCA (Sp) L 404302; MCA 4069 (8-track); **DECCA JAZZ GRD 612; HINDSIGHT HCD 264; JAZZ HERITAGE 514960-T;DUET (E) DCD CD212; KAZ (E) CD 311; MCA (E)GRP 16122; TOPAZ JAZZ (E) TPZ 1041, TPZ 1058;BEST OF JAZZ (FR) 4039; JAZZ ARCHIVES (FR)158532; DECCA JAZZ (JA) MVCR 20008; GIANTS OF JAZZ (CZ) CD 53280; JAZZ GREATS (E) CD 071**

71800-A (N-1752) **Gulf coast blues** aAndy Gibson, Ralph Flanagan
De 18810°; V-Disc (Army) 218; Odeon (Brazil) 288061; Brunswick (E) 03568; WORLD 6279/6283, LP-R 640; *De DL 8098; MCA2 4069°; Affinity (E) AFS 1012; Brunswick (E) LAT 8094; Coral (Ger) 6-22182, PCO 7840, PCO 7995; Queen (It) Q 066; MCA (Ja) 3043; Fanfare LP38 138; Ajax 147; De ED 725;* Hindsight HCS 264; Stack of 78s Stack 73; MCA (Sp) L 404302; MCA 4069 (8-track); **DECCA JAZZ GRD 6712; HINDSIGHT HCD 264; JAZZ HERITAGE 514960-T; KAZ (E) CD 311; MCA (E) GRP 16122; TOPAZ JAZZ (E) TPZ 1041; JAZZ ARCHIVES (FR) 158362, 158532; DECCA JAZZ (JA) MVCR 20008; GIANTS OF JAZZ (CZ) CD 53280; JAZZ GREATS (E) CD 071**; AFRS DOWNBEAT 128
("...*Gulf Coast blues* arrangement, with the exception of the last 24 bars, which were tacked on from another number by Andy Gibson, was the work of Sammy Kaye's staff arranger, Ralph Flanagan" [*Metronome* May 1946])

71801-A **Flat Top flips his lid**
WORLD 7109/7118; Odeon (Brazil) 288.182; Brunswick (E) 03611; *Affinity (E) AFS 1012; Ajax 147;* Stack of 78s Stack 73; **GIANTS OF JAZZ (CZ) CD 53280; STACK OF 78S STACK 73; LIVING ERA (E) CD AJA 5288**

Following this recording session Charlie broke up the band and took a vacation. Uncertainties due to the draft board's interest in Charlie (and apparently his run-down condition) caused him to fall out for awhile. A number of dates were cancelled, including five in Canada. He eventually moved to the Coast.

Hollywood, RKO, ca. March, 1944

"MUSIC IN MANHATTAN"

An RKO black and white feature film starring Ann Shirley and Dennis Day, with Charlie Barnet. 81 minutes. Released ca October 1944.

Charlie Barnet with members of Mischa [Constantine?] Bakaleinakov studio orchestra. Side-liners were used for the filming. (*Sm*)

I like a man who makes music vAnn Shirley

Charlie formed a band whose personnel was approximately:

Al Killian (lead), Wes Hensel, Lyman Vunk, Art House, Peanuts Holland, tpts; Porky Cohen, Ed Fromm, Bill Harris, tbns; Rae DeGeer, Buddy DeFranco, as; Andy Pino, Kurt Bloom, ts; Bob Poland, bar; Dodo Marmarosa, p; Turk van Lake, g; Howard Rumsey, b; Harold Hahn, d.

Bill Harris was in the band from late April into May when it played the Casa Mañana and Slapsy Maxie's. When Charlie was absent, Bill took his solos. (*Howard Rumsey* and *Jim Seidelle*)

Kay Starr joined the band in March. "I was rehearsing with Wingy Manone [at Glenn Wallich's Music City] ... so this guy stuck his head in the door and said, 'Hey, not bad,' he says. 'You wanna audition for Charlie Barnet? We're down in studio A' ... and so when our rehearsal was over with ... I could hear this band—it had so much juice goin' for it, it was comin' through those supposed-to-be soundproof walls, it was comin' through. And I thought, oh God is that wonderful or not? I'm just standin' there, just, but I couldn't really hear it very good, but I could feel it. And so somebody came out of that studio and the doors closed very slowly so they don't make noise ... and before it closed I stuck my foot in there, and I was standin' there, and I thought, this can't bother 'em and I was listening to the band ... and this guy that had yelled at me saw me and he motioned for me to come in the studio ... I was listenin', I was in hog heaven, I loved it, loved it ... and [Charlie] says to me, 'You sing?' and I said, 'Oh, yessir, I do.' He says, 'You got any music?' And he kidded me about this a long time ... I didn't mean to be smart, you know ignorance is bliss, I looked at him, I said, 'Why, haven't you got any?' You know, I didn't mean to be smart, but I mean I saw all this music on the stand, and I'd never owned music in my entire life ... He looked at me, kinda laughed, do you know so and so ... I think so ... I must have sung for 30 minutes ... and he says, well, you got the job. I didn't even know I was auditioning. I just thought I was having fun ... I said 'Who's gonna tell Wingy? I'm not gonna tell him.'" Howard Rumsey observed that Kay Starr never needed any make-up to look gorgeous.

Mar. 29–Apr. 4, 1944: San Francisco, Golden Gate Theater
Apr. 28-30, 1944: Culver City, Casa Mañana
May 2–8, 1944: Hollywood, Slapsy Maxie's
May 19–June 25, 1944: Culver City, Casa Mañana [replaced Bob Crosby]

The Allies landed in Normandy on June 6.

Culver City, Casa Mañana, between May 19 and June 25, 1944

Program content unknown
ONS 243 (mastered May 20, 1944)

As preceding

Johnny come lately
ONS 268 (mastered May 28, 1944)
I'll be seeing you vKay Starr
ONS 268
Oh! Miss Jaxson aAndy Gibson; vPeanuts Holland
ONS 268; PMR 4
Sentimental lady aAndy Gibson
ONS 268
Little John ordinary aHorace Henderson
ONS 268
Star eyes vKay Starr
ONS 268
Washington Whirligig aAndy Gibson
ONS 268
It's love, love, love! vKay Starr
ONS 268
In a mellow tone# aAndy Gibson
ONS 268

Fresno, Camp Pinedale or possibly LeMoore, ca. May 29-30, 1944

Program content unknown

Culver City, Casa Mañana, between May 19 and June 25, 1944

Skyliner aBilly Moore
ONS 281 (mastered June 2, 1944)
Long ago (and far away) (Kern) vKay Starr
ONS 281
Keep the home fires burning aAndy Gibson
ONS 281
Haunted town aBud Estes; vKay Starr [announced as *Haunted house*]
ONS 281; PMR 4
I like to riff aAndy Gibson; vPeanuts Holland
ONS 281
Johnny come lately
ONS 281
Going my way vKay Starr
ONS 281
Washington whirligig aAndy Gibson
ONS 281
Cotton tail aGeorge Siravo
ONS 281
Little John ordinary# aHorace Henderson
ONS 281

As preceding

Redskin rhumba aHead
ONS 298 (mastered June 9, 1944)
The great lie aAndy Gibson
ONS 298
I'll get by aAndy Gibson; vKay Starr
ONS 298
Straighten up and fly right aHarry Rodgers; vPeanuts Holland
ONS 298
I didn't know about you
ONS 298
Skyliner aBilly Moore
ONS 298
A fellow on a furlough vKay Starr
ONS 298
It's love, love, love! vKay Starr
ONS 298

Pompton Turnpike aBilly May
ONS 298

As preceding

The great lie aAndy Gibson
ONS 320 (mastered June 17, 1944)
Sentimental lady aAndy Gibson
ONS 320
It could happen to you vKay Starr
ONS 320
Poinciana
ONS 320
Straighten up and fly right aHarry Rodgers; vPeanuts Holland
ONS 320
I'll get by aAndy Gibson; vKay Starr
ONS 320
Pompton Turnpike aBilly May
ONS 320
Swinging on a star vKay Starr
ONS 320
Skyliner aBilly Moore
ONS 320

As preceding

Rockin' in rhythm aAndy Gibson?
ONS 341 (mastering date unknown)
Oh! Miss Jaxson aAndy Gibson; vPeanuts Holland
ONS 341
Saltin' away my sweet dreams aGeorge Siravo; vKay Starr
ONS 341
I'll get by aAndy Gibson; vKay Starr
ONS 341
Raincheck
ONS 341; *Golden Era 15015* [as *Lame Jack*]; Ajax C-683
Sentimental lady aAndy Gibson
ONS 341; *Golden Era GE 15015*; Ajax C-683
Dear old southland aAndy Gibson
ONS 341
Pompton Turnpike aBilly May
ONS 341

Culver City, Casa Mañana, b'cast (KHJ), June 3, 1944

Unknown vKay Starr
Nowhere aCharlie Barnet
Swinging on a star vKay Starr
Phyllysse aCharlie Barnet
Straighten up and fly right aHarry Rodgers; vPeanuts Holland
Drop me off in Harlem aRalph Burns
Theme (Redskin rhumba) closing

As preceding

Phyllysse aCharlie Barnet
PMR 4
Caravan aRalph Burns
PMR 4
Long ago (and far away) (Kern) vKay Starr
PMR 4
Blue skies aAndy Gibson
PMR 4; *Golden Era GE 15015*; Ajax C-683
Little John ordinary aHorace Henderson
PMR 4; EDDIE CONDON REPLACEMENT 38
(Haunted town—see ONS 281)
Wings over Manhattan# aBilly May
PMR 4

Fresno, Calif., ASC Training Center (Camp Pinedale), Coca Cola Spotlight Bands (549/394), June 21, 1944

Spotlight Bands theme
It's love, love, love! vKay Starr
A fellow on a furlough vKay Starr
Straighten up and fly right aHarry Rodgers; vPeanuts Holland
Blue skies aAndy Gibson
Swinging on a star vKay Starr
Keep the home fires burning# aAndy Gibson

It was probably a similar appearance that elicited the comments in this letter from an Army Air Corps trainee on May 31, 1944:

He can really sing

We are flying BT-15's. That is a Vultee basic trainer. It has a 450 HP engine. Not a bad ship either although it is hard to get used to after flying a primary trainer.

You know this fellow I was telling you about. Well they washed him out Thursday. He hadn't been doing too well, then they took him up for some check rides and I guess he slipped up somewhere and they gave him the axe. The wash-out rate is terrific up here as I imagine it is all over the country. We had Charlie Barnet's band up here at a dance we had. Boy he was really solid too. He has a pretty good Negro trumpet man that can really sing. *(Courtesy of Steve Parque)*

Culver City, Calif., Casa Mañana, between May 19 and June 25, 1944

Redskin rhumba (opening theme)
ONS 375 (mastered June 23, 1944)
Keep the home fires burning aAndy Gibson
ONS 375
I'll walk alone vKay Starr
ONS 375
Skyliner aBilly Moore
ONS 375
Haunted town aBud Estes; vKay Starr
ONS 375
I didn't know about you
ONS 375
Raincheck
ONS 375
I like to riff aAndy Gibson; vPeanuts Holland
ONS 375
Swinging on a star vKay Starr
ONS 375
One o'clock jump#
ONS 375

As preceding

Redskin rhumba (opening theme)
ONS 403 (mastered June 23, 1944)
Skyliner aBilly Moore
ONS 403 [also used on ONS 638]
Long ago and far away (Kern) vKay Starr
ONS 403
Straighten up and fly right aHarry Rodgers; vPeanuts Holland
ONS 403; *First Heard (E) FH 17*; Sandy Hook CSH 2081
Baby, won't you please come home aGeorge Siravo; vKay Starr
ONS 403
Poinciana
ONS 403
Blue skies aAndy Gibson
ONS 403
Saltin' away my sweet dreams aGeorge Siravo; vKay Starr
ONS 403
I'll get by aAndy Gibson; vKay Starr
ONS 403
Drop me off in Harlem aRalph Burns
ONS 403
Redskin rhumba (closing theme)
ONS 403

(Culver City, Casa Mañana, May 19–June 25, 1944?)

I like to riff aAndy Gibson; vPeanuts Holland
AFRS YANK SWING SESSION 111
Skyliner aBilly Moore
First Heard (E) FH 17; *Sandy Hook SH 2081*; Sandy Hook CSH 2081

July 5–??, 1944: Hollywood, Slapsy Maxie's

Peanuts Holland, John Martel, Jack Mootz, Lyman Vunk, tpts; Jerry Foster, Dave Hallett, Burt Johnson,

Skip Moore, tbns; Hal Herzon, Joe Meissner, as; Kurt Bloom, Eddie Pripps, ts; Bob Poland, bar; Dodo Marmarosa, p; Barney Kessel, g; Howard Rumsey, b; Hal Hahn, d

Hollywood, V-Disc recording session, NBC studios, July 13, 1944

Redskin rhumba aHead [issued as *Cherokee*]
V-Disc (A) 307, (N) 87; *Aircheck 30*; *Fanfare LP 38-138*; *Joyce LP 2012*; AFRS BML-P 135; AFRS DOWNBEAT 121, 128; AFRS YANK SWING SESSION 37, 44

Pompton Turnpike aBilly May
V-Disc (A) 307, (N) 87; *Joyce LP 2012*; *First Heard (E) FH 44*; First Heard (E) CFH 44; AFRS BML-P 135; AFRS DOWNBEAT 121; (AFRS MUSIC IN THE MODERN MANNER 298?)

Share croppin' blues aDave Matthews; vKay Starr
V-Disc (A) 326, (N) 106; *Aircheck 30*; *Joyce LP 2012*; Time-Life R138 03; **PICKWICK PK 540301; TIME-LIFE OPCD 4538; RST (AUSTRIA) 91567 2; JASMINE (E) JASCD 837/8**

Bkdown **Skyliner#** aBilly Moore
V-Disc unissued

Skyliner aBilly Moore
V-Disc (A) 458, (N) 238; *Aircheck 30*; AFRS BML-P 144; AFRS DOWNBEAT 121; G.I. JIVE 1137

Blue skies aAndy Gibson
V-Disc (A) 458, 864, (N) 238; *Aircheck 30*; AFRS BML-P 144; AFRS DOWNBEAT 121

Straighten up and fly right aHarry Rodgers; vPeanuts Holland
V-Disc 649; AFRS BML-P 135; AFRS DOWNBEAT 121

Drop me off in Harlem aRalph Burns
V-Disc 649; AFRS BML-P 144; AFRS DOWNBEAT 121

Hollywood, V-Disc recording session, NBC studios, (July 21, 1944 ?)

The great lie (probably recorded at this session)
AFRS BML-P 562

Oh! Miss Jaxson vPeanuts Holland (probably recorded at this session)
AFRS BML-P 562

Bkdown **Until my baby comes back to me/ Saltin' away my sweet dreams#** (3:14) aGeorge Siravo; vKay Starr
Aircheck 30

Bkdown **Until my baby comes back to me/ Saltin' away my sweet dreams#** (1:41) aGeorge Siravo
Aircheck 30

Caravan aRalph Burns (probably recorded at this session)
(Unissued V-Disc?); AFRS BML-P 135; AFRS DOWNBEAT 121; *First Heard (E) FH 17*; *Sandy Hook SH 2081*; Sandy Hook CSH 2081

July 21–23, 1944: Ocean Park, CA, Casino Gardens

"*MELODY PARADE*"

Hollywood, Universal studios, ca July 1944

A Universal short with Charlie Barnet and his orchestra, Dorothy Allen, Kay Starr, the Pied Pipers and dancers Grey and Diane. 15 minutes

Redskin rhumba aHead
Audio: *Joyce 3001*

How am I to know vDorothy Allen
Audio: *Joyce 3001*

Washington whirligig aAndy Gibson
Audio: *Joyce 3001*

Haunted town aBud Estes; vKay Starr
Audio: *Joyce 3001*

Poor Snoqualmie Joe vPied Pipers
Audio: *Joyce 3001*

Skyliner aBilly Moore
Audio: *Joyce 3001*
Video: "Feather on jazz: Strings" (MCA TV, 1967)

ca Aug. 15, 1944: LA, Shrine Theater benefit with Dorseys

Peanuts Holland, Lyman Vunk, John Martel, Jack Mootz, tpts; Gerald Foster, Dave Hallet, Burt Johnson, Charles Coolidge, tbns; Hal Herzon, Joe Meissner, as; Kurt Bloom, Ed Pripps, ts; Bob Poland, bar; Dodo

Marmarosa, p; Barney Kessel, g; Howard Rumsey, b; Harold Hahn, d

Hollywood, Decca recording session, Aug. 3, 1944

L3487-A **Skyliner** aBilly Moore
De 18659°; De 25234; Odeon (Arg) 286364; De (Cz) 03601; De (E) BM 03601; Brunswick (E) 03601; Rhythm (Fi) BM 3601; Brunswick (Ger) A 82458; Brunswick (Nor) 82458; *De DL 8098*; *Franklin Mint 33*; *Franklin Mint Record no.19*; *MCA 27094*;*MCA 2 4069°*; *Reader's Digest RD 184 2, RD4A 113*; *Reader's Digest (C) RD2 710*; *Smithsonian DMM 60610 4 R030*; *Affinity (E) AFS 1012*; *Ace of Hearts (E) AH 157*; *Brunswick (E) LAT 8094*; *Brunswick (Ger) 87099; Coral (E) CDLM 8047*; *MCA (E) MCM 1001*; *Coral (Ger) 6 22182, 6 22569, 6 28203, COPS 6997, PCO 7840, PCO 7995*; *MCA (Ja) 3146*; *Ajax 147*; *De ED 725*; Franklin Mint Tape no.19; Big Bands America 129312; MCA C 27094;Stack of 78s Stack 73; Smithsonian DMK 30610 D RC 030; MCA (Sp) L 404302; MCA 4069 (8-track); **MCA MCAD 20477; MCA MCAM 25196; Decca Jazz GRD 612, 2629; Hip-o HIPD 40073; Jazz Heritage 514960 T;Stack of 78s Stack 73; Smithsonian DMC 40610 4 RD 030; Big Bands America 129320; Topaz (E) TPX 1031; Living Era (E) CD AJA 5169, 5288; Duet (E)DCD CD 212; Classic Jazz (E) CDCD 1271;Kaz (E) CD 311; MCA (E) GRP 16122, 26292;Topaz Jazz (E) TPZ 1041; Best of Jazz (Fr) 4039; Jazz Archives (Fr) 158532; Decca Jazz (Ja)MVCR 20008; Giants of Jazz (Cz) CD 53280; Phontastic (Swed) PHONTCD 7672; Empress (E) RAJCD 898; Avid (E) AMSC 676; Living Era (E) CD AJA 5309**; AFRS MUSIC TRANSCRIPTION LIBRARY P-S 16; AFRS GOLD LABEL LIBRARYP-GL 35; USIA-VOA WORLD OF JAZZ 63; THE MUSIC MAKERS 334

L3488-A **Share croppin' blues** aDave Matthews; vKay Starr
De 24264; *MCA 2 4063, 2 4064*; *MCA 2 4069°*; *Affinity (E) AFS 1012*; *Coral (Ger) 6 22182, PCO 7840*; *Ajax 147*; MCA (Sp) L 404302; MCA 4069 (8-track); **Jasmine (E) JASCD 837/8; Giants of Jazz (Cz) CD 53280; Stack of 78s stack 73;** AFRS DOWNBEAT 272

L3489-A **Come out, come out, wherever you are** vKay Starr
De 18620°; Odeon (Arg) 286304; Odeon (Brazil) 288.020; *Coral (Ger) 6 22182, PCO 7840, PCO 7995*; *Ajax 147*; **Jasmine (E) JASCD 837/8**

L3490-A **What a diff'rence a day made** aGeorge Siravo; vKay Starr
De 18620°; Odeon (Brazil) 288.020; *MCA MCA2 4069°; Smithsonian R 035; Coral (Ger) 6 22182, PCO 7840, PCO 7995; Ajax 147*; Smithsonian RC 035; Smithsonian RC 102; MCA (Sp) L 404302; MCA 4069; (8-track); **Smithsonian RD 102; Jasmine (E) JASCD 837/8**

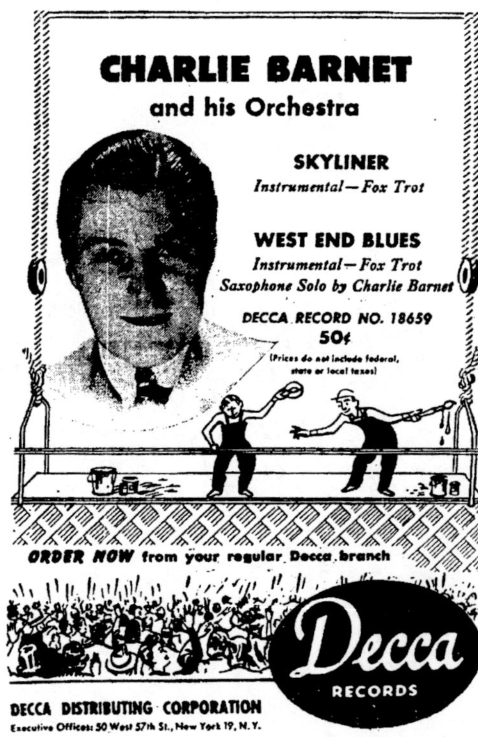

Although the band had featured *Skyliner* in 1944 since early in June as well as recording it for V-Discs in the same month, the Decca recording was not released until June of 1945.

Peanuts Holland, John Martel, Jack Mootz, Lyman Vunk, tpts; Porky Cohen, Ed Fromm, Dave Hallett, Tommy Pederson, tbns; Rae DeGeer, Gene Kinsey, as; Kurt Bloom, Eddie Pripps, ts; Danny Bank, bar; Dodo Marmarosa, p;

Turk Van Lake, g; John Chance, b; Harold Hahn, d

Aug. (25–31?), 1944: Philadelphia, Earle Theater
Sept. 1–Oct. 18, 1944: NYC, Strand Theater

The band which played the Strand was largely an east coast aggregation, "thrown together at short notice when the Mab arrived recently from the Coast ... [and] lacks the precision and kick of the great Barnet bands of the past. It goes through the same old stage routine with the same arrangements.... There was nothing here that hadn't been done better by some earlier Barnet band ... maybe a year or maybe four years ago." (Leonard Feather, *Metronome* Sept. 1944)

It was during this Strand engagement that there were disciplinary problems with the band members: "They tied the hands of the clock in a knot. They figured out a way to jam the pit on the way down. All sorts of weird things. We did Mood indigo in the show at the time and we had the trio up front, the trombone and trumpet player, but actually they weren't playing, they were strobe-light treated instruments, that's all you could see was the instruments there, and there was a real legitimate trio back playing, you know, to be heard. So, these guys got bored while standing up there and they discovered if you take Murine and paint your nose or put it on your face, it reacts to strobe lights, so the audience is breaking up and I couldn't figure out what it was. I got way upstage and looked over, and they are all like clowns up there, standing there. It got so bad that the union came down and collected all the cards, and said, 'One more incident, just one more, and that will be it.'"(*CB, CBC*)

NYC, Strand Theater, stage performance, Sept. 1, 1944

Cherokee aBilly May
Straighten up and fly right aHarry Rodgers; vPeanuts Holland
Time waits for no one vPhil Barton
It happened before vPhil Barton
Is you is, or is you ain't (ma' baby) vKay Starr
Come out, come out, wherever you are vKay Starr

There were plans for the band to make some USO appearances overseas. Physical examinations of all hands were required so over to USO headquarters they trekked. Shortly thereafter Charlie was called by the examining physician who said, "Don't send any more guys over, Charlie. We have already found three dangerous paranoiacs, two dope fiends ... [as to this trip] forget it."

Charlie was a guest on several radio programs during this stint at the Strand: "Dick Gilbert Show" (WHN, Sept. 5); "Jerry Lawrence Show" (WMCA, Sept. 15); "Maggie McNellis Program" (NBC, Sept. 20).

NYC, "For the Record" (NBC), Sept. 11, 1944

Fanfare
Aircheck 30
Say it with music
Aircheck 30
Smiles aAndy Gibson
V-Disc (A) 342, (N) 122; *Aircheck 30*; *Joyce LP 2012*; AFRS BML-P 185
Nobody knows the trouble I've seen aBob Burnet; vKay Starr
V-Disc (A) 364, (N) 150; *Aircheck 30*; *Ajazz 512*; *Joyce LP 2012*; Time-Life R139 39; **PICKWICK PK 540301**; **TIME-LIFE**

OPCD 4537; AFRS BML-P 185; AFRS DOWNBEAT 121

Every day of my life vJohn Conte
Aircheck 30

I like to riff aAndy Gibson; vPeanuts Holland
V-Disc (A) 342, (N) 122; *Aircheck 30*; *Joyce LP 2012*; AFRS BML-P 185; AFRS SOUND OFF 411

I can't get started (aGeorge Siravo?); vKay Starr
V-Disc (A) 482; *Aircheck 30*; *Ajaz 512*; *Joyce LP 2012*; **RST (Austria) 91567-2; Baldwin Street Music (C) BJH 305**; AFRS DOWNBEAT 121

Keep the home fires burning aAndy Gibson
V-Disc (A) 482; *Aircheck 30*; *First Heard (E) FH 17*; *Joyce LP 2012*; *Sandy Hook SH 2081*; Sandy Hook CSH 2081; AFRS DOWNBEAT 121; AFRS BML-P 185

> 11:30-WEAF—Author's Playhouse: Cry for the Hunted
> WOR—Dance Music
> WJZ—Van Cleave Orchestra
> WABC—Mildred Bailey Show: Charlie Barnet, Oscar Petterford, Guests
> WMCA—Dance Music
> WNEW—News: Recorded Music

NYC, "Music till midnight," CBS b'cast, Sept. 22, 1944

Charlie Barnet (as) accompanied by Paul Baron orchestra:

Smiles

NYC, Kate Smith Show (CBS), Sept. 24, 1944

Redskin rhumba (opening theme)
AFRS KATE SMITH 70

In a jam aBob Burnet
AFRS KATE SMITH 70

NYC, Raleigh Room with Hildegarde (NBC), Oct. 3, 1944

Program contents unknown

NYC, Decca/World recording session, Oct. 17, 1944

72450-A **Into each life some rain must fall** aGeorge Siravo; vKay Starr
De 18638; Br (E) 03626; WORLD 300 6704; *Franklin Mint 33, 10; MCA 2 4069º; Coral (Ger) 6 22182, PCO 7840, 7895; Ajax 155*; MUSIC MAKERS 334; Franklin Mint 19; Hindsight HCS 264; MCA (Sp) L 404302; MCA 4069 (8-track); **Decca Jazz GRD 612; Swingsation GRD 9952; Hindsight HCD 264; Jazz Heritage 514960 T; Jasmine (E) JASCD 837/8; MCA (E) GRP 16122; Decca Jazz (Ja) MVCR 20008; Empress (E) RAJCD 888**

72451-A **You always hurt the one you love** (aGeorge Siravo?); vKay Starr
De 18638; Br (E) 03626; WORLD LP-R 613, 300 6705; *Coral (Ger) 6 22182, PCO 7840, 7995; Ajax 155; Tulip TLP 106*; Canco (???); Hindsight HCS 264; **Canco (???); Decca Jazz GRD 612; Decca Jazz GRD 642; Swingsation GRD 6652; Hindsight HCD 264; Jazz Heritage 514960 T; Peaceful BDK 2; Living Era (E) CD AJA 5288; Jasmine (E) JASCD 837/8; MCA (E) GRP 16122; Decca Jazz (Ja) MVCR 20008; Empress (E) RAJCD 888**

72452-A **West End blues** aAndy Gibson
De 18659º, 25234; Br (E) 03611; Br (Ger) A 82458; Br (Nor) 82458; *Affinity (E) AFS 1012; Ajax 155*; **Decca Jazz GRD 612; Jazz Heritage 514960 T; MCA (E) GRP 16122; Decca Jazz (Ja) MVCR 20008; Giants of Jazz (Cz) CD 53280**

72453-A **Desert sands** aGeorge Siravo
De 24264; *MCA 2 4069º; Coral (Ger) 6 22182, PCO 7840, 7995; Ajax 155; Swing Era LP 1019*; MCA 4069 (8-track); **Decca Jazz GRD 612; Jazz Heritage 514960 T; MCA (E) GRP 16122; Decca Jazz (Ja) MVCR 20008**

Trombonist Giff Barnett joined the band at about this time.

Oct. 20–26, 1944: NYC, Apollo Theater

Bridgeport, Conn., Bridgeport Brass Co., Coca Cola Spotlight Bands (661/506), Oct. 30, 1944

Program contents unknown

Nov. 2–8, 1944: Boston, RKO Theater

Victor and Columbia accepted the AFM's terms and signed agreements on November 11, permitting the resumption of recording.

Nov. 9–15, 1944: Newark, NJ, Adams Theater

Nov. 17–20, 1944: Akron, Palace Theater
Nov. 21–23, 1944: Columbus, Palace Theater
Nov. 24–30, 1944: Detroit, Downtown Theater
Dec. 1–7, 1944: Cleveland, Palace Theater
Dec. 8, 1944: London, ON, London Arena
Dec. 9, 1944: Toronto, Queensway Ballroom

Among the musicians who performed in Toronto:

Peanuts Holland, Lyman Vunk, Buddy Hartford, tpts; Porky Cohen, Giff Barnett, Dave Hallet, Ray Montoya, tbns; Rae De Geer, Gene Kinsey, as; Eddie Pripps, Johnny Wade, ts; Dodo Marmarosa, p; John Chance, b; Harold Hahn, d; Kay Starr, vocal (Gerry Lazare's autograph book).

Dec. 15–21, 1944: Chicago, Downtown Theater

The band evidently broke up in December and Charlie returned to the Coast. Contrary to claims, Babs Gonzalez did not work for Charlie in 1944 or at any other time (*Sm*).

Early in 1945 Frances Shirley (tpt) joined the band, remaining for about six months.

Skidding Band B. O. Puzzles Agencies and Leaders

Beneath this ominous January 1945 Variety headline, Bernie Woods noted that the band business was in decline:

"In the past few months ... the band business has been in the deepest b.o. doldrums experienced bandsmen have known since so-called popular music jived its way into big money. There is no apparent reason for the poor grosses being turned in on theatre and one-night dates in areas which heretofore proved fertile ground for reasonably strong names ... Bandleaders and agency executives, too well aware of the anemic b.o. figures being written, are undeniably worried ... This is strictly conjecture, but it's quite possible that the 27-month period ending last November, during which no new recordings were made except by Decca and small disc outfits ... has something to do with the lack of interest by the public as reflected at the b.o. In the past the band public has proved that it is ever on the alert for something new and different. And for almost three years it has been seeing and hearing virtually the same names, faces and styles. Perhaps its appetite is dulled by the same fare day in and day out. If that is the case ... then the situation is due to get darker before the dawn of the postwar band business, envisioned by agency men and experienced leaders as paling the golden era of 1938 to 1944 ... Already some of the bookers of major theatres are considering a change in the construction of stage shows with an aim toward eliminating as often as possible the name bands that cost so much money and too frequently of late have failed to deliver ... There are reasonably good names in the soloist field, around whom an entertaining show can be built for $5,000 or so, giving them a chance to at least come out even on a bad business week. This is not idle conversation. Neither is it a threat. It's being mulled ... If this yarn sounds alarming—it's meant to be..." (*Variety* Jan.3, 1945)

Jan. 17, 1945: San Diego, U.S.Naval Hospital

San Diego, Naval Hospital, Coca Cola Spotlight Bands (729/574), Jan. 17, 1945

Redskin rhumba aHead ***(opening theme)***
SB 574

Poor little rich girl aGeorge Siravo
SB 574; *Aircheck 5; Swing Era LP 1019*; Demand Performance DPC 853; Ajax C-683; **BALDWIN STREET MUSIC (C) BJH 305**

The very thought of you vKay Starr
SB 574; *Aircheck 5*; *Ajaz 512*; Demand Performance DPC 853; **BALDWIN STREET MUSIC (C) BJH 305**

An hour never passes vPhil Barton
SB 574

Obble-ee-eebop aAndy Gibson; vPeanuts Holland
SB 574; *Aircheck 5*

The trolley song vKay Starr
SB 574; *Aircheck 5*; *Ajaz 512*

I didn't know about you
Aircheck 5; *Big Band Archives BBA 1209*; *Limited Edition LP 101*; Ajax C-683

Cherokee aBilly May
SB 574; AFRS CHARLIE BARNET REPLACINGBANDWAGON 158 [incomplete]

Jan. 19–(21?), 1945: San Diego, Pacific Square Ballroom

Peanuts Holland, Lyman Vunk, Jack Mootz, Ernie Figueroa, Frances Shirley, tpts; Dave Hallett, Porky Cohen, Ed Fromm, Giff Barnett, tbns; Rae De Geer, Gene Kinsey, as; Eddie Pripps, Kurt Bloom, ts; Bob Poland, bar; Marty Napoleon, p; John Chance, b; Harold Hahn, d (based on AFM Apr. 23)

Hollywood, "Jubilee" (Jan. 29, 1945?)

Redskin rhumba (opening theme) aHead
JUBILEE 118/214

Obble-ee-eebop aAndy Gibson; vPeanuts Holland
JUBILEE 118/214; *Joyce LP 5003*

Cherokee aBilly May
JUBILEE 118/214; *Joyce LP 5003*; *First Heard (E) FH 44*; *First Heard (E) FHR 1974-12*; First Heard (E) CFH 44

Somebody else, not me vSam Deacon McDaniel [Band in for last chord]
JUBILEE 118/214; *Joyce LP 5004*

Cotton tail aGeorge Siravo
JUBILEE 118/214; *Joyce LP 5004*; *First Heard (E) FH 44*; *First Heard (E) FHR 1974-12*; First Heard (E) CFH 44; Big Band Era (N) 40180

Redskin rhumba (closing theme) aHead
JUBILEE 118/214; *Joyce LP 5004*; *First Heard (E) FH 44*; First Heard (E) CFH 44
[both First Heard issues are edited in such a way as make it seem as if this was an opening theme.]

Jan. 30–Feb. 5, 1945: LA, Orpheum Theater

U. S. Marines landed on Iwo Jima February 19.

The "WHITE DUKE" is Coming!
CHARLIE BARNET and His Orchestra
With "PEANUTS HOLLAND"
THURS. FEB. 22 ♦ ELK'S

Feb. 22, 1945: LA, [Black] Elks Club
Feb. 23–25, 1945: Culver City, Casa Mañana

Culver City, Casa Mañana, Feb. 23?, 1945

Redskin rhumba (opening theme) aHead
ONS 543 (mastered Feb. 24)
Cotton tail aGeorge Siravo
ONS 543
What a diff'rence a day made aGeorge Siravo; vKay Starr
ONS 543
Take the A Train aGeorge Siravo
ONS 543
(Unidentified title) [Neal Hefti may be the composer/arranger as there is a passage in it which matches his work in *The good earth*, although he never re-cycled. Hefti thought it might have been written in 1942]
ONS 543
Smiles aAndy Gibson
ONS 543
He's home for a little while vPhil Barton [Sung as *I'm home...*]
ONS 543
Obble-ee-eebop aAndy Gibson; vPeanuts Holland
ONS 543
West End blues aAndy Gibson
ONS 543
I like to riff aAndy Gibson; vPeanuts Holland
ONS 543
#Cherokee aBilly May
ONS 543

Mar. 2–4, 1945: Culver City, Casa Mañana (with Duke Ellington)

"The bands would get together in the back and they were all drinking together and everything, and Joe Zucca [Casa owner] came back and he said, 'I'm paying for two big bands, what have I got? I've got a stinking trio [Red Callender] out here playing. Now get somebody on this bandstand.'" (*Sm*)

(Culver City, Casa Mañana, ca Feb. 24–Mar. 4, 1945?)

Redskin rhumba aHead
AFRS CHARLIE BARNET REPLACING BAND-WAGON 158 (mastered June 17)
Rockin' in rhythm aBilly May
AFRS CHARLIE BARNET REPLACING BAND-WAGON 158
West End blues aAndy Gibson
AFRS CHARLIE BARNET REPLACING BANDWAGON 158

Culver City, Casa Mañana, Mar. 3, 1945

I like to riff aAndy Gibson; vPeanuts Holland
AFRS EDDIE CONDON 38 REPLACEMENT
Casa Mañana stomp
AFRS EDDIE CONDON 38 REPLACEMENT; *Big Band Archives BBA 1209*
Smiles aAndy Gibson
AFRS EDDIE CONDON 38 REPLACEMENT
#Little John ordinary aHorace Henderson
AFRS EDDIE CONDON 38 REPLACEMENT

Culver City, Casa Mañana, between Feb. 23 and Mar. 11, 1945

Redskin rhumba (opening theme) aHead
ONS 709 (mastered Mar. 10, 1945; announced as emanating from Mission Beach, Calif.); *Joyce JRC 1214*
Poor little rich girl aGeorge Siravo
ONS 709; *Joyce JRC 1214*
Saturday night (is the loneliest night in the week) vKay Starr
ONS 709; *Joyce JRC 1214*
I like to riff aAndy Gibson; vPeanuts Holland
ONS 709; *Joyce JRC 1214*
Sleigh ride in July vKay Starr
ONS 709; *Joyce JRC 1214*
Mellow mood aAndy Gibson
ONS 709; *Joyce JRC 1214*; *First Heard (E) FHR 1974-12*
"C" jam blues
ONS 709; *Joyce JRC 1214*
More and more vPhil Barton
ONS 709; *Joyce JRC 1214*

Just read what the famous swing band leader, Charlie Barnet, says of the U. S. School of Music method:

"Your print-and-picture method of instruction makes music remarkably easy to understand. Everything is so easily explained and illustrated that I do not see how anyone could go wrong.

"What particularly impressed me was the fact that the student started to learn real tunes from the very first. This method of 'learning to play by playing' should appeal to al who dread the old-fashioned drudgery of scales and exercises.

"The lessons are so simple that a beginner should have no trouble with them. Congratulations on taking the hard work out of music for thousands of music lovers."

Take the "A" Train aGeorge Siravo
ONS 709; *Joyce JRC 1214*
One o'clock jump#
ONS 709; *Joyce JRC 1214*

Mar. 9–11, 1945: Culver City, Casa Mañana

(Compiler spent a number of days at Shoemaker as he was shuttled around by the Navy.)

Shoemaker, Calif., U.S. Naval Receiving Station, Coca Cola Spotlight Bands (777/622), March 14, 1945

Redskin rhumba (opening theme) aHead
SB 622; *Aircheck 5*; Joyce Imperfect Series C-05
Rockin' in rhythm aBilly May
SB 622; *Aircheck 5*; *Limited Edition LP 101*; Demand Performance DPC 853; Joyce Imperfect Series C-05
Dream aGeorge Siravo; vGinny Powell
SB 622; *Aircheck 5*; *Joyce 6020*; Demand Performance DPC 853
More and more vPhil Barton
SB 622; *Aircheck 5*; Demand Performance DPC 853
Skyliner aBilly Moore
SB 622; *Aircheck 5*; Demand Performance DPC 853; Joyce Imperfect Series C-05
The story of two cigarettes vGinny Powell, Phil Barton
SB 622; *Aircheck 5*; *Joyce 6020*; Demand Performance DPC 853; Joyce Imperfect Series C-05
Dear old southland aAndy Gibson
SB 622; *Aircheck 5*; *Fanfare 38-138*; Demand Performance DPC 853; Joyce Imperfect Series C-05
Redskin rhumba (closing theme) aHead
SB 622; *Aircheck 5*; *Fanfare 38-138*
Spotlight Bands theme
Fanfare 38-138

(Culver City, Casa Mañana,? ca. Mar. 14–Aug. 1, 1945?)

Dream aGeorge Siravo; vGinny Powell
AFRS CHARLIE BARNET REPLACING BANDWAGON 158

Fresno, ASC Training Center, Coca Cola Spotlight Bands (784/629), Mar. 22, 1945

I ain't got nothin' but the blues vKay Starr
SB 629 [also used on SB 723]
Obble-ee-eebop vPeanuts Holland
SB 629
Skyliner aBilly Moore
SB 629 [also used on SB 723]
Counting the days vKay Starr
SB 629 [also used on SB 723]

Culver City, Casa Mañana, (Mar. 23–25, 1945?)

Redskin rhumba (opening theme) aHead
ONS 674 (mastered March 24, 1945)
Poor little rich girl aGeorge Siravo
ONS 674 [also used on ONS 662]
Dream aGeorge Siravo; vGinny Powell
ONS 674 [also used on ONS 781]
Oh! Miss Jaxson aAndy Gibson; vPeanuts Holland
ONS 674
Things ain't what they used to be aAndy Gibson; vPeanuts Holland
ONS 674 [also used on ONS 781]
Sleigh ride in July vPhil Barton
ONS 674 [also used on ONS 781]
Skyliner aBilly Moore
ONS 674 [also used on ONS 662]
Wings over Manhattan aBilly May
ONS 674 [also used on ONS 662]
Saturday night (is the loneliest night in the week) vGinny Powell
ONS 674

Dear old southland# aAndy Gibson
ONS 674 [also used on ONS 781]

The U. S. Tenth Army and Marines landed on Okinawa on April 1 in what was to be the bloodiest battle in the Pacific Theater.

Culver City, Calif., Casa Mañana, ca. Mar. 23–25, 1945

Redskin rhumba (opening theme)
ONS 638 (mastered March 31, 1945)
Poor little rich girl
ONS 638
There's no you aJerry Fielding; vPhil Barton
ONS 638
Oh! Miss Jaxson aAndy Gibson; vPeanuts Holland
ONS 638
Take the "A" Train aGeorge Siravo
ONS 638
Straighten up and fly right aHarry Rodgers; vPeanuts Holland
ONS 638 [from ONS 298? ca May 14–June 25, 1944?]
Dream aGeorge Siravo; vGinny Powell
ONS 638
Skyliner aBilly Moore
ONS 638 [from ONS 403, May 14–June 25, 1944]
Home for a little while vPhil Barton
ONS 638
Please don't talk about me when I'm gone#
ONS 638

Peanuts Holland, Lyman Vunk, Jack Mootz, Ernie Figueroa, Frances Shirley, tpts; Porky Cohen, Giff Barnett, Dave Hallet, Ed Fromm, tbns; Rae De Geer, Gene Kinsey, as; Kurt Bloom, Ed Pripps, ts; Bob Poland, bar; Marty Napoleon, p; Dave Barbour, g; John Chance, b; Harold Hahn, d

Hollywood, Decca/World recording session, April 4, 1945

L3770-A **Any old time** aJerry Fielding; vPhil Barton
De 18685; WORLD 6979-6980; *Ajax 155*; AFRS GI JIVE 2251
L3771-A **There's no you** aJerry Fielding; vPhil Barton
De 18685; WORLD 6981, LP-R 689; *Ajax 155*; AFRS SWINGTIME (no. unknown)
L3772-A **Mellow mood** aAndy Gibson
WORLD 6982, LP-R 689; *Ajax 155*; *Swing Era LP 1019*; Hindsight HCS 264; **HINDSIGHT HCD 264**
L3773-A **Obble-ee-eebop** aAndy Gibson; vPeanuts Holland
WORLD 6983, LP-R 689

Ernie Edwards in the first Barnet discography notes that *Mellow mood* may have been issued as a 78, De 23618, and subsequently withdrawn. All succeeding editions of the Barnet discographies have repeated this information, however no evidence of a 78 issue has reached this compiler.

The next ONS has been heavily edited with the result that some of the announcements are nonsensical.

Denver, Trocadero Ballroom/Elitch's Gardens, ca. late Mar.–early April 1945

Redskin rhumba (opening theme) aHead
ONS 662 (mastered Apr. 7, 1945)
Smooth sailing [no.1, 1945]
ONS 662
Mellow mood aAndy Gibson
ONS 662
Phyllysse aCharlie Barnet
ONS 662
Number 5000
ONS 662; *Golden Era GE 15015*; Ajax C-683
Dream aGeorge Siravo; vGinny Powell
ONS 662
Skyliner aBilly Moore
ONS 662 [taken from ONS 674, Casa Mañana, ca Feb. 1945]
Poor little rich girl aGeorge Siravo
ONS 662 [taken from ONS 674, Casa Mañana, ca Feb. 1945]
Wings over Manhattan aBilly May
ONS 662 [taken from ONS 674, Casa Mañana, ca Feb. 1945]

Peanuts Holland, Lyman Vunk, Frances Shirley, Ernie Figueroa, tpts; Ed Fromm, Dave Hallet, Giff Barnett, tbns; Rae De Geer, Tiny Rips, Gene Kinsey, as; Kurt Bloom, Eddie Pripps, ts; Bob Poland, bar; (Marty Napoleon?), p; John Chance, b; unknown, g; Harold Hahn, d (Tiny Rips photos)

The band played a number of military installations in the San Joaquin Valley during the spring of 1945. Many of the small towns in that region hosted various kinds of training camps and were the originating points for a number of Spotlight Bands broadcasts. During one stretch Charlie was "off chasing one of his singers" and left the band in charge of lead alto Rae De Geer. The band was due to play in Fresno and desperately needed a lead alto. It was Marshall "Tiny" Rips who was selected as the best alto on the base and he filled in for De Geer, having been placed on "detached service" by the base CO. He played a number of engagements—always in uniform—until Charlie showed up. (Did he catch her? I guess we'll never know.)

Peanuts Holland, Lyman Vunk, Jack Mootz, Frances Shirley, Ernie Figueroa; Dave Hallett, Porky Cohen, Ed Fromm, Giff Barnett, tbns; Rae De Geer, Gene Kinsey, as; Kurt Bloom, Eddie Pripps, ts; Bob Poland, bar; Marty Napoleon, p; Harold Hahn, d; John Chance, b. (AFRS pay records)

Hollywood, "Jubilee" 130/221, April 23, 1945

Redskin rhumba (opening theme) aHead
JUBILEE 130/221 (130 mastered Apr. 23, 1945); *Joyce LP 5003*
Rockin' in rhythm aBilly May
JUBILEE 130/221; *Joyce LP 5003*
There's a small hotel vElla Logan
JUBILEE 130/221; *Joyce LP 5003*
Any old time aJerry Fielding; vPhil Barton
JUBILEE 130/221; *Joyce LP 5003*
On the sunny side of the street vElla Logan
JUBILEE 130/221; *Joyce LP 5003*
Dear old southland aAndy Gibson
JUBILEE 130/221; *Joyce LP 5003*

Eddie Pripps was reported to have left the band in this period.

(Hollywood?), Fitch Bandwagon, ca. May 1945

Dream aGeorge Siravo; vGinny Powell
AFRS BANDWAGON 158 (mastered June 17, 1945)
Dear old southland aAndy Gibson
AFRS BANDWAGON 158
Cherokee aBilly May
AFRS BANDWAGON 158

12 full ounces

We were playing a Coke show. Jack Mootz and the trumpet section were always getting bombed—Lyman Vunk, Jack, Peanuts, and those guys, they were always stoned. Jack said, "Hey, when the guy says 'OK, let's do a run through' [whisper, whisper]" ... So just before air time, the announcer says, "Let's run it down, let's hear the Coke theme," and they played the *Pepsi Cola* theme. This guy got so red in the face, he was ready to kill everybody. "I'm gonna sue you guys, I'm gonna cancel this date." Charlie says, "No, I'll talk to them." (*Marty Napoleon*)

Las Vegas, Army Air Base, Coca Cola Spotlight Bands (822/667), May 5, 1945

Skyliner aBilly Moore
SB 667
I'm beginning to see the light aJerry Fielding; vGinny Powell
SB 667; *Joyce 6020*
There's no you aJerry Fielding; vPhil Barton
SB 667
Any old time aJerry Fielding; vPhil Barton
SB 667
Unidentified instrumental

Singer Patsy Parker may have appeared with the band during this period (*Las Vegas Review Journal* May 5, 1945).

Germany surrendered on May 7.

Benicia, Calif., Benicia Arsenal, Coca Cola Spotlight Bands (827/672), May 11, 1945

Redskin rhumba (opening theme) aHead
SB 672

Skyliner aBilly Moore
SB 672
I'll remember April aConn Humphreys; vPhil Barton
SB 672
How come vGinny Powell
SB 672; *Joyce 6020*
Smooth sailing [no.1, 1945]
SB 672; *IAJRC 17*
Redskin rhumba (closing theme) aHead
SB 672
Unidentified song with vocal by Phil Barton

Santa Maria, Army Air Field,
Coca Cola Spotlight Bands
(831/676), May 16, 1945

Redskin rhumba aHead
SB 676
Caravan aRalph Burns
SB 676
Cherokee aBilly May
SB 676
I'm beginning to see the light aJerry Fielding; vGinny Powell
SB 676
Skyliner aBilly Moore
SB 676
In a mellow tone aAndy Gibson
Blue moon aBill Miller

May 22–June 18, 1945: South Gate, Trianon Ballroom

South Gate, Calif.,
Trianon Ballroom,
May 22–June 18, 1945

#Cherokee#
MC 106
Yesterdays
MC 106
I ain't got nothin' but the blues vGinny Powell
MC 106
Just you—just me
MC 106
Cherokee/Redskin rhumba aBilly May
MC 106

June 22–June 24, 1945: San Diego, Pacific Square

San Diego, Pacific Square,
June 22–24, 1945

Redskin rhumba (opening theme) aHead
MC 55

Skyliner aBilly Moore
MC 55
Any old time aJerry Fielding; vPhil Barton
MC 55
Dream aGeorge Siravo; vBetty Perry
MC 55
Washington whirligig aAndy Gibson
MC 55

June 26–July 8, 1945: Portland, Jantzen Beach

During the Portland appearance, broadcasts were carried almost every night (11:00–11:30PM) by the local CBS affiliate, KOIN. No doubt these programs provided the source material for the Magic Carpet transcriptions.

One evening Charlie jammed with local musicians at The Dude Ranch, a Portland black-and-tan club where he helped Joe and Rose Crane celebrate an anniversary by playing *Honeysuckle rose*.

Portland, Jantzen Beach, between June 26 and July 8, 1945

Redskin rhumba (opening theme) aHead
MC 4
Washington whirligig aAndy Gibson

MC 4 [a partial version of this performance is on MC 21]
There's no you aJerry Fielding; vPhil Barton
MC 4
Blue skies aAndy Gibson
MC 4
Dream aGeorge Siravo; vGinny Powell
MC 4
Take the "A" Train# aGeorge Siravo
MC 4

As preceding

Mellow mood aAndy Gibson
MC 13

Skyliner aBilly Moore
MC 13
I ain't got nothin' but the blues vGinny Powell
MC 13
Any old time aJerry Fielding; vPhil Barton
MC 13
Poinciana
MC 13

<u>*As preceding*</u>

Redskin rhumba (opening theme) aHead
MC 21
There's no you aJerry Fielding; vPhil Barton
MC 21
Skyliner aBilly Moore
MC 21
How come vGinny Powell
MC 21
Yesterdays
MC 21
Washington whirligig# aAndy Gibson
MC 21 [complete version of this performance on MC 4]

<u>*As preceding*</u>

Redskin rhumba (opening theme) aHead
MC 68
Washington whirligig aAndy Gibson
MC 68
Any old time aJerry Fielding; vPhil Barton
MC 68
Obble-ee-eebop aAndy Gibson; vPeanuts Holland
MC 68
Cherokee/Redskin rhumba# aBilly May
MC 68

Ernie Hood, Jr., guitar, joined the band on July 8, the last day of the band's Portland stand. Prior to Hood's joining Charlie was not using a guitar. (Hood did not replace Dave Barbour as noted in other sources.)

July 9, 1945: Seattle, Trianon Ballroom
(July 10, 1945?): Oak Harbor, WA, Ault Field
July 11, 1945: Fife, WA, Century Ballroom

<u>*Tacoma, Fort Lewis, Coca Cola Spotlight Bands (868/715), July 13, 1945*</u>

Unknown title
SB 715
There's no you aJerry Fielding; vPhil Barton
SB 715
Skyliner aBilly Moore
SB 715
How come vGinny Powell
SB 715
Caravan aRalph Burns
SB 715
(Content information on this SB from *Garrod 84*)

Several people sat in during the Fort Lewis performance: Bill Ramsay, as, Tommy Todd, p, and Ted Halleck, d.

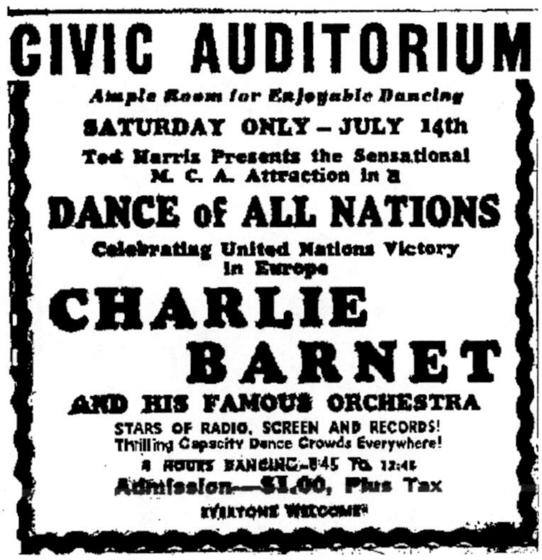

July 14, 1945: Seattle, Civic Auditorium
(July 15, 1945?): Albany, OR, Cottonwood Ballroom
(July 20, 1945?): Long Beach, CA, Auditorium
(July 20, 1945?): Sawtell, CA, Veterans Hosp. (Desi Arnaz, host)
(July 21, 1945?): Los Angeles, [Black] Elks Club

Ernie Hood remembered the personnel as:

Peanuts Holland, Al Killian, Frances Shirley, Jack Mootz, Nelson Shelladay, tpts; Porky Cohen, Ed Fromm, Ken Meisel, tbns; Rae De Geer, Gene Kinsey, as; Kurt Bloom, Eddie Pripps, ts; Bob Dawes, bar; Marty Napoleon, p; Rollo Garberg b; Ernie Hood, g; Hal Hahn, d

Frances Shirley (tpt) left the band approximately July 25. Kay Starr rejoined in late July.

<u>*Point Hueneme, Calif., Camp Rousseau, Coca Cola Spotlight Bands (876/723), Aug. 1, 1945*</u>

Redskin rhumba (opening theme) aHead
SB 723
Just you–just me
SB 723
I ain't got nothin' but the blues vKay Starr
SB 723 [also used on SB 629]
Skyliner aBilly Moore
SB 723 [also used on SB 629]
Counting the days vKay Starr
SB 723 [also used on SB 629]
Take the "A" Train aGeorge Siravo
SB 723
Obble-ee-eebop aAndy Gibson; vPeanuts Holland
Unknown vPhil Barton
Unknown vPhil Barton

An atomic bomb was dropped on Hiroshima on August 6.

"I think we would have played better if there weren't so many boozers in the band—your lip goes, your fingers go." (*Hood*). Jack Mootz and Rae De Geer were among those who did not enjoy reputations of abstemiousness.

<u>*San Francisco, Civic Auditorium, Coca Cola Spotlight Bands (880/727) Aug. 10, 1945*</u>

Redskin rhumba (opening theme) aHead
SB 727
Skyliner aBilly Moore
SB 727
Caravan aRalph Burns
SB 727
On the Atcheson, Topeka and Santa Fe vKay Starr
SB 727; *First Heard (E) FH 17*; *Sandy Hook SH 2081*; <u>Sandy Hook CSH 2081</u>
You was right, baby vKay Starr
SB 727
Back in your own back yard aUnknown ["He looked like a college professor, he was a very facile arranger." (*Hood*)]
SB 727
Caravan# aRalph Burns
SB 727

Harry Babasin, b, replaced Rollo Garberg at about this time.

The band worked its way east in the middle of August by means of Air Force transport planes, paying for its flights by playing various military installations along the way, including: Smyrna and Long Island, Nebraska; Arizona; New Mexico; Texas and Topeka. (*Hood*)

Japan surrendered on August 14.

Aug. 17–23, 1945: Philadelphia, Earle Theater [with Bunny Briggs]

"On the last night that we played a man came out of the audience after Bunny Briggs had done his number and was taking his bows, and the man came up on stage and said, 'Bunny, I want to pass the crown to you,' and it was Bill Robinson and Bunny wept right there in front of everybody." (*Hood*)

Aug. 24–Sept. 27, 1945: NYC, Strand Theater

<u>*NYC, Strand Theater, stage performance, between Aug. 22 and Sept. 27, 1945*</u>

Medley of Barnet hits aAndy Gibson
Back in your own back yard
Skyliner aBilly Moore
In a sentimental mood
Blues vKay Starr and Peanuts Holland
On the Atcheson, Topeka and the Santa Fe vKay Starr
You was right baby vKay Starr

"We would have one rehearsal for a bunch of new arrangements … If there was a new arrangement, we'd run through it once or twice and then it went into the books." (*Hood*)

Sweet (?) Substitute

Charlie had his opening like Duke's band where the piano's in the center stage and before we went into *Cherokee* we would be behind the scrim and there would be a spotlight on my head and I would do four bars, and the trumpets would be standing on a platform and the spotlight would be on the trumpets and they would play a little figure, then the spotlight would go back on me, they would get off, then the trombones, then the saxophones, then the final one with Charlie standing with the spotlight on his head, magnificent handsome guy standing there, and he'd start playing *Cherokee* and he'd walk down and the scrim would open and people went crazy, see. Now one day we came to work and Kurt Bloom says, "Charlie's in jail" and we said, "What happened?" and he said, "Broadway Rose took him up for not paying alimony or something. I think he's going to miss the first show." So where's [lead alto] Rae De Geer? He wasn't even there—he's in the hotel, he's still sleeping—we're supposed to be onstage in 5 minutes so they call him, he wakes up. Now Rae had a big mustache, he comes to the stage, his hair's disheveled, his mustache is messed up and it was obvious he'd slept in his pants, and they were way up over his ankles, and he was wearing slippers and no sox. When he played he used to hunch over, so now we're going through this opening, now comes the spot where Charlie's supposed to be, and all the audience can see is this guy's back and when the curtain opened he came walking out on stage and the people, instead of applauding, just stared—well, we couldn't play, the guys were breaking up, and the people are goin', "What's that?" It was the most outrageous thing you ever saw in your life. (*Marty Napoleon*)

Charlie took part in a jam session at Tommy Dorsey's 400 Restaurant opening on Sept. 6. Others joining in included Buddy Rich, TD, Charlie Shavers, Duke Ellington, Woody Herman and Randy Brooks. (*Stratemann*)

It was probably during the Strand engagement that Kay Starr had very serious problems with her voice and was replaced by Fran Warren. Kay rested her voice, under her doctor's orders, for many months before resuming her career. She once attributed the problem to the many Air Force flights in unheated transport planes as the band went from camp to camp.

Hood noted that marijuana was in wide general use in the band. As for other drugs, "Peanuts was the pharmacist" and source for a number of items. There was also lots of drinking. "Charlie always had a bottle of scotch in his tenor case, in the bell." (*Hood*)

(Sept. 28–Oct. 4, 1945?): Hartford, State Theater

Peanuts Holland, Al Killian, Jack Mootz, Ed Stress, tpts; Nelson Shellady, tpt and tbn; Eddie Aulino, Porky Cohen, Kenny Meisel, tbns; Rae De Geer, Gene Kinsey, as; Kurt Bloom, Ed Pripps, ts; Bob Dawes, bar; Al Haig, p; Ernie Hood, g; Harry Babasin, b; Harold Hahn, d

NYC, Decca/World recording session, Oct. 2, 1945

73067-A **Tell it to a star** vPhil Barton and Satisfiers
De 18736°; Odeon (Brazil) 288134; Brunswick (E) 03742; **EMPRESS (E) RAJCD 898**; WORLD 7269, LP-R 640; *Ajax 155*

CHARLIE BARNET

Tell It to a Star

Xango

Decca 18736

Charlie goes commercial, but with results so pleasing that few should mind. Reminiscent of old Sinatra–Pied Pipers–TD ballads, *Star* combines a particularly nice tune, some wonderful rich-voiced vocalizing by Phil Barton, the Satisfiers accompanying with nice band backgrounds. Charlie inserts a few bars of tenor, restrained and lyrical, yet so typically only Barnet. *Xango* is an unusual number, hard to define. Too long in getting started, once it does go with a good rhythm backing and high-note trumpet work (possibly by Al Killian) it is interesting and different. Both sides are good for Barnet, his first could well prove a sensation. Which is the least this great musician deserves.

CHARLIE BARNET told some race-haters off at an Army camp recently and gets this issue's orchid, or rather, a dozen of them. . . .
(BAND LEADERS, Nov. 1945)

73068-A **Surprise party** vRedd Evans
De 18722; WORLD 7270, LP-R 640; *Ajax 155*
73069-A **Just a little fond affection** vFran Warren
De 18722; WORLD 7271, LP-R 640; *Ajax 155*
73070-A **Xango** aAndy Gibson
De 18736°; Brunswick (E) 03742; WORLD 7272-7273; WORLD LP-5 613; *De DL 8098*; *MCA 2-4069°*; *Affinity (E) AFS 1012*; *Brunswick (E) LAT 8094*; *MCA (Ja) 3146*; *Ajax 155*; Hindsight HCS 264; MCA 4069 (8-track); **HINDSIGHT HCD 264; TOPAZ JAZZ (E) TPZ 1041; GIANTS OF JAZZ (CZ) CD 53280; EMPRESS (E) RAJCD 898**

(Oct. 5–11?, 1945): NYC, Apollo Theater

Tommy Pederson substituted for Porky Cohen during the Apollo engagement. Dorothy Donegan was also on the bill.

"Charlie was a strict disciplinarian when it came to guys playing their parts. He'd let a few bloopers go by but if the guy was obviously lax, or gave him bad looks or back talk, he was prone to violence." (*Hood*)

Ft. Devens, Mass., Lovell General Hospital, Coca Cola Spotlight Bands (908/755), Oct. 15, 1945

Spotlight Bands theme
SB 755; *Fanfare 38-138*
Redskin rhumba (opening theme) aHead
SB 755; *Fanfare 38-138*
Fanfare
SB 755; *Fanfare 38-138*
Just a little fond affection vFran Warren
SB 755; *Fanfare 38-138*
Skyliner aBilly Moore
SB 755; *Fanfare 38-138*
Drop me off in Harlem aRalph Burns [announced as *Drop me off*]
SB 755; *Fanfare 38-138*
Xango aAndy Gibson
SB 755 [incomplete]; *Fanfare 38-138* [complete]

(Oct. 16, 1945?): Detroit, location unknown
(Oct. 17, 1945?): Fargo, ND, Crystal Ballroom
Oct. 27, 1945: Lincoln, NE, The Turnpike
Oct. 30–Dec. 10, 1945: Ocean Park, Casino Gardens

Charlie eliminated the guitar chair so Ernie Hood was let go, probably in October.

Ocean Park, Casino Gardens, between Oct. 30 and Nov. 7, 1945

Redskin rhumba (opening theme) aHead
ONS 781 (mastered Nov. 8, 1945); *Joyce 1105*; Radio Days CACS 1008; **RADIO DAYS CACD 1008**
Dream aGeorge Siravo; vGinny Powell
ONS 781; *Joyce 1105*; Radio Days CACS 1008; **RADIO DAYS CACD 1008**
Just you—just me
ONS 781; *Joyce 1105*; Radio Days CACS 1008; **RADIO DAYS CACD 1008**
Things ain't what they used to be aAndy Gibson; vPeanuts Holland
ONS 781 [taken from ONS 674]; *Joyce 1105*; Radio Days CACS 1008; **RADIO DAYS CACD 1008**
Skyliner aBilly Moore
ONS 781; *Joyce 1105*; Radio Days CACS 1008; **RADIO DAYS CACD 1008**
Tell it to a star vPhil Barton
ONS 781; *Joyce 1105*; Radio Days CACS 1008; **RADIO DAYS CACD 1008**
Keep the home fires burning aAndy Gibson
ONS 781; *Joyce 1105*; Radio Days CACS 1008; **RADIO DAYS CACD 1008**
If I had a dozen hearts
ONS 781; *Joyce 1105*; Radio Days CACS 1008; **RADIO DAYS CACD 1008**
Sleigh ride in July vPhil Barton
ONS 781 [taken from ONS 674]; *Joyce*

1105; Radio Days CACS 1008; **Radio Days CACD 1008**

Strollin'# aHoward McGhee
ONS 781; *Joyce 1105*; Radio Days CACS 1008; **Radio Days CACD 1008**

Dear old southland# aAndy Gibson
ONS 781; *Joyce 1105*; Radio Days CACS 1008; **Radio Days CACD 1008**

(Ocean Park, Casino Gardens, between Oct. 30 and Dec. 10, 1945?)

Redskin rhumba (opening theme) aHead
MC 143

Keep the home fires burning aAndy Gibson
MC 143; Redmond Nostalgia Co. CO 3681

I'll buy that dream vPhil Barton
MC 143; Redmond Nostalgia Co. CO 3681

Xango aAndy Gibson
MC 143; Redmond Nostalgia Co. CO 3681

Tell it to a star vPhil Barton
MC 143; Redmond Nostalgia Co. CO 3681

Skyliner# aBilly Moore
MC 143

Ocean Park, Casino Gardens, (Nov. 14, 1945?)

Skyliner aBilly Moore
First Heard (E) FH 17

As preceding, Nov. 14, 1945 (ABC network)

(This is the first half of a program recorded by United Network, San Francisco)

Redskin rhumba (opening theme) aHead
UNSF

Poor little rich girl aGeorge Siravo
UNSF

If I loved you vPhil Barton
UNSF

Skyliner aBilly Moore
UNSF

Sentimental lady
UNSF

In a jam aBob Burnet
UNSF

At about this time it was noted in the press that Dave Matthews had written some arrangements for Charlie. Les Robinson (as) temporarily replaced Rae De Geer.

Hollywood?, "Truth or Consequences," Dec. 1, 1945

Program contents unknown (Others who took part included Xavier Cugat, Stan Kenton, Mike Riley, Matty Malneck, Alvino Rey and Will Osborne) (*NBC Artist Index*)

Hollywood, Universal Studios, ca. early December, 1945

"Idea Girl"

(Universal feature film starring Alan Mowbray, Julie Bishop, and Laura Deane Dutton, with Charlie Barnet and his orchestra. Running time 60m. Released ca. February 1946.)

Xango aAndy Gibson

I can't get you out of my mind vLaura Deane Dutton

I don't care (if I never dream again) vLaura Deane Dutton

"Laura Deane Dutton sang with us at the Glen Island Casino under the name of Laura Deane ... She wouldn't even speak to me [during the filming]. She had her nose in the air the whole time ... where she had been a friendly girl, she was decidedly unfriendly. Could be that she didn't want anybody to know that she'd been a band singer..." (*Sm*) Al Killian is heard but not seen. Peanuts is also invisible.

Peanuts Holland, Al Killian, Everett McDonald, George Seaburg, Edward Stress, tpts; Porky Cohen, Ed Fromm, Bill Hallar, Tommy Pederson, tbns; Gene Kinsey, Les Robinson, as; Kurt Bloom, Ed Pripps, ts; Bob Dawes, bar; Al Haig, p; Barney Kessel, g; Morris Rayman, b; Harold Hahn, d

Hollywood, Decca/World recording session, Dec. 8, 1945

WL4019-A **Yalta** aJuan Tizol
WORLD 7634-7635; Hindsight HCS 264; **HINDSIGHT HCD 264**

L4020-A **E-bob-o-lee-bob** aAndy Gibson; vPeanuts Holland
De 18761°; Brunswick (E) 03739; Columbia (India) DB 50031; WORLD 7636 [as Be baba leba]; *MCA 2 4069°; Affinity (E) AFS 1012; Coral (Ger) 6 22182, PCO 7840, PCO 7995; Ajax 155*; Hindsight HCS 264; MCA (Sp) L 404302; MCA 4069 (8-track); **DECCA JAZZ GRD 612; JAZZ HERITAGE 514960-T; HINDSIGHT HCD 264; DECCA (E) GRP 16122; JAZZ ARCHIVES (FR) 158532; DECCAJAZZ (JA) MVCR 20008; GIANTS OF JAZZ (CZ) CD 53280; JAZZ GREATS (E) CD 071; EMPRESS (E) RAJCD 898**

L4021-A **Madame Butterball** aAndy Gibson; vPeanuts Holland
De 18862; Brunswick (E) 03751; WORLD 7637; *Ace of Hearts (E) AH 157*; *Ajax 155*

L4022-A **When the one you love (simply won't love back)** aJerry Fielding; vPhil Barton
De 18761°; Odeon (Brazil) 288.134; Brunswick (E) 03739; Columbia (India) DB 50031; WORLD 7638; *Ajax 155*; **EMPRESS (E) RAJCD 898**

Ocean Park, Casino Gardens, between Oct. 30 and Dec. 10, 1945

Redskin rhumba (opening theme) aHead
ONS 821 (mastered Dec. 10, 1945; much evidence of editing); Starline SLC 61018

Some more jive
ONS 821; *Joyce LP 1031*; Starline SLC 61018

Everything but you vFran Warren
ONS 821; *Ajaz 512*; *Joyce LP 1031*; Starline SLC 61018

Xango aAndy Gibson
ONS 821; Starline SLC 61018

Tell it to a star vPhil Barton
ONS 821; Starline SLC 61018

It's never too late to pray vPeanuts Holland
ONS 821; Starline SLC 61018

Just you—just me
ONS 821; Starline SLC 61018

Skyliner aBilly Moore
ONS 821; Starline SLC 61018

I'll buy that dream vPhil Barton
ONS 821; Starline SLC 61018

Strollin' aHoward McGhee
ONS 821; *First Heard (E) FH 44*; *First Heard (E) FHR 1974-12*; Starline SLC 61018; First Heard (E) CFH 44

Dear old southland# aAndy Gibson
ONS 821; Starline SLC 61018

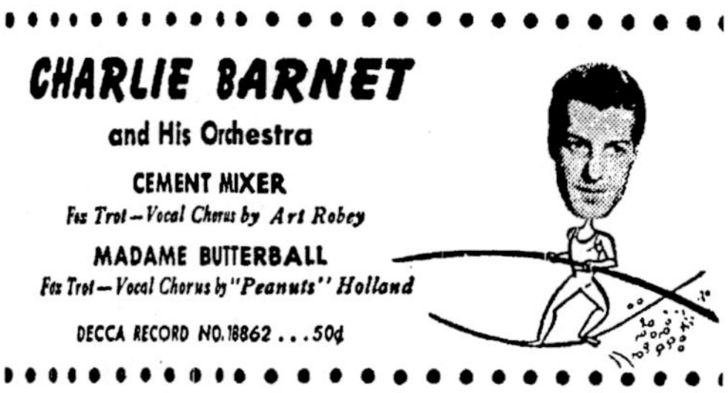

Rae De Geer (as) replaced Les Robinson and Sheldon Smith (p) replaced Al Haig at about this time.

Location and date unknown; "Spotlight Bands" origin

Drop me off in Harlem aRalph Burns
YANK SWING SESSION 118; Radio Yesteryear LD-37

Chapter 5

Things Ain't What They Used to Be 1946–1948

Dec. 31, 1945: San Diego, Mission Beach Ballroom (with Stan Kenton, Peggy Lee and the King Sisters)
Jan. 1, 1946: San Diego, Balboa Stadium (with Kenton, Lena Horne, Peggy Lee and the King Sisters)
Jan. 8–14, 1946: Los Angeles, Orpheum Theater

Los Angeles, Orpheum Theater, performance review, Jan. (11?), 1946

Cherokee aBilly May
The sergeant was shy aBilly May
Pompton Turnpike aBilly May
Drop me off in Harlem aRalph Burns (feat. Al Killian)
If I had a dozen hearts (feat. Tommy Pederson)
E-bob-o-lee-bob aAndy Gibson; vPeanuts Holland
Madame Butterball aAndy Gibson; vPeanuts Holland
Things ain't what they used to be aAndy Gibson
Battle of the trombones
Night and day vPhil Barton
I can't begin to tell you vPhil Barton
11:60 PM vFran Warren
I got it bad (and that ain't good) aAndy Gibson; vFran Warren
That old black magic aAndy Gibson; vFran Warren

Possible line up: Peanuts Holland, Everett McDonald, George Seaburg, Al Killian, tpts; Porky Cohen, Tommy Pederson, Bill Hallar, Ed Fromm, tbns; Rae De Geer, Gene Kinsey, as; Kurt Bloom, Ed Pripps, ts; Bob Dawes, bar; Sheldon Smith, p; Barney Kessel, g; Morris Rayman, b; Harold Hahn, d.

Hollywood, "Jubilee," ca Jan.–Feb. 1946

One o'clock jump (Jubilee opening)
JUBILEE 170; *Joyce LP 5004*; Redmond Nostalgia Co. CO 3619;
Jubilee jump aAndy Gibson
JUBILEE 170; *Joyce LP 5004*; *First Heard (E) FH 17*; *Sandy Hook SH 2081*; Redmond Nostalgia Co. CO 3619; Sandy Hook CSH 2081
Come to baby, do! vLena Horne
JUBILEE 170; *Joyce LP 5004*; *First Heard (E) FH 17*; *Sandy Hook SH 2081*; Redmond Nostalgia Co. CO 3619; Sandy Hook CSH 2081
Xango aAndy Gibson
JUBILEE 170; *Joyce LP 5004*; *First Heard (E) FHR 1974-12*; *Golden Era GE 15015* [as *Tango*]; Redmond Nostalgia Co. CO 3619

E-bob-o-lee-bob aAndy Gibson; vPeanuts Holland
JUBILEE 170; *Joyce LP 5004*; Redmond Nostalgia Co. CO 3619; Big Band Era (N) 40180

Haunted town aBud Estes; vLena Horne
JUBILEE 170; *Joyce LP 5004; First Heard (E) FH 17, FH 44; Sandy Hook SH 2081*; Redmond Nostalgia Co. CO 3619; Sandy Hook CSH 2081; First Heard (E) CFH 44

Zamboanga aAndy Gibson
JUBILEE 170; *Joyce LP 5004*; *First Heard (E) FH 17, FH 44; Sandy Hook SH 2081*; Redmond Nostalgia Co. CO 3619; Sandy Hook CSH 2081; First Heard (E) CFH 44

Redskin rhumba (closing theme) aHead
JUBILEE 170; Joyce LP 5004; First Heard (E) FH 44 [Song is used twice on this LP and on CFH 44; first use is preceded by an announcement by Vince Williams from a Casino Gardens broadcast]; Redmond Nostalgia Co. CO 3619; First Heard (E) CFH 44

Jan. 15–Feb. 10, 1946: Ocean Park, Casino Gardens

Ocean Park, Casino Gardens, between Jan. 15 and Feb. 10, 1946

[Unverified by compiler. Content information from *Garrod 84*.]

Poor little rich girl aGeorge Siravo
MC 269 (*First Heard (E) FH 44?, FHR 1974-12?*)

Skyliner aBilly Moore
MC 269 (*First Heard (E) FH 17?)*

Everything but you vFran Warren
MC 269 (*First Heard (E) FH 44?, CFH 44?*)

Strollin' aHoward McGhee
MC 269

As preceding

[Unverified by compiler. Content information from *Garrod 84*.]

Zamboanga aAndy Gibson
MC 293

I'm just a lucky so-and-so vPhil Barton
MC 293

E-bob-o-lee-bob aAndy Gibson; vPeanuts Holland
MC 293

Everybody knew but me (vFran Warren?)
MC 293

Ocean Park, Casino Gardens, between Jan. 15 and Jan. 26, 1946

Redskin rhumba (opening theme) aHead
ONS 884 (mastered Jan. 27); *Joyce LP 1001*

"C" jam blues
ONS 884; *Joyce LP 1001*; *Limited Edition LP 101*; Ajax C 708

Symphony vPhil Barton
ONS 884; *Joyce LP 1001*

Take the "A" Train aGeorge Siravo
ONS 884; *Joyce LP 1001*; *Limited Edition LP 101*

When the one you love (simply won't love back) aJerry Fielding; vPhil Barton
ONS 884; *Joyce LP 1001*

Day by day vPhil Barton
ONS 884; *Joyce LP 1001*

The sergeant was shy aBilly May
ONS 884; *Joyce LP 1001*; *Limited Edition LP 101*

Nancy vPhil Barton/***Gee, it's good to hold you/A door will open*** vPhil Barton
ONS 884; *Joyce LP 1001*

Shady lady# aAndy Gibson
ONS 884; *Joyce LP 1001*

As preceding, between Jan. 15 and 29, 1946

Redskin rhumba (opening theme) aHead
ONS 862 (mastered Jan. 30); *Joyce LP 1031*; *Radiola 2MR 1314* [clipped]; *Sandy Hook SH 2081* [clipped]; *First Heard (E) FH 17* [clipped]; Sandy Hook CSH 2081 [clipped]

Poor little rich girl aGeorge Siravo
ONS 862; *Joyce LP 1031*
When the one you love (simply won't love back) aJerry Fielding; vPhil Barton
ONS 862
Skyliner aBilly Moore
ONS 862; *Radiola 2MR 1314*
Day by day vPhil Barton
ONS 862
If I had a dozen hearts
ONS 862; *Joyce LP 1031*
Yalta aJuan Tizol
ONS 862; *Joyce LP 1031*
Give me the simple life/More than yesterday vPhil Barton
ONS 862; *Joyce LP 1031*
More and more vPhil Barton
ONS 862; *Joyce LP 1031*
The sergeant was shy aBilly May
ONS 862; *First Heard (E) FH 44*; *First Heard (E) FHR 1974-12*; First Heard (E) CFH 44
Redskin rhumba (closing theme) aHead
ONS 862; *First Heard (E) FH 44; First Heard (E) FHR 1974-12*; First Heard (E) CFH 44

Calgary, Alta., Drill Hall no.11 Equip. Depot, stage performance, Feb. 18, 1946

Cherokee aBilly May
Take the "A" Train aGeorge Siravo
Cotton tail aGeorge Siravo
11:60 PM vFran Warren

Feb. 19, 1946: Edmonton, Alta., Drill Hall, NW Air Command, Kingsway
Feb. 20, 1946: Saskatoon, Alta., The Stadium
Feb. 21, 1946: Regina, Sask., Trianon Ballroom
Feb. 22-23, 1946: Winnipeg, Man., Drill Hall, no. 2 Air Command, St. James
Mar. 1, 1946: Portland, Jantzen Beach

At some point—probably in early March—Art Robey, tpt and vocals, replaced Peanuts Holland.

Shoemaker, CA, U.S. Navy Receiving Station, Coca Cola Spotlight Bands (968/815), Mar. 4, 1946

Spotlight Bands theme
SB 815
Redskin rhumba (opening theme) aHead
SB 815
Symphony vPhil Barton
SB 815
Zamboanga aAndy Gibson
SB 815; *Golden Era GE 15015*; Ajax C 708
Mood indigo aCharlie Barnet
SB 815
Everything but you vFran Warren
SB 815
#Cotton tail#
SB 815

Al Killian, Everett McDonald, Art Robey, Ed Stress, Paul Webster, tpts; Frank Bradley, Porky Cohen, Ed Fromm, Tommy Pederson, tbns; Rae De Geer, Gene Kinsey, as; Kurt Bloom, Kenneth Dehlin, ts; Bob Dawes, bar; Sheldon Smith, p; Irving Lang, b; Mickey Scrima, d (*AFM contract*)

Hollywood, Decca recording session, Mar. 8, 1946

Unidentified song [AFM contract says 4 sides were recorded]
(unissued?)
LA 4113-A **Cement mixer** aAndy Gibson; vArt Robey
De 18862; Odeon (Arg) 286395; Brunswick (Ger) 82584; Brunswick (Nor) 82584; *Ace of Hearts (E) AH 157*; *Coral (Ger) 6 22182, 6 22442, MOPS 8265, PCO 7840, PCO 7995*; *MCA (Ja) 3146*; *Ajaz 201*; **MCA MCAD20477**
LA 4114-A **Baby, you can count on me** aAndy Gibson; vFreddie Stewart
De 18888; *Ajaz 201*
LA 4115-A **Andy's boogie** aAndy Gibson; vArt Robey
De 18888; Brunswick (E) 03751; *MCA 2 4069°*; *Ace of Hearts (E) AH 157*; *Affinity (E) AFS 1012*; *MCA (Ja) 3146*; *Ajaz 201*; MCA 4069 (8-track); **Decca Jazz GRD 612; Jazz Heritage 514960-T; MCA (E) GRP 16122; Decca Jazz (Ja) MVCR 20008**

Billboard's review of Decca 18888 noted that "Andy's boogie" was a "typical race blues set eight-to-the bar ... with Art Robey shouting the back-biting lyrics and the trumpet sharing the instrumental spotlight with the maestro's soprano sax. However, Barnet and his boys never get excited. Neither will the spinner, 'Baby you can count on me'; [it's] a rumba-styled ditty of no great shakes..." The magazine was a little more favorable toward Decca 18541 and 18862. "Decca has re-issued a record made some years ago by the Barnet crew and 'That old black magic,' is still a potent beguine with Frances Wayne doing the interpreting. Arrangement is ageless and it's a welcome oldie ... 'Cement mixer' is a new one from Barnet and a mighty good one. It's in jump tempo and Art Robey does the singing. He sounds tired, but that makes the side all the more amusing." (May 18, 1946)

Al Killian, Everett McDonald, Art Robey, Ed Stress, Paul Webster, tpts; Frank Bradley, Porky Cohen, Ed Fromm, Tommy Pederson, tbns; Rae De Geer, Gene Kinsey, as; Kurt Bloom, Ralph E. Rosenlund, ts; Bob Dawes, bar; Sheldon Smith, p; Wallace Walters, g; Irving Lang, b; Mickey Scrima, d

Hollywood, Monogram Studios, Mar. 9, 1946

"FREDDIE STEPS OUT"

A feature film starring June Preisser and Freddie Stewart with Charlie Barnet and his orchestra. 75 minutes.

#Redskin rhumba aHead (0:22)
Unnamed "sardine song" (0:12) [somewhat of a take-off on the Pepsi Cola jingle of the time]
#Redskin rhumba aHead (0:13)
Dear old southland aAndy Gibson (announced as *Dark bayou*)
Patience and fortitude vFreddie Stewart et al (5:20)

Sideline photography was done on March 10 and 11 with Thomas Daily replacing Al Killian, William Traiant replacing Paul Webster and with Nelson Hall, Justin Johnson, Edward Snyder and J. Rich Chico, violins. No guitar visible on screen. There are several other musical numbers where the accompaniment seems to be by the studio orchestra.

***Delta Rhythm Boys**: Carl Jones, Traverse Crawford, tenors; Kelsey Pharr, baritone; Lee Gaines, bass.*

Hollywood, Decca recording session, March 11, 1946

Unidentified song no. 1 [AFM contract says 4 sides were recorded]
(Unissued?)
Unidentified song no. 2
(Unissued?)
LA 4116-A **Just a-sittin' and a-rockin'** vDelta Rhythm Boys
De 23541; Brunswick (E) 04045; Brunswick (Ger) 82717; *Affinity (E) AFS 1012*; *Coral (Ger) 6-22182, PCO 7840, PCO 7995*; *Ajaz 201*
LA 4117-A **No pad to be had** vDelta Rhythm Boys
De 23541; Brunswick (E) 04045); Brunswick (Ger) 82717; *Coral (Ger) 6-22182, PCO 7840, PCO 7995*; *Ajaz 201*

Hollywood, ca Mar. 15, 1946

"JASPER IN A JAM"

A George Pal Puppetoon featuring Peggy Lee and Charlie Barnet and his orchestra (7 1/2m).

Fanfare/Redskin rhumba aHead (0:40)
JASS J-CD-623
Ol' Man Mose [as *Old Man Mose is dead*] vPeggy Lee (0:50)
JASS J-CD-623
Pompton Turnpike aBilly May (2:14) [Great Killian/Barnet duet]
JASS J-CD-623
Redskin rhumba aHead (2:12)
JASS J-CD-623
Mar. 20–April 16, 1946: NYC, 400 Restaurant

The band was heard nightly from March 26 through April 16 on NBC (*NBC Radio Artist Index*).

Al Killian, Everett McDonald, Paul Webster, Lyman Vunk, Ed Stress, Art Robey, tpts; Porky Cohen, Tommy Pederson, Frank Bradley, Ed Fromm, tbns; Rae De Geer, Gene Kinsey, as; Dave Matthews, Kurt Bloom, ts; Bob Dawes, bar; Bill Miller, p; Dennis Sandole, g; Irving Lang, b; Mickey Scrima, d (*Metronome* May 1946)

NYC, 400 Restaurant, NBC b'cast, between March 20 and April 16, 1946

[Program content from Garrod 1984; not verified by compiler.]

Jubilee jump aAndy Gibson
Do you love me vPhil Barton
Cement mixer aAndy Gibson; vArt Robey
Baby, you can count on me aAndy Gibson; vFran Warren
I love you (aPaul Villepigue?); vPhil Barton
E-bob-o-lee-bob aAndy Gibson; vArt Robey
When you awake/You've got me crying again vFran Warren
The sergeant was shy aBilly May
The frim fram sauce (vArt Robey?)

As preceding, March 26, 1946

Redskin rhumba (opening theme) aHead
Redmond Nostalgia Co. CO 3533
The sergeant was shy aBilly May
Redmond Nostalgia Co. CO 3533
Don't you remember me vPhil Barton
Redmond Nostalgia Co. CO 3533
E-bob-o-lee-bob aAndy Gibson; vArt Robey
Redmond Nostalgia Co. CO 3533
You'd be so nice to come home to vFran Warren
Redmond Nostalgia Co. CO 3533
Skyliner aBilly Moore
Redmond Nostalgia Co. CO 3533
Cement mixer aAndy Gibson
Redmond Nostalgia Co. CO 3533
Do you love me? vPhil Barton
Redmond Nostalgia Co. CO 3533
Cherokee aBilly May
Redmond Nostalgia Co. CO 3533

As preceding, April 2, 1946

Redskin rhumba (opening theme) aHead
Redmond Nostalgia Co. CO 3533
The sergeant was shy aBilly May
Redmond Nostalgia Co. CO 3533
Blue champagne aAndy Gibson
Redmond Nostalgia Co. CO 3533
Baby, you can count on me aAndy Gibson; vFran Warren
Ajaz 512; Redmond Nostalgia Co. CO 3533
Don't you remember me? vPhil Barton
Redmond Nostalgia Co. CO 3533
E-bob-o-lee-bob aAndy Gibson; vArt Robey
Redmond Nostalgia Co. CO 3533
I don't know enough about you vFran Warren
Ajaz 512; Redmond Nostalgia Co. CO 3533
Cement mixer aAndy Gibson; vArt Robey
Redmond Nostalgia Co. CO 3533
Skyliner aBilly Moore
Redmond Nostalgia Co. CO 3533
Strange love#
Redmond Nostalgia Co. CO 3533
Redskin rhumba (closing theme) aHead
Redmond Nostalgia Co. CO 3533

As preceding, April 5, 1946

Redskin rhumba (opening theme) aHead
ONS 957
Skyliner aBilly Moore
ONS 957
When you awake/You've got me crying again vFran Warren
ONS 957
E-bob-o-lee-bob aAndy Gibson; vArt Robey
ONS 957; *First Heard (E) FHR 1974-12*
Baby, you can count on me aAndy Gibson; vFran Warren
ONS 957
The sergeant was shy aBilly May
ONS 957; *First Heard (E) FHR 1974-12*
The frim fram sauce vArt Robey
ONS 957
"C" jam blues aAndy Gibson
ONS 957; *First Heard (E) FHR 1974-12*; Ajax C 683
Blue champagne aAndy Gibson
ONS 957; *Golden Era GE 15015*; *First Heard (E) FHR 1974-12*; Ajax C 708
Shady lady# aAndy Gibson
ONS 957

Around the middle of April Charlie fronted the Goodman band at the Paramount Theater while BG recovered from an illness.

April 18–24, 1946: Newark, NJ, Adams Theater

Newark, NJ, Adams Theater, stage performance, April 20, 1946

Cherokee aBilly May
Andy's boogie aAndy Gibson
The sergeant was shy aBilly May
In the moon mist
You won't be satisfied vFran Warren
I got it bad (and that ain't good) aAndy Gibson; vFran Warren
I'm a big girl now vFran Warren
E-bob-o-lee-bob aAndy Gibson; vArt Robey
Cement mixer aAndy Gibson; vArt Robey
Unknown title no.1 vDanny Payne
Unknown title no.2 vDanny Payne

April 25–May 1, 1946: Boston, RKO Theater

Boston, RKO Theater, stage performance, April 26, 1946

Skyliner aBilly Moore
Cherokee aBilly May
Andy's boogie aAndy Gibson
Drop me off in Harlem aRalph Burns
Unknown titles vFran Warren
Unknown titles vDanny Payne

Down beat mentioned in an article that Tommy Pederson took most of the sweet or melodic solos while the hot work was done by Porky Martin/Cohen.

May 3, 1946: Philadelphia, Convention Hall
May 12–18, 1946: New London, Dance Land (Ocean Beach)

Al Killian, Everett McDonald, Art Robey, Ed Stress, Paul Webster, Lyman Vunk, tpts; Frank Bradley, Porky Cohen, Ed Fromm, Lawrence Brown, tbns; Rae De Geer, Gene Kinsey, as; Dave Matthews, Kurt Bloom, ts; Danny Bank, bar; Bill Miller, p; Dennis Sandole, g; Irving Lang, b; Mickey Scrima, d (Ruppli; D. Mather)

NYC, Decca recording session, May 20, 1946

73584- **Zanesville Zohio ZZZ** aAndy Gibson
DECCA JAZZ GRD 612; JAZZ HERITAGE 514960-T; MCA (E) GRP 16122; DECCA JAZZ (JA) MVCR 20008

73585- **Lonesome as the night is long** [featuring Lawrence Brown]
DECCA JAZZ GRD 612; JAZZ HERITAGE 514960-T; MCA (E) GRP 16122; DECCA JAZZ (JA) MVCR 20008

73586-A **You'd be so nice to come home to** aAndy Gibson; vFran Warren
Coral 60132°; *MCA 2 4069°; Ajaz 201*; MCA (Sp) L 404302; MCA 4069 (8-track); AFRS BML-P 1802

73587-A **Dark bayou** aDennis Sandole
Coral 60132°; *Ajaz 201*; *Swing Era LP 1002, LPS 5001*;**DECCA JAZZ GRD 612; JAZZ HERITAGE 514960-T; MCA (E) GRP 16122; DECCA JAZZ (JA) MVCR20008; JAZZ GREATS (E) CD 071**; AFRS BML-P 1802

Note: Andy Gibson was born in Zanesville, Ohio.

May 24–30, 1946: NYC, Apollo Theater
May 31–June 1, 1946: Sea Girt, NJ, Sea Girt Inn
June 7–16, 1946: Chicago, Rainbo Ballroom
["Spot closed for the summer Sunday (16) with poor 7,000 with Barnet." (*Variety* June 19, 1946)]

Chicago, Rainbo Ballroom, ca. June 7, 1946

Janesville jump

Sometime during the spring Jimmy Pupa (tpt) replaced Lyman Vunk, Johnny McAfee (as, bar, vocal) replaced Bob Dawes and George Jenkins (d) came in for Mickey Scrima.

June 20–26, 1946: Detroit, Downtown Theater

Al Killian, Jimmy Pupa, Everett McDonald, Guy Chiaveri, Paul Webster, Art Robey, tpts; Sam Nestico, Porky Cohen, Ed Fromm, Frank Bradley, tbns; Rae De Geer, Gene Kinsey, as; Kurt Bloom, Dave Matthews, ts; Danny Bank, Johnnie McAfee, bar; Bill Miller, p; Irving Lang, b; George Jenkins, d (Down beat July 15, 1946)

June 27–July 24, 1946: NYC, Aquarium Restaurant

NYC, Aquarium Restaurant, stage performance, June (27?), 1946

Cherokee aBilly May
Blue champagne aAndy Gibson
Skyliner aBilly Moore
Take the "A" Train aGeorge Siravo
Unknown titles vFran Warren
Unknown titles vJohnny McAfee
E-bob-o-lee-bob aAndy Gibson; vArt Robey

As preceding, between June 27 and July 24, 1946

Redskin rhumba (opening theme) aHead
ONS 1071 (mastered Aug. 18, 1946)
Lover, come back to me
ONS 1071; *Golden Era GE 15015*; Ajax C 683
Just you—just me
ONS 1071; *Golden Era GE 15015*; Ajax C 683
Baby, you can count on me aAndy Gibson; vFran Warren
ONS 1071; *First Heard (E) FH 1974-12*
Wherever there's you, there's me vArt Robey
ONS 1071
I can't remember to forget (Leonard Feather)
ONS 1071
Andy's boogie aAndy Gibson
ONS 1071
Skyliner aBilly Moore
ONS 1071
All through the day vJohnny McAfee
ONS 1071
The sergeant was shy aBilly May
ONS 1071
Redskin rhumba (closing theme) aHead
ONS 1071

NYC, Teentimers Club, NBC b'cast, July 20, 1946

Charlie and presumably the band appeared on this program. (*NBC Radio Artist Index*)

Program contents unknown

NYC, Aquarium Restaurant, (MBS?) b'cast, July 24, 1946

All through the day vJohnny McAfee
Washington whirligig aAndy Gibson
You may not love me vJohnny McAfee
In love in vain vJohnny McAfee
Redskin rhumba (closing theme) aHead

[Information on this broadcast from Garrod 1984. Not verified by compiler.]

Aug. 3, 1946: Somers Point, NJ, Orsatti's
Aug. 4–10, 1946: Asbury Park, NJ, Convention Hall

Charlie Barnet: "As far as the band business is concerned ... the party is over." (*Down beat* Aug. 12, 1946)

Charlie and Decca's Jack Kapp agreed to disagree, ending the band's association with the label. From this point forward many of the recordings were done as Barnet enterprises, to be disposed of in the most advantageous manner. Even in those sessions which were done under the auspices of a particular recording company, e.g., Apollo, Charlie was able to claim ownership of the masters. Documentation of these recording sessions is spotty—particularly those that took place in NYC—the one solid record being provided by Bud Shank's diary in which he noted that there were Apollo sessions on November 19 and December 24, 1947. Much of what follows as far as studio recordings are concerned represents the compiler's conclusions based on sometimes very flimsy evidence.

As has been noted in earlier Barnet discographies, the numbers appearing in the wax on Apollo 78s—while they are master numbers—do not reflect recording chronology; if anything, they are an indicator of release chronology, with the suffixes serving to identify stamper numbers.

In August of 1946 an arrangement between Charlie and the newly-formed Cosmo/Cosmopolitan label was effected, with the result that a recording session took place in NYC (probably in the studios of the National Recording Co.) wherein six sides were completed. Personnel is probably about the same as given by *Down beat* for the June 27–July 24 Aquarium stand.

NYC, Cosmo recording session, Aug. 12, 1946

NSC 204 **The new redskin rhumba** aHead
Cardinal 25001; National 25001; *Ajaz 201*
3099 **Caravan** aRalph Burns
Apollo 1070 ["Song hits magazine 'Record of the month'"]; Monogram (C) 116; *Ajaz 209*; *Swing Era LP 1019*
NSC 206 **Cherokee** aBilly May
Cardinal 25001; National 25001; AFRS BML-P 2790; *Ajaz 209*
3098 **Bunny** aAndy Gibson
Apollo 1065; *Clef MG C 638*; *Verve MG V 2027*; *Verve (E) 2317.060*; *Ajaz 201*
3100 **Darktown strutter's ball** aHead
Apollo 1070 ["Song hits magazine 'Record of the month'"];Beaver (C) 1008; Monogram (C) 116; *Bandstand 7106; Ajaz 209*; Stack of 78s Stack 33; **STACK OF 78S STACK 33**
3101 **Atlantic jump** aAndy Gibson
Apollo 1065; *Clef MG C 638*; [as *Atlantic hop*]; *Verve MG V 2027* [as *Atlantic hop*]; *Verve (E) 2317.060*; *Ajaz 209*

Hollywood, Hollywood Bowl, "Music for Wounded," Aug. 24, 1946

An all star band composed of Phil Harris, Lawrence Welk, Freddy Martin, Billy Butterfield, Leonard Sues, Carmen Cavallaro, Harry James and **Charlie Barnet** performed. Other artists included Leopold Stokowski, Igor Stravinsky, Bing Crosby, Frank Sinatra, Mickey Rooney and Lena Horne (who sang *The house I live in*).

Hollywood, United Artists Studio, ca. Sept., 1946

"THE FABULOUS DORSEYS"

A United Artists feature film (87m) released May 1947 starring Jimmy and Tommy Dorsey and Janet Blair. Charlie Barnet appears in a brief jam session scene.

Ziggy Elman, tpt; Tommy Dorsey, tbn; Jimmy Dorsey, cl; ***Charlie Barnet****, ts; Art Tatum, p; Ray Bauduc, d; unidentified, b; unidentified, g*

Art's blues
Audio: *Europa Jazz (It) EJ-1011*; *Extreme Rarities ER-1002*; *Collectors Items (E) 011*; *Sarpe (Argentina) 14*
Video: Republic Pictures VHS 1236; Video Treasures MU 6005

"Oh, yeah. It was a nightclub scene, and at that time the Old Grey Fox, was what we used to call Tommy then, was on the wagon. He wasn't drinking. But everybody else was. All the booze on the tables in the nightclub scene was real. And we had a delightful time there." (*Sm*)

Oct. 8–14, 1946: LA, Lincoln Theater

During the fall, Charlie recorded four sides leading Lionel Hampton's band for the Hamp-Tone label. These sides never seem to have seen the light of day and might be categorized as a PR man's dream were it not for the fact that Lionel recalls this event. The story was reported in *Variety* (Oct. 16, 1946) and *Metronome* (Dec. 1946). The Hampton band of this period was approximately:

Wendell Culley, Duke Garrette, Jimmy Nottingham, Joe Wilder, Leo Shepherd, tpts; Jimmy Wormick, Michael "Booty" Wood, Al Hayse, Andrew Penn, tbns; Bobby Plater, Ben Kynard, as; Arnett Cobb, Johnny Griffin, ts; Milt Buckner, p; Joe Comfort, Charlie Harris, b; Gene "Fats" Heard, d

Hollywood, Hamp-Tone recording session, ca Fall 1946

Four unidentified titles

Hollywood, Charlie Barnet recording session, Oct. 17-18, 1946

Personnel for 1:30–7:30PM session: Irving Lewis, tpt; Tommy Pederson, tbn; Harry Schmidt, Arthur Frantz, Vincent de Rubertis, frh; Arthur C. Smith, fl; George Weidler, George Siravo, as; Don Lodice, ts; Warren David Bahn (ts?); Bob Dawes, bar; William Miller, p; Barney Kessel, g; Nick Fatool, d; Frank Siravo, b
(AFM contract)

3093 **I cover the waterfront** aGeorge Siravo; vMartha Raye
Apollo 1110; *Clef MG C 164* ["Vocal by Margie Reed"]; *Verve MG V 2031*; *Clef (Australia) MG C 164*; *Col (E) 33C 9024*; *Blue Star (Fr) GLP 3521*; *Ajaz 201*; ***Clef EP 243*** ["Vocal by Margie Reed"]; AFRS STATION LIBRARY P3896

3091 **Sweet Lorraine** aGeorge Siravo; vMartha Raye
Apollo 1110; *Clef MG C 164* ["Vocal by Margie Reed"]; *Verve MG V 2031*; *Clef (Australia) MG C 164*; *Col (E) 33C 9024*; *Blue Star (Fr) GLP 3521*; *Ajaz 201*; ***Clef EP 243*** ["Vocal by Margie Reed"]

3102 **As long as I live** aGeorge Siravo; vMartha Raye
Clef MG C 164; *Verve MG V 2031*; *Clef (Australia) MG C 164*; *Col (E) 33C 9024*; *Blue Star (Fr) GLP 3521*; *Ajaz 209*; ***Clef EP 244***

Martha thoughtfully brought along several cases of cold Red Cap ale to share with the musicians. (*Harry Schmidt*)

Personnel for 7:30 session: Irving Lewis, Art Robey, Everett McDonald, Nelson Shelladay, Shorty Rogers, tpts; Tommy Pederson, Burt Johnson, Frank Bradley, Gerald Foster, tbns; Les Robinson, Gene Kinsey, as; Don Raffell, Kurt Bloom, ts; Bob Dawes, bar; Bill Miller, p; Barney Kessel, g; Max Albright, d; Arnold Fishkind, b (*AFM contract*)

3100 **I got it bad (and that ain't good)** aAndy Gibson; vMartha Raye
Clef MG C 164; *Verve MG V 2031*; *Clef (Australia) MG C 164*; *Col (E) 33C 9024*; *Blue Star (Fr) GLP 3521*; *Ajaz 201*; ***Clef EP 243***; AFRS STATION LIBRARY P-3895

3092 **Nobody knows the trouble I've seen** aBob Burnet; vMartha Raye
Clef MG C 164; *Verve MG V 2031*; *Clef (Australia) MG C 164*; *Col (E) 33C 9024*; *Blue Star (Fr) GLP 3521*; *Ajaz 201*; ***Clef EP 244***

(3094?) Unidentified; [She may have also recorded either *Summertime* or *He's funny that way* at this session] vMartha Raye
Unissued

[The following three songs may have been recorded at this 7:30PM session]

3157 **Deep purple**
Apollo 1092; Clef 8980; Mercury 8980°; ***Mercury 8980X45***; *Mercury MG C 114; Verve V 2007; Clef (Australia) MG C 114; Barclay (E) GLP 6592; Blue Star (Fr) GLP 6923; Riviera (Fr) RLP 6592; Verve (Ger) 2304.541; Ajaz 217*; ***Clef EP 138***; AFRS BML-P 2789

3095 **Power steering** [aka *One way passage*] aAndy Gibson
Clef MG C 165; *Verve MG V 2031*; *Verve (E) 2317.060*; *Ajaz 209*; ***Clef EP 236***; ***Karusell (Swed) KEP 254***; AFRS STATION LIBRARY P-3896

3133 **Jubilee jump** aAndy Gibson
Apollo 1092; Mercury 8982°; *Clef MG C 165; Mercury MG C 114; Verve V 2007; Clef (Australia) MG C 114; Barclay (E) GLP 6592; Verve (E) 2317.060; Blue Star (Fr) GLP 6923; Riviera (Fr) RLP 6592; Verve (Ger) 2304.541; Ajaz 209*; ***Clef EP 139; Mercury EP 139; Karusell (Swed) KEP 208***; AFRS BML-P 2790, GL 35

Personnel for 11:45PM session: Shorty Rogers, tpt; Burt Johnson, tbn; Bob Dawes, bar; Bill Miller, p; Arnold Fishkind, b; Max Albright, d

3097 **Juice head blues** aAndy Gibson; vArt Robey
Apollo 1082; *Clef MG C 164* [as *Juice head baby*]; *Verve MG V 2031* [as *Juice head baby*]; *Clef (Australia) MG C 164; Col (E) 33C 9024; Blue Star (Fr) GLP 3521; Ajaz 209*; ***Clef EP 243***; **LIVING ERA (E) CD AJA 5288** [as *Juice head baby*]

Betty Perry, femme vocalist, joined the band in time to make the trip to the Hawaiian Islands.

Oct. 31–Nov. 2, 1946: Honolulu, Civic Auditorium
Nov. 12–18, 1946: LA, Million Dollar Theater

Al Killian, tpt, rejoined, replacing Nelson Shelladay and George Jenkins, d, came in in place of (Max Albright?).

Billboard's reviewer noted that "Barnet crew does typical hot stuff ... Style is good and ork works well, but offerings have too much sameness ... Biz, poor when caught." (Nov. 23, 1946)

SONG HITS' RECORD OF THE MONTH

CHARLIE BARNET'S amazing musical career has taken him and his band to more than one record company. At each of his stops, Charlie has recorded at least one number that hit the top. His versions of "Cherokee," "Comanche War Dance" and "Redskin Rhumba" are highly prized collectors' items. Now that Apollo Records has Charlie recording for their label, he has come through for them as he always has in the past.

It didn't take more than one listen to this Apollo platter of "Caravan" to convince us that this was another collectors' item in the making. That's why we've selected it as Song Hits' Record Of The Month.

The "Mad Mab" or "Cherokee Charlie," as he is variously called, is once more headed for big things—if his newest platters are signs of the future. So, Apollo Record No. 1070 of "Caravan" backed by "Darktown Strutters' Ball" is our number one selection of the month. Look for it at your record shop.

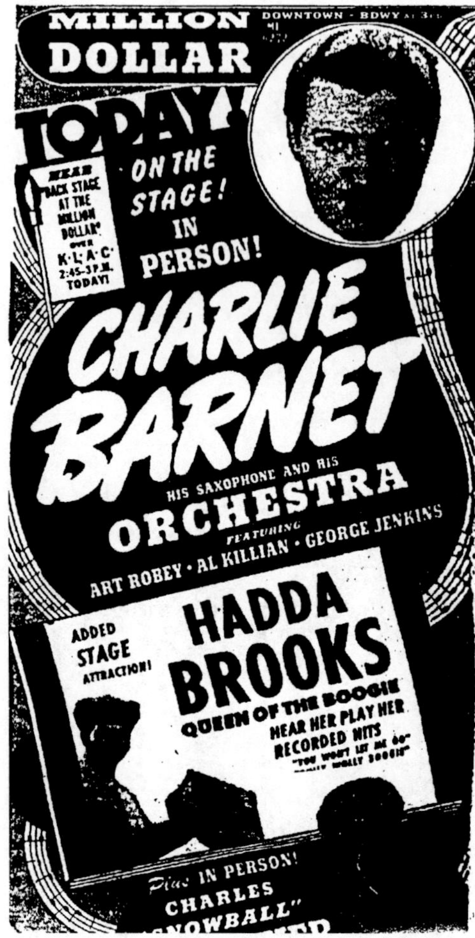

<u>*Los Angeles, Million Dollar Theater, stage performance, Nov. 12, 1946*</u>

Cherokee aBilly May
The sergeant was shy aBilly May
Cotton tail aGeorge Siravo
Things ain't what they used to be aAndy Gibson; vArt Robey
But she's my buddy's chick vArt Robey

<u>*As preceding, Nov. 16, 1946*</u>

Cherokee aBilly May
The sergeant was shy aBilly May
You keep coming back like a song vAlan Lane
I can't get started aAndy Gibson; vAlan Lane
Night and day vAlan Lane
Things ain't what they used to be aAndy Gibson; vArt Robey
But she's my buddy's chick vArt Robey
Juice head blues aAndy Gibson; vArt Robey
Come rain or come shine aAndy Gibson; vBetty Perry
I got it bad (and that ain't good) aAndy Gibson; vBetty Perry
Cotton tail aGeorge Siravo

<u>**Hollywood, Universal Studios, Dec. 12, 1946**</u>

"CHARLIE BARNET AND HIS ORCHESTRA"

A short (14m) featuring Charlie Barnet and his orchestra plus singers Rita Shore and Della Norell, Jeanne Blanch, and dancers Igor and Tania. [Not screened by compiler; information from *Meeker.*]

Irving Lewis, Shorty Rogers, Art Robey, Everett McDonald, Al Killian, tpts; Frank Bradley, Burt Johnson, Claude Graham, Robert Vidoloff, tbns; Gus McReynolds, Gene Kinsey, as; Kurt Bloom, Don Rafell, ts; Bob Dawes, bar; Bill Miller, p; Barney Kessel, g; Arnold Fishkind, b; Jackie Mills, d

For the sideline photography—probably shot Dec. 13—a white player (possibly Jack Winters) was used in place of Al Killian.

I'll remember April
No can do
You're a sweetheart

Rhumba fantasy
I believe in miracles
Murder at Peyton Hall aAndy Gibson

Dec. 13–Jan. 9, 1946/7: Ocean Park, Casino Gardens

Al Killian, Art Robey, Everett McDonald, Irving Lewis, Shorty Rogers, tpts; Burt Johnson, Tommy Pederson, Phil Washburne, Frank Bradley, tbns; Gus McReynolds, Frank Pappalardo, as; Kurt Bloom, Don Raffell, ts; Bob Dawes, bar; Bill Miller, p; Barney Kessel, g; Ed Mihelich, b; Dick Shanahan, d

[Dawes did not play on opening night of this engagement due to a dispute with Tommy Dorsey, who owned the joint. Tommy had it in for Dawes because he had refused to go east with TD a few months earlier. The AFM decided in Dawes' favor and he resumed his chair.]

Ocean Park, Casino Gardens, between Dec. and 29, 1946

Note that a One Night Stand (1261) with exactly the same contents has been noted in the literature (see *Working draft AFRS One Night Stands 1001 thru 2000 by Charles Garrod*). Compiler has not auditioned ONS 1261.

Redskin rhumba (opening theme) aHead
ONS 1240 (mastered Dec. 29)/1261 (mastered Jan. 3)
Murder at Peyton Hall aAndy Gibson; vIrving Lewis
ONS 1240/1261; *First Heard (E) FHR 1974-12*
You keep coming back like a song vAlan Lane
ONS 1240/1261
The best man vBetty Perry
ONS 1240/1261
Strollin' aHoward McGhee
ONS 1240/1261; *First Heard (E) FH 17; Sandy Hook SH 2081*; Sandy Hook CSH 2081
And so to bed vAlan Lane
ONS 1240/1261
Skyliner aBilly Moore
ONS 1240/1261
You're my thrill aBud Estes; vBetty Perry
ONS 1240/1261
Bunny aAndy Gibson
ONS 1240/1261
[an excerpt from this performance was added after *Makin' whoopee* by AFRS]
Makin' whoopee
ONS 1240/1261; *First Heard (E) FH 44*; First Heard (E) CFH 44
#Bunny#
ONS 1240/1261

As preceding between Dec. 13 and Jan. 3, 1946/7

Redskin rhumba (opening theme) aHead
ONS 1247 (prob. mastered Dec. 1946)
Eric the traveler aShorty Rogers [Named after one of Charlie's dogs who went on the road with the band]
ONS 1247; *Golden Era GE 15015*; Ajax C 708
And so to bed vAlan Lane
ONS 1247
Take the "A" Train aGeorge Siravo
ONS 1247
Passé vBetty Perry
ONS 1247
Bunny aAndy Gibson
ONS 1247
The sergeant was shy aBilly May
ONS 1247
You're my thrill aBud Estes; vBetty Perry
ONS 1247
Blue Lou# aAndy Gibson (5:28)
ONS 1247

As preceding

Redskin rhumba (opening theme) aHead
ONS 1254 (prob. mastered Jan. 1947)
The sergeant was shy aBilly May
ONS 1254
The best man vBetty Perry
ONS 1254

This is the night vAlan Lane
ONS 1254
Meadowland
ONS 1254
Coolin' aShorty Rogers
ONS 1254; *First Time Records FTR 1513*
[An excerpt from this performance was added by AFRS after *Bunny*]
The things we did last summer vBetty Perry
ONS 1254
And so to bed vAlan Lane
ONS 1254
Bunny aAndy Gibson
ONS 1254
Coolin'#
ONS 1254

As preceding?

The following 29 second fragment has not been identified but may have originated from this engagement.

Redskin rhumba (opening theme) aHead
First Heard (E) FH 17; Sandy Hook SH 2081; Sandy Hook CSH 2081

Charlie headed east with a few key members of the West Coast band to carry out some jobs using Local 802 men. Thus far no reliable information as to the make-up of this band has been found, beyond the fact that Dorothy Claire was signed on Jan. 24 for $400/week, Billy Usher was the boy singer, and Rex Stewart was featured on cornet. Presumably Kurt Bloom was in one of the tenor chairs and other possibilities are Bill Miller and Dick Shanahan.

NYC, "Vaughn Monroe Show," CBS b'cast, Jan. 18, 1947

Charlie performed on ts with Vaughn's band.

Night and day (not CB head arr)
Unknown song

Jan. 24–Feb. 13, 1947: NYC, Strand Theater (followed V. Monroe and was succeeded by Claude Thornhill)

NYC, Strand Theater, stage performance, Jan. 24, 1947

For sentimental reasons vBilly Usher
Caravan aRalph Burns; featuring Rex Stewart "on talking trumpet"

As preceding, ca. Jan. 25, 1947

Unknown instrumental featuring Rex and Charlie
Pretending vBilly Usher
I only have eyes for you vBilly Usher
Unknown instrumental featuring Rex with "simulated talk on horn"
Kansas City vDorothy Claire
The coffee song vDorothy Claire
Say si si vDorothy Claire
I cain't say no vDorothy Claire
Cherokee/Pompton Turnpike/Smiles

Feb. 14–??, 1947: Philadelphia, Earle Theater

Philadelphia, Earle Theater, stage performance, Feb. 14, 1947

The sergeant was shy aBilly May
Caravan aRalph Burns
For sentimental reasons
Pretending vBilly Usher
Mood indigo vBilly Usher
I only have eyes for you vBilly Usher
Without love vBilly Usher
I'm gonna love that guy vAnn Russell
Unknown instrumental featuring Rex on "talking cornet"

Mar. (8?)–16, 1947: NYC, Aquarium Restaurant

Charlie headed back to the Coast with some of his key men and formed another band whose make-up resembled the following:

Irving Lewis, Neal Hefti, Everett McDonald, Jack Hanson, tpts; Phil

Washburn, Tex Satterwhite, Burt Johnson, tbns; George Weidler, Walt Weidler, as; Kurt Bloom, Don Raffell, ts; Bob Dawes, bar; Bill Miller, p; Ed Mihelich, b; Dick Shanahan, d; Carolyn Scott (Carol Mann), Billy Usher, vocals.

Hollywood, AFRS "Jubilee," ca spring 1947

Redskin rhumba (Opening theme) aHead
JUBILEE 247

Atlantic jump aAndy Gibson
JUBILEE 247; V-disc 823; *First Heard (E) FH 17*; *Sandy Hook SH 2081*; *Dan (Ja) VC 5026*; Sandy Hook CSH 2081; Redmond Nostalgia CO 3657

That's my desire vFrankie Laine
JUBILEE 247; V-disc 810; *First Heard (E) FH 17; Sandy Hook SH 2081; Dan (Ja) VC 5017*; Sandy Hook CSH 2081; Redmond Nostalgia CO 3657; Ajax C 708

Wrap your troubles in dreams vCarolyn Scott
JUBILEE 247; *First Heard (E) FHR 1974-12*; Redmond Nostalgia Co 3657

The gal from Joe's aDuke Ellington
JUBILEE 247; *First Heard (E) FH 17; Sandy Hook SH 2081*; Sandy Hook CSH 2081; Redmond Nostalgia CO 3657

It's a good day vBunny Briggs
JUBILEE 247; Redmond Nostalgia CO 3657

I got it bad (and that ain't good) aAndy Gibson; vCarolyn Scott
JUBILEE 247; Redmond Nostalgia CO 3657

Barnetology: Cherokee/Pompton Turnpike/ Things ain't what they used to be/Smiles
JUBILEE 247; *First Heard (E) FH 17* [*Smiles* lacking]; *Sandy Hook SH 2081* [*Smiles* lacking]; Sandy Hook CSH 2081 [*Smiles* lacking]; Redmond Nostalgia CO 3657

(Hollywood, NBC, "Jubilee," ca. Spring 1947?)

These recordings may have been made for Jubilee but not used.

Tulip or turnip (Tell me, tell me, dream face) aNeal Hefti; vBunny Briggs
V-Disc 811; *First Heard (E) FH 44*; First Heard (E) CFH 44

Prelude to a kiss aCharlie Barnet
V-Disc—unissued

There was a report in *Variety* (Apr. 23, 1947), that "Barnet handed [Apollo] 13 sides he waxed himself some time ago."

Pasadena, "Gene Norman's 'Just jazz,'" Shrine Aud., April 29, 1947

Chuck Peterson, tpt; Vic Dickenson, tbn; Benny Carter, as; ***Charlie Barnet****, ts; Dodo Marmarosa, p; Irving Ashby, g; Red Callender, b; Jackie Mills, d*

Just you—just me
Pandora (Ger) 913137; **GIANTS OF JAZZ (IT) CD 53097; ACE (??) CDBOP 014**

Perdido
Modern 20 660; JUBILEE 261; Jazz Selection (Fr) 633; ***Vogue (E) E 2296***; *Pandora (Ger) 913137; Crown CLP 5008; Swing House (E) SWH 10*; **GIANTS OF JAZZ (IT) CD 53097**

[Note that the performance of *Perdido* lasted a little over 9 minutes and it is in this form that it is heard on the CD release and on the Jubilee transcription. The original 78 and LP issues, though, were edited to remove Dickenson's solo and to cut Charlie's solo in half, resulting in the elimination of about 2 minutes of music. The 78 issue received master numbers 1000-1001 for parts 1 and 2.]

May 2–June 13, 1947: Culver City, Meadowbrook

Everett McDonald, Irving Lewis, Jack Hanson, Neal Hefti, tpts; Phil Washburn, Tex Satterwhite, Oliver Wilson, tbns; George Weidler (lead), Frank Pappalardo, as; Don Raffell, Murray Wald, ts; Bill Miller, p; Ed Mihelich, b; Dick Shanahan, d; Carolyn Scott, Billy Usher, Bunny Briggs, vocals (Billboard May 17, 1947)

Culver City, Meadowbrook, May 3, 1947

Cherokee aBilly May
Pompton Turnpike aBilly May

The Meadowbrook's policy at this time was to have two bands (Murray

McEachern had the other) and vaudeville acts. This approach didn't bring in the expected crowds and it was soon abandoned.

Carolyn Scott left the band in late May.

Everett McDonald, John Best, Jimmy Campbell, Neal Hefti, tpts; Burt Johnson, Ollie Wilson, Phil Washburn, tbns; George Weidler (lead), Frank Pappalardo, as; Don Raffell, Warner Weidler, ts; Bob Dawes, bar; Bill Miller, p; Iggy Shevak, b; Dick Shanahan, d; Jean Louise, Billy Usher, Bunny Briggs, vocals (*Edw 65*)

June 20–21, 1947: Balboa, Rendezvous Ballroom
June 26–27, 1947: Balboa, Rendezvous Ballroom

Chico Alvarez, tpt, is reported to have replaced Neal Hefti in late June (*Edw 65*).

Hollywood, RKO studios, July–Aug. 1947

"A SONG IS BORN"

A feature film starring Danny Kaye and Virginia Mayo with appearances by a number of musicians including Charlie Barnet. 112m. It is believed that Charlie's recording and filming took place between about July 15 and early September. "Originally it was only supposed to be a two-week gig. Well, we were on it seven weeks. So much so that my band finished the Aragon and MCA pulled some strings and let it open … in Portland, at the Jantzen Beach Ballroom, without me, because it overlapped a few days." (*Sm*)

Please note that some—possibly all—of the succeeding music may be on the "Goldwyn reference recordings" cited by Russ Connor in his several BG discographical works.

Charlie Barnet and his orchestra

Jimmy Zito, Jimmy Campbell, Everett McDonald, Chico Alvarez, tpts; Freddie Zito, Phil Washburn, Herbie Harper, tbns; Walt Weidler (lead), Frank Pappalardo, as; Warner Weidler, Jack Henderson, ts; Bob Dawes, bar; unknown, p; Don Tosti, b; (Bob Bain?), g; Dick Shanahan, d.

Redskin rhumba aHead—Version A (0:30) (made up of the first few bars and the last 20 of a recording made for the soundtrack)
"A song is born" ST; Vi (Ja) NB 6013

Redskin rhumba aHead—Version B (2:23) (a complete recording made for the soundtrack but not the same performance as the preceding)
Capitol 10174; WOR 3207 (2:23); **CAP CDP 212558**; WOR 3207 (0:08); *Ajaz 217*

The Capitol 78 was evidently mastered on August 8, 1948, and released shortly thereafter.

The Leaders' orchestra

Louis Armstrong, tpt; Tommy Dorsey, tbn; Benny Goodman, cl; ***Charlie Barnet****, as; Lionel Hampton, vbs; Mel Powell, p; Al Hendrickson, g; Harry Babasin, b; Louie Bellson, d*

A song was born vLouis Armstrong, Jeri Sullivan, Golden Gate Quartet. Note that asterisked issues contain only what wound up on the soundtrack.

Performance A (4:12)
"A song is born" ST [the 8 bar Armstrong solo is taken from this performance]; Vi (Ja) NB 6013*; *RCA (Fr) NL 89279*; *RCA (Fr) FXM1 7083*; *Pumpkin 109**; *Rare Records (Fr) 6**; WOR 3177, pt.A; RCA (Fr) NK 89279; Radio Yesteryear RY 34974*; **RCA (FR) ND 89279**

Performance B (4:51)
"A song is born" ST [the 8 bar Barnet solo is taken from this performance] Vi (Ja) NB 6013*; *RCA (Fr) NL 89279*; *RCA (Fr) FXM1 7083*; *Pumpkin 109**; *Rare Records (Fr) 6**; WOR 3177, pt.A; RCA (Fr) NK 89279; Radio Yester-year RY 34974*; **RCA (FR) ND 89279**

Performance C (4:57)
Capitol 10172; *Cap (Ja) ECJ 50077*

Flying home

Performance A (5:02)
"A song is born" ST (edited to 3:14); WOR 3207 (5:02); *Pumpkin 106**; Radio Yesteryear RY 34974*

Performance B (0:21 fragment)
WOR 3177

Anvil chorus

Performance A (0:25)
"A song is born" ST; Radio Yesteryear RY 34974

Performance B (0:10)
"A song is born" ST; Radio Yesteryear RY 34974

Charlie Barnett interview
WOR 13-1168-D; Radio Yesteryear 2999

The film was released in VHS format on HBO Home Video 084383.

July 1–14, 1947: SF, Edgewater at the Beach
July 18–31, 1947: Ocean Park, Aragon Ballroom (may have been held over)

Variety noted that Charlie and the rest of the band leaders were having to get used to a lot less money than in the halcyon days. "Barnet was here at the Aragon ... not going too well bucking TD ... He's playing more dance music for dancers, not for himself as was his prewar aim." (Aug. 13, 1947)

Ocean Park, Aragon Ballroom, CBS b'cast between July 18–31, 1947

Redskin rhumba (opening theme) aHead
Bunny aAndy Gibson
If my heart had a window vDick Baldwin
Redskin rhumba (closing theme) aHead

As preceding

Redskin rhumba (opening theme) aHead
Heartaches vBunny Briggs
That's where I came in vJean Louise
Andy's jump aAndy Gibson
Redskin rhumba (closing theme) aHead

As preceding

Redskin rhumba (opening theme) aHead
Red silk stockings and the green perfume vBunny Briggs
A midnight masquerade vDick Baldwin
Skyliner aBilly Moore

It was probably in August that Doc Severinsen became the fifth trumpet in the band.

Aug. 19–Sept. 1, 1947: Portland, Jantzen Beach
Sept. 2–3, 1947: Seattle, Trianon Ballroom
Sept. 4, 1947: Yakima, WA, Playland Ballroom
Sept. 5–6, 1947: Spokane, WA, Nat Park
Sept. 10–13, 1947: Salt Lake City, Rendezvous

"Apollo musical director Jerry Jerome to Hollywood for Charlie Barnet record date" (*Billboard,* Sept. 27, 1947)

Hollywood, Apollo recording session, Sept. 20, 1947

Clark Terry, Carl Severinsen, James Nottingham, Joseph Graves, James Campbell, tpts; Zolman Cohen, Herbert Harper, Freddie Zito, tbns; Walter Weidler, Salvatore Dottore, as; Jack Henderson, Donald Raffell, ts; Robert Dawes, bar; Claude Williamson, p; Robert Bain, g; Don Tosti, b; Richard Shanahan, d (*AFM contract*)

There is no documentation as to what was recorded. The session ran from midnight to 3AM. The following may be the songs recorded on this date. See also sessions of Aug. 8 and Oct. 17-18 for other recording sessions germane to the Apollo period.

3096 **Blue Lou** aAndy Gibson
Apollo 1082; Mercury 8980°; ***Mercury 8980X45***; *Mercury MG C 114*; *Verve V 2007*; *Verve VC 3508*; *Metro (Arg) 2356.021*; *Clef (Australia) MG C 114*;*Contour (E) CN 2010, 2870.443*; *Barclay (E)*

GLP 6592; *Verve (E) 2317.060*; *Verve (Eu) 2356.021*; *Metro (Fr) 2355.022*; *Blue Star (Fr) GLP 6923*; *Riviera (Fr) RLP 6592*; *Verve (Ger) 2304.541*; *Ajaz 209*; ***Clef EP 138;*** **LIVING ERA (E) CD AJA 5288**; AFRS BML-P 2789

3130 **East side, west side** aAndy Gibson; vBunny Briggs
Apollo 1084; Monogram (C) 131; *Clef MG C 164,MG V 2031*; *Verve MG V 2031*; *Clef (Australia) MGC 164*; *Franklin Mint 33, Record no. 19*;*Col (E) 33C 9024*; *Blue Star (Fr) GLP 3521*; *Ajaz 209*;***Clef EP 243***; Franklin Mint tape no.19; AFRS REMEMBER 831; AFRTS STATION LIBRARY P 3895; USIA-VOA WORLD OF JAZZ 63

3131 **My old flame** aAndy Gibson; vJean Louise
Apollo 1084; Monogram (C) 131; *Clef MG C 164*; *Verve MG V 2031*; *Clef (Australia) MG C 164*; *Col (E) 33C 9024*; *Blue Star (Fr) GLP 3521*; *Ajaz 209*; ***Clef EP 244*** ["Vocal by Margie Reed"]

3132 **Sleep** aClark Terry
Clef MG C 165; Verve MG V 2031; Ajaz 209; ***Clef EP 237***; AFRTS STATION LIBRARY P 3895

3155 **Moods** aAndy Gibson
Apollo 786; *Clef MG C 165*; *Verve MG V 2031*; *Verve (E) 2317.060*; *Ajaz 209*; ***Clef EP 237***

3156 **Budandy** aBud Estes & Andy Gibson
Apollo 786; *Clef MG C 165*; *Verve MG V 2031*; *Verve (E) 2317.060*; *Ajaz 209*; ***Clef EP 237***; AFRTS STATION LIBRARY P 3895

3194 **Southern fried** aBill Miller
Apollo 1107; Mercury 8982º; ***Mercury 8982X45***; *Mercury MG C 114*; *Verve MG V 2007*; *Clef (Australia) MG C 114*; *Barclay (E) GLP 6592*; *Verve (E) 2317.060*; *Blue Star (Fr) GLP 6923*; *Riviera (Fr) RLP 6592*; *Europa Jazz (It) EJ 1027*; *Sarpe (Sp) (Arg) GJ 34*; *Ajaz 217*; ***Clef EP 139; Mercury EP 139; Karusell (Swed) KEP 208***; I giganti del jazz (It) GJ 34; AFRS BML-P 2790

3195 **Little John ordinary** aAndy Gibson
Apollo 1107; *Clef MG C 165*; *Verve MG V 2031*; *Europa Jazz (It) EJ 1027*; *Sarpe (Sp) (Arg) GJ 34*; *Ajaz 217*; ***Clef EP 236***; ***Karusell (Swed) KEP 254***; I giganti del jazz (It) GJ 34; AFRTS STATION LIBRARY P 3896

3196 **Charleston alley** aAndy Gibson
Apollo 1105; Mercury 8981; Monogram (C) 147; ***Mercury 8981X45***; *Clef MG C 165; Mercury MG C 114; Verve V 2007, MG V 2031; Clef (Australia) MG C 114; Verve (E) 2317.060; Blue Star (Fr) GLP 6923; Riviera (Fr) RLP 6592; Verve (Ger) 2304.541; Europa Jazz (It) EJ 1027; Sarpe (Sp) (Arg) GJ 34; Ajaz 217*; ***Clef EP 139; Clef EP 237; Mercury EP 139; Karusell (Swed) KEP 208***; I giganti del jazz (It) GJ 34; AFRS BML-P 2790

3197 **The gal from Joe's** aDuke Ellington
Apollo 1106; Mercury 8979; ***Mercury 8979X45***; *Mercury MG C 114*; *Verve V 2007*; *Clef (Australia) MG C 114*; *Barclay (E) GLP 6592*; *Verve (E) 2317.060*; *Riviera (Fr) RLP 6592*; *Blue Star (Fr) GLP 6923*; *Verve (Ger) 2304.541*; *Ajaz 217*; ***Clef EP 138***; AFRS BML-P 2789 3198

Rockin' in rhythm aAndy Gibson; vBunny Briggs
Apollo 1106; *Clef MG C 165; Verve MG V 2031*; *Verve (E) 2317.060*; *Europa Jazz (It) EJ 1027*; *Sarpe (Sp) (Arg) GJ 34; Ajaz 217*; ***Clef EP 236; Karusell (Swed) KEP 254***; I giganti del jazz (It) GJ 34; AFRTS STATION LI-BRARY P 3896

3199 **Pompton Turnpike** aBilly May
Apollo 1105; Beaver (C) 1008; Monogram (C) 147; *Clef MG C 165; Verve MG V 2031; Contour (E) 2870.348; Verve (E) 2317.060; Europa Jazz (It) EJ 1027; Sarpe (Sp) (Arg) GJ 34; Ajaz 217*; ***Clef EP 236; Karusell (Swed) KEP 254***; I giganti del jazz (It) GJ 34; USIA-VOA WORLD OF JAZZ 63

4:00–5:30AM

Clark Terry, tpt; Charlie Barnet, ss, as; possibly William Weasel Parker, ts; Claude Williamson, p; Barney Kessel, g; Dick Shanahan, d; Don Tosti, b

R-1301 **Dirty rotten shame blues, pt. 1** aClark Terry
Apollo 814; ***Apollo EP 614***

R-1302 **Dirty rotten shame blues, pt. 2** aClark Terry; vBunny Briggs
Apollo EP 614

R-1303 **Blue moon** aClark Terry
Apollo 814; ***Apollo EP 614***

R-1304 **Bop a boogie** aClark Terry; vBunny Briggs, Clark Terry
Apollo EP 614

[Ernie Edwards in the first edition of the Barnet discography, reported that R-1301 and 1303 were advertised and reviewed (as Apollo 792) but never issued. It's possible that 792 was a white label demo. Compiler has been unable to substantiate this assertion. Apollo 814 was reviewed in *Down beat* (Dec. 31, 1952). It was Clark Terry who suggested Weasel Parker as the ts. Charlie plays soprano on *Dirty* and *Blue moon* and alto on *Bop*. The EP was issued as by "Charlie Barnett and his Cherokee's"]

Down beat reviewed Apollo 1084 in the Dec. 31, 1947 issue. "**East** opens with dancer Bunny Briggs singing a parody on the Sammy Kaye band openings, moving into a bop-syllabled scat chorus, while the band sings the lyrics behind him ... This record is not a great musical side, but should be a terrific juke hit. High trumpet over the Ellington-like reed figures is by Joe Graves. How about the way the Mab always comes up with good wax! **Flame** is sung by Jean Louise, a young lady with a magnificent figure backed by Charlie's soprano."

Bud Shank came in on 4th tenor at about this time. The player in this chair was expected to play Charlie's parts when the leader was off the stand.

The Barnet band was going for $750 or less. (*Billboard* Oct. 25, 1947)

Sept. (19?)–21, 1947: Balboa: Rendezvous
Sept. 23, 1947: Phoenix
Sept. 24, 1947: El Paso
Sept. 25, 1947: Albuquerque
Sept. 26, 1947: Pueblo
Sept. 27, 1947: Wray, CO
Sept. 28, 1947: Day off
Sept. 29, 1947: Omaha
Sept. 30, 1947: Council Bluffs
Oct. 1, 1947: Day off
Oct. 2, 1947: Cedar Rapids
Oct. 4, 1947: Detroit
Oct. 5, 1947: Detroit
Oct. 6, 1947: Fruitport, MI
Oct. 7, 1947: Kitchener, ON
Oct. 8, 1947: Sarnia, ON
Oct. 9, 1947: Buffalo
Oct. 10, 1947: Erie
Oct. 11, 1947: Dayton
Oct. 12, 1947: Fremont (Ohio? Mich?)
Oct. 13, 1947: Chatham, ON
Oct. 14, 1947: Peterborough, ON
Oct. 15, 1947: Toronto, Palace Pier
Oct. 16, 1947: Niagara Falls, ON
Oct. 17, 1947: London, ON, London Arena
Oct. 18, 1947: Lansing
Oct. 19, 1947: Columbia Station, OH
Oct. 20, 1947: Akron
Oct. 21, 1947: Youngstown
Oct. 22, 1947: Pittsburgh
Oct. 23, 1947: Mahanoy City, PA
Oct. 24, 1947: State College, PA
Oct. 25, 1947: Pottstown, PA
Oct. 26, 1947: Bridgeport, CT
Oct. 27, 1947: Day off
Oct. 28, 1947: Rochester, NY
Oct. 29, 1947: Cortland, NY
Oct. 31, 1947: Manchester, NY
Nov. 3–6, 1947: Philadelphia, The Click

Philadelphia, The Click, KYW-NBC b'cast, between Nov. 3 and 6, 1947

East side, west side aAndy Gibson; vClark Terry
Joyce LP 1031
Bunny aAndy Gibson
Joyce LP 1031
The man I love vJean Louise
Joyce LP 1031
Terry tune aNeal Hefti; vClark Terry
The sergeant was shy aBilly May
Joyce LP 1031
That old devil moon v(Dick Baldwin?)
Joyce LP 1031
Atlantic jump# aAndy Gibson

The *Down beat* review of Decca 25234 mentioned the popularity of *Skyliner* in Europe and its use as the theme song of a much listened-to record show, "Midnight in Munich," and that "Barnet plays his head off. Flipover, a band copy of the famous Armstrong-Hines side, devoted to Barnet's alto is even better."

As preceding, November 4, 1947

Program contents unknown

There were 12 network airshots weekly from The Click.

Nov. 7, 1947: Poughkeepsie
Nov. 8, 1947: Long Island
Nov. 9, 1947: New Haven
Nov. 10, 1947: Rumford, ME
Nov. 11, 1947: Providence
Nov. 12, 1947: Boston

Nov. 13, 1947: Day off
Nov. 14, 1947: Providence
Nov. 15, 1947: Troy
Nov. 16, 1947: Lancaster
Nov. 17, 1947: Day off
Nov. 18, 1947: NYC, Arcadia Ballroom

James Campbell, Joe Graves, Clark Terry, James Nottingham, Carl Severinsen, tpts; Porky Cohen, Fred Zito, Edward Benson, tbns; Walt Weidler, Sal Dattore, as; Jack Henderson, Bud Shank, ts; Bob Dawes, bar; Claude Williamson, p; Don Tosti, b; Dick Shanahan, d; Curry Wilson, band boy; Jean Louise, Dick Baldwin, vocals; Neal Hefti and Andy Gibson, arr; Kurt Bloom, band manager (Clark Terry letter, Aug. 11, 1997)

NYC, Arcadia Ballroom, stage performance, Nov. 18, 1947

My old flame vJean Louise
You do vDick Baldwin

NYC, Apollo recording session, Nov. 19, 1947

An Apollo session took place on this date. See also above Sept. 20, 1947.

Nov. 20, 1947: Day off
Nov. 21–27, 1947: Washington, DC, Howard Theater
Nov. 28–Dec. 4, 1947: NYC, Apollo Theater

NYC, Apollo Theater, stage performance, between Nov. 28 and Dec. 4, 1947

You do vDick Baldwin
Begin the beguine vDick Baldwin
Unknown song vJean Louise

NYC, Columbia Pictures studio, Dec. 5, 1947

"Charlie Barnet and his orchestra" (Thrills of Music series)

A short film (11m) featuring Charlie Barnet with vocalists Jean Louise and Jimmy Brown and the Nikolai Dancers.

Redskin rhumba aHead
Pompton Turnpike aBilly May
Stormy weather vJean Louise
Audio: *Joyce 3001*
Civilization vJimmy Brown
Audio: *Joyce 3001*

NYC, "Fred Robbins' One Night Stand," Town Hall, Dec. 6–7, 1947

[Performance began late on the evening of Dec. 6. and was preceded by a Morey Amsterdam comedy routine]

Jimmy Campbell, Joe Graves, Clark Terry, James Nottingham, Doc Severinsen, tpts; Porky Cohen, Fred Zito, Red Benson, tbns; Walt Weidler, Bud Shank, as; Kurt Bloom, Wolfgang Weidler, ts; Bob Dawes, bar; Claude Williamson, p; Don Tosti, b; Dick Shanahan, d

51218 ***Rockin' in rhythm*** aBilly May
Col CL 639°; *Co B 488*
51219 ***Tulip or turnip (Tell me, tell me, dream face)*** aNeal Hefti; vBunny Briggs
Col CL 639°; *Co B 488*
51220 ***My old flame*** aAndy Gibson; vJean Louise
Col CL 639°; *Co P 16741* [7" LP]; *Co B 488*
51221 ***Caravan*** aRalph Burns
Col CL 639°; *Co B 488*
51222 ***Andy's boogie*** aAndy Gibson
Col CL 639°; *Co B 488*
51223 ***Pompton Turnpike*** aBilly May
Col CL 639°; Col JC 36743; Col Musical Treasuries P2M 5193 [mono], *P2S 5194* [elec. stereo], *P7S 5122, Z 173; Harmony HL 7336*; *Col B 2602, B 488*
51224 ***Cherokee/Redskin rhumba*** aBilly May, aHead (5:35)

Col CL 639°; Col P 16741; Col B 2602; B 488

51224 ed ***Cherokee/Redskin rhumba***
Col JC 36742 (4:02); *"Dutch Boy" (XTV-69449-50)* (2:49); ***Col 13 33288*** (3:25)

51225 ***Skyliner*** aBilly Moore
Col CL 639°, P7M 5121, G 30009° [mono, stereo], *JC 36580*; *Col P 16741*; *Col Musical Treasuries P2M 5111*; *Harmony HL 7336*; *Philips (E) BBL 7209*; *Philips (Eu) BO 7227L*; *CBS-Realm (E) RM 52310*; ***Col B 2602***; ***Col 13 33288***; Col CGT 30009; Col PCT 36580; Col Legacy CT 48977; **Col Legacy CK 48977; Col CG 30009; Frémeaux (Fr) FA 078; Sony BUK 50344**

51226 ***East side, west side*** aAndy Gibson; vBunny Briggs
Col CL 639°; ***Co B 489***

51227 ***Terry tune*** aNeal Hefti
Col CL 639°; ***Co B 489***

51228 ***Things ain't what they used to be/Hello baby blues*** aAndy Gibson; vBunny Briggs
Col CL 639°; ***Co B 489***

51229 ***The gal from Joe's*** aDuke Ellington
Col CL 639°, P 16741; ***Co B 489***

51230 ***Barnetology (Cherokee/Pompton Turnpike/Skyliner/Things ain't.../Cornet confab/Smiles)***
Col CL 639°; ***Co B 489***

Since I fell for you vJean Louise
Unissued

Dec. 10–23, 1947: NYC, Strand Theater

NYC, Strand Theater, stage performance, Dec. 10, 1947

The gentleman is a dope vJean Louise
Since I fell for you vJean Louise
East side, west side

As preceding, Dec. 15, 1947

Christmas medley
Barnet medley

Variety's reviewer wrote: "Without disparaging especially the efforts of Charlie Barnet's orchestra ... it's to be emphasized that except for a very few bands, these outfits have dimmed their drawing power." (Dec. 10, 1947)

NYC, Apollo recording session, Dec. 24, 1947

An Apollo session took place on this date. See above September 20, 1947.

Dec. 28, 1947: Washington, DC, Howard Theater
Dec. 29, 1947: Frederick, MD
Jan. 8–14, 1948: Newark, NJ, Adams Theater
Jan. 16–18, 1948: Hartford, State Theater

The band broke up following the State Theater engagement. Charlie returned to the Coast and for a while owned a night club called "The Doll House" in the San Fernando Valley. He formed another band in the spring of 1948 whose approximate personnel was:

Lammar Wright, Jr., Irving Lewis, Dave Nichols, Jack Hanson, tpts; Phil Washburn, Herbie Harper, Karl de Karske, tbns; Walt Weidler, Frank Pappalardo, as; Al Curtis, Bud Shank, ts; Bob Dawes, bar; Claude Williamson, p; Iggy Shevak, b; Dick Shanahan, d

May 28–June 24, 1948: Ocean Park, Casino Gardens
June 25, 1948: South Gate, Trianon Ballroom
June 26–27, July 3-4, 1948: Los Angeles, Avodon Ballroom

Hollywood, Universal-International Studios, July 6 & 8, 1948

"RED SKIN RHUMBA"

A short film (15m) featuring Charlie Barnet and his orchestra with Virginia Maxey and Clark Dennis, vocals.

Audio recording took place on July 6 with the above personnel; sideline photography, with Neal Hefti substituting for Lammar Wright, was done on July 8.

Redskin rhumba aHead (2:31)
Audio: *Joyce 3001*
Video: MCA Home Video 80665 (1:59)
Skyliner aBilly Moore (2:42)
Audio: *Joyce 3001*
Video: MCA Home Video 80666 (2:35); "Feather on jazz: Jazz saxophonists" (MCA TV, 1967)
Jeepers creepers vVirginia Maxey
Audio: *Joyce 3001*
Video: MCA Home Video 80666
Peg o' my heart vClark Dennis
Jealousy vClark Dennis
Pompton Turnpike aBilly May (2:03)
Audio: *Joyce 3001*
Video: MCA Home Video 80666

July 9–10, 1948: South Gate, Trianon Ballroom
July 13–25, 1948: SF, Edgewater at the Beach

San Francisco, Edgewater at the Beach, MBS b'cast, between July 13 and 25, 1948

Redskin rhumba (opening theme) aHead
Now playing
Lonely street aPaul Villepigue
Cherokee/Redskin rhumba#

As preceding

Redskin rhumba (opening theme) aHead
Poor little rich girl aGeorge Siravo
Budandy# aBud Estes and Andy Gibson

July 29–Aug. 4, 1948: Portland, Jantzen Beach Ballroom

Down beat reported that "the crowds were generally so small that Barnet, who came in on a $4,500 guarantee against 60 per cent, never once went into percentage." (Sept. 22, 1948)

Also in the news at this time was the change in ownership of "36 released and unreleased masters" from Apollo to that of Mercury's John Hammond.

Aug. 5, 1948: Pendleton, OR
Aug. 6, 1948: Spokane, Natatorium Park
Aug. 9, 1948: Vancouver, BC, Forum
Aug. 10, 1948: Port Alberni, BC (afternoon) and **Victoria, Booster Club (evening)**
Aug. 11, 1948: Seattle, Trianon Ballroom
Aug. 13, 1948: Eureka, CA
Aug. 14, 1948: Vallejo, CA
Aug. 15, 1948: San Jose, CA
Aug. 16, 1948: Oakland, Sweet's Ballroom
Aug. 20, 1948: Santa Barbara
Aug. 21–28, 1948: Balboa, Rendezvous Ballroom

The band broke up following the Balboa appearance. The press reported that he was going to vacation in South America.

Hollywood, ca. September–October, 1948

"MAKE BELIEVE BALLROOM"

A Columbia feature film (78m) released in 1949 featuring Al Jarvis and Adele Jergens with appearances by Charlie Barnet, Jimmy Dorsey and his orchestra, Frankie Laine, the King Cole Trio, Pee Wee Hunt, Kay Starr, Gene Krupa and his orchestra, Ray McKinley and his orchestra and others.

Charlie Teagarden, tpt; Pee Wee Hunt, tbn; Jan Garber, vn; Jimmy Dorsey, cl; ***Charlie Barnet****, ts; (Harvey Chernap?), b; unknown, g; Ray Bauduc, d*

Joshua fit de battle of Jericho
Video: "Charlie Teagarden" Vernon Prod. (no number); Show 1014

Charlie Teagarden is not seen but made the recording.

The Mab flew into NYC from the Coast and formed a band for an opening at the Carnival on November 19. Rehearsals started on about the 12th.

Sonny Rich, Tommy Allison, Lammar Wright, Doc Severinsen, tpts; Dick Kenney, Ken Martlock, Herb Randell, tbns; Vinnie Dean, lead, Art Raboy, as; Dave Matthews, Kurt Bloom, ts; Danny Bank, bar; Claude Williamson, p; Cliff Leeman, d; Nelson Boyd, b; Frances Lynne, Chuck Clarke, vocals (Edw 65)

Nov. 19–Dec. 16, 1948: NYC, Carnival Ballroom

NYC, Carnival Ballroom, CBS b'cast, Nov. 19, 1948

Redskin rhumba (opening theme) aHead
One morning in May
Say it isn't so vChuck Clarke

As preceding, Nov. 21

Redskin rhumba (opening theme) aHead
#Bunny# aAndy Gibson
Budandy aBud Estes and Andy Gibson

As preceding, Nov. 22

Redskin rhumba (opening theme) aHead
Joyce 1105
Bunny aAndy Gibson
Joyce 1105
Ah, but it happens vChuck Clarke
Joyce 1105
On a slow boat to China vFrances Lynne
Joyce 1105
Skyliner aBilly Moore
Gloria vChuck Clarke
Redskin rhumba (closing theme) aHead

NYC, NBC-TV, Dec. 13, 1948 (8PM EST)

"Eddie Condon's Floor Show no. 13"

Charlie Shavers, tpt; Benny Morton, tbn; ***Charlie Barnet****, ts; Peanuts Hucko, cl; Joe Bushkin, p; Eddie Condon, g; Bob Haggart, b; Buddy Rich, d*

Blues/Ole Miss
Joyce 1035

Dec. 30–Jan. 1, 1948/49: Reading, Rajah Theater

Chapter 6

Be-bop Spoken Here 1949

NYC, Twentieth Century Fox Studios, late 1948, early 1949

"Charlie Barnet and his band"

A "Movietone Melodies" short film (10:25) featuring Charlie Barnet and his orchestra, Frances Lynne, Bunny Briggs, and a dancing couple.

(As seen by viewer:

Tony DiNardi, Doc Severinsen, John Howell, Unidentified, tpts; Ken Martlock, Dick Kenney, Obie Massingill, tbns; Danny Bank, bs; Kurt Bloom, ts; Vinnie Dean, as; [Dave Matthews?], ts; Claude Williamson, p; Cliff Leeman, d; Nelson Boyd, b)

Sideline photography excludes Lammar Wright and Art Raboy.

Redskin rhumba aHead (0:45)
Atlantic jump aAndy Gibson (3:25)
My old flame aAndy Gibson; vFrances Lynne (3:05)
[Melodramatic transition music] (0:14)
East side, west side aAndy Gibson; vBunny Briggs (2:40)

"Charlie Barnet and his band" was also issued by Blackhawk Films in the 1970s.

Jan. 15, 1949: Pottstown, PA, Sunnybrook Ballroom

Dave Burns, Tony DiNardi, John Howell, Doc Severinsen, Lammar Wright, Jr., tpts; Obie Massingill, Ken Martlock, Dick Kenney, tbns; Art Raboy, Vinnie Dean, as; Kurt Bloom, Dave Matthews, ts; Danny Bank, bar; Claude Williamson, p; Eddie Safranski, b; Cliff Leeman, d; Diego Ibarra, bongos; Carlos Vidal, congas

NYC, WMGM Studios, Capitol record session, Jan. 16, 1949

3385 **Eugipelliv** aPaul Villepigue
Cap T 624; *Cap (E) LCT 6018*; *Ajaz 217*; *Cap EAP2 624°*; Smithsonian RC 108; **Cap CDP 212558; Smithsonian RD 108**
3386 **Lonely street** aPaul Villepigue
Cap 15417; *Cap T 624*; *Cap (E) LCT 6018*; *Ajaz 217*; *Cap EAP3 624°*; **Cap CDP 212558**; AFRS BML-P 1293

Jan. 17, 1949: Toronto, Palace Pier
Jan. 21–27,1949: NYC, Apollo Theater
[Wynonie Harris and Bunny Briggs also on bill.]

Dave Burns, tpt, and Carlos Vidal, congas, were replaced by Fern Caron and Francisco Alvarez, resp.

NYC, Apollo Theater, stage performance, between Jan. 21 and 27, 1949

Cherokee aBilly May
Caravan aRalph Burns; feat. Doc Severinsen
Safranski
Rhapsody in blue aJohnny Richards
Smiles/Tea for two

(Jan. 29, 1949?: Columbus, Indian Lake?)

NYC, WMGM Studios, Capitol recording session, Feb. 7, 1949

???? **How high the moon** aDave Matthews
Cap unissued?
3405 **Cu-ba** aGil Fuller
Cap 15417; Cap (E) CL 13151; *Cap T 624*; *Cap (N) and(US) M 11061*; *Cap (E) LCT 6018*; *One Up (E) OU 2008*; *Cap (N) 5C.052 80854*; *Ajaz 217*; *Cap EAP 3 624°*; **Cap CDP 212558**; **Toshiba (Ja) TOCJ 5627**;AFRS BML-P 1265; HERE'S TO VETERANS 107
3406 **Charlie's other aunt** aManny Albam
Cap CDP 212558

Feb. 21–Mar. 13, 1949: NYC, Clique Club

NYC, Clique Club, stage performance, between Feb. 21 and March 13, 1949

Concerto for two trombones feat. Dick Kenney and Obie Massingill
Safranski aPete Rugulo; feat. Safranski
Rhapsody in blue aJohnny Richards
Rockin' in rhythm vBunny Briggs

Charlie Barnet, ts; Claude Williamson, p; Eddie Safranski, b; Specs Powell, d

NYC, "Adventures in Jazz" (WCBS-TV), Feb. 25, 1949

Atlantic jump
East side, west side vBunny Briggs

Wilmington, DE, "Military Ball" (National Guard), ca. early 1949?

Pan-Americana# (6:25)
Good night, ladies

Ray Wetzel, tpt, joined Charlie in late March/early April. It was also about this time that the Gershwin estate ordered Charlie to stop playing *Rhapsody in blue* because "the arrangement was not something to be admired to their way of thinking ... Barnet was also requested to turn parts of the writing over to the executors of the estate so that it could be destroyed. Subsequently the leader changed the title of the music to *Blues on the rhapsody.*" (*Variety* March 9, 1949)

A trumpet-playing friend of Trudy Richards applied for a job with Charlie and brought some audition recordings. Charlie told him the section was full, but "Who's the gal that's singin'?" This was 18-year old Trudy, and she soon wound up with the band. She first had to get permission from her parents and with the understanding that she was to return home by Sept. 1. Trudy remembered, "Later Charlie said, 'OK, now Trudy, do you know a couple of songs, *Easy living*?' I said, 'No.' He said, 'Do you know *Gloomy Sunday*?' I said, 'No.' And he said, 'Well, go out and get Billie Holiday's records and study them. I don't want you to sound like Billie Holiday, but learn these tunes. We're going into a recording session next Thursday for Capitol Records.' I was too young and too dumb to really get scared ... There was a rehearsal at Nola Studios [probably on March 14]. That's when I first heard the band and I was blown away, just blown away. We ran down *Gloomy* and

TELEVISION

8-8:30—Adventures In Jazz: Bill Williams, Charlie Barnet, Bunny Briggs, Fron Warren, Calvin Jackson—WCBS-TV.

Easy living a couple of times, and then all of a sudden we were in a recording studio ... Bobby Sherwood who did the arrangement for 'Easy living' was there." (*Trudy Richards*)

Rolf Ericson, Maynard Ferguson, John Howell, Lammar Wright, Doc Severinsen, tpts; Obie Massingill, Dick Kenney, Ken Martlock, tbns; Vinnie Dean (lead), Art Raboy, as; Kurt Bloom, Dick Hafer, ts; Danny Bank, bar; Claude Williamson, p; Cliff Leeman, d; Eddie Safranski, b; Ivar Jameniz, conga (Edw 65)

NYC, Capitol recording session, March 16, 1949

3727 **Easy living** aBobby Sherwood; vTrudy Richards
Cap 57 592; *Cap (N) and (US) M 11061*; *Cap (E) LCT 6018*; *One Up (E) OU 2008*; *Cap (N) 5C.052 80854*; *Ajaz 217*; **CAP CDP 212558**; AFRS BML-P 1309

3728 **Charlie's other aunt** aManny Albam
Cap (N) and (US) M 11061; *Cap (E) LCT 6018*; *One Up OU 2008*; *Cap (Ja) ECJ 40004*; *Cap (N) 5C.052 80854*; *Ajaz 217*; *Cap EAP1 624º*; **CAP CDP 212558**; **TOSHIBA (JA) TOCJ 5627**; USIA-VOA WORLD OF JAZZ 63

3729 **Overtime** aPete Rugulo
Cap F 15848 (in album CCF 325); *Cap H 325*; *Cap (N) and (US) M 11061*; *Cap (E) LC 6561*; *One Up OU 2008*; *Cap (Eu) T 20396*; *Cap (N) 5C.052 80854*; *Ajaz 217*; *Veteran's Admin. Sound Track Five no.41*; **CAP CDP 212558**; **CAP CDP 98931 2**; **TOSHIBA TOCJ 5627**; HERE'S TO VETERANS 107

3730 **O'Henry** aGil Fuller; vBunny Briggs
Cap 57 592; Cap (E) CL 13151; Cap (Ger) C 80084 [First issue coupled *O'Henry* with *Over the rainbow*. Second issue coupled *O'Henry* with *Pan Americana*]; *Cap T 624*; *Cap (N) and (US) M 11061*; *Cap (E) LCT 6018*; *One Up OU 2008*; *Cap (Eu) T 20396*; *Cap (Ja) ECJ 40004*; *Cap (N) 5C.052 80854*; *Ajaz LP 225*; *Cap EAP2 624º*; **CAP CDP 212558**; **TOSHIBA (JA) TOCJ 5627**; AFRS BML-P 1309; HERE'S TO VETERANS 107

3731 **Portrait of Edward Kennedy Ellington, pt.1** aDave Matthews
Cap 57 60010; Cap (C) 78 144; *Cap T 624*; *Cap (E) LCT 6018*; *Cap (Ja) CR 8811*; *Cap (Ja) ECJ 40004*; *Ajaz LP 225*; *Cap EAP2 624º*; **CAP CDP 212558**; AFRS BML-P 1355

3732 **Portrait of Edward Kennedy Ellington, pt.2** aDave Matthews
Cap 57 60010; Cap (C) 78 144; *Cap T 624*; *Cap (E) LCT 6018*; *Cap (Ja) CR 8811*; *Cap (Ja) ECJ 40004*; *Ajaz LP 225*; *Cap EAP2 624º*; **CAP CDP 212558**; AFRS BML-P 1355

3733 **Rhapsody in blue, pt.1** aJohnny Richards
Swing Era LP 1019; *Ajaz LP 225*; Ajax C 708; **TOSHIBA (JA) TOCJ 5627**

3734 **Rhapsody in blue, pt.2** aJohnny Richards
Swing Era LP 1019; *Ajaz LP 225*; Ajax C 708; **TOSHIBA (JA) TOCJ 5627**

Mar. 18–24, 1949: Washington, DC, Howard Theater

Mar. 29–? , 1949: Chicago, Music Bowl

A silence in Maryland

While the band was based in NYC, it played an engagement at Chesapeake Beach, MD and Terry Slater noted that "...he opened with his new book to an absolute lack of interest by any of those attending. He was greeted with almost a stony silence. Finally, after a set or a set and a half, he looked at the crowd, shrugged his shoulders, and played *Cherokee/Redskin rhumba*. The crowd immediately responded and he went back to his old book for most of the rest of the evening." (*Terry Slater*)

(Mar. 31, 1949?): Canton, OH, Meyers Lake Park

One of Maynard Ferguson's specialties was "Someone to watch over me" and as might be expected it worked up to a high (and higher) note climax. He put himself into it with all his power, and even sometimes beyond it: there were times when he'd black out and Johnny Howell would pull him back into his seat. Manny Albam recalled hearing a clicking noise behind him during one of Maynard's high altitude flights—it was the trumpet players tossing quarters into a derby betting on when Maynard would pass out (*Albam*).

After the appearance in Canton, Maynard jammed at an after-hours place in Cleveland.

NYC, "Here's to Veterans" session, ca. late March–early April, 1949

Redskin rhumba (opening theme) aHead [0:33]
HERE'S TO VETERANS 167
Skyliner aBilly Moore
HERE'S TO VETERANS 167
Cornucopia aPaul Villepigue
HERE'S TO VETERANS 167; *Swing Era LP 1019*
We're in the money (The gold digger's song) [0:08]
Claude reigns aManny Albam
HERE'S TO VETERANS 167
Redskin rhumba (closing theme) aHead [2:15]
HERE'S TO VETERANS 167

For a trumpet specialty four horns would come to the mike. Wetzel would fake having trouble and would miss a note or two, look at his horn, and take out one of the valves. John Howell would then shoot him, and Maynard would walk over Ray's body capping the performance with high notes.

Band members were eating at an all-night diner in Washington when Ray and Reuben Leon started arguing. Ray headed for the door but was shot by Reuben, to the great distress of the waitress who called the police. Charlie thought this gag was hilarious.

April 1–(3?), 1949: Hartford, State Theater
[Wetzel's avoirdupois caused bandstand to collapse]

Rolf Ericson, Doc Severinsen, Ray Wetzel, John Howell, tpts; Maynard Ferguson, tpt and tbn; Obie Massingill, Dick Kenney, Bob "Butter" Burgess, tbns; Ken Martlock, btb; Vinnie Dean, lead, Reuben Leon, as; Dick Hafer, Kurt Bloom, ts; Danny Bank, bar; Claude Williamson, p; Eddie Safranski, b; Cliff Leeman, d; Carlos Vidal, conga

NYC, Capitol recording session, April 2, 1949

3772 **Be-bop spoken here** aPete Rugulo; vDave Lambert, Buddy Stewart; Charlie and Trudy speak
Cap 57 640; Cap (Fr) 325; Cap (E) CL 13128; *Cap (N) and (US) M 11061*; *Cap (N) 5C.052 80854*; *Ajaz LP 225*; **CAP CDP 212558**; **TOSHIBA (JA) TOCJ 5627**; AFRS BML-P 1355
3773 **Gloomy Sunday** aPete Rugulo; vTrudy Richards
Cap 57 640; *Cap (E) CL 13128*; *Ajaz LP 225*; **CAP CDP 212558**; AFRS BML-P 1355

Pete Rugulo had originally arranged *Gloomy Sunday* for Stan Kenton but it became part of Charlie's library due to Stan's inactivity.

April 6–19, 1949: NYC, Paramount Theater

The scene is backstage at the Paramount, Charlie's dressing room, where he is in the depths of a severe hangover. The men are warming up for the first show. Charlie—with his "V" painfully throbbing—storms in and orders quiet. Then just before the second show, several of the men sneak up to his dressing room door and let go a huge blast of sound, which Charlie takes good-naturedly, possibly having taken something to cure his hangover (the juice of a bottle of Dewar's?). (*Dean*)

Bobby Sherwood filled in for two days while Charlie recovered from a strep throat. Bunny Briggs appeared with the band.

May 2, 1949: Providence, RI, Sheraton-Biltmore Hotel (Providence College Junior Prom)
May 8, 1949: New London, Dance Land
May 26–June 8, 1949: NYC, Bop City

Also on the Bop City bill were Billy Eckstine and the Milt Jackson Trio. Variety noted that "Barnet has a hard-driving expertly-trained crew ... Their decibel rating is a bit too high for the ringsiders'

Junior Promenade Souvenir Edition

DANCING
9:00—1:00

THE COWL

GRAND MARCH
11:00 P.M.

VOL. XI, No. 19—TWO PAGES. PROVIDENCE COLLEGE, PROVIDENCE, R. I., MAY 2, 1949 Complimentary Copy

PROMSTERS SWAY THE BARNET WAY

Vocalist

Trudy Richards

Maestro

Charlie Barnet

350 COUPLES ATTEND GALA PROM FORMAL

QUEEN TO BE CHOSEN AFTER GRAND MARCH

Acclaimed by many critics as the greatest sax man of this generation, Charlie Barnet, who plays at the Providence College Junior Prom this evening, has attained a lofty position at the top of the musical ladder by his unfailing insistence on good music above every other consideration.

Tonight's formal festivities will be highlighted by the Grand March at 11:00 p. m. led by the red-sashed committee members and their guests. Immediately after the Grand March the Queen of the Prom will be announced and crowned with appropriate ceremony. The lucky and beautiful first lady will be presented with a silver loving-cup as a momento of the occasion. The Queen's Court will also be chosen at this time.

Guests invited to the Sheraton-Biltmore on this festive night include Governor and Mrs. John O. Pastore, Mayor Dennis J. Roberts, The Very Reverend Robert J. Slavin, O.P., Rev. Jeremiah T. [illegible], O.P. [illegible]

eardrums but this music is tailored to the modern style. Large share of the bebopping is supplied by Barnet's ace trumpeter, Maynard Ferguson…" (*Variety* June 8, 1949).

On hearing his 1936 recording of *Cross patch* during a *Metronome* blindfold test, Charlie responded to Leonard Feather, "What is this? Fletcher Henderson trying to play a pop song? … OH! … I didn't recognize it until that vocal. Well, all I can say is, ever since I quit singing I've been working steadily." (May 1949)

June 10–16, 1949: Virginia Beach, VA, Surf
June 19–25, 1949: Atlantic City, Steel Pier

Danny Bank had asked Manny Albam to write a challenging piece for him—one that was demanding, in a difficult key, etc. *Lemon drop* was the result. Shortly thereafter, Manny replaced Bank (possibly during the Steel Pier stand) and in addition to his sideman duties, he had agreed to contribute two arrangements a week. He found this difficult to do as the road schedule was demanding but he worked on his days off and at odd hours and kept his part of the bargain (though he owed Charlie two charts at the end). A couple of days after Bank had gone, Charlie called *Lemon drop* and Manny had big-time trouble executing the difficult piece. To which Charlie's bland response was, "Well, you wrote it didn't you?"

Charlie asked Manny to write an extended piece not over 20 minutes in length. This turned out to be *Pan Ameri-*

cana which in its original form ran about 18 minutes.

Personnel as preceding but Tiny Kahn (d), replaced Cliff Leeman; Bob Burgess (tbn) left as did Carlos Vidal (cga) and Dave Lambert (v).

Atlantic City, Steel Pier, b'cast, June 22, 1949

Redskin rhumba (opening theme) aHead
Lemon drop aManny Albam
Alamac QSR 2446; Alamac QSR 2446; Drive DE4 42446; **DRIVE DE2 42446**
Portrait of Edward Kennedy Ellington aDave Matthews
Alamac QSR 2446; Alamac QSR 2446; Drive DE4 42446; **DRIVE DE2 42446**
Bebop spoken here aPete Rugulo; vBuddy Stewart, Ray Wetzel
Alamac QSR 2446; Alamac QSR 2446; Drive DE4 42446; **DRIVE DE2 42446**
All the things you are aDennis Farnon
Alamac QSR 2446; Alamac QSR 2446; Drive DE4 42446; Big Band Era (N) 40180; **DRIVE DE2 42446**
The hucklebuck aAndy Gibson
Smooth sailing [no.2, 1949] aManny Albam

On one occasion, Vinnie Dean rose to take a flute solo, and his chair came with him—Charlie having tied the chair to Vinnie's coat, engendering a lot of guffaws.

The following broadcast, reported by Garrod in the 1973 Barnet discography, may have originated from The Steel Pier. It has not been verified by the compiler.

As preceding, b'cast, between June 19 and 25, 1949?

Nobody loves a fat man (until he starts to blow) a(Ray Wetzel?)
Lemon drop aManny Albam
Smooth sailing [no.2, 1949] aManny Albam
Nostalgia aPaul Villepigue
Budandy aBud Estes and Andy Gibson

June 29, 1949: Sandusky, Cedar Point Ballroom

Dave Matthews was reported to have composed "The sextet from Lower Trombovia," a concerto for six trombones. Lyman Vunk, "now an op, busy converting the Great Neck ice rink, on Long Island, to a summer terpery." (*IM* Aug. 1949)

ca. July 15, 1949?: Elk Mountain, Wyo.

July 29–Aug. 28, 1949 (weekends only): Balboa, Rendezvous Ballroom

Balboa, Rendezvous Ballroom, MBS b'cast, between July 29 and Aug. 28, 1949

Redskin rhumba (opening theme) aHead
Wilson—that's all aManny Albam
Rhubarb# aAl Cohn; feat. Rolf Ericson
East side, west side aAndy Gibson; v(Ray Wetzel?)

As preceding

Over the rainbow# aTiny Kahn
Chas me blues aManny Albam
Redskin rhumba (closing theme) aHead

As preceding

Swell and super#
Alamac QSR 2446; Alamac QSR 2446; Drive DE2 42446; **DRIVE DE2 42446**
Laughing boy vBuddy Stewart
Eric the traveler aShorty Rogers
Redskin rhumba (closing theme) aHead

As preceding, July 29, 1949

Bebop spoken here aPete Rugulo; vBuddy Stewart, Ray Wetzel
Alamac QSR 2446; Alamac QSR 2446; Drive DE2 42446; **DRIVE DE2 42446**
Durango aKen Hanna
Alamac QSR 2446; Alamac QSR 2446; Drive DE2 42446; **DRIVE DE2 42446**
Lord Nelson aManny Albam; feat. Eddie Safranski
Alamac QSR 2446; Alamac QSR 2446; Drive DE2 42446; **DRIVE DE2 42446**
Some enchanted evening vTrudy Richards
Lonely street aPaul Villepigue
Alamac QSR 2446; Alamac QSR 2446; Drive DE2 42446; **DRIVE DE2 42446**
T-bone for two#
Alamac QSR 2446; Alamac QSR 2446; Drive DE2 42446; **DRIVE DE2 42446**
Raffles# aAndy Gibson
Alamac QSR 2446; Alamac QSR 2446; Drive DE2 42446; **DRIVE DE2 42446**

<u>*As preceding, July 30, 1949*</u>

Rolf Ericson, Doc Severinsen, Ray Wetzel, Maynard Ferguson, John Howell, tpts; Obie Massingill, Dick Kenney, Kent Larson, tbns; Ken Martlock, btb; Vinnie Dean, (lead), Ruben Leon, as; Dick Hafer, Kurt Bloom, ts; Manny Albam, bar; Claude Williamson, p; Eddie Safranski, b; Tiny Kahn, d; (Carlos Vydal, conga?) (Treichel)

Bop City aManny Albam
Joyce LP 1012
Ill wind aPete Rugulo; vTrudy Richards
Joyce LP 1012
Bebop spoken here aPete Rugulo; vBuddy Stewart, Ray Wetzel
Joyce LP 1012
Claude reigns aManny Albam
Joyce LP 1012
Redskin rhumba (closing theme) aHead
Joyce LP 1012

Add Woody Herman band:

Stan Fishelson, Al Porcino, Shorty Rogers, Ernie Royal, Charlie Walp, tpts; Bill Harris, Earl Swope, Ollie Wilson, tbns; Bart Varsalona, btbn; Sam Marowitz, as; Gene Ammons, Jimmy Giuffre, Buddy Savitt, ts; Serge Chaloff, bar; Lou Levy (and Stan Kenton?), p; Mert Oliver, b; Shelly Manne, d; Terry Gibbs, vbs (Treichel)

Ornithology/More moon aShorty Rogers, et al [announced as *How high the moon*]
Joyce LP 1012

Charlie Barnet and his orchestra

<u>*As preceding, Aug. 5, 1949*</u>

Redskin rhumba (opening theme) aHead
Smooth sailing [no.2, 1949]# aManny Albam
Portrait of Edward Kennedy Ellington aDave Matthews
Lush life vBuddy Stewart

<u>*As preceding, August 6, 1949*</u>

Redskin rhumba (opening theme) aHead
What's this vBuddy Stewart, Ray Wetzel
All the things you are aDennis Farnon; feat. Maynard Ferguson
You're driving me crazy aManny Albam?; vTrudy Richards
Cherokee aBilly May

<u>*As preceding, August 13, 1949*</u>

Contents unknown

Rolf Ericson, Doc Severinsen, Ray Wetzel, John Howell, Maynard Ferguson, tpts; Harry Betts, Dick Kenney, Herbie Harper, tbns; Ken Martlock, btb; Vinnie Di Vittorio (lead), Reuben Leon, as; Dick Hafer, Kurt Bloom, ts; Manny Albam, bar; Claude Williamson, p; Eddie Safranski, b; Tiny Kahn, d; Carlos Vidal, conga (Edwards 65)

<u>**Hollywood, Capitol recording session, August 16, 1949**</u>

4898 **Over the rainbow** aTiny Kahn
Cap 1404; Cap 57 744; Cap (C) 78 153; Cap (E) CL 13477; Cap (Fr) 375; Cap (Ger) C 80084 [First issue coupled *O'Henry* with *Over the rainbow.* Second issue coupled *O'Henry* with *Pan Americana*]; ***Cap F 1404***; *Cap T 624; Sam Goody DNFR 7836; Franklin Mint 93-96; Cap (E) LCT 6018; Cap (Ja) CR 8812, ECJ 40004, ECJ 50073; Ajaz LP 225;* <u>*Cap EAP 3 624*</u>; **Cap CDP 212558; TOSHIBA (JA) TOCJ 5627**; AFRS GI JIVE 2310
4899 **All the things you are** aDennis Farnon
Cap 843; LeeJay 8007; Q-T OfergO-A; Cap (E) CL 13281; ***Cap F 843***; *Sam Goody DNFR 7836; Longines Symphonette Soc. SVS 5386; Moonlight KH1 2; Ajaz LP 225; Swing Era LP 1002, LPS 5001*; **CAP CDP 212558; TOSHIBA (JA) TOCJ 5627 EMI JAZZ 7243 8 55142 27**
4900 **Pan Americana** aManny Albam
Cap 57 744; Cap (C) 78 153; Cap (Fr) 375; Cap (Ger) C 80084 [see note for *Over the rainbow*]; ***Cap F 15609***; *Cap H 235, T 624, T 667; Sam Goody DNFR 7836; Cap (Australia) T 667, H235; CLP 001; Cap (E) LC 6510, LCT 6018; Cap (Ja) CR 8812, ECJ 40004, ECJ 50073; Cap (not US) ST 23346, ST 23737, ST 24630; Ajaz LP 225;* <u>*Cap EAP1 624°*</u>; <u>*Cap EBF 235*</u>; **CAP CDP 212558; TOSHIBA (JA) TOCJ 5627**; AFRS BML-P 1632; AFRS GOLD LABEL LIBRARY P-GL 35

4901 **Ill wind** aPete Rugulo; vTrudy Richards
Cap 843; Cap (E) CL 13281; ***Cap F 843***; *Ajaz LP 225*; **CAP CDP 212558**

4902 **Claude reigns** aManny Albam
Cap 7 1222; Cap (C) 7C 589; Cap (E) CL 13477; ***Cap 6F 1222***; *Cap T 624*; *Cap (N) (US) M 11061*; *Cap (E) LCT 6018*; *One Up (E) OU 2008*; *Cap (Ja) CR 8812, ECJ40004, ECJ 50073*; *Cap (N) 5C.052 80854*; *Ajaz LP225*; *Cap EAP1 624°*; **CAP CDP 212558**; **TOSHIBA (JA) TOCJ 5627**; AFRS BML-P 1802; AFRS GOLD LABEL LIBRARY P-GL 36; HERE'S TO VETERANS 107

4903 **Really?** aManny Albam
Cap 7 1222; Cap (C) 7C 589; ***Cap 6F 1222***; *Cap T 624*; *Cap (N) & (US) M 11061*; *Cap (E) LCT 6018*; *One Up (E)OU 2008*; *Cap (Ja) CR 8812, ECJ 40004, ECJ 50073*; *Cap (N) 5C.052 80854*; *Ajaz LP 225*; *Cap EAP3 624°*; **CAP CDP 212558**; **TOSHIBA (JA) TOCJ 5627**; AFRS BML-P 1802

Capitol 843 and F843 were released in early 1950 but soon withdrawn due to objections by Kern's widow. The two bootleg 78s—Q-T and LeeJay—were probably issued late in 1950. At some later point, perhaps in 1955, at least 100 copies were pressed by Capitol under terms of an arrangement by which record dealers could order out-of-print discs in quantities of at least 100. Capitol personnel unwittingly re-issued this suppressed disc and until these copies came on the market, collectors were paying around $25 for an acetate or pirate issue.

Pete Rugulo had arranged *Ill wind* for the Kenton band but Charlie bought it from him. *Claude reigns* is said to be based on the chords for *The way you look tonight.*

The following broadcasts were reported by Charles Garrod in the 1973 edition of the discography; compiler has not determined if they were preserved in any form.

Balboa, Rendezvous Ballroom, CBS b'cast, Aug. 19, 1949

Redskin rhumba (opening theme) aHead
Swell and super
Ill wind aPete Rugulo; vTrudy Richards
The hucklebuck aAndy Gibson
The four winds and the seven seas
Bebop spoken here aPete Rugulo; vBuddy Stewart, Ray Wetzel
Again
Bunny aAndy Gibson
Lonely street aPaul Villepigue

As preceding MBS b'cast, Aug. 20, 1949

Cherokee aBilly May
Rockin' chair vBuddy Stewart
There'll be some changes made aDave Matthews?
Portrait of Edward Kennedy Ellington aDave Matthews
Nobody loves a fat man (until he starts to blow) a(Ray Wetzel?)
Redskin rhumba aHead

As preceding, between July 30 and Aug. 27, 1949

Chas me blues# aManny Albam
Alamac QSR 2446; Alamac QSR 2446; Drive DE4 42446; Big Band Era (N) 40180; **DRIVE DE2 42446**

Around this time Claude Williamson (p) left the band and was replaced by Gil Barrios. Claude noted that "He'd start the band off with Cherokee, do a couple of tunes and go backstage and drink a while and come back out and play a couple of tunes. Nobody worried about anything, the band swung ... I enjoyed the whole two years..." (Williamson)

Another departee was Trudy Richards who returned to her home on the east coast and was not replaced.

Ray Wetzel, Maynard Ferguson, Doc Severinsen, John Howell, Rolf Ericson, tpts; Dick Kenney, Charles Etter, Ken Martlock, tbns; Vinnie

Di Vittorio, lead, Ruben Leon, as; Dick Hafer, Kurt Bloom, ts; Manny Albam, bar; Gil Barrios, p; Eddie Safranski, b; Tiny Kahn, d; Carlos Vidal, conga; Buddy Stewart, vocals (*Down beat* Oct. 7, 1949)

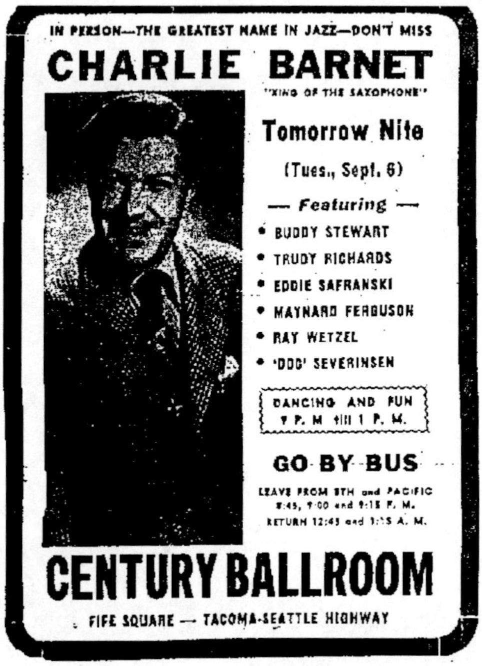

Sept. 3–4, 1949: Portland, Jantzen Beach Ballroom
Sept. 6, 1949: Fife, WA, Century Ballroom
Sept. 7, 1949: Vancouver, BC, The Auditorium
Sept. 8, 1949: Seattle, Trianon Ballroom
Sept. 9, 1949: Yakima, WA, National Guard Armory
Sept. 10, 1949: Spokane, Natatorium Park
Sept. 17, 1949: Bainville, MT

Ken Hanna was reported to have briefly replaced Ray Wetzel. Eddie Safranski, b, left the band and was replaced by Red Kelly "somewhere in the corn fields ... I joined the band in some town in Iowa. They were having a pig festival or something. They were having a whole bunch of pigs in this lot, under tents and things." (*Red Kelly*)

The band came in third in a contest conducted by *Down beat*. Woody was first and Duke second.

Oct. 3–16, 1949: Columbus, Deshler-Wallick Hotel

<u>*Columbus, Deshler-Wallick Hotel, MBS b'cast, between Oct. 3–16, 1949*</u>

Chas me blues aManny Albam
That lucky old sun a(Dave Matthews?); vBuddy Stewart
Bebop spoken here aPete Rugulo; vBuddy Stewart, Ray Wetzel

<u>*As preceding*</u>

Lush life vBuddy Stewart
Chas me blues aManny Albam
That lucky old sun a(Dave Matthews?); vBuddy Stewart
Pan-Americana aManny Albam

While at the Deshler-Wallick the band played the dining room which was downstairs. Charlie liked to go across the street and have a couple of drinks before performing. On a particular evening Tiny Kahn was stationed just inside the hotel watching for the Mab's arrival, and when he was just about to head downstairs, the whole band—armed with cap and water

pistols—on Tiny's signal gunned Charlie down as punishment for his announced decision to break up the band. He went along with the gag (and perhaps summoning up his alleged experiences in Hollywood westerns), yelled, "Ya got me" and fell down the stairs.

The band played for the dinner crowd, about 7–8PM. There were complaints about the loudness of the music so Charlie brought in some stock arrangements that were more in keeping with the staid setting, but after hearing a couple of them, he stopped the band and called one of the loudest things in the book—he just couldn't stand the corn. The management threatened never to hire him again, and he responded, "I don't want to ever work here again."

Oct. 17, 1949: Toronto, Palace Pier
Oct. 18, 1949: London, ON, The Arena
(Oct. 21–28?) 1949: NYC, Apollo Theater

Rolf Ericson, Doc Severinsen, Ray Wetzel, John Howell, Maynard Ferguson, tpts; Chuck Etter, Dick Kenney, tbns; Ken Martlock, btb; Vinnie Di Vittorio (lead), Ruben Leon, as; Dick Hafer, Kurt Bloom, ts; Manny Albam, bar; Gil Barrios, p; Red Kelly, b; Tiny Kahn, d (Edw 65)

NYC, Apollo Theater, b'cast, Oct. 28, 1949

Really aManny Albam
Alamac QSR 2446; Alamac QSR 2446; Drive DE4 42446; **DRIVE DE2 42446**
Nostalgia aPaul Villepigue
Budandy aBud Estes and Andy Gibson
Redskin rhumba (closing theme) aHead

To the great disappointment of the players Charlie broke up the band at the end of the Apollo engagement. On the final night tears flowed as *Redskin rhumba* was played for the last time by that edition of the Barnet aggregation. Vinnie Di Vittorio remembers that The Mab was depressed.

Charlie later ruminated, "As great as that trumpet section was and as startling as the band was, I wasn't too happy with it. That band got out of my control. It was doing things well, but it wasn't doing the things I wanted it to do. I was uncomfortable with the band, although I appreciated it and I was very proud to stand there every night. You'd have to be ... I had arrangers writing for me that were great arrangers, but what they were writing wasn't what I really would [like to have had them do] ... I let the band run me for the first time. And that is why I broke it up ... They were running me. I wasn't running it." (*Sm*)

Chapter 7

Barnetology 1950–1966

Charlie went to work for Carlos Gastel who had helped him out following the Palomar fire in 1939. He came in as a personal manager.

Late in 1949 the "Charlie Barnet All-Stars" was formed using part of Charlie's library. This was a combo which at various times included Ernie Royal, Dave Matthews, Tommy Todd, Delores Parker, Chet Ball and Bud Shank and was led by Bob Dawes. They were active into the early part of 1950 playing the Avadon, Casino Gardens, Shrine Auditorium, Million Dollar Theater and the Pasadena Civic Auditorium.

Ernie Royal, tpt; ***Charlie Barnet****, ts; Nat Cole, p; Irving Ashby, g; Joe Comfort, b; Earl Hyde, d*

Hollywood, Capitol record session, Jan. 5, 1950

Nat King Cole and Nellie Lutcher

5366 **For you my love** vNat Cole, Nellie Lutcher
Cap 847; Cap (E) CL 13275; ***Cap F 847; Cap (E) 12CL 351*** [this is a 12" 45 rpm disc]; ***Cap (E) CL 351;*** *Mosaic MR27 138*; *Official (Den) 12003*; *Music for Pleasure (E) MFP 5198, 1432*; *Kat Wisker (E) NC 1002*; **CAP CDP 96693 2; MOSAIC MD 18 138; OFFICIAL (DEN) 8 12003; BEAR FAMILY (GER) 15910; TOSHIBA (JA) TOCJ 5698; Cap (Ja) ???**

5371 **Can I come in for a second?** vNat Cole, Nellie Lutcher
Cap 847; Cap (E) CL 13275; ***Cap F 847***; *Mosaic MR27 138*; *Official (Den) 12003*; **THE ENTERTAINERS CD 372; CAP CDP 96693 2; MOSAIC MD 18 138; OFFICIAL (DEN) 8 12003; BEAR FAMILY (GER) 15910**

Buddy Stewart was killed in a car accident near Albuquerque on Feb. 1, 1950; Charlie headed up a campaign to raise money for interment.

The Charlie Barnet Septet

Neal Hefti, tpt; Eddie Shu, tpt, cl, as, ts, harmonica; Bob Dawes, bar; Sheldon Smith, p; Charlie Drayton, b; Barret Deems, d; Frances Wayne, vocal

Feb. 13–(19?), 1950: San Diego, Tops
Feb./Mar. 1950: Carrizo, AZ
Feb./Mar. 1950: El Paso
Feb./Mar. 1950: Albuquerque

Frances and Neal left the group after the Albuquerque engagement and headed east. Ray Wetzel came in in place of Hefti.

It was about this time that *All the things you are* was recalled.

Ray Wetzel, tpt; Eddie Shu, reeds, etc.; Bob Dawes, bar; Dick Kenney, tbn; Sheldon Smith, p; Dick Guyat, g; Charlie Drayton, b; Barrett Deems, d

April 6–12, 1950: San Jose, Melody
April 13–26, 1950: San Francisco, New Orleans Swing Club
April 28–May 4, 1950: Pittsburg, CA, Argentine

It was around this time that Charlie began organizing a big band, temporarily headquartering in Sacramento:

Ray Wetzel, John Cappola, Marvin Rosen, John Howell, tpts; Dave Wells, Dick Kenney, Ken Martlock, tbns; Dick Meldonian, Chester Ball, as; Dick Hafer, Claude Gilroy, ts; Bob Dawes, bar; Don Trenner, p; Red Kelly, b; John Markham, d; Bill Derry and Helen Carr, vocals.

May 14, 1950: Portland, Jantzen Beach
June 4, 1950: Dallas, Louann's

The band trekked east, many of the men buoyed on the one-nighters by infusions of maryjane. One evening in Oklahoma City they were "loaded" on the bus waiting for Charlie's Cadillac to show so the caravan could get under way. CB saw all the smoke and shenanigans and Bob Dawes came over and asked them to at least wait till the bus got out of town. From then on the cry in the band was, "Hey Bob, are we out of town yet?" (*Dave Wells*)

Al Porcino was added to the trumpet section by the time the band opened at Bop City. Ray Wetzel and Dick Hafer may have left prior to the eastern trip.

On June 25, 1950, The People's Republic of Korea (North) invaded The Republic of Korea (South).

July 5–18, 1950: NYC, Bop City

It was during this engagement (July 8) that Charlie lost it. "I got in a bind with a wife of mine [Rita Merrit—and the management wanted to pull Bill Derry, who by Charlie's account, was "killing" singer Bill Farrell who was also on the bill] so I don't know, I was drinking and I flipped, and I walked out, we started to play the opening number and I absolutely flipped. I walked out in the middle of the stage in Bop City and I stopped the band. I said, 'I've been wanting to do this all my life. You can all go f--- yourselves.' And I took my soprano and I broke it over my knee and walked out of the club ... got in a taxicab and went to the airport and took a plane to California. Now, that is exactly what happened." The problem with his relationship with Rita may have stemmed from rumors which linked her with Stan Kenton. While in California, a somewhat haggard and unshaven CB showed up at one of Stan's performances at the Rendezvous and after a big production number, the Mab's sepulchral voice was heard from the audience, "Yeah, but it don't swing." *(Wells)*

Domestic bliss was not to come to Charlie until his second marriage to Betty and the road traveled until then was marked by incidents that made life pleasant and unpleasant for both Charlie and his several partners. On one occasion he returned to the hotel room he shared with his wife to find all his socks and underwear cut in pieces. On another, one of his wives "summoned police when she believed Barnet had tried to kill himself because their reconciliation was not working out. She said he had swallowed 21 tablets of a drug prescribed for her. 'I just put them in the side of my mouth to scare her,' Barnet told the investigating officers. 'Then I went outside and spit them out.' He often joked that most of his marriages didn't count because they ended with annulment rather than divorce." (Apropos of not very much, the scissor-wielder was reputed by one of Charlie's band leader colleagues to be extraordinarily skilled in certain intimate practices.)

On about the 12th of July, our man returned to Bop City to finish the engagement. During the interim Curry Wilson, "my valet of 18 years," had arranged to have the soprano repaired.

ca July 22, 1950: Boston area

Carleton McBeath, tpt, and Jack Laird, ts, came into the band at about this time. (*Edw 65*)

NYC, "Dumont Cavalcade of Bands," Dumont telecast, July 25, 1950

Program contents unknown. Mildred Bailey also appeared.

Aug. 3, 1950: Newport, VT, International Club

Apparently the band "one-nightered" its way back the Coast where Charlie broke it up.

Subsequently he used an aggregation which included his long-time associate, Al Killian.

Sept. 2, 1950: Bakersfield, CA, Melody Bowl

Al was part of the group which appeared in Bakersfield, and it was shortly after this engagement—September 5—that he was murdered. "He was, for the record, murdered here in an apartment house in Los Angeles, on East 35th Street, by a janitor who had a death list, and on the death list were a great many members of the Ellington band, but apparently he never got to finish his list." (*Sm*)

Sept. 9, 16, 1950: Los Angeles, Avodon

John Cappola, Buddy Childers, Al Del Simone, tpts; Gene Roland, tpt, vtbn; Lewis McCreary, Dick Kenney, Ken Martlock, tbns; Dick Meldonian, René Bloch, as; Jack Laird, Bill Holman, ts; Bob Dawes, bar; Arnold Ross, p; Ed Mihelich, b; Frank Bode, d; Helen Carr, Bill Derry, vocals.

(Oct. 22–28, 1950: SF, Edgewater???)

Hollywood, Snader Telescriptions session, November 3, 1950 (7–11:36AM)

"SNADER TELESCRIPTIONS"

Skyliner aBilly Moore
Video: Snader Telescription 2901; Swingtime Video 114; Storyville 6005
Audio: *Camay CA 3024*; *New World (E) 5024*

Cherokee aBilly May
Video: Snader Telescription 2902; Swingtime Video 114; Storyville 6005
Audio: *Camay CA 3024*; *New World (E) 5024*

Andy's boogie aAndy Gibson
Video: Snader Telescription 2903; Swingtime Video 114; Storyville 6005
Audio: *Camay CA 3024*; *New World (E) 5024*

Caravan vBill Derry
Video: Snader Telescription 2904
Audio: *Camay CA 3024*; *New World (E) 5024*

My old flame aAndy Gibson; vHelen Carr
Video: Snader Telescription 2905; Storyville 6005; Swingtime Video 114
Audio: Joyce LP 3001

John Capolla, Al Del Simone, tpts; Dick Kenney, Dave Wells, Ken Martlock, tbns; Donn Trenner, p; Ed

Mihelich, b; John Markham, d; Lou Raderman, Paul Nero, Werner Callies, Dave Gelfand, Chuck Clark, Allan Harshman, Bill Spear, Stan Spiegelman, strings

Hollywood, Capitol recording session, Dec. 4, 1950

6877 **Spain** aPaul Villepigue
Cap 1404; ***Cap F1404***; *Cap T 624*; *Cap (E) LCT 6018*; *Cap (Ja) ECJ 40004*; *Ajaz 225*; *Cap EAP1 624°*; **CAP CDP 212558**
6890 **My crime** vBill Derry
CAP CDP 212558
6891 **Theme for Cynthia** aPaul Villepigue
Cap 1394; Cap (C) C 611; ***Cap F1394***; *Ajaz 233*; **CAP CDP 212558**; AFRS BML-P 1802; AFRS GOLD LABEL LIBRARY P-GL 35
6892 **I'm a dreamer, aren't we all?** aPaul Villepigue
Cap 1394; Cap (C) C 611; ***Cap F1394***; *Ajaz 233*; **CAP CDP 212558**; AFRS BML-P 1802

For a southern tour a band was formed in NYC by contractor Hal Miles. There isn't any reliable information as to either the locations played, beyond Phil Woods' comment that it was "the tobacco warehouse circuit," or just when this trip took place. It was in the early 1950s. The men who made this tour may have been about as follows:

Dick Sherman, John Eardley, one other, tpts; Frank Rehak, one other (Urbie Green?), tbns; Phil Woods, as, ts; Shelly Gold, as; Chasey Dean, ts; Hal Miles, bar; Hal Serra, p; Sol Gubin, d; Chuck Andrus, b

"We had a great Manny Albam arrangement of 'Gone with the wind.' It began with eight bars of improvised soprano sax by the Mab. Frank Rehak decided to play along with Charlie's improvisation, which by now was a set piece … the veins started to stick out of Charlie's neck [and the "V" was probably in evidence]. He waved Frank out, but Frank dogged every turn of phrase and nuance and aped Charlie's solo … Charlie turned around and attacked the trombone section. Slides flew everywhere as people screamed and ladies fainted. Charlie got off a right cross to Frank's head and Frank countered with a vicious uppercut … We didn't get paid that night because Charlie stormed out and away. We eventually got our bread." (*Woods*)

Before heading south the band made a second appearance on the Dumont TV Network.

John Cappola, Carleton McBeath, Al Del Simone, Dick Collins, tpts; Ziggy Elmer, Dave Wells, Lew McCreary, tbns; Dick Meldonian, René Bloch, as; Bill Holman, Eddie Wasserman, ts; Bob Dawes, bar; Claude Williamson, p; Ed Mihelich, b; John Markham, d; Adele Frances, Bill Derry, vocals (Down Beat March 9, 1951)

NYC, "Dumont Cavalcade of Bands," Dumont telecast, Feb. 6, 1951

Redskin rhumba (opening theme) aHead
Skyliner aBilly Moore
Pompton Turnpike aBilly May
You're just in love vAdele Frances, Bill Derry
I get a kick out of you
Cherokee aBilly May
Redskin rhumba (closing theme) aHead

Trudy Richards was on this tour, riding with Charlie in his car rather than on the bus with the men—this was part of the deal between the two. During one performance Charlie alerted Trudy to be ready to leave the place early in just what she was wearing (a pink tulle ball gown) and to meet him at his car. Then ensued a mad drive to the Chesapeake Bay ferry as Charlie wanted to get together with a hooker from Washington he'd known for some time. As luck would have it the ferry had left the dock and was on its way to its other terminus. Charlie was furious: "The red "V" was bright enough to light up the place" and he yelled at the ferry "f--- you" repeatedly. This meant a much longer trip to DC and a crimp on his date.

Feb. 7, 1951: Baltimore (site unknown)
Feb. 8, 1951: Clemson, SC, Clemson Univ.
Feb. 9–(21?): Various southern locations
Feb. 22–28, 1951: Apollo Theater
March 8–14, 1951: Washington, Howard Theater

Hollywood, recording session at Capitol studios, March 5, 1951

C747 **Cherokee** aBilly May
Mercury 8981; ***Mercury 8981X45***; *Verve V2007*; *Mercury MG C 114*; *MGM E 4219* (mono), *SE 4219* (stereo); *MGM (E) C 990*; *Clef (Australia) MG C 114*; *Barclay (E) GLP 6592*; *Verve (E) 2317.060*; *Blue Star (Fr) GLP 6923*; *Riviera (Fr) RLP 6592*; *Verve (Ger) 2615.044*; *Verve (Ger) 2304. 541*; *Ajaz 233*; *Clef EP 139*; *Mercury EP 139*; *Karusell (Swed) KEP 208*; THE MUSIC MAKERS 334

C748 **Skyliner** aBilly Moore
Mercury 8979; ***Mercury 8979X45***; *Mercury MG C 114*; *Verve V 2007*; *Clef (Australia) MG C 114*; *Verve (E) 2317.060*; *Blue Star (Fr) GLP 6923*; *Barclay (Fr) GLP 6592*; *Riviera (Fr) RLP 6592*; *Verve (Ger) 2304. 541*; *Ajaz 233*; *Mercury EP 138*; *Mercury EP 114*; VERVE (GER) 833281 2; AFRS BML-P 2789

??? **Tennessee waltz for fun**
Unissued

??? **Redskin rhumba** aHead
Unissued

Vernon Smith, John Cappola, Carleton McBeath, Al Del Simone, tpts; Lewis McCreary, Ziggy Elmer, Dave Wells, tbns; Dick Meldonian, René Bloch, as; Dick Hafer, Ed Wasserman, ts; Bob Dawes, bar; Bob Harrington, p; Paul Saramento, b; John Markham, d; Bill Derry, Adele Frances, vocal (Edw 65)

A band evidently organized for an east coast tour in early May was composed of the following:

Dick Sherman, Dale Pierce, Lyman Vunk, John Vohs, Ziggy Schatz, tpts; Dave Dweck, Jimmy Knepper, Carl Raetz, tbns; Dick Meldonian, Andy Cicalese, as; Dick Hafer, Charlie Kennedy, ts; Bob Dawes, bar; Lou Pagani, p; Art Mease, b; Harold Hahn, d; Eleanor "Ellye" Russell, Bill Derry, vocals (Down beat June 1, 1951)

ca. late May, 1951: Fort Eustis, VA

John Markham, d, replaced Harold Hahn and Vinnie Dean took over the lead alto spot from Dick Meldonian. Trumpeters Kenny Winslet and Al Stewart replaced Vunk and Pierce. Later on Conte Candoli came in for Dick Sherman. Moe Koffman was reported to have replaced Dean.

July 11, 1951: Cobourg, ON, Cobourg Pavilion

Charlie broke up the band on July 12 and at about the same time made final arrangements to give Norman Granz the rights to approximately 24 sides recorded over the last five years. He then headed back to the Coast. A marital note: his divorce from Rita Merritt took place at about this time.

Ray Wetzel died in a car accident on August 17.

Buddy Childers, John Cappola, Carleton McBeath, Jimmy Salco, tpts; Herbie Harper, Ziggy Elmer, Dave Wells, tbns; Dick Meldonian, René Bloch, as; Bill Holman, Jack Laird, ts; Bob Dawes, bar; Claude Williamson, p; Don Prell, b; John Markham, d (Edw 65)

Sept. 1–16 (weekends), 1951: Ocean Park, Casino Gardens

Charlie began lining up a combo for some east coast dates. Reports in the music press and elsewhere mentioned Buck

Clayton and Tyree Glenn as prospective members but the group sorted out about as follows:

Vernon "Geechie" Smith, tpt; Ziggy Elmer, tbn; Bob Harrington, p; Paul Saramento, b; John Markham, d (Edw 67)

(Sept 1951?): El Paso, officers' club
(Oct. 1?)–7, 1951: Philadelphia, Ciro's
Oct. 8–14, 1951: Providence, Celebrity

NYC, Abbey recording session (ca. late October, 1951?)

G 1009 **These foolish things**
Abbey 15063; *Ajaz 233*
G 1010 **Cherokee Trail** [*In a mellow tone*]
Abbey 15063; *Ajaz 233*
Unknown instrumental no.1
Unissued
Unknown instrumental no.2
Unissued

A review in *Down beat* noted that "Robbins Music should be interested in *Cherokee Trail.* They published *In a mellow tone*, composed by Duke Ellington, which is 12 years older than *Cherokee Trail* (composed by Barnet, Gibson, and Johnson) and has the identical melody, the whole 32 bars almost note for note. The lawyers should make more out of this one than Barnet will; musically it ain't that great. Trumpet solo, probably Vernon Smith, provides the best moments. *Things* is a tenor solo. On this kind of thing Charlie has an awful lot of competition nowadays. All in all, a slightly less than sensational debut for the Mab's sextet."

early Nov., 1951: Chicago, Silhouette (17 days)
Nov. 21–25, 1951: Cleveland, Skybar
Nov. 27–Dec. 3, 1951: Boston, Storyville

The following recordings—suspect as to their Barnet content—were probably made in 1951. The labels read "Linda Shannon sings ... Charlie Barnet and the Skyliners" but there's no CB to be heard.

Charlie Barnet and the Skyliners

NYC? Jubilee recording session (1951?)

JB1294 **A million ways to forget** vLinda Shannon
Jubilee 5144
JB1295 **How d'ya do do do** vLinda Shannon
Jubilee 5144

A band was formed for a series of engagements on the Coast:

Vernon Smith, Hal Moe, O'Neill Dell, Stuart Williamson, tpts; Tex Satterwhite, Don Maddox [soon replaced by Chuck Etter], Karl De Karske, tbns; Dick Meldonian, Dick Paladino, as; Bill Holman, Otto Stampe, ts; Bob Dawes, bar; Bob Harrington, p; Johnny Markham, d; Paul Saramento, b; Jeri Brock, vocals

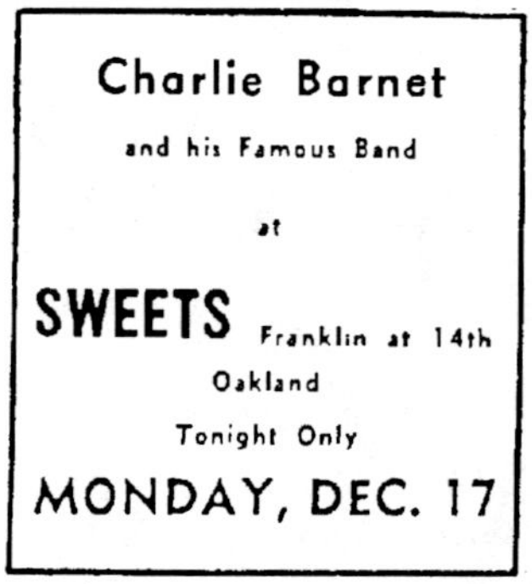

Dec. 15, 1951: LA, Zenda Ballroom
Dec. 17, 1951: Oakland, Sweet's
(Dec. 19?, 1951): Coos Bay, OR, Elks' Club
Dec. 21, 1951: Eugene, OR, Fern Ridge Ball Room
Dec. 22, 1951: Portland, Jantzen Beach
(Dec. 23, 1951?): Lewiston, ID, (Elks' Club?)

A *Down beat* report indicated that Charlie had a combo at The Harlem in Philadelphia late in December. This hasn't been confirmed.

Ernie Edwards in his 1967 edition of the Barnet discography noted that a rehearsal band was formed early in 1952 in Hollywood made up of these players:

Vernon Smith, Stu Williamson, Charles Caudle, Bill Castagnino, tpts; Herbie Harper, Dick Kenney, Dave Wells, tbns; Dick Paladino, as; Bill Holman, Kurt Bloom, ts; Don Davidson, bar; Bob Harrington, p; Don Prell, b; John Berger, d

Personnel unknown.

Hollywood, Decca recording session, April 11, 1952

Peter Lind Hayes with orchestra directed by Charlie Barnet

L6721-A **Beware of the bear (with the chartreuse hair)** vPeter Lind Hayes
De 28205°; *De 9 28205°*; AFRS BML-P 2420

(The other side of this disc, *You're so much a part of me* with vocal by Hayes and Mary Healy, does not credit the accompaniment. Charlie is not audible on either song. His name may have been included on *Beware* because the song was published by his firm, Indigo Music.)

Unidentified tpt, tbn, saxophone, piano, bass, drums

Charlie Barnet and his sextet

Hollywood, "AFRS Jubilee," ca. early May 1952

In a mellow tone
AFRS JUBILEE 369
Chico's surprise
AFRS JUBILEE 369

In the spring of 1952 Willie Smith had left Duke Ellington to join Billy May's big band and this brought about an interesting "Might Have Been": it seems that the Duke entertained the idea of replacing Willie with Charlie. "He offered me a job … He called me and said, 'I know I can't pay you what you're used to getting, but, would you consider coming with the band for a while?' And I think I would have except I already had a tour booked with my own band and I couldn't." (Palm Springs *Desert Sun*, Aug. 24, 1989)

May 6–June 8, 1952: Hollywood, Royal Room

Guy Key (Chiaverini), Ken Winslet, Charlie Caudle, tpts; Dick Taylor,

John Soltaine, Dick Kenney, tbns; Bud Shank (lead), Stan Seckler, as; Red Norman, Dick Paladino, ts; Don Davidson (preceded by Bob Dawes), bar; Bob Harrington, p; Bob Peterson, b; Bill Dolney, d

The band went on tour starting from Long Beach. The Air Force flew the band to its first two dates.

June 10, 1952: Mountain Home, ID, AFB
June 11, 1952: Marfa, TX , Texas Club
June 13–26, 1952: Galveston, Pleasure Pier
June 27, 1952: Shreveport, Crystal Ballroom (W.Y. Hotel)
June 28, 1952: Greenville, MS, AFB
June 29, 1952: Shreveport, Officers' Club, Barksdale Field June 30, 1952: Ft. Worth, Will Rogers Aud.
July 1, 1952: Magnolia, AR, Magnolia Country Club
July 2, 1952: Mountain Home, AR, HS Gym
July 3, 1952: Tulsa, Tulsa Country Club
July 4, 1952: Oklahoma City, Persian Room Skirvin Tower Hotel
July 5, 1952: Ft. Worth, Casino
July 6, 1952: Shreveport, NCO Club, Barksdale Field
July 8, 1952: Houston, Plantation Club
July 9, 1952: Yorktown, TX, Cotton Patch

Bud Shank left the band on July 10 and was replaced by Dick Paladino who moved into the lead alto chair. Paladino's tenor spot was filled by Kurt Bloom. It may have been at this time that Marilyn Moore, vocals, joined.

July 10, 1952: San Antonio, Seven Oaks
July 12–13, 1952: Ft. Worth, Casino
July 15, 1952: Biloxi, Keesler Field
July 17, 1952: San Antonio, Sunken Gardens
July 18, 1952: San Marcos, TX, NCO Club, AFB
July 19, 1952: Ft. Worth, Casino
July 20, 1952: Wichita Falls, TX, NCO Club, Sheppard Field
July 21, 1952: Ardmore, OK, Club Willow

Guy Key (tpt) and Dick Taylor (tbn) left and were replaced by Bobby Nichols and O. B. Massingill.

July 23–27, 30, 1952: Wichita, KS, Mambo Club
Aug. 2, 1952: Clarksville, TN, Dunbar Cave
Aug. 6, 1952: Ft. Benning, GA, Post Theater—Officers' Club
Aug. 7, 1952: Camp Rucker, AL, Shows Theaters 1-3
Aug. 8, 1952: Selma, AL, NCO Club, Craig AFB
Aug. 9, 1952: Panama City, FL, Officers' Club, Tyndall AFB
Aug. 10, 1952: Panama City, FL, NCO Club, Tyndall AFB
Aug. 11–13, 1952: Jacksonville, FL, Officers' Mess, USNAS
Aug. 14, 1952: Milton, FL, EM Club, USNAS Whiting Field
Aug. 15, 1952: Moultrie, GA, S.E. Tobacco Festival
Aug. 16, 1952: Selma, AL, Officers' Club, Craig AFB
Aug. 17, 1952: Montgomery, AL, Progressive Club
Aug. 18, 1952: Ft. Benning, NCO Mess, Pine Lodge
Aug. 19, 1952: Camp Rucker, AL, Officers' Mess
Aug. 20, 1952: Sumter, SC, NCO Mess, Shaw AFB
Aug. 21, 1952: Savannah, Moose Club
Aug. 22, 1952: Columbia, SC, Officers' Mess, Fort Jackson
Aug. 23, 1952: Greenville, SC, Officers' Mess, Donaldson AFB
Aug. 24, 1952: Sumter, SC, Officers' Mess, Shaw AFB
Aug. 25, 1952: Columbia, SC, NCO Club, Fort Jackson
Aug. 26–28, 1952: Norfolk, VA, Officers' Club, USNAS
Aug. 29, 1952: Cherry Point, NC, USMC Air Station
Aug. 30, 1952: Hadnot Point, Camp LeJeune

On Aug. 31 Al Porcino and Dick Sherman "da muscle from da Apple" (as Porcino described the two) came in and Caudle and Winslet left.

Aug. 31, 1952: Washington, NCO Open Mess, Bolling AFB
Sept. 1, 1952: Glen Echo, MD, Glen Echo Park

Further changes were made for the Verve recording session with the addition of Doc Severinsen and others so that the personnel were as follows:

Dick Sherman, Al Porcino, Doc Severinsen, Wayne Nichols, Charlie Shavers, tpts; Obie Massingill, Dick Kenney, John Soltaine, tbns; Dick Paladino, Stan Seckler, as; Ray Norman, Kurt Bloom, ts; Don Davidson, bar; Hank Jones, p; Mundell Lowe, g; Bob Peterson, b; Don Lamond, d

NYC, Reeves Studio, Verve recording session, Sept. 2–4, 1952

YB853-5 **Durango** aKen Hanna? [Tbn solo by Dick Kenney]
Mercury 89015; ***89015X45***; *Clef MG C 139*; *Clef (Australia) MG C 139*; *Ajaz 233*; *Swing Era LP 1002, LPS 5001*; ***Clef EP 156***

YB854-7 **St. Louis blues** aAndy Gibson
Clef MG C 139; *Verve V 2007*; *Clef (Australia) MG C 139*; *Verve (Ger) 2304.541*; *Ajaz 233*

YB855-3 **Swingin' down the lane** aPaul Villepigue
Mercury/Clef 89049; ***Mercury 89049X45***; *Clef MG C 139*; *Verve V 2007*; *Clef (Australia) MG C 139*; *Verve (Ger) 2304.541*; *HMV (E) CLP 1143*; *World Record Club (E) T 303* [mono and stereo]; *Ajaz 233*

YB856-1 **Who's sorry now** aPaul Villepigue
Clef MG C 139; *Verve V 2007*; *Clef (Australia) MG C 139*; *Verve (Ger) 2304.541*; *Ajaz 233*

YB857-9 **Let's blow the blues** aGene Roland
Mercury 89015; ***Mercury 89015X45***; *Clef MG C 139*; *Verve V 2007*; *Clef (Australia) MG C 139*; *Verve (Ger) 2304.541*; *HMV (E) CLP 1143*; *World Record Club (E) T 303* [mono and stereo]; *Ajaz 233*; ***Clef EP 156***

YB858 **Fur trapper's boogie** aAndy Gibson
Mercury 89016; ***Mercury 89016X45***; *Clef MG C 139*; *Verve V 2007*; *Clef (Australia) MG C 139*; *Verve (Ger) 2304.541;jaz 233*; ***Clef EP 156***

YB859-3 **Rhubarb** aAl Cohn [ts solo by Ray Norman]
Clef/Mercury 89049; ***Mercury 89049X45***; *Clef MG C 139*; *Verve V 2007*; *Clef (Australia) MG C 139*; *Verve (Ger) 2304.541*; *HMV (E) CLP 1143*; *World Record Club (E) T 303* [mono and stereo]; *WS (E) TP 330*; *Ajaz 233*

YB860-3 **Rose room** aPaul Villepigue
Clef MG C 638; *Verve MG V 2027*; *Ajaz 273*

YB861-6 **I love you** (Wright, Forrest) aPaul Villepigue
Clef MG C 638; *Verve MG V 2027*; *Ajaz 273*

YB862-8 **Wosie posie** aAndy Gibson
Clef/Mercury 89016; ***Mercury 89016X45***; *Clef MG C 139*; *Clef (Australia) MG C 139*; *Verve V 2007*; *Verve (Ger) 2304.541*; *Ajaz 273*; ***Clef EP 156***; USIA-VOA WORLD OF JAZZ 63

YB863-3 **Sleepy time gal** aPaul Villepigue [Tbn solo by Dick Kenney]
Clef MG C 638; *Verve MG V 2027*; *Ajaz 273*

YB864-6 **Keep the home fires burning** aAndy Gibson
Clef MG C 638; *Verve MG V 2027*; *HMV (E) CLP 1143*; *World Record Club (E) T 303*; *WS (E) TP 330*; *Ajaz 273*

"On a break between the two dates on the second day, Charlie's mother came in to the studio with a large cart full of booze, ice and mixes for the band which was her contribution to successful recordings." (*Don Davidson*)

The tour resumed with approximately the pre-recording session line-up.

Sept. 5–12, 1952: St. John's, NF, Pepperrell AFB

While in Newfoundland Marilyn Moore had appendicitis and was replaced by Lois "Torchy" Barcroft for about a week. Hard liquor sold for 50 cents a fifth on the base but mixes—imported from the States—were very expensive. (*Don Davidson*)

Sept. 13–17, 1952: Argentia, Nfld., McAndrews AFB

Sept. 18, 1952: St. John's, Nfld., Pepperrell AFB

Sept. 20–21, 1952: Hartford, State Theater (with R.Q. Lewis)

Sept. 26–Oct. 2, 1952: Washington, Howard Theater

Oct. 3–9, 1952: NYC, Apollo Theater
(Others on the bill: Slim Gaillard, Bunny Briggs, Pigmeat Markham, Marilyn Moore, and The Dyerettes)

"During the Apollo stand Dick Sherman brought in test records of the Reeves Studio efforts including *Durango* and *Sleepytime gal*, both of which had beautiful solos by Dick Kenney, and Kenney made the comment, after hearing *Sleepytime*, 'That's pretty good. I'll have to write that out and learn it!'" (*Don Davidson*)

Don Davidson, bar, left the band on Oct. 13.

Oct. 24–25, 1952: Hamilton, ON, Brant Inn

Dick Sherman, Al Porcino, Doc Severinsen, Sonny Rich, Bill Castagnino, tpts; Obie Massingill, Dick Kenney, John Soltaine, tbns; Dick Paladino, Shelly Gold, as; Ray Norman, Kurt Bloom, ts; Sol Schlinger, bar; Harvey Leonard, p; Bob Carter, b; Sol Gubin, d (*Edw 65*)

Hamilton, ON, Brant Inn, CHML b'cast, Oct. 25, 1952

Redskin rhumba (opening theme) aHead
Swingin' down the lane aPaul Villepigue
Be anything but be mine vMarilyn Moore
Rose room aPaul Villepigue
Laura
That old black magic aAndy Gibson; vMarilyn Moore
Sleepy time gal aPaul Villepigue
Walkin' my baby back home vMarilyn Moore
Wosie posie aAndy Gibson
All of me
Redskin rhumba (closing theme) aHead

In approximately December further changes took place when Paul Webster, tpt, replaced Dick Sherman.

During the first quarter of 1953 the band's line-up looked something like this:

Kenny Winslet, Dick Hoffman, Al Stuart , Jerry Marshall, Bill Castagnino, tpts; Obie Massingill, Dick Kenney, John Soltaine, tbns; Shelly Gold, Phil Woods, as; Ray Norman, Kurt Bloom, ts; Hal Miles, bar; John Williams, p; Phil Leshin or Chuck Andrus, b; Frank Widder (later replaced by Phil Arabia), d (*Edw 67* and *Down beat* Mar. 25, 1953)

This band is believed to have toured the south.

By April Charlie had switched to a combo to take advantage of an offer to play Martha Raye's Five O'clock Club.

Charlie Barnet and his Quartet

Dick Kenney, tbn and b; Jerry Marshall, tpt; Hal Serra, p; Sol Gubin,d

Apr. 22–ca Aug., 1953: Miami, Five O'clock Club
Sept. 22–Oct. 18, 1953: Detroit, Crest Lounge

Jack Hitchcock, tbn and vbs; Hal Serra, p; Karl Kiffe, d; Roy Shaine, b

Oct. 19–24, 1953: Toronto, Colonial

Karl Kiffe, d, was replaced by Jo Jones at about this time.

Nov. 1953?: Boston, Hi Hat Club

Boston, Hi Hat Club, b'cast, ca. Fall 1953

Caravan
Blues#
Ol' Man River

As preceding

Perdido
Ol' Man River
Jumpin' with Symphony Sid#
Lover, come back to me

Dec. 2–6, 1953: Chester, PA, El Rancho
(Dec. 29?)–Jan. 5, 1954: East St. Louis, IL, Terrace Lounge

Munroe Shain, tpt; Jack Hitchcock, tbn and vbs; Sir Charles Thompson, p; Jo Jones, d

(Jan. 6?, 1954)–??: NYC, Café Society

Neal Hefti and his orchestra

Billy Butterfield, Bernie Privin, tpts; Lou McGarity, tbn; Charlie Barnet, as; Hank D'Amico, cl & as; Boomie Richman, ts; Danny Bank, bar; Lou Stein, p; Danny Perri, g; Chet Amsterdam, b; Jimmy Crawford, d; Ray Charles Singers, vocals

NYC, Columbia recording session, March 9, 1954

51030 **Redskin rhumba** (aNeal Hefti?)
Epic LG 1013, LG 3113, LN 3440; Philips (N) 21699 H; Epic EG 7064, EG 9006

Charlie Barnet and his quartet

Possible personnel:

Munroe Shain, tpt; Jack Hitchcock, tbn and vbs; Sir Charles Thompson, p; Jo Jones, d

Apr. 20–26, 1954: Washington, DC, Club Trinidad

Band with unidentified personnel—save possibly for Phil Woods—played at the Apollo Theater May 14–20.

Down beat (July 15, 1954) reported that Charlie was in the Bay Area "for a series of June one-nighters."

Charlie Barnet Quintet

Buddy Childers, tpt; Bob Harrington, p; Ralph Pena, b; Artie Anton, d; Ann Richards, vocals

June 25–ca. July 10, 1954: Las Vegas, El Rancho

One of the couples in the El Rancho audience was honeymooning and enjoying the music when the groom saw a bald-headed guy with a beautiful young lady on each arm come into the lounge and exchange greetings with Charlie. He soon realized that this was none other than Artie Shaw who was also performing in LV (at the Sahara) and who had dropped by on a break to say hello. (Artie and Red Norvo had been "best men" at one of Charlie's early marriages.)

Nov. 16–Nov. (26?), 1954: Hollywood, Celebrity Club

Charlie Barnet and his orchestra

Pete Candoli, Buddy Childers, Maynard Ferguson, John Best, tpts; Herbie Harper, Si Zentner, Tommy Pederson, Milt Bernhart, tbns; Willie Smith, Fred Falensby, as; George Auld, Chuck Gentry, ts; Bob Dawes, bar; Bob Harrington, p; Tony Rizzi, g; Sam Cheifetz, b; Alvin Stoller, d

Hollywood, Victor recording session, Nov. 29, 1954

E4VB 4594-4 **Lullaby of Birdland** aPaul Villepigue
Vi LPM 1146; Big Band Archives BBA 1209; Ajaz 273; Vi EPA 673

E4VB 4595-5 **By the waters of Minnetonka** aPaul Villepigue
Vi LPM 1091; Vi (Australia) L 10033; Fresh Sound (Sp) NL 45977; Ajaz 273; Vi EPB 1091 2°; RCA (Sp) 74321421292

E4VB 4596-13 **Comanche war dance** aBilly May (1954)
Vi LPM 1091; *Vi (Australia) L 10033*; *Fresh Sound (Sp) NL 45977*; *Ajaz 273*; ***Vi EPB 1091 1°***; **RCA (SP) 74321421292**

Pete Candoli, Conrad Gozzo, Buddy Childers, Maynard Ferguson, Carleton McBeath, tpts; Milt Bernhart, Si Zentner, Tommy Pederson, Herbie Harper, tbns; Willie Smith, as; Georgie Auld, Fred Falensby, ts; Bob Dawes, bar; Bob Harrington, p; Tony Rizzi, g; Sam Cheifetz, b; Alvin Stoller, d

Hollywood, Verve recording session, Dec. 1, 1954

2093-4 **Who's your hoosier** aBilly May
Clef MG C 638; *Verve MG V 2027*; *HMV (E) CLP 1143*; *World Record Club (E) T 303* [mono and stereo]; ***Clef EP 276***

2094-2 **Argo** aBilly May
Clef MG C 638; *Verve MG V 2027*; *HMV (E) CLP 1143*; *World Record Club (E) T 303* [mono and stereo]; ***Clef EP 276***

2095-1 **Bluehound bus greys** aBilly May [6:10]
Clef MG C 638; *Verve MG V 2027*; *HMV (E) CLP 1143*; *World Record Club (E) T 303* [mono and stereo]; ***Clef EP 275***

2096-4 **Things ain't what they used to be** aAndy Gibson
Clef MG C 638; *Verve MG V 2027*; *HMV (E) CLP 1143*; *World Record Club (E) T 303* [mono and stereo]; *Verve (Eu) 2352.099*; ***Clef EP 275***

Conrad Gozzo, Buddy Childers, Maynard Ferguson, John Best, tpts; Herbie Harper, Si Zentner, Tommy Pederson, Dick Nash, tbns; Willie Smith, Fred Falensby, as; Georgie Auld, Chuck Gentry, ts; Bob Dawes, bar; Bob Harrington, p; Tony Rizzi, g; Joe Mondragon, b; Alvin Stoller, d

Hollywood, Victor recording session, Dec. 6, 1954

E4VB 5227-6 **Wahoo's lament** aBilly May
Vi LPM 1091; *Vi (Australia) L 10033*; *Fresh Sound (Sp) NL 45977*; *Ajaz 273*; ***Vi EPA 612°***; **RCA (SP) 74321421292**

E4VB 5228-5 **Indian love call** aBilly May
Vi LPM 1091; *Vi (Australia) L 10033*; *Fresh Sound (Sp) NL 45977*; *Ajaz 273*; ***Vi EPB 1091 2°***; **RCA (SP) 74321421292**

E4VB 5229-5 **Iroquois** aBilly May
Vi LPM 1091; *Vi (Australia) L 10033*; *Fresh Sound (Sp) NL 45977*; *Ajaz 273*; ***Vi EPB 1091 1°***; **RCA (SP) 74321421292**

E4VB 5230-3 **Cherokee** aBilly May (1954)
Vi LPM 1091; Vi (Australia) L 10033; Fresh Sound (Sp) NL 45977; Ajaz 273; ***Vi EPB 1091 2°***; **RCA (SP) 74321421292**

E4VB 5231-10 **Indian summer** aBilly May
Vi LPM 1091; *Vi (Australia) L 10033*; *Fresh Sound (Sp) NL 45977*; *Ajaz 273*; ***Vi EPB 1091 1°***; **RCA (SP) 74321421292; READER'S DIGEST RBD 114/CDI**

Personnel as above except Milt Bernhart replaced Dick Nash, Sam Cheiftez replaced Joe Mondragon and Jack Costanzo, bongoes, was added.

Hollywood, RCA Victor recording session, Dec. 20,1954

E4VB 5248-4 **Pale moon** aBilly May
Vi LPM 1091; *Vi (Australia) L 10033*; *Fresh Sound (Sp) NL 45977*; *Ajaz 273*; ***Vi EPA 612°***; **RCA (SP) 74321421292**

E4VB 5249-5 **From the land of the sky-blue water** aPaul Villepigue
Vi LPM 1091; *Vi (Australia) L 10033*; *Fresh Sound (Sp) NL 45977*; *Ajaz 273*; ***Vi EPB 1091 1°***; **RCA (SP) 74321421292**

E4VB 5250-4 **Seminole** aBilly May (1954)
Vi LPM 1091; *Vi (Australia) L 10033*; *Fresh Sound (Sp) NL 45977*; ***Vi EPB 1091 2°°***; **RCA (SP) 74321421292**

E4VB 5251-5 **Along the Santa Fe Trail** aBilly May
Vi LPM 1091; *Vi (Australia) L 10033*; *Fresh Sound (Sp) NL 45977*; ***Vi EPA 612°***; **RCA (SP) 74321421292**

E4VB 5252-11 **Redskin mambo** aBilly May
Vi LPM 1091; *Vi (Australia) L 10033*; *Fresh Sound (Sp) NL 45977*; ***Vi EPA 612°***; **RCA (SP) 74321421292**

Personnel unknown.

Feb./Mar. 1955: Southgate, Trianon Ballroom (weekends)

Allen Smith, tpt; Richard Wyands, p; Eric Miller, g; Vernon Alley, b; Gus Gustafson, d (*Down beat* Apr. 20, 1955)

March 14–ca. March 27, 1955: SF, Fack's

A tour by a band fronted by Charlie and Ike Carpenter took place sometime during the 1950s. Each would lead the band when playing his own charts. The band lasted about two months, toured the Pacific Northwest and broke up at Lake Tahoe after an engagement there. "Hey Ike, leave me a few notes to play, huh?" was Charlie's remark after Ike had played one of his ornamental specials. (*Ernie Small*) The lineup for this band may have been about as follows:

Diz Mullens, Carleton McBeath, Buddy Ptacheck, tpts; Richie Gillum, Charlie Fite, tbns; Bob Jung, as; Lanny Morgan, as and bar; Ken Downing, Jack Kernan, ts; Ernie Small, tbn and bar; Ike Carpenter, p; Don Payne, b; Gary Frommer, d (*Edw 65*)

Personnel unknown.

May 1, 1955: Cleveland, Crystal Beach
(May 1955?): Sandusky, Cedar Point

NYC, "Friday with Garroway," NBC-TV, June 3, 1955

Program content unknown

Other bands which appeared on this occasion were those of Ozzie Nelson, Glen Gray, the Dorseys, Larry Clinton and the Glenn Miller orch.

Lee Castle, Al Stewart, Doc Severinsen, Ernie Royal, Charlie Shavers, tpts; Harry Di Vito, Obie Massingill, John Soltaine, tbns; Vinnie Dean, Buzzy Brauner, as; Peanuts Hucko, George Berg, ts; Charlie Fowlkes, bs; Howard Smith, p; Bob Carter, b; Louis Bellson, d (Hall 70)

NYC, "America's Greatest Bands" (Paul Whiteman), CBS-TV, July 30, 1955

Comanche war dance aBilly May (1954)
Joyce 1081
Bluehound bus greys aBilly May
Joyce 1081
Skyliner aBilly Moore
Joyce 1081; Big Band Era 40180 (Neth)

NYC, "Jackie Gleason Show," CBS-TV, Aug. 8, 1955

Seminole aBilly May
Bluehound bus greys aBilly May
Skyliner aBilly Moore

Personnel unknown for this appearance:

Aug. 19, 1955: SF, Civic Auditorium

Charlie headed a combo for this appearance:

ca. Oct. 1955: Hollywood, Melody Room

Lee Mack and Kenny Hing and possibly Sam Schlichting, reeds; Fred McKinney, p; others unknown (These men were from Portland and totaled about 12 players)

Oct. 29, 1955: Bellingham, WA, National Guard Armory (WWCE homecoming)

A combo which included Buddy Childers and Harry Babasin played various engagements in the Pacific Northwest.

Charlie Barnet and his All Stars

Buddy Childers, tpt; Arnold Ross, p; Paul Saramento, b; Boone Stines, d

Dec. 23, 1955–Jan. 12, 1956: Miami Beach, Dream Bar

Miami, "Steve Allen Show" (NBC-TV), Jan. 13, 1956

Cherokee
Joyce 1081; Big Band Era (N) 40180
Perdido

Fine and dandy
Joyce 1081; Big Band Era (N) 40180

Jan. 17–23, 1956: Nassau, Bahamas, Cat and Fiddle
Jan. 26–Feb. 8, 1956: Palm Beach, Monte Cristo Hotel
(March?) 1956: Hollywood, Peacock Lane

Personnel unknown.

Hollywood, Universal Studios, ca. late April 1956

"BRIGHT AND BREEZY"

A Universal short film with Charlie Barnet and his orchestra, Romo Vincent, The King Sisters and The Sportsmen Quartet. (15m)

Skyliner aBilly Moore (1:27)
You were meant for me vRomo Vincent (1:49)
Lullaby of Birdland vKing Sisters (1:49)
Smooth sailing [no.2, 1949] aManny Albam (1:25)
Shadrack vSportsmen Quartet (2:56)
Easy street vRomo Vincent (2:06)
Open up your heart vRomo Vincent, King Sisters, Sportsmen Quartet (1:36)

Possible personnel:

Ray Triscari, John Audino, Al Porcino, Joe Triscari, Jack Holman, tpts; Juan Tizol, vtb; Frank Lane, Lewis McCreary, Walt Malzahn, tbns; Bob Jung, as; Lanny Morgan, as & bar; Dave Madden, Jack Kernan, ts; Bob Dawes, bar; Buddy Motsinger, p; Harry Babasin, b; Jack Sperling, d

Los Angeles, "Stars of jazz" KABC-TV telecast, May 15, 1956

Skyliner aBilly Moore
Audio: *Calliope 3031*
Argo aBilly May
Audio: *Calliope 3031*
My old flame aAndy Gibson; vMary Lou Martin
Audio: *Calliope 3031*
Who's your Hoosier aBilly May
Audio: *Calliope 3031*
Cherokee aBilly May
Audio: *Calliope 3031*

"Of course we never played [the Palladium] because they wouldn't hire a band that was mixed. Well, I lost the Palladium, but I don't consider it a loss, because at that time there were so many other ballrooms in California that actually paid just as good or better money ... but I later played it and without any problems." He played the Palladium for the first time on June 20. Shorty Rogers and his Giants were also on the week-end bill.

Ralph Mullins, Ollie Mitchell, Carleton McBeath, Buddy Ptacheck, tpts; Bob Burgess, Dave Wells, Roy Anderson, tbns; Dick Paladino, as; Ernie Small, tbn, as, bar; Bill Holman, Ken Downing, ts; Bob Dawes, bar; Norman Pockrandt, p; Red Wooten, b; Jackie Mills, d; Mary Lou Martin and Lynn Franklin, vocals (*Edw 65*)

June 20, 1956–July 1: Hollywood, Palladium

"Is this a record? Orchestra leader Charlie Barnet tells me that none of his nine unsuccessful marriages has ever cost him alimony. Two did result in settlements. Incidentally, two of Charlie's ex-wives, Rita Barnet and Betty Reilly, attended his opening at the Palladium." (*Harrison Carroll, LA Herald,* June 22, 1956)

Hollywood, Palladium, NBC b'cast, June 23, 1956

Redskin rhumba (opening theme) aHead
I get a kick out of you aBill Holman
My old flame aAndy Gibson; vLynn Franklin
Who's your Hoosier aBilly May
You'd be so nice to come home to aRuss Garcia; vLynn Franklin
Moonglow/Picnic aBill Holman
Wosie posie aAndy Gibson
Too close for comfort vLynn Franklin
The great lie aAndy Gibson
Redskin rhumba (closing theme) aHead
[recorded by Wally Heider]

As preceding, June 30, 1956

Redskin rhumba (opening theme) aHead
Lullaby of Birdland aBilly May
You'd be so nice to come home to aRuss Garcia; vLynn Franklin
Comanche war dance aBilly May (1954)
Mister Wonderful vLynn Franklin
Creole love call aAndy Gibson
Stella by starlight aNeal Hefti
Too close for comfort vLynn Franklin
Skyliner aBilly Moore
Redskin rhumba (closing theme) aHead

As preceding?

Program contents unknown
ONS 4676A

As preceding?

[Note that these songs were reported by Edwards as being aired from the Palladium; they appear to be from more than one broadcast. Not researched by compiler. It isn't known if these were preserved in any form]

A Sunday kind of love vMary Lou Martin
All of me
Canadian sunset
Come rain or come shine vMary Lou Martin
Deep purple
I got it bad (and that ain't good) vMary Lou Martin
Jubilee jump
Lemon twist
Now! baby, now! vMary Lou Martin
Sure thing aNeal Hefti
A beautiful friendship vMary Lou Martin

Ralph Mullins, tpt; Dave Wells, tbn; Ernie Small, bar & tbn; Norman Pockrandt, p; unidentified, b; Boone Stines, d

July 2–Sept. 2, 1956: Avalon (Santa Catalina Is.), Casino

During this engagement the band played the ship on and off the island, jazzing up *Aloha oe* etc., but the management objected and told them to play the stuff straight. This was not at all to Charlie's liking, and he later said he would have told them to shove it had it not been that Dave Wells, his wife and new baby—with all their accoutrements—had set up housekeeping on the island. Dave never forgot this. (*Dave Wells*)

Carleton McBeath, Conrad Gozzo, Ralph Mullins, tpts; Richard Nash, Dave Wells, Bob Burgess, Ernest Small, tbns; Willie Smith, as; Willis Holman, ts; Bob Dawes, bar; Eudice Shapiro, Robert Sushel, Amerigo Rickey Marino, William R. Kurasch, Tibor Zelig, Benny Gill, vns; Allan Harshman, Louis Kievman, Dan Lube, vlas; Raphael Ray Kramer, cello; William Miller, Norman Pockrandt, Russ Garcia, p; Robert Bain, g; Lawrence Wootten, b; Bill Richmond, d (AFM contract)

Hollywood, Verve recording session, Sept. 24, 1956

20405-4 **The moon was yellow** aRuss Garcia
Verve MG V 2040 [as *The moon is yellow*]
20406-11 **Myna** aRuss Garcia
Verve MG V 2040; ***Verve V 10036X45***
20407-6 **You'd be so nice to come home to** aRuss Garcia
Verve MG V 2040
20408-10 **Phyllysse** aRuss Garcia
Verve MG V 2040

Ralph Mullins, Bob Clark, Carleton McBeath, Buddy Ptacheck, tpts; Bob Burgess, Dave Wells, Roy Anderson, tbns; Dick Paladino, as; Bill Holman, Ken Downing, ts; Bob Dawes, bar; Ernie Small, tbn, as, bar; Norman Pockrandt, p; Red Wootten, b; Jackie Mills, d; Lynn Franklin, vocal (Edw 67)

Oct. 17–ca. Nov. 4, 1956: Hollywood, Palladium

Hollywood, Palladium, (NBC?) b'cast, Oct. 17–ca. Nov. 4, 1956

Argo aBilly May
Indian summer aBilly May
The blimp aAndy Gibson
Skyliner aBilly Moore
Moonglow/Picnic aBill Holman
You go to my head vLynn Franklin
Redskin rhumba (closing theme) aHead

As preceding

Who's your Hoosier aBilly May
A Sunday kind of love vLynn Franklin
Moonglow/Picnic aBill Holman
The great lie aAndy Gibson
Along the Santa Fe Trail aBilly May
I'm gonna laugh you right out of my life vLynn Franklin
Seminole aBilly May
Redskin rhumba (closing theme) aHead

As preceding

Redskin rhumba (opening theme) aHead
Rhubarb aAl Cohn
A Sunday kind of love vLynn Franklin
Who's sorry now aPaul Villepigue
On a slow boat to China vLynn Franklin
I get a kick out of you aBill Holman
My old flame aAndy Gibson; vLynn Franklin
Moonglow aBill Holman
Wosie posie aAndy Gibson
The great lie aAndy Gibson
Redskin rhumba (closing theme) ahead

Gene Duermeyer, tpt, may have alternated with Buddy Ptacheck during this period. Ken Downing, ts, was replaced by Bill Trujillo and Bill Bradley, d, came in for Mills. Bob Starrett, vocals, was reported by *Down beat* to be a member of the band at about this time. Charlie and Lynn Franklin probably worked at the La Paz Hotel in Palm Springs sometime during the fall.

Maynard Ferguson, Ralph Mullins, Carleton McBeath, Oliver Mitchell, tpts; Leroy Anderson, Dave Wells, Bobby Burgess, Richard Nash, tbns; Willie Smith, Dick Paladino, as; Bill Holman, William Trujillo, ts; Bob Dawes, bar; Norman Pockrandt, p; Barney Kessel, g; Red Wootten, b; Alvin Stoller, d (AFM contract)

Hollywood, Verve recording session, Nov. 8, 1956

20460-5 **Blue rose** aBill Holman
Verve MG V 2040; *HMV (E) CLP 1143*; *World Record Club (E) T 303* [mono & stereo]; *WS (E) TP 330*
20461-4 **Lemon twist** aBill Holman
Verve MG V 2040; *HMV (E) CLP 1143*; *World Record Club (E) T 303* [mono & stereo]; *WS (E) TP 330*
20462-2 **Lumby** aBilly May (1956)
Verve MG V 2040; *HMV (E) CLP 1143*; *World Record Club (E) T 303* [mono & stereo]; *WS (E) TP 330*
20463-2 **Hear me talkin' to you** aBuddy Childers
Verve MG V 2040; *HMV (E) CLP 1143*; *World Record Club (E) T 303* [mono & stereo]; *WS (E) TP 330*

Ralph Mullins, Bob Clark, Carleton McBeath, Buddy Ptacheck, tpts; Bob Burgess, Dave Wells, Roy Anderson, tbns; Dick Paladino, as; Bill Holman, Ken Downing, ts; Bob Dawes, bar; Ernie Small, tbn, as, bar; Norman Pockrandt, p; Red Wootten, b; Jackie Mills, d; Lynn Franklin, vocal (Edw 67)

Nov. 10, 1956: San Diego, Mission Beach Ballroom

Russ Garcia, conductor; David Wells, bass tpt; Marion Bacon, David Frisina, Heimann Weinstine, Tibor Zelig, Amerigo Rickey Marino, Werner Callies, Dixie Blackstone, Robert Sushel, Gerald Vinci, Victor Arno, Joachim Chassman, vns; David Sterkin, Allan Harshman, Dan Lube, vlas; George Neikrug, Raphael Kramer, Armand Kaproff, cellos; William Miller, Norman Pockrandt, p; Barney Kessel, g; Lawrence Wootten, b; Alvin Stoller, d. [Note that Wells is not heard at all on *Lonely street.*]

Hollywood, Verve recording session, Nov. 19, 1956

20464-10 **I gotta right to sing the blues** aRuss Garcia
Verve MG V 2040
20465-6 **Serenade in blue** aRuss Garcia
Verve MG V 2040
20466-2 **Lonely street** aRuss Garcia
Verve MG V 2040; ***Verve V 10036X45***
20467-7 **Isn't this a lovely day—to be caught in the rain** aRuss Garcia
Verve MG V 2040

He probably played the La Paz Hotel in Palm Springs with a small group during the fall.

NYC, "Jackie Gleason show: A tribute to Tommy Dorsey" CBS-TV, Dec. 1, 1956

Charlie was among the performers on this show.

Dinah
Audio: *Sounds Great SG 8014*

> **"The V"**
>
> A Barnet band was playing a one nighter in Yreka, Calif. (possibly in early 1957) when some local police officers showed up in the dance hall and took Charlie down to the station. It seems one of his lady friends of that time had called the police long distance in order to get her man on the phone. This caused the famous Barnet "V" to appear. (During his absence Lee Mack took over the band.) (*Lee Mack*)

This group played a number of southern California locations such as Long Beach, Bakersfield and the LA Biltmore Hotel during the spring of 1957:

Don Manning, d; other Portland area musicians probably including Art Abrams, Lee Mack and Wally Heider.

ca. early May, 1957: Portland, Jantzen Beach Ballroom

"Well, this happened to be at the time that Duke had the thing with Paul Gonsalves where he played all the choruses, *Diminuendo in blue*, you know ... Charlie had a long thing built in front of the bandstand with a carpet ... out into the crowd ... It was a wild night ... because he went out on the end of this thing, and he was blowin', and blowin' and blowin', and he was trying not to exactly copy Gonsalves but the idea of getting the crowd roaring with a whole bunch of blues choruses, and building and building like that, and it went over really well." (*Manning*)

Ralph Mullins, Bob Clark, Ollie Mitchell, Carleton McBeath, tpt; Dave Wells, Bob Edmondson, Roy Anderson, Juan Tizol, tbns; Dick Paladino, as; Lanny Morgan, as and bar; Ken Downing, Jack Kernan, ts; Bob Dawes, bar; Buddy Motsinger, p; Red Kelly, b; Don Manning, d; Joy Windsor, vocals

May 4, 1957: Stockton, Calif.

Charlie married (for the 9th? time) in Yuma. The bride was the former Joy Windsor and the knot was tied May 9. "The newlyweds will have to wait until Sunday to start a planned honeymoon of one week. Tonight, they and the band have to play a party at the Beverly Hilton Hotel." (*Harrison Carroll*, May 10, 1957)

May 10, 1957: Hollywood, Beverly Hilton Hotel

A late-night one-nighter was played early one morning in Las Vegas with with many Local 369 musicians in the audience.

(May 20?) 1957: Las Vegas

Diz Mullins (soloist), Jack Hohlman, Art Depew (lead), Bobby Clark, tpts; George (???), one or two others, tbns; Bob Jung, Bob Dawes, two or three others, reeds; Fred Massey, p; Don Prell, b; Don Manning, d. Lynn Franklin, vocals.

May 30–June 8, 1957: Salt Lake City, Saltair Ballroom

Salt Lake City, Saltair Ballroom, between May 30 and June 8, 1957 (recorded in stereo by Wally Heider)

#Wosie posie aAndy Gibson
Wosie posie aAndy Gibson
Cherokee/Redskin rhumba
Cherokee/Redskin rhumba
Swingin' down the lane aPaul Villepigue
Deep purple
Moonglow aBill Holman
C'est la vie vLynn Franklin
What is this thing called love
Stella by starlight aNeal Hefti
Jazz Hour JH 3005
After all aRalph Burns
Jazz Hour JH 3005
Warm valley/Chelsea Bridge aRalph Burns
Jazz Hour JH 3005
Lemon twist aBill Holman
Jazz Hour JH 3005
Robbins' nest
Jazz Hour JH 3005
Blue rose aBill Holman
Over the rainbow aTiny Kahn
Seminole aBilly May (1954)
Sure thing aNeal Hefti
Sometimes I'm happy
Imagination [part of a medley]
Claude reigns aManny Albam
Who's your Hoosier aBilly May
Nowhere aCharlie Barnet
Mister Wonderful vLynn Franklin
In a mellow tone aAndy Gibson
Bakiff aAndy Gibson
Love vLynn Franklin
Creole love call aBilly May

Salt Lake City, Saltair Ballroom, KDYL b'cast, June 5, 1957

Redskin rhumba (opening theme) aHead
Jazz Hour JH 3005
Jubilee jump aAndy Gibson
Jazz Hour JH 3005
You'd be so nice to come home to aAndy Gibson; vLynn Franklin
Jazz Hour JH 3005
Along the Santa Fe Trail aBilly May
Jazz Hour JH 3005
Myna aRuss Garcia
Jazz Hour JH 3005
Indian summer aBilly May
Love letters in the sand vLynn Franklin
Bakiff aAndy Gibson
The great lie aAndy Gibson
Redskin rhumba (closing theme) aHead

Charlie was not at all happy with the way the Saltair engagement turned out. Crowds were very sparse (as is evident from the recordings). He was testy with the patrons—few though they were—and apparently also took it out on the musicians. He blamed inadequate publicity for one thing, but the dancing public, shrunken in size from the glory days, simply didn't show up during his stay.

Don Manning left at this point and headed east to join the Gene Roland band.

June 14–15 and 21–22, 1957: Hollywood, Palladium

Approximate personnel:

Ralph Mullins, Bobby Clark, Ollie Mitchell, Carleton McBeath, tpts;

Dave Wells, Bob Edmondson, Walt Malzahn, tbns; Bob Jung, as; Lanny Morgan, as & bar; Ken Downing, Jack Kernan, ts; Bob Dawes, bar; Buddy Motsinger or Fred Massey, p; Harry Babasin, b; Jackie Mills, d (Edw 65)

Hollywood, Universal Studios, ca. July 1957

"THE BIG BEAT"

A Universal feature film which included Charlie Barnet and his orchestra, the Mills Brothers, Russ Morgan, Freddy Martin and numerous others. (82m)

You're being followed vMills Brothers
Unidentified instrumental (on cutting room floor)

"We did a number then we did a number with the Mills Brothers ... then Freddy Martin came in the studio, and strangely enough he used my band..." (*Sm*)

Art Depew, tpt; Murray McEachern or Ernie Small, tbn; Bob Dawes, bar; Fred Massey, p; Don Simpson, b; Bill Richmond, d

Hollywood, "The Charlie Barnet show" (USMC), Aug. 5–7, 12, 1957

Each program begins and ends with a brief statement of *Redskin rhumba*.

Rosetta
NO. 1; NO. 13
I only have eyes for you
NO. 1; **TOTAL TRCD 3004**
Cherokee
NO. 2
Tenderly
NO. 2; **TOTAL TRCD 3004**
Who's your Hoosier (announced as *Indiana*)
NO. 3
These foolish things
NO. 3
It's only a paper moon
NO. 4
G7th mambo
NO. 4; *Golden Era 15082*; **LASERLIGHT 15764**
Perdido
NO. 5
You're my thrill vLynn Franklin
NO. 5; **TOTAL TRCD 3004**
A foggy day
NO. 5; **TOTAL TRCD 3004**
Gone with the wind
NO. 5; **TOTAL TRCD 3004**
Fine and dandy
NO. 6
Star dust (featuring Murray McEachern)
NO. 6; **TOTAL TRCD 3004**
Skyliner
NO. 7
Makin' whoopee
NO. 7; **TOTAL TRCD 3004**
Cotton tail
NO. 8; *Redwood Records (C) RWJ 1001*; <u>Masters of Music BCCS 309</u>; **MASTERS OF MUSIC BCCD 309**; **TOTAL TRCD 3004**
One for my baby (and one more for the road) vLynn Franklin
NO. 8
Three little words
NO. 8
C'est la vie vLynn Franklin
NO. 8
Let's blow the blues
NO. 9
Moonglow
NO. 9
Zing! went the strings of my heart
NO. 10
Dancing on the ceiling
NO. 10
Lumby
NO. 11
Pennies from heaven
NO. 11
Blue moon
NO. 12
I hadn't anyone till you (Charlie not heard on this one)
NO. 12
S'posin'
NO. 12
You're driving me crazy vLynn Franklin
NO. 12
Night and day
NO. 13

A singer is featured on each disc (June Christy on nos. 1, 3, 6, 9 and 11, Peggy King on nos. 2, 4, 7, 10 and 13, and Lynn Franklin on nos. 5, 8 and 12) and with the exception of Lynn, each is accompanied by a three or four-piece rhythm section. For example, it is Benny Aronov who plays for June Christy and Howard Roberts is part of the group behind Peggy King.

A further footnote on the Marine Corps discs: Ernie Small substituted for McEachern on some of the sessions. In some cases he played transcriptions of McEachern's solos; he felt honored that Charlie called him to take the place of the great McEachern. (Their styles were very similar as can be heard on these recordings.)

Aug. 2-4, 9-10, 1957: Balboa, Rendezvous Ballroom
Aug. 30–31, Sept. 1, 1957: Hollywood, Palladium

Personnel unknown

Hollywood, Palladium, b'cast, (between Aug. 30 and Sept. 1, 1957?)

Redskin rhumba (opening theme) aHead
ONS 4686 (4786?)
You call it madness/You're blasé/Time on my hands
ONS 4686 (4786?)
Bakiff aAndy Gibson
ONS 4686 (4786?)
A beautiful friendship vLynn Franklin
ONS 4686 (4786?)
Myna#
ONS 4686 (4786?)
Balance of program undocumented

As preceding

Redskin rhumba (opening theme) aHead
ONS 4756; Joyce JRC C 1476
Skyliner aBilly Moore
ONS 4756; Joyce JRC C 1476
C'est la vie vLynn Franklin
ONS 4756; Joyce JRC C 1476
Wild mab of the fish pond aBud Estes
ONS 4756; Joyce JRC C 1476
Serenade to May aBill Holman
ONS 4756; Joyce JRC C 1476
Spanish kick aBilly Moore
ONS 4756; Joyce JRC C 1476
One for my baby (and one more for the road) vLynn Franklin
ONS 4756; Joyce JRC C 1476
Southern fried aBill Holman
ONS 4756; Joyce JRC C 1476
Redskin rhumba (closing theme) aHead
ONS 4756; Joyce JRC C 1476

As preceding?

Program contents unknown
ONS 4782

A fifteen piece band toured the east coast, briefly, during this period, the line-up including:

Don Ellis, Bobby Nichols, Ralph Mullins, tpts; Ephi Resnick, tbn; Sam Firmature, ts; Jake Hanna, d (*Edw 65*)

Ordinarily Bob Dawes would have been in the band but he had started work as Edsel sales manager in Hollywood.

Charlie Barnet orchestra

Personnel is unknown beyond the fact that Fred Massey is the pianist. Diz Mullins may be one of the trumpeters.

Hollywood, Universal Studios, ca. October 1957

"RECORD HOP"

A Universal short featuring Charlie Barnet and his orchestra, The Lancers, Tex Williams, Alan Copeland and Ella Mae Morse.

Redskin rhumba (opening theme) aHead
Every night vTex Williams
Charm bracelet vThe Lancers
Audio: *Joyce LP 3001*
Claude reigns aManny Albam
Audio: *Joyce LP 3001*
Will you still be mine vAlan Copeland
Ac-cent-tchu-ate the positive vElla Mae Morse
Audio: *Joyce LP 3001*
Myna aRuss Garcia [string parts re-scored for reeds]
Audio: *Joyce LP 3001*

Our man embarked on another string of one-nighters, traveling in a caravan of three Edsel station wagons which carried the band, and a single Chevy station wagon driven by bandboy "Champ" with the instruments.

Sanford Skinner, Bobby Clark, Marvin Brown, Diz Mullins, tpts; Vincent Diaz, Tommy Hodges, one other, tbns; Bob Jung, lead as; Don Davidson, as & bar; Jack Kernan, one other, ts; Lenny Mitchell, bar; John Bannister, p; Paul Gormley, b; Jackie Mills, d (*Davidson*)

Oct. 4, 1957: Oklahoma City, Skirvin Tower Hotel
Oct. 5, 1957: Lawton, OK, Officers' Club, Ft. Sill
Oct. 6, 1957: San Antonio, Officers' Club, Lackland AFB
Oct. 8, 1957: Thibodeaux, LA, College Inn
Oct. 9, 1957: Pensacola, Pensacola Beach Casino
Oct. 10, 1957: Clearwater, FL, Municipal Aud.
Oct. 11, 1957: Montgomery, AL, Maxwell Field Officers' Club
Oct. 12, 1957: Panama City, FL, Officers' Club, Tyndall AFB
Oct. 13, 1957: Mobile, AL, Jewish Progressive Club
Oct. 14, 1957: Pensacola, USNAS
Oct. 15, 1957: Jackson, AL, Country Club
Oct. 16, 1957: Augusta, GA, Bon Air Hotel
Oct. 17, 1957: Greenville, SC, Donaldson AFB
Oct. 18, 1957: Norfolk, VA, Langley Field
Oct. 19, 1957: Raleigh, NC, Reynolds Coliseum
Oct. 20–21, 1957: Washington, Annapolis Hotel
Oct. 22, 1957: Morgantown, WV, V.F.W.
Oct. 23, 1957: Crisfield, MD, Armory
Oct. 24, 1957: Staten Island, Wagner College
Oct. 25, 1957: NYC, Waldorf Astoria Hotel, Adelphi College
Oct. 26, 1957: College Park, MD, Univ. of Maryland
Oct. 27, 1957: South River, NJ, Liberty Ballroom
Oct. 28, 1957: Bangor, ME, Dow AFB
Oct. 29–30, 1957: Limestone, ME, Loring AFB
Oct. 31, 1957: NYC, Floyd Bennett Field
Nov. 1, 1957: Blacksburg, VA, Memorial Hall—V.P.I.
Nov. 2, 1957: Onanock, VA, Armory
Nov. 3, 1957: Goldsborough, NC, Seymour Johnson AFB
Nov. 6, 1957: Tyler, TX, American Legion Hall
Nov. 7, 1957: Abilene, TX, Abilene HS
Nov. 9, 1957: Lubbock, TX, Texas Tech Coliseum
Nov. 10, 1957: Oklahoma City, Hillcrest Golf and CC
Nov. 12, 1957: Plainview, TX, Country Club
Nov. 13, 1957: Chickasaw, OK, Chickasaw CC
Nov. 14, 1957: Abilene, TX, Country Club
Nov. 15, 1957: Amarillo, TX, Amarillo CC
Nov. 16, 1957: Sherman, TX, Municipal Ballroom
Nov. 17, 1957: Amarillo, TX, Aviatrix Club
Nov. 18, 1957: Roswell, NM, Officers' Club, Walker AFB
Nov. 19, 1957: Lubbock, TX, Lubbock CC
Nov. 20, 1957: Wichita Falls, TX, M.B. Corral
Nov. 21, 1957: Stillwater, OK, Oklahoma State University
Nov. 22, 1957: Wichita, KS, Moose Lodge
Nov. 23, 1957: Salina, KS, Officers' Club, Smoky Hill AFB
Nov. 24, 1957: Wichita, Trig Ballroom
Nov. 27–(Dec. 3?), 1957: Chicago, Blue Note

Around Jan. 23 he and Joy Windsor (wife no. 9) were divorced.

Approximately early 1958 Charlie married Betty Thompson. In sharpest contrast to what had gone before, the two were together for 33 years—a record in anybody's league—and were separated only by his death.

Also early in the year Charlie once more got involved in personal management, working with singer-comedienne Pat Morissey and violinist Stuff Smith.

Charlie Barnet

Clark Terry, tpt; Paul Gonsalves, ts; Sir Charles Thompson, p; George D. Wright, g; Harry Babasin, cello; Ben Tucker, b; Bill Douglass, d (*AFM contract*)

Hollywood, "The Navy Swings," Feb. 24, 1958

[Note that each show begins and ends with a brief statement of *Redskin rhumba*]

I'll remember April# (CB does not play on this tune)
SHOW 13
Easy pickin's aHarry Babasin
SHOW 13
Lester leaps in# (no CB)
SHOW 14
On Bear Hill aHarry Babasin (no CB)
SHOW 14
Clap hands! Here comes Charley!
SHOW 15
An evening in Azerbaijan aHarry Babasin
SHOW 15
Rapscallion aHarry Babasin
SHOW 16
Hoppy aHarry Babasin
SHOW 16

Jeri Southern is also heard on each show, singing two numbers with rhythm accompaniment. Her pianist and bass were probably Buddy Motsinger and Don Kitzmiller, as their names also appear on the AFM contracts.

Sanford Skinner, Al Porcino, Ray Triscari, Stu Williamson, tpts; Juan Tizol, Walt Malzahn, Dick Nash, Joe Cedeño, tbns; Bob Dawes, Teddy Lee, Bob Jung, Jack Kernan (and possibly Bill Perkins), reeds; John Bannister, p; Harry Babasin, b; Jack Sperling, d

Hollywood, "Stars of Jazz," KABC-TV, May 5, 1958

Cherokee aBilly May
Audio: *Calliope 3026*; *Joyce 1081*; AFRTS STARS OF JAZZ NO.7
Video: Classic Music TV #5005; Video Yesteryear 510
Bakiff aAndy Gibson
Audio: *Calliope 3026*; *Joyce 1081*; AFRTS STARS OF JAZZ NO.7
Video: Classic Music TV #5005; Video Yesteryear 510
Lemon twist aBill Holman
Audio: *Calliope 3026*; *Joyce 1081*; AFRTS STARS OF JAZZ NO.7; CALIF. INST. FOR THE PRESERVATION OF JAZZ [UNNUMBERED]
Video: Classic Music TV #5005; Video Yesteryear 510
Skyliner aBilly Moore
Video: Classic Music TV #5005; Video Yesteryear 510

Mel Tormé does *Cross your heart* and *Looking at you* playing his own piano accompaniment with the help of Harry Babasin and Jack Sperling. Both numbers were issued as above. *Cross your heart* was also issued on a cassette, Big Band Era 40180.

A band which probably included the following played the Palladium in August:

Diz Mullins, tpt; Dave Wells, bass tpt and tbn; Bob Jung, as; Lanny Morgan, as and bar; Bob Dawes, bar; Harry Babasin, b; Lynn Franklin, vocals (Edw 65)

Aug. 1–2, 1958: Hollywood, Palladium

Clark Terry, Al Stewart, Marky Markowitz, Charlie Shavers, tpts; Billy Byers, Bobby Byrne, Frank Sarracco, tbns; Vinnie Dean (lead), Pete Mondello, as & bar; Dick Hafer, Kurt Bloom, ts; Danny Bank, bar; Nat Pierce, p; Chubby Jackson, b; Terry Snyder, d (Edw 65)

NYC, Everest recording session, Aug. 5, 1958

Blue juice aBill Holman
Everest BR 5008, SDBR 1008, FS 333; *Top Rank (E) 35/037*; *World Record Club (E) T 141*; *Ariola (Ger) S 701177 1T*; *Everest (Ger) 70176 1T*; EVEREST STBR 1012 (open reel tape); **Evidence ECD 22065 2**; EASTER SEALS 2 [announced as *Skyliner*]
Charleston alley aBill Holman
Everest BR 5008, SDBR 1008, FS 333; *Top Rank (E) 35/037*; *World Record Club (E) T 141*; *Ariola (Ger) S 701177 1T*; *Everest (Ger) 70176 1T*; *I Grandi del Jazz GdJ 08*; ***Everest BREP 102***; EVEREST STBR 1012 (open reel tape); EVIDENCE **ECD 22065** 2; EASTER SEALS 2

Code 288A aBill Holman
Everest BR 5008, SDBR 1008, FS 333; Top Rank (E) 35/037; World Record Club (E) T 141; Ariola (Ger) S 701177 1T; Everest (Ger) 70176 1T; EVEREST STBR 1012 (open reel tape); **Evidence ECD 22065 2**

Moten swing aBill Holman
Everest BR 5008, SDBR 1008, FS 333; Top Rank (E) 35/037; World Record Club (E) T 141; Ariola (Ger) S 701177 1T; Everest (Ger) 70176 1T; I Grandi del Jazz GdJ 08; MP Records (Ger) 33013; EVEREST STBR 1012 (open reel tape); **Evidence ECD 22065 2**

Skyliner aBilly Moore
Everest 29375*; Everest BR 5008, SDBR 1008, FS 282; Murray Hill M56761; K-tel (N) TN 1241; Top Rank (E) 35/037; World Record Club (E) T 141; Ariola (Ger) S 701177 1T; Everest (Ger) 70176 1T; I Grandi del Jazz GdJ 08;* ***Everest BREP 102****;* Capitol CDP 7243 27813 4; Murray Hill 55124; EVEREST STBR 1012 (open reel tape); **Capitol CDP7243 8 27813 2 5; Evidence ECD 22065 2**

East side, west side aAndy Gibson; vBunny Briggs
Everest BR 5008, SDBR 1008, FS 333; Top Rank (E) 35/037; World Record Club (E) T 141; Ariola (Ger) S 701177 1T; Everest (Ger) 70176 1T; I Grandi del Jazz GdJ 08; EVEREST STBR 1012 (open reel tape); **Evidence ECD 22065 2**; EASTER SEALS 2

Jimmy Nottingham (tpt) replaced Shavers. Don Lamond (d) replaced Snyder.

NYC, Everest recording session, Aug. 6, 1958

Cherokee/Redskin rhumba aBilly May [6:59]
Everest 29375 [7" LP; 3:48 excerpt)]; *Everest BR 5008, DBR 1008, BR 5042, ER 8, FS 282, FS 333, 359, SDBR 1001/5, SDBR 1042; Collectables 5096; Sunset SUM 1150, SUS 5150; Murray Hill 927942, M 56761; Nostalgia Lane NLR 1601; Showcase LCA 0002* [2:18], *SH 3301; Sunset (E) SLS 50037 E; Top Rank (E) 35/037; World Record Club (E) T 141; Ariola (Ger) S 701177 1T; Everest (Ger) 70176 1T; I Grandi del Jazz (It) GdJ 08;* ***Everest BREP 102****;* GAS GAS 779; Everest FS 359; Radio Classics AFP 7140 AC [3:22]; Murray Hill 55124; Tennessee (Arg) 45619; EVEREST STBR 1012 (open reel tape); Capitol CDP 7243 27813 4; **Capitol CDP 7243 8 27813 2 5; Collectables COL CD 5096; Evidence ECD 22065 2; Tradition (C) 1035; EASTER SEALS 2**

Pompton Turnpike aAndy Gibson, Bob Jung
Everest BR 5008, SDBR 1008, FS 282, FS 367; Murray Hill M 567761; Collectables 5097; Pickwick SH 3305 3; Top Rank (E) 35/037; World Record Club (E) T 141; Ariola (Ger) S 701177 1T; Everest (Ger) 70176 1T; GAS GAS 779; Capitol CDP 7243 27813 4; Murray Hill 5124; EVEREST STBR 1012 (open reel tape); **Capitol CDP 7243 8 27813 2 5; Collectables COL-CD 5097; Evidence ECD 22065 2; K-tel 3406 2**; EASTER SEALS 2

Serenade to May aBill Holman
Everest BR 5008, SDBR 1008, FS 333; Top Rank (E) 35/037; World Record Club (E) T 141; EVEREST STBR 1012 (open reel tape); **Evidence ECD 22065 2**

Smiles aAndy Gibson
Everest BR 5008, SDBR 1008, FS 333; Sunset SUM 1150, SUS 5150; Sunset (E) SLS 50249, SUS 50037; Top Rank (E) 35/037; World Record Club (E) T 141; Ariola (Ger) S 701177 1T; Everest (Ger) 70176 1T; EVEREST STBR 1012; **Evidence ECD 22065 2**

Southern fried aBill Holman
Everest BR 5008, SDBR 1008, FS 333; Sunset SUM 1150, SUS 5150; Sunset (E) SLS 50037 E; EVEREST STBR 1012; **Evidence ECD 22065 2**; *Top Rank (E) 35/037; World Record Club (E) T 141* [last two issues as *Hairy Joe jump*]

John Bello, Doc Severinsen, Dick Sherman, Charlie Shavers, tpts; Billy Byers, Frank Rehak, Chauncey Welsh, tbns; Phil Woods, as; Dick Meldonian, as & bar; Dick Hafer, Kurt Bloom, ts; Danny Bank, bar; Nat Pierce, p; Barry Galbraith, g; Milt Hinton, b; Don Lamond, d (*Edw 65*)

NYC, Everest recording session, Sept. 3, 1958

Evergreens aBill Holman
Everest BR 5059, SDBR 1059; Everest (Arg) SDBR 1059; **Evidence ECD 22112 2**

Goodbye aBill Holman
Everest BR 5059, SDBR 1059; Everest (Arg) SDBR 1059

Star dust aBill Holman
Everest BR 5059, SDBR 1059, FS 282; Everest Arg) SDBR 1059; Sunset SUM 1150, SUS 5150; Sunset (E) SLS 50037 E; I Grandi del Jazz (It) GdJ 08; GAS GAS 779; AMERICAN TAPE 28 04128; AMERICAN TAPE PIC 3573; EVIDENCE **ECD 22112 2**

Take the "A" Train aBill Holman
Everest BR 5059, SDBR 1059, FS 282; Everest (Arg) SDBR 1059; Mark 56 553 B; Everest (Ger)76177; K-tel (N) TN 1241; Ariola (Ger) S 701177 1T; Everest (Ger) 70176 1T; I Grandi del Jazz (It) GdJ 08; EVIDENCE **ECD 22112 2**

George Duvivier, b, replaced Milt Hinton.

NYC, Everest recording session, Sept. 4, 1958

Begin the beguine aBill Holman
Everest BR 5059, SDBR 1059, FS 333; Everest (Arg) SDBR 1059; Sunset SUM 1150, SUS 5150; Sunset (E) SLS 50037 E; EVIDENCE **ECD 22112 2**

Early autumn aBill Holman
Everest BR 5059, SDBR 10593; Everest (Arga) SDBR 1059; Sunset SUM 1150, SUS 5150; Sunset (E) SLS 50037 E; EVIDENCE **ECD 22112 2**

Flying home aBill Holman
Everest BR 5059, SDBR 1059, FS 282; Everest (Arg) SDBR 1059; Everest (Ger) 76177; Sunset SUM 1150, SUS 5150; Sunset (E) SLS 50037 E; Ariola (Ger) S 701177 1T; Everest (Ger) 70176 1T; I Grandi del Jazz (It) GdJ 08; EVIDENCE **ECD 22112 2**

I can't get started aBill Holman
Everest BR 5059, SDBR 1059, FS 282; Everest (Arg) SDBR 1059; Sunset SUM 1150, SUS 5150; Sunset (E) SLS 50037 E; I Grandi del Jazz (It) GdJ 08; EVIDENCE **ECD 22112 2**

Sept. (5–6?), 1958: Hollywood, Palladium

Diz Mullins, Al Porcino, Sanford Skinner, Stu Williamson, tpts; Walt Malzahn, Dave Wells, Frank Lane, tbns; Bob Jung, Lanny Morgan, as; Jack Kernan, Dave Madden, ts; Bob Dawes, bar; Buddy Motsinger, p; Harry Babasin, b; Jack Sperling, d; Lynn Franklin, vocals (Edw 65)

Hollywood, Palladium, KFI b'cast, Sept. 5, 1958

Redskin rhumba (opening theme) aHead
Joyce LP 1052

Evergreens aBill Holman
Joyce LP 1052

Early autumn aBill Holman
Joyce LP 1052

Goodbye aBill Holman
Joyce LP 1052

Begin the beguine aBill Holman
Joyce LP 1052

Take the "A" Train aBill Holman

Darn that dream aBill Holman

Flying home aBill Holman

As preceding, Sept. 6, 1958

Program contents unknown

John Bello, Jimmy Maxwell, Al Derisi, Charlie Shavers, tpts; Billy Byers, Frank Rehak, Chauncey Welsh, tbns; Phil Woods, as; Dick Meldonian, as & bar; Dick Hafer, Kurt Bloom, ts; Danny Bank, bar; Nat Pierce, p; Barry Galbraith, g; Wendell Marshall, b; Don Lamond, d (Edw 65)

NYC, Everest record session, Sept. 29, 1958

Darn that dream aBill Holman
Everest BR 5059, SDBR 1059; Everest (Argentina) SDBR 1059; EVIDENCE **ECD 22112 2**

Harlem nocturne aBill Holman
Everest BR 5059, SDBR 1059, FS 282; Everest (Arg) SDBR 1059; Sunset SUM 1150, SUS 5150; Murray Hill M 56761; Sunset (E) SLS 50037 E; I Grandi del Jazz (It)GdJ 08; GAS GAS 779; Murray Hill 55124; EXCELSIOR **EXL 10582**; RETRO **SLD23122**; EVIDENCE **ECD 22112 2**

Midnight sun aBill Holman
Everest BR 5059, SDBR 1059, FS 282; Everest (Arg) SDBR 1059; EVIDENCE **ECD 22112 2**

One o'clock jump aBill Holman
Everest BR 5059, SDBR 1059, FS 282; Everest (Arg) SDBR 1059; Sunset SUM 1150, SUS 5150; Sunset (E) SLS 50037 E; Ariola (Ger) S 701177 1T; Everest (Ger) 70176 1T; I Grandi del Jazz (It) GdJ 08; GAS GAS 779; EVIDENCE **ECD 22112 2**

(Sept.–Nov. 1958?): Hollywood, Palladium
(Fall 1958?): Palm Springs, La Paz Hotel

Personnel unknown

Hollywood, Palladium, Sept., 1958

Redskin rhumba (opening theme) aHead
ONS 4916 (mastered Sept. 25, 1958); Joyce JRC C1476
Charleston alley aBill Holman
ONS 4916; Joyce JRC C1476
Come rain or come shine aAndy Gibson; vLynn Franklin
ONS 4916; Joyce JRC C1476
Southern fried aBill Holman
ONS 4916; Joyce JRC C1476
Serenade to May aBill Holman
ONS 4916; Joyce JRC C1476
You stepped out of a dream vLynn Franklin
ONS 4916; Joyce JRC C1476
Lemon twist aBill Holman
ONS 4916
Robbins' nest
ONS 4916
I hadn't anyone till you vLynn Franklin
ONS 4916
Redskin rhumba (closing theme) aHead

As preceding, (Oct.?) 1958

Redskin rhumba (opening theme) aHead
ONS 4922; *Swing House (E) SWH6*; Swing House (E) CSWH 6
Blue juice aBill Holman
ONS 4922; *Swing House (E) SWH6*; Swing House (E) CSWH 6; **Jazz Hour JH 3005**
One for my baby (and one more for the road) vLynn Franklin
ONS 4922; *Swing House (E) SWH6*; Swing House (E) CSWH 6; Big Band Era (N) 40180
Jubilee jump aAndy Gibson
ONS 4922; *Swing House (E) SWH6*; Swing House (E) CSWH 6
Easy living/For heaven's sake
ONS 4922; *Swing House (E) SWH6*; Swing House (E) CSWH 6
Skyliner aBilly Moore
ONS 4922
You'd be so nice to come home to aAndy Gibson; vLynn Franklin
ONS 4922
Moten swing aBill Holman
ONS 4922; *Swing House (E) SWH6*; Swing House (E) CSWH 6; **Jazz Hour JH 3005**
Spanish kick# aBilly Moore
ONS 4922; *Swing House (E) SWH6*; Swing House (E) CSWH 6

As preceding, Oct.–Nov. 1958

Redskin rhumba (opening theme) aHead
ONS 4966 (mastered Dec. 4, 1958); *Joyce LP 1052*
Charleston alley aBill Holman
ONS 4966; *Joyce LP 1052*; *Golden Era LP 15037*
But beautiful aNeal Hefti
ONS 4966; *Joyce LP 1052*; *Golden Era LP 15037*
Moonglow aBill Holman
ONS 4966; *Joyce LP 1052*; *Golden Era LP 15037*
Fair and warmer
ONS 4966; *Joyce LP 1052*; *Golden Era LP 15037*
Come rain or come shine aAndy Gibson; vLynn Franklin
ONS 4966; *Joyce LP 1052*; *Golden Era LP 15037*
Moten swing aBill Holman
ONS 4966; *Joyce LP 1052*; *Golden Era LP 15037*
Lemon twist aBill Holman
ONS 4966; *Joyce LP 1052*; *Golden Era LP 15037*
Redskin rhumba (closing theme) aHead
ONS 4966; *Joyce LP 1052*

As preceding, (late Nov.?), 1958

Redskin rhumba (opening theme) aHead
ONS 4971 (mastered Dec. 11, 1958)
Bangtail
ONS 4971; *Swing House (E) SWH6*; Swing House (E) CSWH 6; **Jazz Hour JH 3005**
You're my thrill aBud Estes; vLynn Franklin
ONS 4971
Smiles aAndy Gibson
ONS 4971; *Swing House (E) SWH6*; Swing House (E) CSWH 6; Big Band Era (N) 40180; **Jazz Hour JH 3005**
Serenade to May aBill Holman
ONS 4971; *Swing House (E) SWH6*; Swing House (E) CSWH 6
Skyliner aBilly Moore
ONS 4971; *Swing House (E) SWH6*; Swing House (E) CSWH 6
My old flame aAndy Gibson; vLynn Franklin
ONS 4971; *Swing House (E) SWH6*; Swing House (E) CSWH 6
Southern fried aBill Holman
ONS 4971; *Swing House (E) SWH6*; Swing House (E) CSWH 6

East side, west side# aAndy Gibson
ONS 4971

<u>*Hollywood, Palladium, Nov.–Dec. 1958*</u>

Contents unknown
ONS 5082

Joe Gooden (tbn) was a member of the band at this time. Jake Hanna was also reported to be on the roster.

<u>*As preceding, Nov.–Dec. 1958*</u>

Redskin rhumba (opening theme) aHead
ONS 5087
Take the "A" Train aBill Holman
ONS 5087
Come rain or come shine aAndy Gibson; vLynn Franklin
ONS 5087
Charleston alley aBill Holman
ONS 5087
Star dust aBill Holman
ONS 5087
I hadn't anyone till you vLynn Franklin
ONS 5087
Darn that dream aBill Holman
ONS 5087
Begin the beguine aBill Holman
ONS 5087
My old flame aAndy Gibson; vLynn Franklin
ONS 5087
Code 288A aBill Holman
ONS 5087; *Golden Era LP 55001* [Title given as *King Porter stomp*]

<u>*Hollywood, Palladium, b'cast, Oct.–Nov. 1958*</u>

Redskin rhumba (opening theme) aHead
ONS 5106
Evergreens aBill Holman
ONS 5106
Early autumn aBill Holman
ONS 5106
You stepped out of a dream vLynn Franklin
ONS 5106
Goodbye aBill Holman
ONS 5106
Begin the beguine aBill Holman
ONS 5106
Lover man a(Andy Gibson?); vLynn Franklin
ONS 5106
Take the "A" Train aBill Holman
ONS 5106
Darn that dream aBill Holman
ONS 5106
Flying home aBill Holman
ONS 5106

<u>*As preceding*</u>

Contents unknown
ONS 5112

ca fall/winter 1958: Saints and Sinners Room, La Paz Hotel, Palm Springs
Jan. 2–3, 8, 1959: Hollywood, Palladium

Ralph Mullins, Ollie Mitchell, Sanford Skinner, Stu Williamson, tpts; Vince Diaz, Dave Wells, Frank Lane, tbns; Bob Jung, as; Lanny Morgan, as & bar; Don Davidson, Jack Kernan, ts; Bob Dawes, bar; Buddy Motsinger, p; Carson Smith, b; Dick Shanahan, d; Lynn Franklin, vocals (*Edw 65*)

<u>*Hollywood, Palladium, KFI b'cast, Jan. 2, 3 and 8, 1959*</u>

Contents unknown (*Edw 65*)

During the 1959-60 period Art Abrams (tpt) and Cy Touff (tbn) traveled with the band.

Apr. 4–5, 1959: Hollywood, Palladium

Ralph Mullins, John Audino, Bill Mattison, tpts; Bobby Clark, tpt and v; Gil Falco, Ray Klein, Walt Malzahn, tbns; Bob Jung, as; Lenny Mitchell, as & bar; Bob Killian, Jack Kernan, ts; Bob Dawes, bar; Buddy Motsinger, p; Harry Babasin, b; John Markham, d; Lynn Franklin, vocals (*Edw 65*)

<u>*Hollywood, Palladium, KFI broadcasts, Apr. 4–5, 1959*</u>

Contents unknown (*Edw 65*)

Personnel information is lacking for these September broadcasts:

<u>*Hollywood, Palladium, KFI b'cast, Sept. 11, 1959*</u>

Evergreens aBill Holman
Early autumn aBill Holman
Goodbye aBill Holman
Begin the beguine aBill Holman
Take the "A" Train aBill Holman
Darn that dream aBill Holman
Flying home aBill Holman

As preceding, Sept. 12, 1959

Redskin rhumba (opening theme) aHead
Jazz Hour JH 3005
Skyliner aBilly Moore
Jazz Hour JH 3005
Midnight sun aBill Holman
Jazz Hour JH 3005
Evergreens aBill Holman
Jazz Hour JH 3005
One o'clock jump aBill Holman
Jazz Hour JH 3005
Redskin rhumba (closing theme) aHead
Jazz Hour JH 3005

Personnel for the Reno engagement is probably the same as for the Crown recording session.

Sept. 25–Oct. 14, 1959: Reno, Theater Lounge, Holiday Hotel

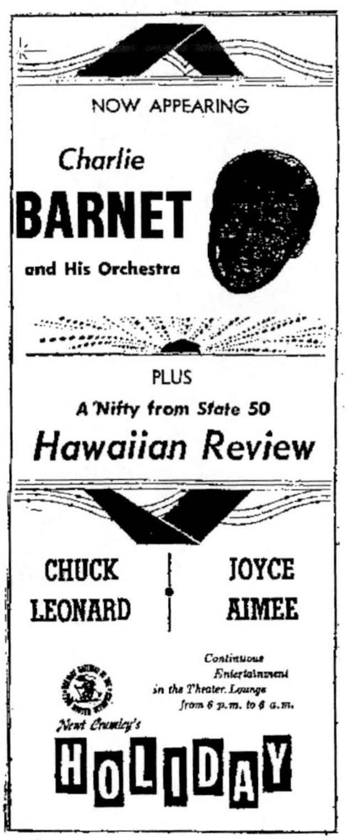

Big bands had slipped out of fashion by the time **CHARLIE BARNET** recorded **MORE CHARLIE BARNET** (Evidence ECD-22112) for Everest in 1958. It features a fine band (Barnet, as, ss; Phil Woods, as; Dick Meldonian, as, bari s; Dick Hafer, Kurt Bloom, ts; Danny Bank, bari s; Charlie Shavers, John Bellow, Jimmy Maxwell, Doc Severinsen, Al De Risi, Dick Sherman, tpt; Billy Byers, Frank Rehak, Chauncey Welsch, tbn; Nat Pierce, p; Barry Galbraith, g; Milt Hinton, George Duvivier, Wendall Marshall, b; Don Lamond, d; Bill Holman, arr) and good solos by Shavers (whose ballad feature on "I Can't Get Started" and fiery few choruses on "One O'Clock Jump" are highlights of the record), Byers, and Barnet himself, who recalls Pete Brown on the up-tempo numbers. But despite this the record does little except evoke a pleasant feeling of nostalgia and an appreciation for the band's flawless execution of the material. The "big bands greatest hits" feel of the song selection doesn't help (Evergreens/ Stardust/ Take The "A" Train/ Goodbye/ Early Autumn/ Flying Home/ I Can't Get Started/ Begin The Beguine/ Darn That Dream/ Midnight Sun/ One O'Clock Jump/ Harlem Nocturne – 39:03; NYC). Perhaps the presence of a couple more soloists who were as fired up as Charlie Shavers would have spared this date the designation "nice but forgettable."

(*Cadence* Sept. 30, 1995)

Bill Mattison, tpt; Joe Cadena, tbn; Bob Jung, bar; Al Marlow(e), p; Carson Smith, b; Roy Roten, d; Lynn Franklin, vocals

Hollywood, Crown recording session, Oct. 19, 1959

[Crowd noises dubbed]

Redskin rhumba (opening theme)
Crown CST 167, CLP 5134; Koala KO 14276; Bright Orange X-BO 719; Telehouse TS 77100; Classics 7691; OMEGATAPE DSST 823 (open reel tape); Bright Orange BO 7819 (8-track); **Classics 7691**

Caravan
Crown CST 167, CLP 5134; Koala KO 14276; Bright Orange X-BO 719; Telehouse TS 77100; Golden Hour (E) GH 868; Classics 7691; OMEGA TAPE DSST 823 (open reel tape); Bright Orange BO 7819 (8-track); **Classics 7691**

E O eleven blues
Crown CST 167, CLP 5134; Koala KO 14276; Bright Orange X-BO 719; Telehouse TS 77100; Classics 7691; OMEGA TAPE DSST 823 (open reel tape); Bright Orange BO 7819 (8-track); **Classics 7691**

Gone with the wind vLynn Franklin
Crown CST 167, CLP 5134; Koala KO 14276; Bright Orange X-BO 719; Telehouse TS 77100; Classics 7691;OMEGA

On February 15, 1959, *Down beat* ran an enthusiastic review of Barnet's new album, *Cherokee* (Everest SDBR 1008). "Here again is nostalgia revisited," said the reviewer, noting that the album "successfully manages to bridge the years and carry one back to the early '40s."

The musicians offered "verve and spirit galore," and the reviewer called it "a field day" for trumpet soloists, noting also the good trombone solo in "Juice."

Down beat's rating:

★ ★ ★

TAPE DSST 823 (open reel tape); Bright Orange BO 7819 (8-track); **CLASSICS 7691**

I got it bad (and that ain't good) vLynn Franklin
Crown CST 167, CLP 5134; *Koala KO 14276*; *Bright Orange X-BO 719*; *Telehouse TS 77100*; Classics 7691;OMEGA TAPE DSST 823 (open reel tape); Bright Orange BO 7819 (8-track); **CLASSICS 7691**

Let the good times roll
Crown CST 167, CLP 5134; Koala KO 14276; Bright Orange X-BO 719; Telehouse TS 77100; Classics 7691; OMEGA TAPE DSST 823 (open reel tape); Bright Orange BO 7819 (8-track); **CLASSICS 7691**

Mughunters' ball [Title refers to a golf tournament that took place during band's engagement.]
Crown CST 167, CLP 5134; *Koala KO 14276*; *Bright Orange X-BO 719*; *Telehouse TS 77100*; Classics 7691; OMEGA TAPE DSST 823 (open reel tape); Bright Orange BO 7819 (8-track); **CLASSICS 7691**

One for my baby (and one more for the road) vLynn Franklin
Crown CST 167, CLP 5134; *Koala KO 14276*; *Bright Orange X-BO 719, BO 7819*; *Telehouse TS 77100*; Classics 7691; Classics 7742; OMEGA TAPE DSST 823 (open reel tape); Bright Orange BO 7819 (8-track); **CLASSICS 7691, 7742**

Rockin' in rhythm
Crown CST 167, CLP 5134; *Koala KO 14276*; *Bright Orange X-BO 719*; *Telehouse TS 77100*; Classics 7691;Classics 7743; OMEGA TAPE DSST 823 (open reel tape); Bright Orange BO 7819 (8-track); **CLASSICS 7691, 7743**

Skyliner
Crown CST 167, CLP 5134; Koala KO 14276; Bright Orange X-BO 719; Telehouse TS 77100; Classics 7691; OMEGA TAPE DSST 823 (open reel tape); Bright Orange BO 7819 (8-track); **CLASSICS 7691**

The lady is a tramp vLynn Franklin
Crown CST 167, CLP 5134; Koala KO 14276; Bright Orange X-BO 719; Telehouse TS 77100; Classics 7691; Classics 7744; OMEGATAPE DSST 823 (open reel tape); Bright Orange BO 7819 (8-track); **CLASSICS 7691, 7744**

Redskin rhumba (closing theme)
Crown CST 167, CLP 5134; Koala KO 14276; Bright Orange X-BO 719; Telehouse TS 77100; Classics 7691; OMEGA TAPE DSST 823 (open reel tape); Bright Orange BO 7819 (8-track); **CLASSICS 7691**

Leader: Billy May. Pete Candoli, Frank Beach, Vito Mangano, Manny Klein, tpts; Si Zentner, Tommy Pederson, Murray McEachern, Ed Kusby, tbns; Phil Stephens, brass bass; Skeets Herfurt, Heinie Beau, Bill Ulyate, Fred Falensby, Jerome Kasper, ***Charlie Barnet****, reeds; Paul Smith, Jimmy Rowles, p; Al Hendrickson, Jack Marshall, g; Joe Mondragon, Ralph Pena, b; Alvin Stoller, Stan Levey, d; Jud Conlon Rhythmaires with Jesse White*

Hollywood, Capitol recording session, Nov. 30, 1959

Stan Freberg, featuring Jesse White

32809 **The old payola roll blues, pt. 2 (Like—the End)** vStan Freberg, Jud Conlon Rhythmaires

Capitol F4329; *Capitol (Australia) CP 1399*; *Capitol ST 23867*; *Capitol (E) EMS 1321*; *Raven (Australia) RVLP 1019*; *Capitol (NZ) EMI HITS 22, AXIS 48*; Capitol (E) TCEMS 1321; **CAPITOL (E) CDP7 91929 2**

Leader: Billy May. ***Charlie Barnet****, ts; Milt Raskin, p; Jack Marshall, g; Ralph Pena, b; Stan Levey, d*

Stan Freberg, featuring Jesse White

As preceding Dec. 1, 1959

32812 **The old payola roll blues, pt. 1 (Like—the Beginning)** vStan Freberg, Jud Conlon Rhythmaires
Capitol F4329; Capitol (E) CL 15122; Capitol (Australia) CP 1399; *Capitol ST 23867; Capitol (E) EMS 1321; Raven (Australia) RVLP 1019; Capitol (NZ) EMI HITS 22, AXIS 48*; Capitol (E) TCEMS 1321; **CAPITOL (E) CDP7 91929 2**

[Note that Part 1 has elements that were recorded on Nov. 30 and Dec. 1, as well as some additions recorded by Stan on Dec. 4. Further editing was carried out for the English issue CL 15122, deleting the reference to "Payola"; this was assigned master number 33231. Information on these sessions is transcribed from Jack Mirtle's *The music of Billy May: a discography*, with thanks.]

Oct. 23–ca. Spring, 1959: Palm Springs, La Paz Hotel

The Charlie Barnet Quartet

Arnold Ross, p; Bob Berteaux, b; Roy Roten, d

Palm Springs, La Paz Hotel, ca. late Nov. 1959

I only have eyes for you/There will never be another you vLynn Franklin
Unissued
Makin' whoopee
Unissued
Rosetta
Unissued
33567 ***Anything goes***
Unissued
Gone with the wind vLynn Franklin
Unissued
33662 ***In a mellow tone***
Capitol T/ST 1403
Redskin rhumba (0:38)
Unissued
33661 ***Rosetta***
Capitol T/ST 1403
Cherokee
Unissued
Don't worry 'bout me vLynn Franklin
Unissued
33654 ***Night and day***
Capitol T/ST 1403
33656 ***On the sunny side of the street***
Capitol T/ST 1403
33655 ***Take the "A" Train***
Capitol T/ST 1403
33664 ***Let the good times roll***
Capitol T/ST 1403; *PRO 1592* [mono]
Things ain't what they used to be
Unissued
In a mellow tone
Unissued
Lover man (oh, where can you be?) vLynn Franklin
Unissued
On the sunny side of the street
Unissued
The lady is a tramp vLynn Franklin
Unissued
Jive at five
Unissued
Rosetta
Unissued
Caravan
Unissued
Don't worry 'bout me vLynn Franklin
Unissued
Honeysuckle rose
Unissued
One for my baby (and one more for the road) vLynn Franklin
Unissued
Charlie's blues
Unissued
It's only a paper moon
Unissued
Gone with the wind vLynn Franklin
Unissued
East side, west side
Unissued
I hadn't anyone till you vLynn Franklin
Unissued

Let the good times roll
Unissued
Anything goes
Unissued
One for my baby (and one more for the road) vLynn Franklin
Unissued
Take the "A" Train
Unissued
Cherokee
Unissued
Moonlight in Vermont/That old feeling vLynn Franklin
Unissued
33658 ***It's only a paper moon***
Capitol T/ST 1403
33660 ***Things ain't what they used to be***
Capitol T/ST 1403; ***PRO 1592*** [mono]
Lover man (oh, where can you be?) vLynn Franklin
Unissued
Let the good times roll
Unissued
Makin' whoopee
Unissued
When Sunny gets blue vLynn Franklin
Unissued
In a mellow tone
Unissued
Night and day
Unissued
33659 ***Jive at five***
Capitol T/ST 1403
33663 ***Honeysuckle rose***
Capitol T/ST 1403
33665 ***Charlie's blues***
Capitol T/St 1403
Rosetta
Unissued
One for my baby (and one more for the road) vLynn Franklin
Unissued
On the sunny side of the street
Unissued
Gone with the wind vLynn Franklin
Unissued
Jive at five
Unissued
Caravan
Unissued

Capitol engineers recorded the group on five successive nights, utilizing recording equipment in a van parked outside the Hotel.

Al Marlow(e) sometimes subbed for Ross.

Down beat reviewed Charlie's album *Jazz Oasis* (Capitol T/ST 1403) on November 24, 1960. "The relaxed, congenial atmosphere is noteworthy," said the reviewer of this live album recorded at Palm Springs.

The reviewer notes that Barnet's inspirations—including Johnny Hodges and Coleman Hawkins—are much in evidence and are blended with Barnet's own "exuberance." The overall effect, according to reviewer B.G., is "Barnet ... as a lecturing veteran showing off his mettle and reminding us of his contribution...." Still, the album is "well executed and ... good listening."

Down beat rating:

★ ★ ★ ½

There apparently was a brief eastern tour by a big band at about this time including a late February date at the Howard Theater in Washington, DC which was a three-show, one-day only appearance. *Down beat* reported that "The lively show also included the Zoot Sims-Al Cohn group." One of the audience members recalled that Charlie "played an afternoon date at the Howard Theater along with the then Al Cohn/Zoot Sims

Quintette. I kid you not, the attendance was not more than fifty and I think less. However, Charlie made the announcement that, although he obviously was disappointed in the turnout, they would play a full show. And, of course, they did." (*Slater*)

[Charlie Barnet Septet]

(also described as "Charlie Barnet and his Mad Mabs" and "Charlie Barnet Octet")

Bob Jung, as; Stu Williamson (or Don Fagerquist), tpt; Dave Wells (or Dick Nash), tbn; possibly Buddy Motsinger or John Bannister, p; Harry Babasin, b; Unidentified, d

Hollywood, "The Swingin', Singin' Years" (Ford Star Time Theater), CBS-TV telecast, March 8, 1960

Redskin rhumba (opening theme)
Video: Vintage Jazz Classics VJC 2003
Audio: *Sounds Great 8003*; *Joyce LP 3008*
Wanderin' blues
Video: Vintage Jazz Classics VJC 2003
Audio: *Sounds Great 8003*; *Joyce LP 3008*

There is no personnel information for the following broadcast.

Hollywood,Palladium, KFI b'cast, March 25, 1960

Redskin rhumba (opening theme) aHead
Flight of the foo birds
Sophisticated lady
Main stem
Unidentified instrumental

A big band was used for the following engagements:

April 13–26, 1960: Chicago, Blue Note
April 29, 1960: West Long Branch, NJ, Monmouth College
April 30, 1960: Trenton, NJ, Infantry Armory
May 1, 1960: NYC, Tuxedo Ballroom
May 3, 1960: Suffolk, VA, Suffolk Shrine Club
May 4, 1960: Virginia Beach, VA, Moose's Tropicana Club
May 6, 1960: Charlottesville, VA, Univ. of Virginia
May 7, 1960: Spartanburg, SC, Municipal Building
May 8, 1960: Greenville, SC, Donaldson AFB, Officers' Club
May 10, 1960: St. Simons Island, GA, King and Prince Hotel
May 11, 1960: Charleston, SC, Naval Station, Officers' Club
May 12, 1960: Charleston, SC, Naval Station, Enlisted Men's Club
May 13, 1960: Clemson, SC, Clemson College
May 14, 1960: Charlotte, NC: Park Center
May 15, 1960: Savannah, GA: Hunter AFB, Service Club
May 17, 1960: White Sulphur Springs, WV, Greenbrier Hotel
May 18, 1960: State College, PA, Hecla Park Ballroom

On the 19th, the band took a jet to California for an engagement at the Palladium, opening May 21. Bob Jung recalls that big band arrangements had been written for several of the tunes done on Capitol T/ST 1403, "Jazz Oasis."

May 21–22, 27–28, June 10–11, 1960: Hollywood, Palladium

Charlie and Betty took a vacation in late June.

Stu Williamson, Al Porcino, Frank Huggins, Bud Brisbois, tpts; Lewis McCreary, Bob Edmondson, Dick Kenney, tbns; Pat Chartrand, Charlie Kennedy, as; Med Flory, Lenny Mitchell, as; Bob Jung, bar; Lou Levy, p; Max Bennett, b; Mel Lewis, d; Lynn Franklin, Al Porcino, vocals (Edw 65)

(Aug.–Sept. 1960, weekends?): Hollywood, Palladium

Hollywood, Palladium, broadcasts, Sept. 9–10, 1960

Program contents unknown

Replacements were reported by Ernie Edwards (*Edw 65*): Jack Laubach (tpt) for Brisbois, Bob Fitzpatrick and Frank Rosolino (tbns) for Edmondson and Kenney, and Victor Feldman (p) for Levy.

<u>*As preceding, ca. late Sept., 1960*</u>

Redskin rhumba (opening theme) aHead
Cotton tail aMaxwell Davis
S'posin' (aBilly May?)
Other titles unknown

Juliette Gardner, pac and vocals, is reported to have worked for Charlie. (*D. A. Handy*, p. 251)

Bobby Nichols, tpt; Mickey Gravine, tbn; probably Harvey Estrin, woodwinds; Ray Alexander, vbs; Steve Little, d; unidentified bass [from Atlanta]; Herbie Wasserman, tympani and other percussion; Nat Pierce, p (Alexander)

Oct. 6–Nov. 2, 1960: NYC, Basin Street East

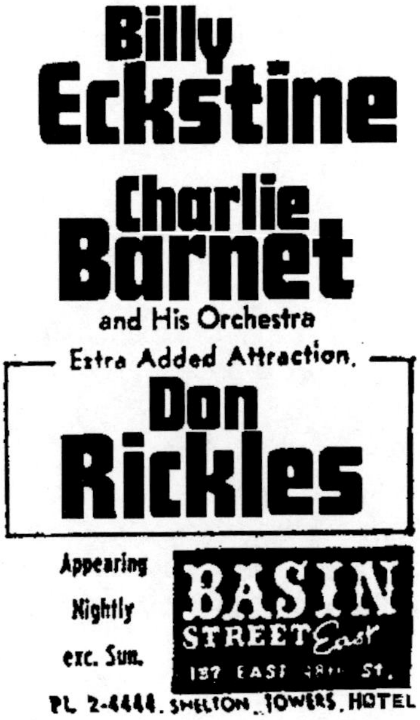

Charlie remarked in *TSY* that this "Sauter-Finegan" type band marked a departure from his convictions. Marty Paich wrote the book. Even *The New Yorker* looked somewhat askance, describing it as "Charlie Barnet's medium-sized band doing arrangements by Rosemarie De Paris" and describing the music as "spun-sugar" and "sugar-coated."

There is no personnel information available for this next appearance:

Nov. 20, 1960: Palm Springs, Notre Dame HS Auditorium

At a one-nighter in Palm Springs Charlie led a small group which included Dave Wells (tbn), a tpt and a rhythm section. The band wore Charlie's uniforms which had an unusual inside pocket. One of the band members kept his pot pipe in this pocket, and after bending over to pick up something, out fell the pipe which rolled and clattered across the dance floor. Charlie pointedly looked the other way, saying, "I didn't see that." After the job the band adjourned to Charlie's house for a drink and Charlie gave Dave and his passenger a bottle of Dewar's (Charlie's drink) to take along on their way back to LA.

The Out Islanders

Leaders: Billy May and Charlie Barnet. Vincent DeRosa, John Cave, James Decker, William Hinshaw, frh; ***Charlie Barnet****, Justin Gordon, Willie Schwartz, Ted Nash, reeds; Jimmy Rowles, p; Bob Gibbons, Al Hendrickson, Alvino Rey, g; Ralph Pena, b; Frank Flynn, Irving Cottler, Emil Richards, perc*

<u>**Hollywood, Capitol Recording session, Feb. 27, 1961**</u>

35476 **Sand in my shoes** aBilly May
Capitol T/ST 1595
35477 **Return to paradise** aBilly May; vMarni Nixon
Capitol T/ST 1595
35478 **Little island** aBilly May
Capitol T/ST 1595

35479 **Beyond the reef** aBilly May
Capitol T/ST 1595
35480 **Beyond the reef**—breakdown
35481 **Sand in my shoes**—breakdown

Arthur Franz (frh) replaced DeRosa and Larry Bunker (d) replaced Richards.

As preceding, Feb. 28, 1961

35482 **Honorable rock of Hong Kong** aBilly May
Capitol T/ST 1595; CAPITOL **CDP8 37596 2**
35483 **Ebb tide** aBilly May
Capitol T/ST 1595; CAPITOL **CDP8 37598 2**

Leaders: Billy May and Charlie Barnet. James Perissi, Arthur Franz, James Decker, William Hinshaw, frh; ***Charlie Barnet****, Justin Gordon, Harry Klee,Ted Nash, reeds; Jimmy Rowles, p; Jack Marshall, H. J. Timbrell, Alvino Rey, g; Ralph Pena, b; Frank Flynn, Irving Cottler, Emil Richards, perc*

As preceding, March 16, 1961

35560 **Poinciana** aBilly May
Capitol T/ST 1595
35561 **Sea breeze** aBilly May
Capitol T/ST 1595
35561 **China Sea** aBilly May
Capitol T/ST 1595

Leaders: Billy May and Charlie Barnet. Vincent DeRosa, John Cave, James Decker, William Hinshaw, frh; ***Charlie Barnet****, Justin Gordon, Willie Schwartz, Harry Klee, reeds; Jimmy Rowles, p; Bob Gibbons, H. J. Timbrell, Alvino Rey, g; Ralph Pena, b; Frank Flynn, Irving Cottler, Emil Richards, perc*

As preceding, March 18, 1961

35568 **The moon of Manakoora** aBilly May; vLoulie Jean Norman
Capitol T/ST 1595
35569 **My tane** aBilly May
Capitol T/ST 1595
35570 **Moon mist** aBilly May; vLoulie Jean Norman
Capitol T/ST 1595

Lee Katzman, Al Porcino, Bud Brisbois, Joe Burnett, tpts; Joe Cadena, Bob Edmondson, Dick Kenney, tbns; Bob Jung, Charlie Kennedy, as; Med Flory, Bill Perkins, ts; Lenny Mitchell, bar; Buddy Motsinger, p; Max Bennett, b; Larry Bunker, d; Lynn Franklin, vocals (*Edw 65*)

Mar. 17–18, 1961: Hollywood, Palladium

Hollywood, Palladium, NBC b'cast, March 18, 1961

Cherokee aBilly May
Skyliner aBilly Moore
Pompton Turnpike aAndy Gibson, Bob Jung
Why not (aNeal Hefti?)
Gone with the wind aManny Albam; vLynn Franklin
Middle man
Flight of the foo birds
Redskin rhumba (closing theme) aHead

Stu Williamson, Al Porcino, Frank Huggins, Joe Burnett, tpts; Joe Cadena, Bob Edmondson, Dick Kenney, tbns; Bob Jung, Charlie Kennedy, as; Med Flory, Lenny Mitchell, ts; Jack Nimitz, bar; Buddy Motsinger, p; Joe Comfort, b; Larry Bunker, d; Lynn Franklin, vocals (*Edw 65*)

April 14–15, 1961: Hollywood, Palladium

As preceding, April 14–15, 1961

Program contents unknown

As preceding, ca. June 30, 1961

Redskin rhumba (opening theme) aHead
ONS 5377
Begin the beguine aBill Holman
ONS 5377; *Golden Era LP 15037*
Darn that dream aBill Holman
ONS 5377; *Golden Era LP 15037*
Close your eyes vLynn Franklin
ONS 5377; *Golden Era LP 15037*
Sophisticated lady
ONS 5377; *Golden Era LP 15037*
The gal upstairs
ONS 5377; *Golden Era LP 15037*; Ajax C 708
Everything happens to me vLynn Franklin
ONS 5377; *Golden Era LP 15037*
Basieville aNat Pierce
ONS 5377; *Golden Era LP 15037*
Redskin rhumba (closing theme) aHead
ONS 5377

Personnel for the next program is unverified.

Hollywood, Palladium, KFI b'cast, ca July 21, 1961

Redskin rhumba (opening theme) aHead
ONS 5392; *Golden Era LP 55001*
Charleston alley aBill Holman
ONS 5392
Come rain or come shine aAndy Gibson; vLynn Franklin
ONS 5392
Indian love call aBilly May
ONS 5392; *Golden Era LP 55001*
Main stem
ONS 5392; *Golden Era LP 55001; Limited Edition LP 101*; Ajax C 708
Goodbye aBill Holman
ONS 5392; *Golden Era LP 55001*
I'm gonna laugh you right out of my life vLynn Franklin
ONS 5392; *Golden Era LP 55001*
Bouncing with Boots
ONS 5392; *Golden Era LP 55001*
Why not# (aNeal Hefti?)
ONS 5392; *Golden Era LP 55001*

Gil Falco or Joe Cadena, tbn; Bob Jung or Lenny Mitchell, bar; Buddy Motsinger and Arnold Ross, p; Charlie Haden, b; Dick Shanahan, d; Lynn Franklin, vocals (Lynn Franklin)

ca. Oct. 1961–early 1962: Anaheim, CA, Domino Club

Gil Falco, tbn; Don Raffell, ts; Bob Jung, bar; Ernie Freeman, p, org; Max Bennett, b; Larry Bunker, vbs; Jack Sperling, d (AFM contract)

(Tommy Wolf's name also appears on the contract but he may have assisted Jackie Mills in producing the sessions.)

Hollywood, Choreo recording session, May 24, 1962

Cherokee raid (Who's your Hoosier)
Choreo/äva *A/AS 10*
5104-C **Mood indigo**
Choreo/äva *A/AS 10*
5105-C **Jazz skyliner**
Choreo/äva *A/AS 10*
5106-C **The great gong of Hong Kong**
Choreo/äva *A/AS 10*
5107-C **Murder at Peyton Hall**
Choreo/äva *A/AS 10*
5108-C **Coachella blue**
Choreo/äva *A/AS 10*
5109-C **Tappin' at the Tappa**
Choreo/äva *A/AS 10*

As preceding, May 25, 1962

5110-C **Leapin' at the Lincoln**
Choreo/äva *A/AS 10*
5111-C **Indianapolis**
Unissued
5112-C **I love Paris**
Unissued
5113-C **East side, west side**
Choreo/äva *A/AS 10*
5114-C **Things ain't what they used to be (Time's a-wastin')**
Choreo/äva *A/AS 10*

An appearance at Disneyland by a band whose personnel has not been determined took place in June.

Anaheim, Disneyland, "Cavalcade of Big Bands," stage perf., June 2-6, 1962

Cherokee aBilly May
Pompton Turnpike aBilly May
Deep purple
Southern fried aBill Holman

(These were among the songs performed according to a Disneyland press release.)

July 6, 1962: Santa Monica, Seaview Ballroom

Bill Harris, tbn; Gerry Wiggins, p; Max Bennett, b; Larry Bunker, d (AFM contract)

(Tommy Wolf's name also appears on the contract but he may have assisted Jackie Mills in producing the session.)

Hollywood, Choreo recording session, Sept. 13, 1962

5178-C **Seminole**
Koala AW 14158
5178-? **Seminole**
Unissued
5179-C **Bronx blues** (actually *After all*)
Koala AW 14158
5180-C **Manhatten** *[sic]* **blues** (actually *Wanderin' blues*; issued as *Taxi driver*)
Koala AW 14158
5181-C **Igor's dream from Wings over Manhattan** (actually *Serenade to May*; issued as *Wings over Manhattan*)
Koala AW 14158
5181-? **Igor's dream from Wings over Manhattan**
Unissued
5182-C **Don't worry 'bout me**
Unissued
5183-C **Warm valley**
Unissued
5184-C **Strip city**
Unissued
5185-C **I got it bad (and that ain't good)**
Unissued
5186-C **Cotton tail**
Unissued

The remaining 4 tracks on Koala AW 14158 are by an unidentified big band recorded live, with a male singer who sounds a lot like Sammy Davis, Jr. The tunes are *Butterball*, *Toe tappin'*, *September in the rain* and *Star dust*.

Feb. 4–Mar. 4, 1963: Las Vegas, Edie Adams show, Riviera Casino

Charlie's part consisted of appearing twice each night with the Jack Cathcart orchestra playing a 5-minute medley of his big hits. "Easiest job I've ever had," he said, "I'm out of work 23 hours and 50 minutes a day."

Las Vegas, "Edie Adams show," ABC-TV, b'cast Feb. 26, 1963 (taped earlier, ca. Feb. 1963)

Cherokee/Pompton Turnpike/Skyliner

Ray Triscari, Conrad Gozzo, John Audino, Joe Burnett, tpts; Vernon Friley, Bob Edmondson, Ernie Tack, tbns; Joe Maini, Art Howland, fl and as; Lenny Mitchell, Bill Perkins, ts; Bob Jung, bar; Jimmy Rowles, p; Don Bagley, b; Freddy Potter, d (Edw 65)

Hollywood, Palladium, NBC b'cast, March 29, 1963

Why not (aNeal Hefti?)
Everything happens to me vLynn Franklin
Begin the beguine aBill Holman
Darn that dream aBill Holman
Skyliner aBilly Moore
Come rain or come shine aAndy Gibson; vLynn Franklin
Basieville# aNat Pierce

As preceding, March 30, 1963

Cherokee aBilly May
Charleston alley aBill Holman
One for my baby (and one more for the road) vLynn Franklin
The lamp is low aBill Holman
Early autumn aBill Holman
Close your eyes vLynn Franklin
Our love aBill Holman
Fantail
Redskin rhumba (closing theme) aHead

Ray Anthony All Star Orchestra

Jack Laubach, Conrad Gozzo, Ray Triscari, John Audino, tpts; Lloyd Elliot, Frank Rosolino, Lew McCreary, George Roberts, tbns;

Charlie Barnet, ss; Joe Maini, Abe Most, as; Bob Hardaway, Dave Pell, ts; Leo Anthony, bar; Nick Ceroli, d; Don Simpson, b; Kellie Greene, p; Al Hendrickson, g

Hollywood, "Club Anthony" (syndicated TV program), April 27, 1963 (aired June 1)

Cherokee/Pompton Turnpike/Skyliner
Video: Aero Space Home Video AS 1001

15-piece band included:
Ray Triscari, Conrad Gozzo, Al Porcino, tpts; Bob Fitzpatrick, tbn; Bob Jung, as; Bill Perkins, ts; Jack Nimitz, bar; Jimmy Rowles, p; Alvin Stoller, d; Lynn Franklin, vocals.(*Edw 65*)

June 1, 1963: Anaheim, Disneyland, "Cavalcade of big bands"
Dec. 11, 1963: San Diego [Charlie did not appear as his mother died on this date]

17-piece band included:

Mickey Mangano, Conrad Gozzo, Bobby Guy, tpts; Lloyd Elliot, Joe Howard, Herbie Harper, tbns; Art Howell, as; Gene Cipriano, ts; Marty Berman, bar; Tony Rizzi, g; Rollie Bundock, b; Jack Sperling, d. (*Edw 65*)

Hollywood, NBC-TV, ca. February 1964

Cherokee aBilly May
Pompton Turnpike aAndy Gibson, Bob Jung

Charlie threw a party in Palm Springs at the San Jacinto Country Club. The invited guests totaled about 70 and included Billy May, Stan Kenton, Leonard Feather, Carlos Gastel, Ben Pollack and Billy Strayhorn. The Ellington band was flown in from San Francisco to entertain the guests. (This was on Sept. 29, 1964.)

He played a New Year's Eve job somewhere in Arizona, probably Dec. 31, 1965. The instruments didn't arrive.

The Mab philosophized in 1966, "I was leading dance bands until I just couldn't take it any more. It got to the point where if a young fellow came up to the bandstand, I'd say, 'Drop dead' [others have reported that his language was much stronger] before he had a chance to say anything … Funny thing … it's possible he might have wanted an autograph or to tell me he thinks the band is the greatest. I won't go on tour, but I'll work any dates where I don't have to play for dancing." (*Down beat* Nov. 17, 1966)

Chapter 8

The Last Jump 1967

The Mab formed a 16-piece band which included:

Al Porcino, Conte Candoli, tpts; Bob Fitzpatrick, tbn; Willie Smith, as;Willie Maiden, ts; Max Bennett, b and Fender; Jack Wilson, Jr., p; Jack Sperling, d; Lynn Franklin, vocals.

Oct. 14–23, 1966: Hollywood, Chez Supper Club

Conte Candoli, Jack Laubach, Larry McGuire, Al Porcino, Dalton Smith, tpts; Bob Fitzpatrick, Richard Hyde, Ernie Tack, Peter Meyers, tbns; Allen Lasky, Willie Smith, as; Willie Maiden, Lennie Mitchell, ts; Bob Jung, bar; Jack Wilson, Jr., p; Max Bennett, b; Jack Sperling, d

Hollywood, Worcester Records session, Oct. 29, 1966

Rabble rouser aBilly Byers [2:12]
Vault 9004; *Creative World ST 1056*; *Vocalion (E) SAE-L 604, LAE-L 604*; *Karusell (Ger) 635.077*; Jazz Heritage 313097 M; ORIGINAL MASTER RECORDING **MFCD 841**; JAZZ HERITAGE **513097 H**

Satin doll aBilly Byers [5:23]
Vault 9004; *Creative World ST 1056*; *Vocalion (E) SAE-L 604, LAE-L 604*; *Karusell (Ger) 635.077*; Jazz Heritage 313097 M; ORIGINAL MASTER RECORDING **MFCD 841**; JAZZ HERITAGE **513097 H**

Something to live for aBilly Byers; vRuth Price (dubbed) [2:37]
Vault 9004; *Creative World ST 1056*; *Vocalion (E) SAE-L 604, LAE-L 604*; *Karusell (Ger) 635.077*; Jazz Heritage 313097 M; ORIGINAL MASTER RECORDING **MFCD 841**; JAZZ HERITAGE **513097 H**

Something to live for (alt. dubbing) aBilly Byers; vRuth Price [2:37]
Unissued

It had to be you aBilly Byers [3:12]
Unissued [Lynn Franklin was to have dubbed the vocal to this accompaniment recording but was unable to because of illness.]

Clap hands! here comes Charley! aBill Holman
Vault 9004; *Creative World ST 1056*; *Vocalion (E) SAE-L 604, LAE-L 604*; *Karusell (Ger) 635.077*; Jazz Heritage 313097 M; ORIGINAL MASTER RECORDING **MFCD 841**; JAZZ HERITAGE **513097 H**

Pete Candoli, Conte Candoli, Larry McGuire, Al Porcino, tpts; Bob Fitzpatrick, Dick Hyde, Ernie Tack, Peter Myers, tbns; Wilbur Schwartz, Allen Lasky, Willie Smith, as; Willie

Maiden, Lennie Mitchell, ts; Bob Jung, bar; Jack Wilson, Jr., p; Max Bennett, b; Jack Sperling, d

As preceding, Nov. 2, 1966

A flower is a lovesome thing aBilly Byers [3:49]
Unissued [Instrumental accompaniment for a vocal that was to have been performed by Lynn Franklin. Willie Smith plays in her place.]

Introduction to an ending aBill Holman [3:36]
Vault 9004; *Creative World ST 1056*; *Vocalion (E) SAE-L 604, LAE-L 604*; *Karusell (Ger) 635.077*; Jazz Heritage 313097 M; ORIGINAL MASTER RECORDING MFCD 841; JAZZ HERITAGE 513097 H

When the world was young aBilly Byers [2:09]
Unissued [Was to have been a Lynn Franklin vocal]

Upper Manhattan Medical Group aBilly Byers [2:40]
Vault 9004; *Creative World ST 1056*; *Vocalion (E) SAE-L 604, LAE-L 604*; *Karusell (Ger) 635.077*; Jazz Heritage 313097 M; ORIGINAL MASTER RECORDING MFCD 841; JAZZ HERITAGE 513097 H

Snowfall aBilly Byers [no piano solo] [2:17]
Unissued

Mab 66 [2:52]
Unissued

Personnel for next sessions is the same as for Oct. 29.

As preceding, Nov. 9, 1966

Rabble rouser aBilly Byers
Unissued

As preceding, Nov. 12, 1966

'Deed I do aDon Rader
Vault 9004; *Creative World ST 1056*; *Vocalion (E) SAE-L 604, LAE-L 604*; *Karusell (Ger) 635.077*; MUSIC MAKERS 334; Jazz Heritage 313097 M; ORIGINAL MAS-TER RECORDING MFCD 841; JAZZ HERITAGE 513097 H

Boomerang aBilly Byers
Vault 9004; *Creative World ST 1056*; *Vocalion (E) SAE-L 604, LAE-L 604*; *Karusell (Ger) 635.077*; Jazz Heritage 313097 M; ORIGINAL MASTER RECORDING MFCD 841; JAZZ HERITAGE 513097 H

Snowfall aBilly Byers [3:26]
Unissued

Snowfall aBilly Byers [with piano overdub; 3:22]
Vault 9004; *Creative World ST 1056*; *Vocalion (E) SAE-L 604, LAE-L 604*; *Karusell (Ger) 635.077*; Jazz Heritage 313097 M; ORIGINAL MASTER RECORDING MFCD 841; JAZZ HERITAGE 513097 H

Bali Bali buck dance aBill Holman [no CB solo; 3:00]
Unissued

Bali Bali buck dance aBill Holman [CB solo; 2:48]
Vault 9004; *Creative World ST 1056*; *Vocalion (E) SAE-L 604, LAE-L 604*; *Karusell (Ger) 635.077*; Jazz Heritage 313097 M; ORIGINAL MASTER RECORDING MFCD 841; JAZZ HERITAGE 513097 H

Dec. 15–31, 1966: NYC, Basin Street East

Snooky Young (lead), Clyde Reasinger, Clark Terry, George Triffon, Randy Brecker, tpts; Jimmy Cleveland, Herb Wise, Billy Tole, tbns; Jackie Jeffers, btbn; Willie Smith (lead), Dick Meldonian, as; Richie Kamuca, Stan Edson, ts; Danny Bank, bar; Steve Little, d; Nat Pierce, p; Eddie Jones, b

NYC, Basin Street East, b'cast Dec. 24, 1966

BASIN STREET EAST, 137 E. 48th St. (PL 2-4444): The show must go on—but of its own momentum, for no one tells the performers when to start or to stop. Still, with any luck, you will get to see the Baja Marimba band (Mexico), the Geezinslaw Brothers (jocularity), and Marty Richards (song). The plan is to disband on Saturday, Dec. 10, but to resume on Thursday, Dec. 15, with Charlie Barnet's band (memories, memories!) and the Four Tops, whose carolling is cacophonic.

... **BASIN STREET EAST**, 137 E. 48th St. (PL 2-4444): In this year of celebrated reruns, we now acquire Charlie Barnet's band, which has come in out of the unknown cold for the first time in six years. The Four Tops, whose songs are shots heard around the world, are likewise in residence. Closed Sundays.

It had to be you aBilly Byers
Hep (E) HEP 2005
Mumbles vClark Terry
Hep (E) HEP 2005
I can't get started aBill Holman
Hep (E) HEP 2005
Jeep's blues
Hep (E) HEP 2005
Cotton tail aMaxwell Davis
Hep (E) HEP 2005
Introduction to an ending aBill Holman
Hep (E) HEP 2005

As preceding, Dec. 25, 1966

Rabble rouser aBilly Byers
Hep (E) HEP 2005
Bali Bali buck dance aBill Holman
Hep (E) HEP 2005
Satin doll aBilly Byers
Hep (E) HEP 2005
Basieville aNat Pierce
Hep (E) HEP 2005
Mab medley (Cherokee/Southern fried/East side, west side/Things ain't what they used to be/Skyliner/Pompton Turnpike/Smiles)
Hep (E) HEP 2005

NYC, Basin Street East, between Dec. 15 & 31, 1966

#Mab 66

"Now we'd like to present our only—oh, I gotta tell ya—there's four sexes: male, female, homosexuals, then there's girl singers. I wanna tell you that the girl singers that I have had have destroyed my bands so many times [laughter] … never mind mentionin' the names, fellas.

"I would like to present our one and only vocalist, one of Rudolph Bing's rejects, but he's beautiful, and I'm sure you've heard his record of this. Mr. Clark Terry and 'Mumbles.'"

Mumbles vClark Terry
I can't get started

11:30 (2) Late Show: "The Deadly Mantis" (1957), Craig Stevens, William Hopper. His special effects are all right (R)
(4) Tonight: Johnny Carson is host to Kaye Stevens, the Charlie Barnett Orchestra, others
(7) Best of Broadway: "The True Story of Jesse James". (1957), Robert Wagner. Psychological

UDB084 (27)(31)SYA611
SY FGA202 PD WHITESTONE NY 31 407P EST
CHEROKEE CHARLIE BARNETT
DELIVER BASIN ST EAST 137 E 48 ST NYK
HAPPY NEW YEAR COULDNT GETBY WORKED THE SAME HOURS AT EDDIE
CONDONS WISH YOU COULD CALL ME BEFORE YOU LEAVE FLUSHING 82504
LOVE AND KISSES
CLIFF LEEMAN
PS DOES THE DRUMMER GET A DRESSING ROOM

As preceding, Jan. 1, 1967

Redskin rhumba (opening theme) aHead
Basieville aNat Pierce
Blue rose aBill Holman
'Deed I do aDon Rader
Early autumn aBill Holman
Upper Manhattan Medical Group aBilly Byers
(Moonlite (E?) KH1 2?)
It had to be you aBilly Byers
Introduction to an ending aBill Holman

Sam Herman, g, was added for the film.

NYC, 20th Century Fox Studios and Basin Street East, Jan. 3-5, 1967

"Charlie Barnet in concert"

A short film (about 60m) featuring Charlie Barnet and his orchestra with Anita Ortez, and The Fabulous Flippers (a rock group). So far as is known, it has never been released commercially. The title has also been cited as "Mr. Charlie" and "Here comes Charlie."

Main title (fragments of *Redskin rhumba*, *Cherokee*, etc., interspersed with some excerpts from performances by Anita Ortez and The Fabulous Flippers) (2:05)
Clap hands! here comes Charley! aBill Holman (4:05)
It had to be you aBilly Byers (3:36)
Introduction to an ending aBill Holman (4:15)
[Anita Ortez: *Malagueña*]
Bali Bali buck dance aBill Holman (4:35)
[Fabulous Flippers: *Harlem shuffle*]
Cotton tail (aMaxwell Davis?) (4:24)
Mumbles vClark Terry (1:56)
Jeep's blues (3:25)
I've got my love to keep me warm vAnita Ortez (2:29)
Rabble rouser aBilly Byers (2:10)
[Fabulous Flippers: *Tell the truth*]

Mab 66 (including Anita Ortez doing *East side, west side*) (12:20)
Redskin rhumba aHead (1:50)
#It had to be you aBilly Byers (2:58)

<u>**NYC, "Bring back the big bands" (Social Security Admin.), ca. Jan. 1967**</u>

Redskin rhumba (opening theme) aHead
PROGRAM 49, 50, 51, 52
Rabble rouser aBilly Byers
PROGRAM 49
Satin doll aBilly Byers
PROGRAM 49
Bali Bali buck dance aBill Holman
PROGRAM 49
I can't get started aBill Holman
PROGRAM 49
Redskin rhumba (closing theme) aHead
PROGRAM 49, 50, 51, 52
Cotton tail aMaxwell Davis
PROGRAM 50
Jeep's blues
PROGRAM 50
Upper Manhattan Medical Group
PROGRAM 50
Introduction to an ending aBill Holman
PROGRAM 50
Clap hands! here comes Charley! aBill Holman
PROGRAM 51
'Deed I do aDon Rader
PROGRAM 51
Early autumn aBill Holman
PROGRAM 51
Goodbye aBill Holman
PROGRAM 51
Blue rose aBill Holman
PROGRAM 52
It had to be you aBilly Byers
PROGRAM 52
Cherokee aBilly May
PROGRAM 52
Skyliner aBilly Moore
PROGRAM 52

To fulfill a Las Vegas commitment, Charlie had Raoul Romero put together a band of local musicians, with the subsequent addition of Snooky Young. The line-up included:

Carl Saunders or Snooky Young, lead, Ron Towell, and three or four others, tpts; Jimmy Guinn (lead), and two or three others, tbns; Raoul Romero, ts and four others, reeds; Eddie Wied, p; Ernest E. McDaniel, b; Karl Kiffe, d

Feb. 3–16, 1967: Las Vegas, Blue Room, Tropicana

Also on the bill was singer Tommy Leonetti. The Modernaires were among those to "drop in to dig his torrid big band sound in the Trop's Blue Room." (*Las Vegas Review Journal*). Charlie followed a bill which included Maynard Ferguson and Mel Tormé and he in turn was followed by Guy Lombardo. The following broadcast was reported by George Hall (*Hall 70*):

<u>*Las Vegas, Blue Room, Tropicana, CBS b'cast, between Feb. 3 and 16, 1967*</u>

Redskin rhumba (opening theme) aHead
Rabble rouser aBilly Byers
Satin doll aBilly Byers
A wonderful day like today vTommy Leonetti
Joey vTommy Leonetti
That warm and tender glow vTommy Leonetti
It had to be you aBilly Byers
Clap hands! here comes Charley! aBill Holman

Chapter 9

In a Mellow Tone 1967–1991

"The First Annual Charlie Barnet International Golf Tournament and Happening" was staged at the San Jacinto Country Club in mid–June 1967. "The Ellington program ... had an audience of celebrities." (*Stratemann*)

On July 5, 1968 he appeared in front of the Ellington band at the Newport Jazz Festival.

Duke Ellington and his orchestra

Cat Anderson, Cootie Williams, Herbie Jones, Mercer Ellington, Money Johnson, Clark Terry, tpts; Lawrence Brown, Chuck Connors, Buster Cooper, tbns; Russell Procope, as, cl; Johnny Hodges, as; Paul Gonsalves, ts, cl; Harold Ashby, ts; Harry Carney, bar, cl, bcl; Nat Pierce (for Duke), p; Steve Little (for Rufus Jones), d; Jeff Castleman, b

Newport, CT, "Newport Jazz Festival," July 5, 1968

Cherokee/Southern fried/East side, west side/ Things ain't what they used to be/Skyliner/ Pompton Turnpike/Smiles

Charlie Barnet and his orchestra

Conte Candoli, Larry McGuire, John Audino, Ray Triscari, Don Fagerquist, tpts; Dick Hyde, Richard Nash, Phillip Teele, tbns; Bud Shank, James Cook, as; Thomas Scott, Pete Christlieb, ts; Bob Jung, bar; Pete Jolly, p; Max Bennett, b; Herb Ellis, g; John Guerin, d; Larry Bunker, perc

Hollywood, Reader's Digest recording session, Dec. 1, 1969

A hard day's night aBilly May
Reader's Digest RDS 6872, RD3/4 034 1, RD3/4 106; Reader's Digest RD8 5231; READER'S DIGEST RD05 106 1 (8-track)

Call me aBilly May
Reader's Digest RD4 169, RDS 6872, RD3/4 112

Music to watch girls by aBilly May
Reader's Digest RDS 6872, RD3/4 112, RD4 169; Reader's Digest RD8 5233

The beat goes on aBilly May
Reader's Digest RDS 6872, RD3/4 112, RD4 169

As preceding, Dec. 2, 1969

Charade aBilly May
Reader's Digest RDS 6872, RD3/4 034 1,

RD3/4 106; Reader's Digest RD8 5231; READER'S DIGEST RD05 106 1 (8-track)

Come together aBilly May

Reader's Digest RDS 6872, RD3/4 106; RD4 169; Reader's Digest RD8 5233; READER'S DIGEST RD05 106 1 (8-track)

Little green apples aBilly May

Reader's Digest RDS 6872, RD4 169, RD 233, RD 113 [As "Billy May and his orchestra. Saxophone solo by Charlie Barnet"], *RD 3/4 103, RD3/4 112, RD4 46 10*; *Bulldog (E) BDL 2025* [As "Billy May and his orchestra"]; *Capitol (C) RD (S) 2 832, RB233*; *Warwick (E) WW2070*; Bulldog (E) AJKL 2025; Reader's Digest (C) RD4 832 3; **SONY A 19995**

The girl from Ipanema aBilly May

Reader's Digest RDS 6872, RD4 169, RD3/4 112, **SONY A 19995**

Charlie appeared with the Mort Lindsay band on the Merv Griffin Show.

Mort Lindsay band

Included Pete Candoli, Herb Ellis, Kai Winding, Ted Nash, Jack Sheldon, and possibly Richie Kamuca

Hollywood, "The Merv Griffin Show," CBS-TV, Jan. 18, 1971

Cherokee/Pompton Turnpike/Skyliner
South Rampart Street parade
Take the "A" Train
On the sunny side of the street vConnie Haines

Guido Basso Band

Guido Basso flhn & tpt, Arnie Cykowski or Eric Traugott, Al Stanwyk, Bruce Cassidy, tpts; Teddy Roderman, Rob McConnell, Butch Watanabe, Ron Hughes or Bob Livingstone, tbns; Moe Koffman, Rudy Toth or Bernie Piltch, as; Eugene Amaro, Rick Wilkins, ts; Gary Morgan, bar; Jimmy Coxon, p; Don Thompson, b; Terry Clarke, d

Toronto, "In the Mood" CBC-TV, taped ca. Dec. 13, 1971; televised Jan. 13, 1972

Clap hands! here comes Charley!
Cherokee/Pompton Turnpike/Skyliner
Satin doll
It had to be you
Charleston alley
Bali Bali buck dance (omitted from show as broadcast)

Personnel is unknown for next appearance.

Hollywood, "The Merv Griffin Show," May 25, 1972 (b'cast May 29)

Program contents unknown

In a band assembled for an appearance at Disneyland, the personnel included:

Cat Anderson and Al Aarons, tpts; Med Flory, Rod Cradit, Don Menza, Bob Jung, reeds; Britt Woodman, tbn; Monte Budwig, b; Jack Sperling, d

"I went overboard on rehearsals. I paid them myself, and spent everything I was paid and a little bit more, because I wanted to be proud standing in front of that band." (New York News World, Aug. 30, 1978). A member of the Basie band, which was to follow Charlie, was around for some of the rehearsals and warned the Count that Charlie was loaded for bear and that the Basie band had better shape up as Charlie was "serious."

May 27–28, 1972: Disneyland, "11th Annual Big Band Festival," Plaza Gardens, 9P–1A.

Charlie appeared again with the Guido Basso band:

Guido Basso Band

Guido Basso, tpt and flh, Bruce Cassidy, Al Hendricks, Al Stanwyk, Eric Traugott, Cat Anderson, tpts; Rob McConnell, Teddy Roderman, Butch Watanabe, Ron Hughes, tbns; Eugene Amaro, Jerry Toth, Moe

Koffman, Rick Wilkins, Gary Morgan, reeds; Bruce Harvey, p; Terry Clarke, d; Don Thompson, d

Aug. 24–25, 1973: Toronto, CNE Bandshell

Toronto, CNE Bandshell, CBL-FM b'cast, Aug. 25, 1973

Redskin rhumba (opening theme) aHead
Rabble rouser aBilly Byers
Satin doll aBilly Byers [not broadcast]
It had to be you aBilly Byers
Skyliner aBilly Moore
Pompton Turnpike aBilly May
The birth of the blues
Cotton tail# aMaxwell Davis
All heart [not broadcast]
One o'clock jump aBill Holman [not broadcast]
I can't get started aBill Holman
Flying home aBill Holman
Things ain't what they used to be# [not broadcast]
Goodbye aBill Holman
Cherokee aBilly May
Unidentified instrumental

"I told Cat, I said, 'Look, now, I don't want you to play any high notes until after I introduce you on your number.' I said, 'Don't blow the show, you know.' So he's back there and he's very good, and I finally introduced him, and he's doing that thing he does in Birth of the blues, which of course he picks up all by himself. And I gave him a big buildup in the announcement, you know, so forth and so on, the greatest lip in the world, and he got up and he, splat, split, splat, splat, da-da, you know [laughter] the guys in the band broke up. They recovered in time, but he of course acquitted himself nobly after that, but what an awful thing to happen after the build up." (Sm)

Our man fronted the Kenton band for an ailing Stan sometime during the week of Sept. 1–7, 1974 for a Disneyland date. Charlie did not play.

Late in 1979 he gave his band library—about 270 arrangements—to College of the Desert, Palm Desert, Calif.

During his retirement from the music business he spent a good deal of time deep-sea fishing on the *Betty B. I* and *Betty B. II*, doing crossword puzzles as a joint activity with Betty, playing the horses, listening to music on his state-of-the-art sound system—he most liked the old swing bands—having one martini before dinner and no more than one scotch and water afterwards, traveling and otherwise enjoying the fruits of his labors and inheritance.

Reputedly his last public performance was in 1981 in a basement club in Singapore. Winton Fillmore, a local DJ and entrepreneur, organized an afternoon jam session in Charlie's honor. The club was packed to the gunnels, to such an extent that movement of any kind was extremely difficult but somehow Charlie made it to the stand where he played *Things ain't what they used to be* on a borrowed horn.

He died a month short of his 78th birthday.

This is to inform you that

my beloved husband of 33 years

Charlie Barnet

passed away September 4, 1991

of Alzheimer's and Pneumonia.

I trust he will be remembered

with love as he is by me.

Betty Barnet

The Mab, age 4 (ca. 1917; courtesy of Betty Barnet).

"Got the world in a jug" (ca. 1924; courtesy of Betty Barnet).

Frank Wine-gar band at the Village Barn, NYC, 1931 (by arrangement with Duncan Schiedt). *Left to right:* Evan Young, vn; Horace Diaz, Jr., p; CHARLIE BARNET, ts (sitting in guitarist Scoop Thomson's place); Bill Wyder, brass bass; Frank Wine-gar, leader; Gordon Tully, tpt; Gable Gelinas, sax; Walt Ottinger, d; Eddie Wade, tpt; Willard "Skrooy" Brady, sax; Huffert Allen, tbn; Norman "Pal" Campbell, sax; "Hank," vocalist.

"I had a new Auburn and five men riding with me." (TSY p. 53; courtesy of Betty Barnet.)

Cocoanut Grove, Park Central Hotel, NYC, 1934 (courtesy of Herb Baschung). ***Left to right:*** **(Chris Griffin?), tpt; (Neil Reed?), tbn; Ruth Robbins, vocal; Milt Laufer, as; Pete Peterson, b; CB; Nat Brown, as; Jackie Martin, ts.**

Denizens of Sloppy Joe's (Havana, 1935; courtesy of Betty Barnet). Left to right: Jerry Johnson, (Mark Steele?), CB.

Soaking it up (Havana, 1935; courtesy of John Brechler).

New Penn Club, Liberty, PA, 1938 (courtesy of Frank Driggs). *Tpts:* Johnny Mendel, Johnny Owens, Bobby Burnet. *Tbns:* Bob Fishel, Ben Hall, Don Ruppersberg. *Saxes:* James Lamare, Joe Estren, Rocque Dominick, Henry Saltman. *Rhythm:* Graham Forbes, p; Bob Elden, b; Wesley Dean, d.

Palomar, LA (ca. September 1939; by arangement with Wayne Knight). Bob Burnet, Don McCook, Kurt Bloom, Ray Michaels.

Dorothy Lamour, CB, Lee Wiley at the Onyx Club (spring 1939; by arrangement with Wayne Knight).

Bobby Burnet, Boddy Tate (ca. 1940; by arrangement with Wayne Knight).

Bob Carroll (ca 1941; by arrangement with Wayne Knight).

"Juke Box Jenny" (1941; by arrangement with Wayne Knight). *Tpts:* Bernie Privin, (Paul McCoy?), (Cy Baker?), Bob Burnet (behind CB). *Saxes:* Kurt Bloom, (Ray Hopfner?), Conn Humphreys, James Lamare. *Tbns:* Bill Robertson, (Spud Murphy?), (Tommy Reo?), Ford Leary. *Rhythm:* Bill Miller, p; Phil Stephens,b; (Jack LeMaire?), g; Cliff Leeman, d.

Above: 1942 (courtesy of Joe Ferrante). *Tpts:* Sidney De Paris, Joe Ferrante, Bud McQuinness, Neal Hefti. *Tbns:* Bill Robertson, Kahn Keene, Wally Barron, Russ Brown. *Saxes:* Kurt Bloom, George Bohn, Conn Humphreys, Jimmy Lamare. *Rhythm:* Bill Hiller, p; (Olin Anderhold?), b; Jackie Mills, d; Tom Moore, g. *Vocals:* Al Lane, Hazel Bruce.

Right: State Theater, Hartford, 1942 (courtesy of Tony De Bonee).

Left: Peanuts Holland (by arrangement Wayne Knight).

Below: Schlitz Brewery, Milwaukee, November 27, 1942 (courtesy of Mac Marlow). *Left to right (back row):* Unidentified, Irving Berger, Steve Cole, Chubby Jackson, Max Gussak, Walter McGuffin, Unidentified. *Front row:* Sam Kublin, Mac Marlow, Tony Lala, Kurt Bloom, CB, Anita Bradley, Cliff Leeman, Unidentified, Andy Gibson.

Top: Howard Theater, Washington, D.C., May 1943 (courtesy Frank Driggs). *Tpts:* Dick Vance, Peanuts Holland. *Tbns:* Bob Swift, Eddie Bert, Ed Fromm. *Saxes:* Kurt Bloom, George Siravo, Steve Cole, Mike Goldberg. *Rhythm:* Lou Fromm, d; Chubby Jackson, b; Ralph Burns, p. *Bottom:* 1944–1945 (by arrangement with Wayne Knight). Kay Starr, Rae DeGeer, Harold Hahn, CB.

Top: Victorville, CA, NCO Club, spring 1945 (courtesy of Frances Shirley). *Saxes:* Bob Poland, Kurt Bloom, Rae DeGeer, Gene Kinsey, (Pripps behind Frances Shirley). *Tpts:* Frances Shirley, Peanuts Holland, Jack Mootz, Lyman Vunk, Ernie Figueroa. *Tbns:* Ed Fromm, Dave Hallet. *Vocalists:* Ginny Powell, Phil Barton. *Bottom:* Fresno, 1945 (courtesy of Tiny Rips). *Rhythm:* Unidentified, g; Hal Hahn, d; John Chance, b. *Saxes:* Bob Poland, Kurt Bloom, Rae DeGeer, Tiny Rips, Gene Kinsey, Eddie Pripps. *Tpts:* Peanuts Holland, Frances Shirley, Ernie Figueroa. *Tbns:* Ed Fromm, Dave Hallet.

Top: Victoria, BC, 1948 (courtesy of Eric Gee). *Tpts:* (Lammar Wright, Jr.?), Irving Lewis, Dave Nichols, Jack Hansen. *Tbns:* Herbie Harper, Phil Washburne, Karl De Karske. *Saxes:* Bob Dawes, Bud Shank, Walt Weidler, Frank Pappalardo. *Vocalist:* Jean Louise. *Bottom:* Washington, D.C., 1949 (courtesy of Vinnie Dean). *Tpts:* Johnny Howell, Tony Di Nardi, Doc Severinsen, Fern Caron, Lammar Wright, Jr. *Tbns:* Obie Massingill, Dick Kenney, Ken Martlock. *Saxes:* Danny Bank, Kurt Bloom, Vinnie Dean, Art Raboy, Dave Matthews. *Rhythm:* Claude Williamson, p; Eddie Safranski, b; Cliff Leeman, d (behind CB). *Vocalists:* Bunny Briggs, Unidentified male, Unidentified female.

Above: Apollo Theater, NYC, October 1949 (courtesy of Vinnie Dean). *Border (clockwise):* Pearl Bailey, CB, Unidentified, Pigmeat Markham or Flip Wilson, Unidentified, Reuben Leon, Kurt Bloom, Maynard Ferguson, Carlos Vidal, Ray Wetzel, Boddy Stewart, Bunny Briggs, Reuben Leon, (Chuck Etter?), Unidentified tpt; Gil Barrios, p; Rolf Ericson, Ray Wetzel, Johnny Howell, Maynard Ferguson, Kurt Bloom, Manny Albam, (Chuck Etter?), Dick Kenney. *Inner circle:* Doc Severinsen, CB, Reuben Leon, Vinnie Dean, Dick Hafer.

Left: Trudy Richards (courtesy of Trudy Richards).

Top: Pepperell AFB NCO Club, 1952 (courtesy of Don Davidson). *Tpts:* Dick Sherman, Al Porcino, Wayne Nichols, Bill Castagnino (behind Soltain). *Tbns:* Obie Massingill (behind CB), Dick Kenney, John Soltain. *Saxes:* Red Norman, Stan Seckler, Dick Paladino, Kurt Bloom, Don Davidson. *Rhythm:* Bob Harrington, p; Bob Peterson, b; Bill Dolny, d. *Bottom:* Catalina, 1956 (courtesy of Dave Wells). CB; Ralph Mullens, tpt; Boone Stines, d; Norman Parker, p; Ernie Small, tbn & bar; Dave Wells, tbn; Unidentified, b.

Right: La Paz Hotal, Palm Springs, ca. 1962 (courtesy of Lynn Winiecki).

Below: "Charlie Barnet and His Orchestra in Concert" (1967; by arrangement Jack Brady). *Tpts:* Randy Brecker, Clyde Reasinger, Snooky Young, George Triffon, Clark Terry. *Tbns:* Jack Jeffers (btbn), Jimmy Cleveland, Herb Wise, Billy Tole. *Saxes:* Danny Bank, Richie Kamuca, Willie Smith, Dick Meldonian, Stan Edson. *Rhythm:* Nat Pierce, p; Sam Herman, g; Eddie Jones, b; Steve Little, d.

Betty and The Mab

Toronto, 1973

Reflections (by arrangement with Wayne Knight).

Postscript

Betty once remarked to him that he could say that he'd really made it if his name turned up in a crossword puzzle. Check out 43 down.

ACROSS

1 Girl, in Aussie slang
7 —— jongg
10 Audi rival
13 Novelist
14 "Our Gang" schoolteacher Miss ——
17 Alfalfa, for one
18 Least sissyish
19 French satellite launcher
20 Arena tops
21 Head squeeze
22 Suffolk's county seat
24 Children's classic
27 1936 Medicine Nobelist Otto
28 "Evil Woman" rock grp.
29 Answer incorrectly
32 Subj. of three of the six Nobel Prizes
34 Adm.'s milieu
35 Pavement caution
36 Clover site
37 Not flabby
39 TV show set in Springfield
47 Little lobster's look-alike
48 Kitchen implement
49 First name in comedy
50 Get in
51 Pertaining to construction
54 "—— in the Rain"
55 Aeschylus trilogy
56 Fume
57 Curved path
58 Party staple
59 Ethyl acetate and others

DOWN

1 Surprised with, with "on"
2 Eavesdropper
3 Preserve, as fodder
4 If
5 Rest against
6 A Francis
7 Year the Paris Métro opened
8 Heavenly neighbor of Scorpius
9 Shop tools
10 Word with knee or riding
11 Slop site
12 Marked by drinking
15 Shown up unexpectedly
16 Not exactly outgoing
22 1939 hit "—— for That"
23 False
25 "Russlan and Ludmilla" composer
26 Low
29 Pointy shoe wearer
30 Rude ones, at the dinner table
31 Exhausting existences
32 Dutch oven
33 Blocked (off)
38 Kind of user
40 Does' mates
41 Razorfish, e.g.
42 39-Across, e.g.
43 Charlie of swing
44 Foreign fleer
45 Tennessee's first governor, John ——
46 Courses
51 Familiar tapper
52 Article of the Constitution regarding the judiciary
53 Topper

ANSWER TO PREVIOUS PUZZLE

Puzzle by Frank Longo

(©New York Times 1998. Used by permission)

(Correct answers courtesy Karyl Mather)

So long, Charlie. We miss you.

Album Listing

78 ALBUMS

Apollo A 133	*Charlie Barnet, etc.*
Capitol CC 106	*Giants of jazz*
Mercury C 114	*Charlie Barnet plays Charlie Barnet*

45 ALBUMS

Capitol CCF 235	*Battle of the bands*
Capitol CCF 325	*Classics in jazz—the modern idiom*
Mercury C 114 X 45	*Charlie Barnet plays Charlie Barnet*
Vi WP 217	*Theme songs*

LPs

Ace of Hearts (E) AH 157	*Skyliner*
Affinity (E) AFS 1012	*Big band bounce & boogie: Skyliner—Charlie Barnet*
Aircheck 5	*Charlie Barnet and his orchestra*
Aircheck 30	*Charlie Barnet and his orchestra "On the air" vol. 2*
Ajax 104, 106, 140, 147,155, 201, 209, 217, 225, 233, 273	*Charlie Barnet in disco order, vol. 1-2, 16-24*
Ajazz 512	*Big band singers—Fran Warren and Kay Starr*
Alamac QSR 2435	*Charlie Barnet and his orchestra—1938*
Alamac 2446	*Charlie Barnet and his orchestra—1949*
Ariola (Ger) S 701177 1T	*Charlie Barnet and his orchestra*
BBC (E) REB 666	*The classic years in digital stereo: Swing—small groups*

Bandstand 7106	*Screwballs of swingtime*
Bandstand 7118	*Musical madness*
Bandstand 7123	*Charlie Barnet and his orchestra 1936-1941*
Barclay (E) GLP 6592	*(Album title unknown)*
Big Band Archives 1209	*Swingin' on nothin'*
Big Band Archives LP 2204	*The big band scene: and all that jazz*
Big Bands (Time-Life) STBB 07	*Charlie Barnet*
BLU-DISC T 1012	*The unheard Benny Goodman, vol. 6, 1939-45*
Blue Heaven BH-1 106	*Wings over Manhattan*
Blue Heaven BH-6 604	*A legend*
Blue Heaven BH-7 702	*Encore*
Blue Star (Fr) GLP 3521	*Dance session #2*
Blue Star (Fr) GLP 6923	*Charlie Barnet plays Charlie Barnet*
Bluebird AXM2 5526, 5577, 5581, 5585, 5587, 5590	*The complete Charlie Barnet, vol.1-6*
Boulevard (E) 4113	*(Album title unknown)*
Bright Orange X-BO 719	*On stage live—Charlie Barnet and his orch.*
Bright Orange BO 7819	*On stage with Charlie Barnet and his orchestra*
Brunswick (E) LAT 8094	*Hop on the Skyliner!!*
Brunswick (G) 87099	*Golden book of classic swing, vol. 3*
Bulldog (E) BDL 2025	*Twenty golden pieces of Billy May and his orchestra*
CBS (Fr) (N) 88210	*The complete Duke Ellington, vol. 9—1937*
CBS-Realm (E) RM 52310	*Theme songs of the great bands, vol. 1*
CBS-Sony (Ja) SOPM 188	*Metronome all-stars*
Calliope CAL 3026	*Sessions, live: Charlie Barnet/Mel Tormé*
Calliope CAL 3031	*Sessions, live: Charlie Barnet/Les Brown*
Camay CA 3024	*Basie greets Barnett*
Camden CCL2 0619 (e)	*The big band sound*
Camden CAL 389	*Charlie's choice*
Camden CAL°/CAS 811	*Original recordings by great bands of our time*
Capitol H 235	*Battle of the bands*
Capitol H 325	*Classics in jazz—the modern idiom*
Capitol T/ST 1403	*Jazz oasis—The Charlie Barnet Quartet*
Capitol T/ST 1595	*Polynesian fantasy*
Capitol ST 23867	*(Album title unknown)*
Capitol T 624	*Classics in jazz—Charlie Barnet and his orch.*
Capitol T 667	*Battle of the big bands*
Capitol (Australia) CLP 001	*(Album title unknown)*
Capitol (Australia) H 235	*Battle of the bands*

Capitol (Australia) T 667	*Battle of the big bands*
Capitol (E) EMS 1321	*Stan Freberg: The best of the Capitol years*
Capitol (E) LC 6510	*Battle of the bands*
Capitol (E) LC 6561	*Classics in jazz—the modern idiom*
Capitol (E) LCT 6018	*Charlie Barnet and his orchestra*
Capitol (Eu) T 20396	*Ten tasty tenors*
Capitol (Ja) CR 8811	*Capitol collector's items*
Capitol (Ja) CR 8812	*Bebop professors*
Capitol (Ja) ECJ 40004	*Classics in jazz—Charlie Barnet and his orch.*
Capitol (Ja) ECJ 50073	*Bebop professors*
Capitol (Ja) EDJ 50077	*A song was born*
Capitol (N) 5C.052 80854	*Bebop spoken here*
Capitol (N) & US M 11061	*Bebop spoken here*
Capitol (not US) ST 23346	*(Album title unknown)*
Capitol (not US) ST 23737	*(Album title unknown)*
Capitol (not US) ST 24630	*(Album title unknown)*
Choreo/äva A/AS 10	*Charlie Barnet ? ! ? ! ? ! ? (Following the initial release of these recordings on the Choreo label an east coast dance studio with the same name protested so the label name was changed to "äva". The albums exist with a variety of stickers, different labels, and different jackets.)*
Cicala-"Serie Jazz Live" (It) BLJ 8008	*The Charlie Barnet orchestra*
Circle CLP 65	*Charlie Barnet and his orchestra 1941*
Clef MG C 139	*Dance with Charlie Barnet*
Clef MG C 164	*Charlie Barnet dance session #2*
Clef MG C 165	*Charlie Barnet dance session*
Clef MG C 638	*One night stand*
Clef MG V 2031	*For dancing lovers*
Clef (Australia) MG C114	*Charlie Barnet plays Charlie Barnet*
Clef (Australia) MG C 139	*Dance with Charlie Barnet*
Clef (Australia) MG C 164	*Charlie Barnet dance session #2*
Col CB 4	*Jazz at Columbia—Swing*
Col CG 33557	*Boss of the bass*
Col CL 2528	*Metronome all stars*
Col CL 639°	*Town Hall jazz concert*
Col G 30009°	*Big bands' greatest hits*
Col J2 15596	*The big bands are back*
Col JC 36580	*Let's dance*
Col JC 36742	*Dance the night away*

Col JC 36743	*Come dance with me*
Col JSN 6042	*Swing Street*
Col LG 3128	*Red Norvo and his all stars*
Col P 16741	*The best of the big bands, vol. 5*
Col P2M 5111	*Best of the big bands*
Col P7M 5121	*The big bands revisited*
Col (E) 33-SX 1511	*Swing street*
Col (E) 33C 9024	*Dance session*
Col Musical Treasuries D 450	*The great bands: The kings of swing*
Col Musical Treasuries P2M 5111	*The best of the big bands*
Col Musical Treasuries P2M 5193	*The best of the big bands*
Col Musical Treasuries P2S 5194	*The best of the big bands*
Col Musical Treasuries P7S 5122	*Big bands revisited*
Col Musical Treasuries Z 173	*Best of the big bands and best of the big band singers*
Col Record Prod. [unnumbered]	*When they brought down the house*
Collectables 5096	*Big bands of the swinging years, vol. 1*
Collectables 5097	*Big bands of the swinging years, volume 2*
Collectors Items (E) 011	*(Album title unknown)*
Contour (E) 2870.348	*Explosive sounds of the big bands*
Contour (E) CN 2010	*The golden sounds of the big bands, volume 1*
Contour (E) CN 2870.443	*The golden sounds of the big bands*
Coral (E) CDL 8024	*(Album title unknown)*
Coral (E) CDLM 8046	*(Album title unknown)*
Coral (E) CDLM 8047	*(Album title unknown)*
Coral (E) MCM 1001	*(Album title unknown)*
Coral (Ger) 6 22182	*Charlie Barnet and his orchestra*
Coral (Ger) 6 22442	*(Album title unknown)*
Coral (Ger) 6 22569	*(Album title unknown)*
Coral (Ger) 6 28203	*(Album title unknown)*
Coral (Ger) COPS 6997	*(Album title unknown)*
Coral (Ger) MOPS 8265	*(Album title unknown)*
Coral (Ger) PCO 7840	*Charlie Barnet and his orchestra*
Coral (Ger) PCO 7995	*(Album title unknown)*
Creative World ST 1056	*Charlie Barnet big band 1967*
Crown CLP 5008	*Jazz surprise: The modern jazz stars*
Crown CLP 5134	*On stage with Charlie Barnet*
Crown CST 167	*On stage with Charlie Barnet*
DJM (E) DJML 061	*C.B.*
Dan (Ja) VC 5017	*The favorite pop songs of the 40s*

Dan (Ja) VC 5026	*The great swing bands of the 40s*
Decca DL 8098	*Hop on the Skyliner!*
Epic BN 24029	*Swing Street*
Epic JEE 22009	*Red Norvo and his all stars*
Epic JSN6042	*Swing street*
Epic LG 1013	*Neil Hefti—Singing instrumentals*
Epic LG 3113	*Neil Hefti—Singing instrumentals*
Epic LG 3128	*Red Norvo and his all stars*
Epic LN 3440	*Singing instrumentals*
Europa Jazz (It) EJ 1011	*(Album title unknown)*
Europa Jazz (It) EJ 1027	*Europa jazz: Erskine Hawkins...*
Everest BR 5008	*Cherokee*
Everest BR 5042	*Pop parade*
Everest BR 5059	*More Charlie Barnet*
Everest ER 8	*Big band era*
Everest FS 282	*Charlie Barnet*
Everest FS 333	*Charlie Barnet, volume 2*
Everest FS 359	*Big bands of the swinging years*
Everest FS 367	*Big bands of the swinging years, volume 2*
Everest SDBR 1001/5	*That's jazz*
Everest SDBR 1008	*Cherokee*
Everest SDBR 1042	*Pop parade*
Everest SDBR 1059	*More Charlie Barnet*
Everest (Argentina) SDBR 1059	*Mas Charlie Barnet*
Everest (Ger) 70176 1T	*Charlie Barnet and his orchestra*
Everest (Ger) 76177	*(Album title unknown)*
Extreme Rarities ER 1002	*Hot jazz on film vol. 1*
Fanfare 38 138	*Charlie Barnet and his orchestra featuring Roy Eldridge—Al Killian*
First Heard (E) FH 17	*Charlie Barnet and his orchestra 1944-1947* (or *Charlie Barnet vol. 2)*
First Heard (E) FH 44	*"Showcase" Charlie Barnet and his orchestra*
First Heard (E) FH 1974 12	*Charlie Barnet and his orchestra*
First Time Records FTR 1504	*Charlie Barnet and his orch. (1938)*
First Time Records FTR 1513	*Big band collector's choice (1938-1946)*
First Time Records FTR 2501	*Big band themes on the air*
Franklin Mint 33	*The greatest recordings of the big band era: Charlie Barnet & his orchestra*
Franklin Mint 93-96	*Big band jazz: Fletcher Henderson—Buddy Rich*

Franklin Mint Record no. 19	*The greatest recordings of the big band era: Charlie Barnet & his orchestra*
Fresh Sound (Sp) NL 45977	*Redskin romp*
Golden Era 15015	*Charlie Barnet and his orchestra 1944–1949*
Golden Era GE 15015	*Charlie Barnet and his orchestra 1944–1949*
Golden Era GE 15082	*The small groups*
Golden Era LP 15037	*Charlie Barnet and his orchestra: Fair and warmer*
Golden Era LP 55001	*The big bands play again*
Golden Hour (E) GH 868	*Skyliner: the big band sounds of Charlie Barnet and Billy May*
I Grande del Jazz (It) GdJ 08	*Charlie Barnet*
HMV (E) CLP 1143	*(Charlie Barnet?)*
Harmony HL 7044	*Metronome all stars*
Harmony HL 7336	*Theme songs of the great bands, volume 1*
Hep (E) HEP 2005	*Charlie Barnet live at Basin Street East*
Hollywood Soundstage HS 5014	*Jam session/Reveille with Beverly*
IAJRC 8	*Charlie Barnet and his orch.*
IAJRC 14	*Radio Rhythm, volume 1*
IAJRC 17	*The swinging war years*
Jazz Archives JA 9	*Frankie Newton Swinging on 52nd Street 'Emperor Jones'*
Jazz Band (Fr) 8008	*The Charlie Barnet orchestra*
Jazz Bird JAZ 2016	*Charlie Barnet—King of the Saxophone*
Joyce 1035	*One night stand with Eddie Condon*
Joyce 1081	*One night stand with Charlie Barnet; on the air in the fifties*
Joyce 1105	*One night stand with Charlie Barnet at the Casino Gardens*
Joyce 1152	*One night stand with Charlie Barnet at the Famous Door, July 1939*
Joyce 2017	*Downbeat with Charlie Barnet*
Joyce 6020	*The big bands' greatest vocalists*
Joyce JRC 1214	*Charlie Barnet at Mission Beach*
Joyce LP 1001	*One night stand with Charlie Barnet*
Joyce LP 1012	*One night stand with the battle of the bands*
Joyce LP 1031	*One night stand with Charlie Barnet, volume 2*
Joyce LP 1052	*One night stand with Charlie Barnet at the Palladium*
Joyce LP 2012	*Radio discs of Charlie Barnet 1944*
Joyce LP 3001	*Film tracks of Charlie Barnet*
Joyce LP 5003	*Charlie Barnet's jubilee*
Joyce LP 5004	*Charlie Barnet's second Jubilee*

K-tel (N) TN 1241	*Kings of swing*
Karusell (Ger) 635.077	*Manhattan—Charlie Barnet big band*
Karusell (Swed) K 1039	*(Album title unknown)*
Koala AW 14158	*Wings over Manhattan*
Koala KO 14276	*Caravan*
Limited Edition Records LP 101	*Charlie Barnet plays Duke Ellington*
Longines Symph. Soc. SVS 5386	*The years to remember: The kings of swing*
MCA 1927	*Get out those old records*
MCA 27094	*Best of the big bands*
MCA MCA2 4063	*Leonard Feather encyclopedia of jazz on records, vol. 5*
MCA MCA2 4064	*Singin' the blues*
MCA MCA2 4069°	*The best of Charlie Barnet*
MCA (E) MCM 1001	*(Album title unknown)*
MCA (Ja) MCA 3043	*Swing and bop*
MCA (Ja) MCA 3146	*Skyliner: Charlie Barnet and his orchestra*
MGM SE/E 4219	*The very best of the big bands*
MGM (E) C 990	*The very best of the big bands*
MP Records (Ger) 33013	*The best of the big bands*
Mark 56 553 B	*(Album title unknown)*
Mercury MG C 114	*Charlie Barnet plays Charlie Barnet*
Meritt LP 3	*Featured performances by Teddy Wilson, Benny Goodman & Harry James*
Meritt 8	*The trumpet album, volume 1*
Metro (Argentina) 2356.021	*Twelve big band classics by 12 classic big bands*
Metro (Fr) 2355.022	*(Album title unknown)*
Moonlite KH1 2	*(Album title unknown)*
Mosaic MR27 138	*The complete Capitol recordings of the Nat King Cole Trio*
Murray Hill 927942	C*ollector's history of classic jazz*
Murray Hill M 56761	*Big bands of the swinging years*
The Music Makers	Program 334 *Charlie Barnet*
Music for Pleasure (E) MFP 1432	*(Album title unknown)*
Music for Pleasure (E) MFP 5198	*(Album title unknown)*
Narwood Productions Program 334	*Charlie Barnet*
Neiman-Marcus DMM4 0261	*First Edition (Jazz series)*
Neiman-Marcus DMM4 0405	*First Edition/Third series*
Neiman-Marcus DMM4 0456	*First Edition/4th series: Jazz*
New World (E) 5024	*Basie greets Barnett*
Nostalgia Lane NLR 1601	*Big band salute*
Official (Den) 12003	*Havin' fun with (rare duets)*

One Up (E) OU 2008	*(Album title unknown)*
Onward to Yesterday OTY 1504	*Charlie Barnet and his orch. (1938)*
Pandora (Ger) 913137	*The famous Gene Norman's "Just Jazz" concerts*
Parnaso (Argentina) 13032	*El rey del Saxofon*
Philips (E) BBL 7209	*Dazzlin' jazz—the big sound*
Philips (Eu) BO 7227L	*(Album title unknown)*
Philips (N) 21699 H	*Neil Hefti—Singing instrumentals*
Philips (N?) BBL 7077	*(Red Norvo and his swing septet/octet?)*
Phontastic (Swed) NOST 7610	*The alternate Goodman II*
Pickwick SH 3305 3	*Swingin' big bands*
Pumpkin 109	*New discoveries*
Queen (It) Q 066	*Little Jazz special*
RCA PRM/PRS 401	*The big bands live again*
RCA PRS 356	*Sentimental journey*
RCA VPM 6043°	*This is the big band era*
RCA (Fr) FXM1 7083	*Benny Goodman vol. 10 Echoes of the swing era (1935-48)*
RCA (Fr) NL 89279	*Louis Armstrong: From the big band to the all stars (1946 1956)*
RCA (Fr) NL 89483 2	*The indispensable Charlie Barnet, volumes 3/4 (1935–1939)*
RCA (Fr) PM 42041	*Charlie Barnet "The Duke's ideas" vol. 1 (1939-1941)*
RCA (Fr) PM 42401	*Charlie Barnet "Swing Street strut" vol.2 (1935-1942)*
RCA (Fr) PM 43259	*Harlem, l'age d'or 1926-1957*
RCA (Fr) PM 45689	*The indispensable Charlie Barnet, volumes 1/2 (1935–1939)*
RCA (Ger) LPM 551	*Charlie Barnet, vol. I*
RCA (Ger) LPM 567	*Charlie Barnet vol. II*
RCA (It) EDP 1004	*Jazz, Musica del nostro tempo*
RCA (It) LPM 34022	*(Album title unknown)*
RCA (Ja) RA 60-68	*The sounds of swing*
RCA (Ja) RJL 2019-20	*The swing*
RCA Spec. Prod. DMM1 0698	*Music of the Yank years—Big bands*
RCA Spec. Prod. (C) DPM2 0813	*In the mood: greatest hits of the big band era*
RCA Victor LPT 3062°	*Charlie Barnet plays Duke Ellington*
RCA Victor PRS 401 (e)	*The big bands live again*
RCA Victor (Argentina) AVLT 7	*Charlie Barnet interpreta a Duke Ellington*
RCA Victor (E) RD 7965	*Charlie Barnet, vol. I*
RCA Victor (E) RD 8088	*Charlie Barnet, vol. II*
Radiola 2MR 1314	*Radio band remotes*

Rare Records LP-6	*Louis Armstrong rare session 1934 & rare films*
Raretone (N) RTE 23006	*Barney Bigard*
Raven (Australia) RVLP 1019	*Stan Freberg vs Rock 'n' roll*
Rdr's Digest 2 776	*All star jazz festival*
Rdr's Digest RB4 84	*These were our songs—the early 40s*
Rdr's Digest RB4 136	*These were our songs—the late 30s*
Rdr's Digest RD 113	*Sweet with a beat*
Rdr's Digest RD 184 2	*Original hits of the big bands*
Rdr's Digest RD 233	*Big band memories*
Rdr's Digest RD3 112	*The big bands are back swinging today's hits*
Rdr's Digest RD4 21	*The swing years*
Rdr's Digest RD4 25 1	*The great band era (1936-1945)*
Rdr's Digest RD4 34 1	*Still swinging! The big bands play songs of the 60's*
Rdr's Digest RD4 44 1/2	*Great hits of the great bands*
Rdr's Digest RD4 45	*In the groove with the kings of swing*
Rdr's Digest RD4 78	*Fabulous memories of the fabulous 40s*
Rdr's Digest RD4 106	*Happiness is*
Rdr's Digest RD4 112	*The big bands are back swinging today's hits*
Rdr's Digest RD4 113	*The best of the swing years*
Rdr's Digest RD4 169	*Great songs! Great bands!*
Rdr's Digest RDS 6872	*(Album title unknown)*
Rdr's Digest (C) RD2 627	*In the groove with the kings of swing*
Rdr's Digest (C) RD2 710	*Original hits of the big bands*
Rdr's Digest (C) RD2 776	*All star jazz festival*
Rdr's Digest (C) RD2 832	*They're playing our song*
Rdr's Digest (E) RD 46	*Happiness is*
Rdr's Digest (E) RDM 265	*In the groove*
Rdr's Digest (E) RDM 2173	*The Glenn Miller years*
Rdr's Digest (Ja) 9S	*The great band era (1936-1945)*
Redwood Records (C) RWJ 1001	*Jazz Giants*
Riviera (Fr) RLP 6592	*Charlie Barnet plays Charlie Barnet*
Roy (E) Br C-2	*(Album title unknown)*
Roy (E) LP 1	*(Album title unknown)*
Saga (E) ERO 8014	*Billie Holiday volume 2 Lady Day*
Saga (E) PAN 6918	*Billie Holiday volume 2 Lady Day*
Sam Goody DNFR 7836	*Capitol music treasuries deluxe 6-record set*
Sandy Hook SH 2081	*Charlie Barnet and his orchestra: Rare recordings 1944–1947*
Sarpe (Sp) GJ 34	*Erskine Hawkins, Charlie Barnet, Bud Freeman*

Showcase LCA 0002	*Fifty great hits of the 30's and 40's*
Showcase SH 3301	*Those swingin' days of the big bands*
Smithsonian DMM 6 0610 4 R030	*Big band jazz*
Smithsonian R 035	*Singers and soloists of the swing bands*
Sony (Ja) NP 50419	*Album title unknown*
Sound Track Five 41	*Program no.535: The Charlie Barnett show*
Sounds Great 8003	*More sounds of the swing years*
Sounds Great SG 8014	*Tommy Dorsey—a tribute*
Sounds of Swing LP 103	*Charlie Barnet and his orchestra, vol. 1*
Sounds of Swing LP 122	*Artie Shaw: the sideman years*
Sunset SUM 1150	*Cherokee*
Sunset SUS 5150	*Cherokee*
Sunset (E) SLS 50037 E	*Cherokee*
Sunset (E) SLS 50249	*(Album title unknown)*
Swing Era LP 1002	*Charlie Barnet and his orchestra: "Some like it hot"*
Swing Era LP 1019	*Charlie Barnet and his orchestra—Rhapsody in Barnet*
Swing Era LPS 5001	*The big bands play again*
Swing House (E) SWH 6	*Charlie Barnet and his orchestra: Dance date*
Swing House (E) SWH 10	*A live Dodo*
Tax (Swed) m 8023	*Barney goin' easy*
Tax (Swed) m 8039	*(Album title unknown)*
Telehouse TS 77100	*Let the good times roll*
Time-Life STLJ 14	*Red Norvo—giants of jazz*
Top Rank (E) 35/037	*Cherokee*
Trip TLP 5804	*King of the saxophone*
Tulip TLP 106	*The best of the big band singers, volume 1*
Vault 9004	*Charlie Barnet big band—1967*
Verve MG V 2007	*Dance bash*
Verve MG V 2031	*For dancing lovers*
Verve MG V 2040	*Lonely street*
Verve VC 3508	*Jazz spectrum, vol.5 12 big band classics by 12 classic big bands*
Verve (E) 2317.060	*The big band sound of Charlie Barnet*
Verve (E) 2352.099	*A big band spectacular*
Verve (Eu) 2356.021	*(Album title unknown)*
Verve (Ger) 2304.541	*Dance bash*
Verve (Ger) 2615.044	*(Album title unknown)*
Vi LEJ 1	*The RCA-Victor encyclopedia of recorded jazz, album 1*
Vi LJM 1008	*Jazz for people who hate jazz*

Vi LPM 1091	*Redskin romp*
Vi LPM 1146	*Lullaby of Birdland*
Vi LPM 2081	*The great dance bands of the 30's and 40's—Charlie Barnet and his orchestra*
Vi LPT 1°	*Theme songs*
Vi LPV 551°	*Charlie Barnet, volume 1*
Vi LPV 567°	*Charlie Barnet vol. II*
Vi PR 111	*Golden anniversary album*
Vi PR 125	*The music of Life*
Vi (Australia) L 10033	*Redskin romp*
Vi (Australia) L 10051	*Jazz for people who hate jazz*
Vi Special Products DPL1 0013	*(Album title unknown)*
Vocalion (E) LAE-L 604	*Charlie Barnet big band 1967*
WOR 13 1168 D	*"A song is born" Charlie Barnett/Louis Armstrong interview*
WS (E) TP 330	*(Album title unknown)*
Warwick (E) WW 2070	*Marrakesh express*
World Record Club (E) T 141	*Cherokee*
World Record Club (E) T 303	*Charlie Barnet*

EPs

Apollo EP 614	*Charlie Barnett and his Cherokee's [sic]*
Camden CAE 432	*Charlie's choice*
Capitol EAP1/2/3 624°	*Classics in jazz—Charlie Barnet and his orchestra*
Capitol EBF 235	*Battle of the bands*
Clef EP 138	*Charlie Barnet plays Charlie Barnet [vol. 1] /Charlie Barnet and his orchestra*
Clef EP 139	*Charlie Barnet plays Charlie Barnet [vol. 2]/ Charlie Barnet and his orchestra*
Clef EP 156	*Dance with Charlie Barnet*
Clef EP 236	*Charlie Barnet dance session*
Clef EP 237	*Charlie Barnet dance session*
Clef EP 243	*Charlie Barnet dance session #2*
Clef EP 244	*Charlie Barnet dance session album #4*
Clef EP 275	*One night stand (vol. 2)*
Clef EP 276	*(Album title unknown—possibly One night stand [vol.3])*
Co B 488	*Town Hall jazz concert, vol.1*
Co B 489	*Town Hall jazz concert, vol.2*

Co B 2602	*Charlie Barnet and his orchestra*
Decca ED 725	*Hop on the skyliner!*
Epic EG 7064	*Neal Hefti—Singing instrumentals*
Epic EG 9006	*Neal Hefti—Singing instrumentals*
Everest BREP 102	*(Album title unknown)*
Karusell (Swed) KEP 208	*(Album title unknown)*
Karusell (Swed) KEP 254	*(Album title unknown)*
Mercury EP 114	*(Album title unknown)*
Mercury EP 138	*Charlie Barnet plays Charlie Barnet*
Mercury EP 139	*Charlie Barnet plays Charlie Barnet*
RCA (E) RCX 1008	*Charlie Barnet and his orchestra*
RCA (N?) 21 016	*Theme songs*
RCA Victor EPA 612	*Redskin rumpus*
RCA Victor EPA 5001	*Gold standard series: Charlie Barnet*
RCA Victor EPBT 3062	*Charlie Barnet plays Duke Ellington*
Vi EJC 1008	*Jazz for people who hate jazz*
Vi EPA 673	*Lullaby of Birdland, vol. 3*
Vi EPAT 1	*Theme songs*
Vi EPAT 404	*Charlie Barnet Cherokee*
Vi EPAT 433°	*Four big ideas*
Vi EPB 1091 1	*Redskin romp*
Vi SPD 17-9074	*(Album title unknown)*
Vi WEJ 1	*The RCA-Victor encyclopedia of recorded jazz, album 1*
Vi WPT 1	*(Album title unknown)*

CASSETTES

Ajax C 668	*The unissued Charlie Barnet, volume 1*
Ajax C 671	*The unissued Charlie Barnet, volume 2*
Ajax C 679	*The unissued Charlie Barnet, volume 3*
Ajax C 683	*The unissued Charlie Barnet, volume 4*
Ajax C 708	*The unissued Charlie Barnet volume 5*
Ajax C 712	*The complete Charlie Barnet, volume 3*
Ajax C 716	*The complete Charlie Barnet, volume 4*
Alamac QSR 2435	*Charlie Barnet and his orchestra—1938*
Alamac QSR 2446	*Charlie Barnet and his orchestra—1949*
Big band era (N) 40180	*Charlie Barnet: One for my baby*
Big band renaissance RC 108	*Big band renaissance—the evolution of the jazz orchestra*

Big Bands (Time-Life) 4TBB 07	*Charlie Barnet*
Big Bands (Time-Life) 4TL-0011 R959-11	*Charlie Barnet*
Big bands America 129312	*Big bands America, disc 1*
Bluebird 61059 4	*Cherokee*
Bluebird 61109 4	*Masters of the big bands*
Bluebird AXK2 5526	*The complete Charlie Barnet, vol. 1*
Bluebird AXK2 5577	*The complete Charlie Barnet, vol. II 1939*
Bluebird AXK2 5581	*The complete Charlie Barnet, vol. III 1939-1940*
Bluebird AXK2 5584	*The complete Charlie Barnet, vol. IV 1940*
Bluebird AXK2 5587	*The complete Charlie Barnet, vol. V 1940-1941*
Bluebird AXK2 5590	*The complete Charlie Barnet, vol. VI 1941-1942*
CDS (E) RPMC 611	*Battle of the big bands*
CHG 0155 32789 1	*Big bands of the war years—1*
Canco	*Fifty big bands! Fifty sweet songs!*
Capitol CDP 7243 27813 4	*Big bands in hi fi, volume 1—Let's dance*
Capitol CDP 7243 27816 4	*Big bands in hi-fi, volume 2—In the mood*
Capitol (E) TCEMS 1321	*Stan Freberg: The best of the Capitol years*
Castle (E) MAC MC 358 4	*Big band theme tunes*
Classics 7691	*Skyliner*
Classics 7742	*Big bands volume 1*
Classics 7743	*Big bands volume 2*
Classics 7744	*Big bands volume 3*
Col CGT 30009	*Big bands' greatest hits*
Col CT 45476	*Big band sampler*
Col PCT 36580	*Let's dance*
Col RJ 44118	*Red Norvo featuring Mildred Bailey*
Col Legacy C3T 52862	*Swing time! The fabulous big band era 1925-1955*
Col Legacy CT 48977	*Big band instrumentals—16 most requested songs*
Demand Performance DPC 853	*Charlie Barnet*
Drive DE2 42446	*Charlie Barnet and his orchestra—Swell and super*
ESX JCT 7004	*Those wonderful years—Sentimental journey*
ESX JCT 7006	*Those wonderful years—Swingtime*
Everest FS 359	*Big bands of the swinging years*
First Heard (E) CFH 44	*Charlie Barnet and his orchestra: Showcase*
Franklin Mint Tape no.19	*The greatest recordings of the big band era: Charlie Barnet & his orchestra*
GAS GAS 779	*Charlie Barnet*
I giganti del jazz (It) GJ 34	*Erskine Hawkins, Bud Freeman, Charlie Barnet*

Good Music 143818 2	*The big band singers tape 2*
Hindsight HCS 264	*Those swinging years*
Intersound PCD 1014	*Themes of the big bands*
J.C. Entertainment JCS 110	*Big band romance: 40 great love songs*
Jazz Heritage 313097 M	*Charlie Barnet big band 1967*
Joyce JRC C 1476	*Charlie Barnet at the Palladium*
Joyce JRC C 1521	*Charlie Barnet transcriptions vol.1*
Joyce JRC C 1523	*Charlie Barnet transcriptions vol.2*
Joyce Imperfect Series C 05	*Strong/Pastor/Barnet: Spotlight bands from 1945*
MCA C 27094	*Best of the big bands*
MCA (Sp) L 404302	*The best of Charlie Barnet*
Masters of music BCCS 309	*Brooklyn boogie*
Murray Hill 55124	*Big bands of the swinging years*
RCA 1055 4	*Stompin' at the Savoy*
RCA 68507	*Big band—greatest hits*
RCA PK 5099	*This is the big band era*
RCA (Fr) NK 89279	*Louis Armstrong: From the big band to the all stars (1946–1956)*
Radio Classics AFP 7140 AC	*The best of the big bands vol. 1*
Radio Classics AFP 7141 AC	*The best of the big bands vol. 2*
Radio Days CACS 1008	*Charlie Barnett orchestra Casino Gardens…*
Radio Yesteryear 2999	*A song is born (air trailer)*
Radio Yesteryear 34974	*A song is born*
Radiola 10CMR 2	*Radio band remotes*
Razor and Tie 89023 4	*Swing America, tape 1*
Rdr's Digest RD 3	*The great band era (1936-1945)*
Rdr's Digest RD 72	*The best loved bands of all time*
Rdr's Digest RD 78	*Fabulous memories of the fabulous 40s*
Rdr's Digest (C) RD4 832 3	*They're playing our song*
Redmond Nostalgia Co. CO 3533	*Charlie Barnet and his orchestra from the 400 Club in New York*
Redmond Nostalgia Co. CO 3619	*Jubilee 170 and 149*
Redmond Nostalgia Co. CO 3657	*Jubilee 247*
Redmond Nostalgia Co. CO 3681	*Magic Carpet 132—Lucky Millinder; 143—Charlie Barnet*
Redmond Nostalgia Co. CO 4390	*Barnet, Krupa and Clinton*
Redmond Nostalgia Co. CO 4391	*Ray Noble and Charlie Barnet*
Sandy Hook CSH 2081	*Charlie Barnet and his orchestra: Rare recordings 1944–1947*

Smithsonian DMK 3 0610 C/D RC 030	*Big band jazz*
Smithsonian RC 035	*Singers and soloists of the swing bands*
Smithsonian RC 102	*Swing that music*
Sony Music Special Products P2T-26670/PT-26672	*The big band singers tape 2*
Stack of 78s Stack 33	*Swinging madness*
Stack of 78s Stack 73	*Skylining with Charlie Barnet*
Starline SLC 61018	*Charlie Barnet live*
Swing House (E) CSWH 6	*Charlie Barnet and his orchestra: Dance date*
Tennessee (Argentina) 45619	*Las grandes bandas*
Time-Life 164	*Your hit parade 1941*
Time-Life R138 03	*V-Disc: The songs that went to war*
Time-Life R139 39	*V-Disc: The songs that went to war*
Vi CAK 811	*Original recordings by great bands of our time*

Open Reel Tapes

American Tape 28 04128	*(Album title unknown)*
American Tape PIC 3573	*(Album title unknown)*
Everest STBR 1012	*Cherokee*
Omegatape DSST 823	*On stage with Charlie Barnet*

8-Track Tapes

Bright Orange BO 7819	*On stage with Charlie Barnet and his orchestra*
MCA (4069?)	*The best of Charlie Barnet*
Rdr's Digest RD5 78	*Fabulous memories of the fabulous forties*
Rdr's Digest RD5 025-1/1-4	*The great band era*
Rdr's Digest RD5 106 1	*Happiness is*

CDs

Ace CDBOP 014	*Way out Wardell*
Aero Space RACD 7123	*Make believe ballroom 1936-1941*
Affinity (E) CD AFS 1036 4	*One hundred greatest jazz and swing hits, 1917-1942*
Affinity (E) CD AFS 1017	*Knock on wood*
Allegro (Fr) 151832	*Jazz anthology 1940*

Arista 886281	*(Album title unknown)*
L'art vocal (Fr) 11	*Lena Horne 1936-1941*
Avid (E) AMSC 676	*The classic swing collection: All the cats join in*
Avid (E) AVC 540	*Classic big band jazz: Swing that jazz*
B&C Records 74081 2	*Charlie Barnet: Swing back with Charlie Barnet—1940s*
BBC (E) REB 666	*The classic years in digital stereo: Swing-small groups*
BMG 09026 63345 2	*More big bands greatest hits*
BMG JCD 7006	*Those wonderful years: Swingtime*
Baldwin Street Music (C) BJH 305	*Kay Starr: The complete Lamplighter recordings*
Bear Family (Ger) 15910	*Nellie Lutcher and her rhythm*
Best of Jazz (Fr) 4039	*Charlie Barnet*
Big band renaissance RD 108	*Big band renaissance—the evolution of the jazz orchestra*
Big bands TCD 0011 R960 11	*Charlie Barnet*
Big bands America 129320	*Big bands America, disc 1*
Bluebird 61059 2	*Cherokee*
Bluebird 61109 2	*Masters of the big bands*
Bluebird 6273 2-RB	*Clap hands, here comes Charlie*
CBS RK 44118	*Red Norvo featuring Mildred Bailey*
CDS (E) 541	*(Album title unknown)*
CDS (E) RPCD 611	*Battle of the big bands*
CDS (E) RPCD 641	*The best of Robert Parker*
CDS (Ger) CD 666	*The classic years in digital stereo: swing-small groups*
CDS (Ger) RPCD 305	*The classic years in digital stereo: swing-small groups*
Canco (no. unknown)	*Fifty big bands! Fifty sweet songs!*
Capitol CDP 212558	*Charlie Barnet: The Capitol big band sessions*
Capitol CDP 32563 2	*Mondo exotica*
Capitol CDP 37596 2	*Cocktail capers*
Capitol CDP 37598 2	*Saxophobia*
Capitol CDP 96693 2	*Jazz encounters*
Capitol CDP 98931 2	*Capitol jazz 50th anniversary collection*
Capitol CDP 7243 8 27813 2 5	*Big bands in hi-fi, volume 1—Let's dance*
Capitol CDP 7243 8 27816 2 2	*Big bands in hi-fi, volume 2—In the mood*
Capitol (E) CDP7 91627 2	*Stan Freberg: The best of the Capitol years*
Capitol (Ja) ?	*Capitol vocal classics*
Castle (E) MAC MC 358 2	*Big band theme tunes*
Circle CCD 65	*Charlie Barnet and his orchestra 1941*
Circle CCD 112	*Charlie Barnet and his orchestra 1942*
Classic Jazz (E) CDCD 1239	*Big band blast*
Classic Jazz (E) CDCD 1271	*Big band ballads*

Classics 7691	*Skyliner*
Classics 7742	*Big bands volume 1*
Classics 7743	*Big bands volume 2*
Classics 7744	*Big bands volume 3*
Classics (Fr) 1085	*Red Norvo and his orchestra 1933-1936*
Col CG 30009	*Big bands' greatest hits*
Col RK 44118	*Red Norvo featuring Mildred Bailey*
Col Legacy 52862	*Swing time! The fabulous big band era 1925-1955*
Col Legacy CK 48977	*Big band instrumentals—16 most requested songs*
Collectables COL-CD 5096	*Big bands of the swinging years, vol. 1*
Collectables COL-CD 5097	*Big bands of the swinging years, vol. 2*
Decca GRD 639	*A piano anthology*
Decca Jazz GRD 612	*Charlie Barnet and his orchestra: Drop me off in Harlem*
Decca Jazz GRD 642	*The legendary big band singers*
Decca Jazz GRD 2 629	*An anthology of big band swing 1930-1955*
Decca Jazz (Ja) MVCR 20008	*Charlie Barnet and his orchestra: Drop me off in Harlem*
Drive DE2 42446	*Charlie Barnet and his orchestra—Swell and super*
Duet (E) DCD CD 212	*Fifty big band classics*
EMI Jazz 7243 8 55142 27	*Big band jazz*
ESX JCD 7004	*Those wonderful years—Sentimental journey*
ESX JCD 7006	*Those wonderful years—Swingtime*
Emporio (E) DEMPCD 011	*The big band collection*
Empress (E) RAJCD 829	*Hits of 1943*
Empress (E) RAJCD 898	*Skyliner*
The Entertainers CD 372	*Nat King Cole*
Evidence ECD 22065 2	*Cherokee*
Evidence ECD 22112 2	*More Charlie Barnet*
Excelsior EXL 10582	*(Album title unknown)*
Flapper (E) PAST CD 7091	*The lady and her music*
Flapper (E) PAST CD 9787	*Stateside sweet music*
Frémeaux (Fr) 078	*Swing era big bands—1934—1947*
Giants of Jazz (Cz) CD 53277	*Charlie Barnet and his orchestra 1939-1940: "Cherokee"*
Giants of Jazz (Cz) CD 53280	*Charlie Barnet and his orchestra 1940-1945: "Skyliner"*
Giants of Jazz (It) CD 53097	*An unforgettable session*
Giants of Jazz (It) CD 53274	*Charlie Barnet 1935-1939*
Giants of Jazz (It) CD 53283	*Red Norvo 1933-1944*
Good Music 143826	*The big band singers*
Hep (E) CD 53	*Charlie Barnet: The transcription performances 1941*
Hep (E) CD 1044	*Dance of the octopus*

Hindsight HCD 264	*Those swinging years*
Hip-o HIPD 40073	*The swingingest sounds ever heard*
Hollywood Soundstage 4007	*Reveille with Beverly/Jam session*
Homecoming 1945 GMCD 80037 1	*Homecoming 1945—disc 1*
Intersound CDC 1014	*Themes of the big bands*
Intersound CDC 1041	*Best of the big bands*
Intersound (C) CDC 1046	*The war years*
J.C. Entertainment JCD 110	*Big band romance: 40 great love songs*
JCI 42446	*Those wonderful years: sentimental journey*
Jasmine (E) JASCD 337/8	*A rising Starr*
Jasmine (E) JASMCD 2540	*Boogie woogie volume 3—the big bands*
Jass J-CD 623	*Halloween stomp*
Le Jazz (E) 8102	*The complete Charlie Barnet 1933-1936*
Jazz Archives (Fr) 30	*Charlie Barnet vol.1*
Jazz Archives (Fr) 158362	*Little Jazz*
Jazz Archives (Fr) 158532	*Charlie Barnet vol. 2*
Jazz Archives (Fr) 3891092	*Frankie Newton Swinging on 52nd Street 'Emperor Jones'*
Jazz Band 2260	*Swingdance, vol.1*
Jazz Greats (E) CD 071	*Clap hands, here comes Charlie*
Jazz Heritage 513097 H	*Charlie Barnet big band 1967*
Jazz Heritage 514150 X	*A piano anthology*
Jazz Heritage 514960 T	*Charlie Barnet and his orchestra: Drop me off in Harlem*
Jazz Hour JH 3005	*Charlie Barnet and his orchestra*
K-tel 3406 2	*Swingin' big bands*
Kaz (E) CD 311	*Charlie Barnet: The classic tracks*
Laserlight 15764	*The small groups*
Living Era (E) CD AJA 5141	*Twenty-one swing band all-time greats*
Living Era (E) CD AJA 5169	*Hits of '44*
Living Era (E) CD AJA 5238	*Fabulous*
Living Era (E) CD AJA 5247	*Battle of the saxes*
Living Era (E) CD AJA 5288	*Charlie Barnet and his orchestra: Cherokee*
Living Era (E) CD AJA 5309	*I'm in the mood for swing*
Living Era (E) CD AJA 5341	*Red Norvo: Knockin' on wood*
MCA MCAD 20477	*Big bands, vol. 1*
MCA MCAMD 25196	*Swing: The best of the big bands*
MCA (E) GRP 16122	*Charlie Barnet and his orchestra: Drop me off in Harlem*
MCA (E) GRP 26292	*An anthology of big band swing 1930-1955*
Masters of Jazz (Fr) CD 59	*Benny Carter volume 4 1934-35*
Masters of Music BCCD 309	*Brooklyn boogie*

Mobile Fidelity MFCD 841	*Charlie Barnet big band 1967*
Mosaic MD18 138	*The complete Capitol recordings of the Nat King Cole Trio*
Official (Den) 8 12003	*Havin' fun with (rare duets)*
PILZ (Ger) 44 2042 2	*Charlie Barnet*
Peaceful BDK 2	*50 sweet bands! 50 sweet songs!*
Phontastic (Swed) PHONTCD 7668	*Frenesi*
Phontastic (Swed) PHONTCD 7672	*1944—I'm beginning to see the light*
Pickwick PK 540301	*Original V-Disc collection; American forces original recordings/1*
Qualitone JTD 102 401	*In the mood*
RCA 1055 2	*Stompin' at the Savoy*
RCA 2128562 2	*Victor jazz history vol.8: Swing big bands*
RCA 44546	*Best of big band era, 1940*
RCA 44547	*Best of big band era, 1941*
RCA 63115	*Love songs greatest hits*
RCA 63116	*Number 1 hits: greatest hits*
RCA 63119	*The fabulous big band collection*
RCA 63445	*More fabulous swing*
RCA 63446	*More fabulous big band*
RCA 68502 2	*Idiot's guide to jazz*
RCA 68507	*Big band—Greatest hits*
RCA 68987	*The fabulous swing collection*
RCA 9855 2-R	*Nipper's greatest hits—The 40's, volume 1*
RCA 9972 2-R	*Nipper's greatest hits—The 30's volume 2*
RCA 2128562 2	*Victor jazz history vol.8: Swing big bands*
RCA 09026 63119 2	*The fabulous big band collection*
RCA 09026 63342 2	*Wicked swing*
RCA 09026 68778 2	*RCA Victor 80th anniversary, vol. 2 1930-1939*
RCA 7863 66746 2	*Swingin' uptown*
RCA (E) 86273	*Clap hands, here comes Charlie*
RCA (E) ND 90441	*The legendary Lena 1941-1958*
RCA (Fr) 7432135553 2	*The indispensable Charlie Barnet, volumes 3/4 (1935–1939)*
RCA (Fr) 7432135554 2	*The indispensable Charlie Barnet, volumes 1/2 (1935–1939)*
RCA (Fr) ND 89279	*Louis Armstrong: From the big band to the all stars (1946–1956)*

RCA (Sp) 7432142129 2	*Redskin romp*
RST (Austria) 91567 2	*Rare V-Discs vol. 3: "The girls"*
Radio Days CACD 1008	*Charlie Barnett orchestra Casino Gardens...*
Rdr's Digest RB-7 002	*The best loved bands of all time*
Rdr's Digest RBD 114/CDI	*The big bands swing your all time favorites*
Rdr's Digest RDD 25/CD11	*The great band era (1936-1945)*
Rdr's Digest (E) ND 90441	*The legendary Lena 1941-1958*
Rdr's Digest (E) RDCD 123	*The Bing Crosby years—Reminiscing with the stars 1939–1941*
Retro SLD 23122	*The big band sound*
Rhino R2 70722	*Legends of guitar jazz volume 2*
Second Street SSP 1204	*Jazz saxophone classics*
Smithsonian DMC 4 0610 4 RD 030	*Big band jazz*
Smithsonian RD 102	*Swing that music*
Sony A 19995	*The big bands: Moonglow*
Sony BUK 50344	*Sentimental journey*
Sony Special Prod.	*The big band singers*
Stack of 78s Stack 33	*Swinging madness*
Stack of 78s Stack 73	*Skylining with Charlie Barnet*
Swing Time (E)? 9807	*Dick McDonough and his orchestra*
Swingsation GRD 9952	*Charlie Barnet and Jimmy Dorsey*
Tax (Swed) CD 3715-2	*Charlie Barnet 1938*
Time-Life 162	*Your hit parade 1941*
Time-Life OPCD 4537	*V-Disc: The songs that went to war*
Time-Life OPCD 4538	*V-Disc: The songs that went to war*
Topaz (E) TPZ 1028	*Swing into bop*
Topaz (E) TPZ 1031	*The great bands*
Topaz Jazz (E) TPZ 1041	*Charlie Barnet and his orchestra—Skyliner*
Topaz Jazz (E) TPZ 1058	*Dodo lives*
Toshiba (Ja) TOCJ 5627	*Capitol jazz classics: Bop goes white*
Toshiba (Ja) TOCJ 5698	*Capitol vocal classics 1942-1955*
Total TRCD 3004	*June Christy and Charlie Barnet Sextet*
Tradition (C) 1035	*Big bands of the swinging years*
Verve (Ger) 833.281 2	*Compact jazz—Best of the big bands*
Victor 68735	*Jazz greatest hits of the 30s*
Viper's Nest VN 1002	*Charlie Barnet and his orchestra: "Wings over Manhattan"*
Viper's Nest VN 1010	*Swingin' the classics*
Zeta (Ger) ZET 749	*Charlie Barnet vol.1*

Video

Aero Space Home Video AS 1001	*Story of the big band era*
Classic Music TV 5005	*Stars of jazz*
HBO Home Video 084383	*A song is born*
MCA Home Video 80665	*Swing: The best of the big bands, volume I*
MCA Home Video 80666	*Swing: The best of the big bands, volume II*
Republic Pictures VHS 1236	*The fabulous Dorseys*
Show 1014	*Charlie Teagarden*
Storyville 6005	*The Snader telescriptions: The big bands, vol. 2*
Swingtime Video 114	*Meet the bandleaders*
VJC 2003	*The swingin', singin' years*
Video Treasures MU 6005	*The fabulous Dorseys*
Video Yesteryear 510	*Stars of jazz*

Pseudo-Charlie

Among the things ushered in during the LP era was the practice of using studio bands to record big band hits in high fidelity and stereo. A number of albums were issued which contained performances of Charlie's hits performed by top musicians, many of whom had worked for him over the years (it is almost easier to list the musicians who *didn't* work for him). The album covers usually inferred that Charlie was present—by displaying his name prominently and sometimes by using a mug shot. In other instances, e.g., Glen Gray, there was no attempt to deceive the record buyer. In spite of the impression one might get from the album covers or from the music itself, Charlie does not play on any of these recordings.

Kenny Baker and his orchestra

Allen Franks, Harry Lathman, Stan Roderick, Kenny Baker, tpts; Jack Bentley, Lad Bushby, Jimmy Coombes, Harry Rocher, tbns; Leslie Gilbert, Reg Owens, as; Johnny Gray, ts; Norman Stenfalt, p; Dave Goldberg, g; Charlie Short, b; Jack Parnell, d

London, Oriole recording session, April 1946

9134 **Skyliner**
Oriole (E) 1007
9137 **Pompton Turnpike**
Oriole (E) 1006

Glen Gray and his orchestra

Pete Candoli, Conrad Gozzo, Manny Klein, Shorty Sherock, tpts; Benny Benson, Joe Howard, Si Zentner, Murray McEachern, tbns; Gus Bivona, Skeets Herfurt, as; Babe Russin, Plas Johnson, Julie Jacobs, ts; Chuck Gentry, bar; Ray Sherman, p; Jack Marshall, g; Mike Rubin, b; Nick Fatool, d

Hollywood, Capitol recording session, early 1958

Cherokee
Capitol W1022, SM 1022

The next session used the Harry James band which at the time was performing in Las Vegas. At 4AM the band members flew to Hollywood, without Harry's knowledge. There, augmented by Hoyt Bohannon and others and a subsequently dubbed string section, they took part in a recording session produced by Charlie Barnet, who is remembered as being in the glassed-in control room.

Transcriptions of the James arrangements were made, possibly by Maxwell Davis, and it was from these that the band worked. The musicians were paid scale. The trombone solos were played by Ray Sims. Shorty Sherock played Harry's ballad solos and Rob Turk took the rest. The band returned to Las Vegas and played that night. When Harry found out, "he was sore as Hell." *(Jack Perciful)*

(Harry James orchestra) ("Charlie Barnet presents a tribute/salute to Harry James")

Nick Buono, Ollie Mitchell, Bob Rolfe, John Audino, Shorty Sherock, Rob Turk, tpts; Hoyt Bohannon, Ray Sims, Ernie Tack, Bob Edmondson, tbns; Willie Smith, Ernie Small, as; Sam Firmature, Herb Lorden, ts; Bob Poland, bar; Jack Perciful, p; Dave Coone, g; Joe Comfort, b; Jackie Mills, d.

Hollywood, Crown recording session, July 7, 1958

Bangtail
Bright Orange BO 710; Crown CST 146, CLP 5114; Eros (E) ERL/ERLS 50014; CROWN ST-111 (open reel tape)

Blues for sale
Bright Orange BO 715; Crown CST 160, CLP 5127

Cherry
Bright Orange BO 710, 724; Crown CST 146, CLP 5114; Eros (E) ERL/ERLS 50014; Michelle 5607-TC; CROWN ST-111 (open reel tape); **MICHELLE 5607-CD**

Ciribiribin
Bright Orange BO 710, 725; Crown CST 146, CLP 5114; Eros (E) ERL/ERLS 50014; Riviera (Fr) STR 003; CROWN ST-111 (open reel tape)

Easter parade
Bright Orange BO 715; Crown CST 160, CLP 5127

Flatbush Flanagan
Bright Orange BO 715; Crown CST 160, CLP 5127

Here's one
Bright Orange BO 710; Crown CST 146, CLP 5114; Eros (E) ERL/ERLS 50014; CROWN ST-111 (open reel tape)

Just lucky
Bright Orange BO 710; Crown CST 146, CLP 5114; Eros (E) ERL/ERLS 50014; CROWN ST-111 (open reel tape)

Music makers
Bright Orange BO 715; Crown CST 160, CLP 5127; Michelle 5601-TC; **MICHELLE 5601-CD**

One on the house
Bright Orange BO 715; Crown CST 160, CLP 5127

Palladium party
Bright Orange BO 710; Crown CST 146, CLP 5114; Eros (E) ERL/ERLS 50014; CROWN ST-111 (open reel tape)

Sleepy lagoon
Bright Orange BO 715; Crown CST 160, CLP 5127; Michelle 5601-TC; **MICHELLE 5601-CD**

The Mole
Bright Orange BO 715; Crown CST 160, CLP 5127

Trumpet blues
Bright Orange BO 710; Crown CST 146, CLP 5114; Eros (E) ERL/ERLS 50014; Michelle 5602-TC; CROWN ST-111 (open reel tape); **MICHELLE 5602-CD**

Two o'clock jump
Bright Orange BO 710, 720; Crown CST 146, CLP 5114; Modern M7005, MS 805; Eros (E) ERL/ERLS 50014; Baccarola (Ger) 77835; Michelle 5604-TC; CROWN ST-111 (open reel tape); **MICHELLE 5604-CD**

Ultra
Bright Orange BO 710; Crown CST 146, CLP 5114; Eros ERL/ERLS 50014; CROWN ST-111 (open reel tape)

You made me love you
Bright Orange BO 710, 722; Crown CST 146, 173, CLP 5114, 5140; Modern M7005, MS 805; Eros ERL/ERLS 50014; CROWN ST-111 (open reel tape)

Members of the Charlie Barnet orchestra (Maxwell Davis, leader)

Collective personnel

Bob Clark, Don Fagerquist, Morey Harris, Ray Linn, Al Porcino, Zeke Zarchey, tpts; Milt Bernhart, Murray McEachern, Dick Noel, Dick Nash, Tommy Pederson, tbns; Skeets

Herfurt, ss, as; Bob Jung, as; Teddy Lee, as, bar; Plas Johnson, ts; Fred Falensby, ts; Bob Dawes, bar; Claude Williamson, p; Allan Reuss, Al Hendrickson, g; Phil Stephens, b; Dick Shanahan, Jack Sperling, d

Hollywood, Crown recording session, ca Dec. 23-24, 1958

Charleston alley aHorace Henderson
BMC 5178; Bright Orange X-BO 706; Crown CST 131, 531, CLP 5094, 5531; Eros (E) ERL/ERLS 50012; FM Verisonics VS 102; Golden Hour (E) GH 868; Modern M 7002, MST 802; Big Band Classics CBB 3005; Bright Orange BOC 706; Michelle 5607-TC; BRIGHT OR-ANGE BO 8706 (8-track tape); MODERN TST; 105 (open reel tape); **MICHELLE 5607-CD**

Charlie's other aunt aManny Albam
BMC 5174; Bright Orange X-BO 706; Crown CST 131, 531°, CLP 5094, 5531; FM Verisonics; Modern M 7002, MST 802; Eros (E) ERL/ERLS 50012; Golden Hour (E) GH 868; Big Band Classics CBB 3005; Bright Orange BOC 706; Michelle 5605-TC; BRIGHT ORANGE BO 8706 (8-track tape); MODERN TST 105 (open reel tape); **MICHELLE 5605-CD**

Cherokee aBilly May
BMC 5171; Bright Orange X-BO 706, BO 721; Crown CLP 5094, 5531, CST 131, 531°; FM Verisonics VS 102; Modern M 7002, MS/MST 802; The Big Band Era LSP 4608; Eros (E) ERL/ERLS 50012; Golden Hour (E) GH 868; Big Band Classics CBB 3005; Michelle 5608-TC; MODERN TST 105 (open reel tape); Bright Orange BO 8706 (8-track tape); **B&C RECORDS 74081-2; MICHELLE CDW 421, 5608-CD; PILZ (GER) 44 2042 2**

Claude reigns aManny Albam
BMC 5177; Bright Orange X-BO 706; Crown CST 131, 531°; CLP 5094, 5531; FM Verisonics VS 102; Modern M 7002, MST 802; Eros (E) ERL/ERLS 50012; Golden Hour (E) GH 868; Big Band Classics CBB 3005; Bright Orange BOC 706; Michelle 5609-TC; MODERN TST 105 (open reel tape); BRIGHT ORANGE BO 8706 (8-track tape); **MICHELLE 5609-CD**

East side, west side aAndy Gibson; vBunny Briggs
Bright Orange X-BO 706; Crown CST 131, 531°, CLP 5094, 5531; FM Verisonics VS 102; Modern M 7002, MST 802; Eros (E) ERL/ERLS 50012; Big Band Classics CBB 3005; Bright Orange BOC 706; Michelle 5610-TC; MODERN TST 105 (open reel tape); BRIGHT OR-ANGE BO 8706 (8-track); **B&C RECORDS 74081-2; MICHELLE 5610-CD; PILZ (GER) 44 2042 2**

Lonely street aPaul Villepigue
Bright Orange X-BO 706; Crown CST 131, 531°, CLP 5094, 5531; FM Verisonics VS 102; Modern M 7002, MST 802; Eros (E) ERL/ERLS 50012; Golden Hour (E) GH 868; Big Band Classics CBB 3005; Bright Orange BOC 706; MODERN TST 105 (open reel tape); BRIGHT ORANGE BO 8706 (8-track)

Pompton Turnpike aBilly May
BMC 5173; Bright Orange X-BO 706, BO 722; Crown CST 131, 531°, CLP 5094, 5531; Modern M 7002, MST 802; FM Verisonics VS 102; Eros (E) ERL/ERLS 50012; Golden Hour GH 868; Big Band Classics CBB 3005; Bright Orange BOC 706; Michelle 5604-TC; MODERN TST 105 (open reel); BRIGHT ORANGE BO 8706 (8-track); **B&C RECORDS 74081-2; MICHELLE 5604-CD; PILZ (GER) 44 2042 2**

Really aManny Albam
Bright Orange X-BO 706; Crown CST 131, 531°, CLP 5094, 5531; FM Verisonics VS 102; Modern M 7002, MST 802; Eros (E) ERL/ERLS 50012; Golden Hour (E) GH 868; Big Band Classics CBB 3005; Bright Orange BOC 706; MODERN TST 105 (open reel); BRIGHT ORANGE BO 8706 (8-track)

Redskin rhumba aHead
BMC 5176; Bright Orange BO 723, 725; Crown CST 131, 159, 531°, CLP 5126, 5531; FM Verisonics VS 102; Modern M 7002, MST 802; Custom (E) CS 1094; Eros (E) ERL/ERLS 50012; Golden Hour (E) GH 868; Riv-iera (Fr) STR 003; Big Band Classics CBB 3005; Bright Orange BOC 706; Michelle 5603-TC; MODERN TST 105 (open reel); BRIGHT ORANGE BO 8706 (8-track); **MICHELLE 5603-CD**

Skyliner aBilly Moore
BMC 5172; Bright Orange X-BO 706, 723; Crown CST 131, 173, 531°, CLP 5094, 5140, 5531; Modern M 7002, 7005, MST 802, 805; FM Verisonics VS 102; Eros (E) ERL/ERLS 50012; Golden Hour (E) GH 868; Big Band Classics CBB 3005; Bright Orange BOC 706; Michelle 5606-TC; MODERN TST 105 (open reel); BRIGHT ORANGE BO 8706 (8-track);

B&C RECORDS BMC 74081 2; COMPOSE 9056; MICHELLE 5606-CD; RETRO (C) SLD 23302

Glen Gray and his orchestra

Conrad Gozzo, Shorty Sherock, Joe Graves, Uan Rasey, tpts; Milt Bernhart, Ed Kusby, Joe Howard, Lew McCreary, tbns; Skeets Herfurt, Abe Most, as; Plas Johnson, Babe Russin, Justin Gordon, ts; Chuck Gentry, bar; Ray Sherman, p; Jack Marshall, g; Mike Rubin, b; Irv Cottler, d

Hollywood, Capitol recording session, Oct. 8, 1962

38485 **Redskin rhumba** aHead
Capitol T/ST 1812, SXA 1812; Capitol SM 1812; CAPI-TOL ZT 1812 (open reel); CAPITOL 8M 1812 (8-track)

Unidentified big band

Outdoor live performance, (ca 1962?)

Butterball
Koala 14158
September in the rain vMale
Koala 14158
Star dust
Koala 14158
Toe tappin'
Koala 14158

Glen Gray and his orchestra

Collective personnel:
Manny Klein, Joe Graves or Pete Candoli, Shorty Sherock, tpts; Ed Kusby, Milt Bernhart or Lew McCreary, Joe Howard, tbns; Skeets Herfurt, Abe Most, as; Babe Russin or Justin Gordon, Plas Johnson, ts; Chuck Gentry, bar; Jack Marshall, g; Ray Sherman, p; Mike Rubin, b; Nick Fatool, d.

Hollywood, Capitol recording session, ca 1963

The sweetest sounds aLarry Wagner or Van Alexander, in the style of Charlie Barnet
Capitol T/ST 1938

As preceding

Charade aLarry Wagner or Van Alexander, in the style of Charlie Barnet's "Cherokee"
Capitol T/ST 2014
Your other love aLarry Wagner or Van Alexander, in the style of Charlie Barnet's "Skyliner"
Capitol T/ST 2014

Billy May orchestra

Billy May, leader; Pete Candoli, Shorty Sherock, Ray Triscari, Joe Graves, tpts; Lew McCreary, Hoyt Bohannon, Francis Howard, Ed Kusby, tbns; Skeets Herfurt, Abe Most, as; Plas Johnson, Justin Gordon, ts; Chuck Gentry, bar; Ray Sherman, p; Jack Marshall, g; Roland Bundock, b; Nick Fatool, d

Hollywood, Capitol recording session, Dec. 9, 1969

73614 **Pompton Turnpike** aBilly May
Time-Life STA/STL 345; Time-Life 4TL 345; TIME-LIFE 8TL 345 (8-track tape); **TIME-LIFE CDTL 345**

Billy May, leader; Pete Candoli, Shorty Sherock, John Audino, Frank Beach, Uan Rasey, tpts; Joe Howard, Dick Nash, Lew McCreary, Milt Bernhart, tbns; Skeets Herfurt, Abe Most, as; Justin Gordon, Plas Johnson, ts; Chuck Gentry, bar; rhythm section as preceding.

As preceding, May 12, 1970

74503 **Charleston alley** aHorace Henderson, transcribed Carl Brandt
Time-Life STA/STL 346; Time-Life 4TL 346; TIME-LIFE 8TL 346 (8-track tape)

Billy May, leader; Shorty Sherock, John Best, Uan Rasey, John Audino, Bud Brisbois, tpts; Joe Howard, Lew McCreary, Lloyd Ulyate, Dick Nash, tbns; Skeets Herfurt, Les Robinson, Abe Most, as; Justin Gordon, Plas Johnson,ts; Chuck Gentry, bar; rhythm section as preceding.

As preceding, Sept. 9, 1970

75390 **Skyliner** aBilly Moore, transcribed by Sammy Nestico
Time-Life STA/STL 348; Time-Life 4TL 348; TIME-LIFE 8TL 348 (8-track tape)

Billy May, leader; John Best, Shorty Sherock, Ray Triscari, Uan Rasey, Pete Candoli, tpts; Lloyd Ulyate, Dave Wells, Gil Falco, tbns; Marshall Royal, Abe Most, as; Justin Gordon, Nat Brown, Plas Johnson, ts; Chuck Gentry, bar; rhythm section as preceding.

As preceding, Sept. 13, 1971

77328 **Night and day** aHead, transcribed by Billy May
Time-Life STA/STL 351; Time-Life 4TL 351; TIME-LIFE 8TL 351 (8-track tape)

Billy May, leader; John Best, Zeke Zarchy, Uan Rasey, George Werth, tpts; Joe Howard, Dick Nash, Lew McCreary, tbns; Les Robinson, Wilbur Schwartz, Abe Most, Justin Gordon, Plas Johnson, reeds; Ray Sherman, p; Jack Marshall, g; Morty Corb, b; Nick Fatool, d.

As preceding, Feb. 7, 1972

78066 **Southern fried** aBill Miller, transcribed by Billy May
Time-Life STA/STL 353; Time-Life 4TL 353; TIME-LIFE 8TL 353 (8-track tape)

Bibliography

Books

Barnet, Charlie. *1000 one nighters or (I didn't raise my boy to be a musician)* ("Some names and places have been changed so as to protect the guilty") Undated manuscript in Charlie's hand. **MS**

Barnet, Charlie. *The swing era: The golden age of network radio.* New York: Time-Life Records, 1971.

Barnet, Charlie, with Stanley Dance. *Those swinging years: the autobiography of Charlie Barnet.* Baton Rouge: Louisiana State University Press, 1984; New York: Da Capo, 1992. **TSY**

Edwards, Ernest. *Charlie Barnet and his orchestra.* Jazz Discographies Unlimited, 1965. **Edw 65**

Edwards, Ernest. *Charlie Barnet and his orchestra.* Jazz Discographies Unlimited, 1967. **Edw 67**

Garrod, Charles. *Charlie Barnet and his orchestra.* Zephyr Hills, FL: Joyce Music, 1984. **Garrod 84**

Hall, George. *Charlie Barnet and his orchestra.* Jazz Discographies Unlimited, 1970. **Hall 70**

Handy, D. Antoinette. *Black women in American bands and orchestras.* Latham, MD: Scarecrow Press, 1998. **D. A. Handy**

Inman, Robert. *[Scrapbooks and correspondence.]* **Inman**

McKenzie, Harry and Lothar Polomski. *One Night Stand series, 1-1001.* New York: Greenwood, 1991

Meeker, David. *Jazz in the movies.* [New enl. ed.] New York: Da Capo Press, Inc.; London: Talisman Books, 1981. **Meeker**

Ruppli, Michel. *The Decca labels: a discography, v.1-3.* New York: Greenwood, 1996. **Ruppli**

Rust, Brian A. L. *Jazz records 1897–1942.* New Rochelle, NY: Arlington House, 1978. **Rust JR**

Scott, Jeff. [*Liner notes for The complete Charlie Barnet*] (Bluebird AXM2-5526, etc.).

Sears, Richard S. *V-discs—A history and discography.* Westport, CT: Greenwood, 1980.

Sears, Richard S. *V-discs—First supplement.* Westport, CT: Greenwood, 1986.

Stratemann, Klaus. *Duke Ellington: Day by day and film by film.* Copenhagen: Jazz-Media ApS, 1992. **Stratemann**

Treichel, James A.: *Keeper of the flame: Woody Herman and the Second Herd, 1947-1949.* Zephyr Hills, FL: Joyce Music, 1978.

Vail, Ken: *Lady Day's diary: The life of Billie Holiday, 1937-1959.* Castle Communications, c1996. **Lady Day's diary**

Magazines

Bank, Danny. *Danny Bank* (taken and transcribed by Bob Rusch). Cadence, July 1996. **DBank**

Briggs, John. *Charlie Barnet.* Song hits, vo.3, no.5, Oct. 1939, p.22.

Brown, Betty. *Man with a sax.*Song hits, v.9, no.9, p.12, 18, Feb. 1946.

Clare, Don. *The Charlie Barnet story.* Jazz journal intl., Nov. 1996.

Crosbie, Ian. *Clap hands, here comes Charlie, pts. 1-2.* Jazz journal intl., v.26, no.5, May 1973, p.10-12; v.26, no.7, July 1973, p.25-28.

(Dexter, Dave ?) *New Mab music best since '39?* Capitol news, v.7, no.5, May 1949.

Feather, Leonard. *Barnet took Basie's beat, Duke's harmonics.* Down beat, Sept. 21, 1951. **Feather 51**

Feather, Leonard. *Whatever happened to Charlie Barnet?* Down beat, Apr. 11, 1963. **Feather 63**

Lees, Gene. *Bright laughter: Billy May.* Gene Lees Jazzletter, v.16, no.6, June 1997.

Levin, Floyd. *The Palomar Ballroom fire.* IAJRC journal, v.29, no.2, Spring 1996.

May, Billy. *Big band memories: Billy May interview.* Jazz journal intl., v.35, May 1982, p.6-8.

Morgan, Lanny. *Lanny Morgan: a career appraisal* (interviewed by Stan Woolley). Jazz journal intl., Oct. 1999.

Tynan, John. *Charlie Barnet.* Down beat, June 26, 1958.

Waters, Howard J. *Frank Wine-gar: architect of dance bands.* Storyville 103 (Oct.-Nov. 1982). **Waters**

Williamson, Claude. *Claude Williamson.* Cadence, v.23, no.3, March 1997. **Williamson**

Woods, Phil. *Reflections in E-flat—Redskin rumble.* Saxophone journal, Mar.-Apr. 1996, p.12-13 (also appeared in Gene Lees Jazzletter, Nov. 1996 [v. 15, no.11]). **Woods**

Newspapers

Carroll, Harrison. *[LA Herald Express columns]*

Laurence, Robert P. *Charlie Barnet remembers big bands.* NY News world, v.3, no.242, Aug. 30, 1978.

Interviews

Albam, Manny. *Phone conversation, Apr. 21, 1999.* **Albam**

Alexander, Ray. *Phone conversation, Apr. 27, 1999.* **Alexander**

Atwood, Harlow. *Phone conversations, 1998.* **Atwood**

Barnet, Charlie. *Canadian Broadcasting Corporation interview.* **CB, CBC**

Barnet, Charlie. *Interviewed by Jack Cullen, July 15, 1980.* **Cullen**

Barnet, Charlie. *Interview with Charlie Barnet by Patricia Willard, Apr. 23, 1978.* **Sm**

Bert, Eddie. *Phone conversations, correspondence, 1997.* **Bert**

Davidson, Don. *Phone conversation, corrrespondence, 1999.* **Don Davidson**

De Julius, Rudy. *Phone conversation and correspondence, 1998.* **DeJ**

Dean, Vinnie. *Phone conversation, Apr. 20, 1999.* **Dean**

Griffin, Chris. *Phone conversations, April 2000.* **Griffin**

Hood, Ernie, Jr. *Interviewed by Don Manning.* **Hood**

Kelly, Red. *Interview, 1997.* **Red Kelly**

Manning, Don. *Interview, 1998.* **Manning**

May, Billy. *Interviewed by Chuck Cecil.* **Cecil**

May, Billy. *Interview, 1999.* **Billy May**

Napoleon, Marty. *Record Research presentation.* (1960s?) **Marty Napoleon**

Richards, Trudy. *Phone conversations,1998/99.* **Trudy Richards**

Rugulo, Pete. *Phone conversation, Apr. 22, 1999.* **Rugulo**

Shank, Bud. *Interview, 1998.* **Shank**

Slater, Terry. *Letter, Jan. 17, 1996.* **Slater**

Small, Ernie. *Phone conversation, 1998.* **Ernie Small**

Van Lake, Turk. *Interview.* (1970?) **Van Lake**

Wells, Dave. *Phone conversation, correspondence, 1998.* **Dave Wells**

Recording Units Index

Adrian Rollini and his orchestra 11

Barney Bigard and his Jazzopators 26

California Ramblers 24
Charles Barnet and his orchestra 8, 15
Charles Barnett and his orchestra 10, 11, 12, 17
Charlie Barnet and his Glen Island Casino orchestra 18, 19
Charlie Barnet and his orchestra 22, 24, 27, 33, 34, 35, 36, 37, 38, 39, 40, 41, 42, 44, 45, 46, 47, 48, 49, 51, 54, 55, 56, 58, 59, 62, 63, 64, 65, 68, 70, 71, 80, 82, 87, 88, 90, 92, 95, 96, 101, 103, 105, 107, 108, 110, 112, 117, 118, 119, 120, 122, 126, 128, 129, 132, 137, 140, 141, 145, 147,148, 151, 153, 158, 159, 160, 163, 170, 171, 173, 177
Charlie Barnet and his quartet 165
Charlie Barnet and his sextet 143
Charlie Barnet and the Skyliners 142
Charlie Barnet King of the Saxes and his orchestra 57, 60, 71
Charlie Barnet orchestra 39, 61
The Charlie Barnet quartet 165
The Charlie Barnet septet 137

Dick McDonough and his orchestra 23
Duke Ellington and his orchestra 177

Frank Wine-gar and his orchestra 5

Leith Stevens and his orchestra 27

Lionel Hampton and his orchestra 112

Metronome all star band 45
Metronome all star leaders 88

Neil Hefti and his orchestra 147

The out islanders 168

Peter Lind Hayes and his orchestra 143

Red Norvo and his swing septet 13
Rhythm makers orchestra 28, 30

Saturday Evening Post all-American jazz band 69, 70
Stan Freberg, featuring Jesse White 165

Program Index

Adams Theater 57, 110
Adventures in Jazz 127
America's Greatest Bands 49
Apollo Theater 44 .74, 79, 122, 123, 127, 136
Aragon Ballroom 119
Arcadia Ballroom 122

Band Wagon 93
Basin St East 174, 175
Blue Room, Tropicana 176
Brant Inn 146
Bring Back the Big Bands 176

Calgary Drill Hall 107
Canadian National Exhibition 179
Carnival Ballroom 125
Casa Manana 64
Cavalcade of Big Bands 170
Cedar Point Ballroom 53
Charlie Barnet Show 155
Chicago Theater 78
Circle Theater 75
The Click 121
Clique Club 127
Club Anthony 172

Deschler-Wallick Hotel 134
Dumont Cavalcade of Bands 139, 140

Earle Theater 116
Eastwood gardens 53
Eddie Condon Floor Show 125
Edgewater at the Beach 124
Edie Adams Show 171, 172

Famous Door 35, 35
Fiesta Danceteria 53, 54
Fitch Bandwagon 60, 82, 96
For the Record 89
Ford Star Time 167
Fred Robbins One Night Stand 122
Friday with Garroway 149
400 Restaurant 109

Glen Island Casino 18, 19, 20, 21, 22

Hi-Hat Club 146

In the Mood 178

Jackie Gleason Show 149, 153
Jubilee 92, 96, 105, 106, 117, 142, 143
Just Jazz 117

Kate Smith Show 90

La Paz Hotel 165, 166
Lincoln Hotel 46, 49, 52

Magic Carpet 97, 98, 99, 103, 106
Magic Key 35, 39
Make Believe Ballroom 21, 22, 23, 57
Meadowbrook (CA) 117
Merv Griffin Show 178
Military Ball 127
Million Dollar Theater 114
Monte Proser Dance Carnival 63
Music for Wounded 112
Music Till Midnight 90

The Navy Sings 158
NBC-TV 172
Newport Jazz Festival 177

One Night Stand 84, 85, 86, 93, 94, 95, 102, 104, 106, 107, 109, 111, 115, 116, 156, 161, 162, 170
Orpheum Theater 65, 105

Pacific Square 97
Palace Theater (Cleveland) 78
Palladium Hollywood 150, 151, 154, 160, 167, 172
Palomar Ballroom 41
Paramount Theater 50
Park Central Hotel 79
PMR 85
Providence 58

Rainbo Ballroom 110
Raleigh Room 90
Rendezvous Ballroom 131, 132, 133
RKO Theater 73, 110

Saltair Ballroom 154
Shea's Theater (Buffalo) 56
Show of the Week 51
South Weymouth 78
Spotlite Bands 67, 75, 85, 90, 92, 94, 96, 97, 99, 100, 102, 104, 107
Stanley Theater 80
Stars of Jazz 150, 158
Steel Pier 70, 71, 131
Steve Allen Show 149
Strand Theater 72, 81, 89, 100, 116, 123

Teentimers' Club 111

Uncle Sam's Christmas Tree 74
United Network San Francisco 103

Vaughn Monroe Show 116

WBZ 69
WEAF 23, 25, 26
WNEW 57
World's Fair 52

Yank Swing Session 86, 104

Song Title Index

Ac-cent-chuate the positive 156
Admiration 26, 27
Afraid to say hello 59, 60
After all 154
After looking at you 31
Afternoon of a moax 48, 50, 51, 54
Ah but it happens 125
Ain'tcha comin' out? 39
All God's chillun got rhythm 24
All heart 179
All I desire 57
All I need is you 72, 73
The all-night record man 40
All of me 146, 151
All or nothing at all 79
All the things you are 131, 132, 138
All this and heaven too 49, 51, 53
All through the day 111
Along the Santa Fe Trail 148, 152, 154
Always 20, 22
And so do I 51, 53
And so to bed 115, 116
Andy's boogie 110, 111, 122, 139
Andy's jump 119
Anvil chorus 119
Any old time 95, 96, 98, 99
Anything goes 20, 165, 166
An apple for the teacher 38, 39
Are we burnt up? 42
Argo 148, 150, 151
Art's blues 112
As long as I live 113
Asleep or awake 36
At a Dixie roadside diner 52
Atlantic jump 112, 117, 121, 126, 127
Avalon 51, 54
Aviation suite 52

Baa, baa black sheep 61
Baby take a bow 12
Baby you can count on me 107, 109, 111
Baby's birthday party 4
Back in your own back yard 100
Bakiff 82, 154, 156, 158
Bali Bali buck dance 174, 175, 176
Bangtail 161
The bar is now open 64
Barcarolle 64
Barnetology 117, 123
Basieville 175
Battle of the trombones 105
Bay won't you please come home 82, 86
Be anything 146
The beat goes on 177
A beautiful friendship 151, 156
Be-bop spoken here 129, 131, 132, 133, 134
Begin the Beguine 49, 53, 54, 122, 160, 162, 163
The best man 115
Between 18th and 19th on Chestnut St 44
Between the devil and the deep blue sea 19, 21
Beware of the bear 143
Beyond the reef 169
Birmingham breakdown 60
The birth of the blues 179
Blame it on my last affair 35
The blimp 151
Blue champagne 109, 111
Blue juice 57, 58, 61, 158, 161
Blue Lou 115, 119
Blue moon 21, 82, 97, 120, 155
Blue rose 152, 154, 175, 176
Blue skies 20, 21, 85, 86, 87, 98
Blue turning grey over you 29
Bluehound bus greys 148, 149
Blues in the night 165
Body and soul 4, 79
Boomerang 174
Bop a boogie 120
Bop city 132
The breeze and I 48
Bronx blues 171
Buckin' the wind 10
Budandy 120, 124, 125, 131
Buffy boy 55, 61
Bunny 112, 115, 116, 119, 121, 125
Busy as a bee 45, 46
But beautiful 161
But definitely 18
But she's my buddy's chick 114
Butterfingers 11
By the waters of Minnetonka 147
Bye-bye baby 20, 21

"C" Jam blues 93, 106, 109
Call me 177
Can I come in for a second? 137
Canadian sunset 151
The captain and his men 58
Caravan 26, 71, 80, 85, 87, 97, 99, 100, 112, 116, 122, 127, 139, 146, 163, 165, 166
Carelessly 26
Casa Mañana stomp 93
Castle of dreams 46, 47
Cement mixer 107, 109, 110
C'est la vie 154, 155, 156
Charade 177
Charleston alley 57, 58, 59, 120, 158, 161, 162, 178
Charlie's blues 165, 166
Charlie's other aunt 127, 128
Charm bracelet 156
Chas me blues 131, 133, 134
Chatterbox 29
Cheatin' on me 72, 73
Chelsea Bridge 154
Cherokee 39, 46, 50, 51, 65, 72, 73, 74, 75, 78, 79, 89, 92, 93,

96, 97, 99, 105, 107, 109, 110, 111, 112, 114, 116, 117, 122, 123, 124, 127, 132, 133, 139, 140, 141, 142, 148, 149, 150, 154, 155, 158, 159, 165, 166, 176, 177, 178, 179
Chico's surprise 143
China Sea 169
Chris and his gang 24
Christopher Columbus 19, 23
Civilization 122
Clap hands! Here comes Charley! 44, 158, 173, 175, 176, 178
Clarinet lament 25
Class will tell 36
Claude reigns 129, 132, 133, 154, 156
Code 288A 159, 162
The coffee song 116
Comanche war dance 45, 50, 65, 148, 149, 151
Come out, come out wherever you are 88, 89
Come rain or come shine 114, 151, 161, 162
Come to baby do 105
Come together 178
Concerto for two trombones 127
Conga del moaxo 59
Consider yourself kissed 62, 63
Coolin' 116
Cornet confab 1123
Cornucopia 129
Corporal Moax 53
Cotton tail 71, 84, 92, 93, 107, 114, 155, 168, 171, 175, 176, 179
Counting the days 94, 100
The Count's idea 41, 46
Creole love call 151, 154
Cross patch 17, 20, 130
Cu-ba 127
Cuban boogie woogie 42

Dancing on the ceiling 155
Danger in the dark 38, 39
Dardanella 50
Dark avenue 48
Dark bayou 110
Darktown strutters' ball 21, 112
Darn that dream 160, 162, 163
Day by day 106, 107
Dear old Southland 19, 21, 25, 75, 85, 94, 96, 103, 104, 108
Deed I do 47, 174, 175, 176
Deep purple 35, 113, 154
Desert sands 90
Devil may care 51
Dick Tracy liquidates 88 keys 78
Did I remember 21
Did you mean it? 22, 23
Dinah 153
Dirty rotten shame blues 120
The Dixieland band 19, 20, 21, 23
Do you know? 68
Do you love me? 109
Do you wanna jump children? 31
Don't be afraid to tell your mother 16
Don't let that moon get away 29
Don't send my boy to prison...4
Don't worry 'bout me 165, 171
Don't you remember me 109
Down Argentina way 57
Down South camp meetin' 19, 21, 24
Dream 94, 95, 96, 98, 102
Dream lullaby 18, 20
Drop me off in Harlem 82, 85, 86, 87, 102, 104, 105, 110
The Duke's idea 41, 47
Durango 131, 145
Dutch kitchen stomp 63

Early autumn 160, 162, 163, 176
East side, west side 120, 121, 123, 126, 127, 131, 159, 162, 165, 177
Easy living 128, 161
Easy pickin's 158
Easy street 150
Ebb tide 169
E-bob-o-lee-bob 104, 105, 106, 109, 110, 111
Ebony rhapsody 38, 39
Echoes of Harlem 26, 29, 34, 36, 39
Eleven sixty pm 105, 107
Emaline 11
Emperor Jones 27
Empty saddles 19
E-O eleven blues 163
Eric the traveler 115, 131
Eugipelliv 126
An evening in Azerbaijan 158
Evergreens 159, 160, 162, 163
Every day of my life 90
Every night 156
Every tub 34
Everybody knew but me 106
Everything but you 104, 106, 107
Ev'ry Sunday afternoon 46, 47
Ev'rything I love 69
Exactly like you 57

The fable of the rose 48
Fair and warmer 161
Fanfare 89
Fantasia 57, 61
Fare thee well, Annabelle 16
A fellow on a furlough 84, 85
Fifty million nickels 65, 66
Fine and dandy 150, 155
The first time I saw you 24
Flat top flips his lid 83
Flight of the foo birds 167
A flower is a lovesome thing 174
Flying home 49,50, 51, 53, 69, 119, 160, 162, 163, 179
A foggy day 155
Fools fall in love 48
Fools rush in 52
For heaven's sake 151
For sentimental reasons 116
For tonight 40
For you my love 137
Four or five times 21, 22
The four winds and the seven seas 133
The frim fram sauce 109
From another world 47, 58
From the land of the sky-blue water 148
Fur trapper's boogie 145

G 7th mambo 155
The gal from Joe's 34, 35, 117, 120, 123
The gentleman is a dope 123
The girl from Ipanema 178
The girl with pigtails in her hair 42
Give me the simple life 107
Give out 66
Gloomy Sunday 127, 129
Gloria 125
Going my way 84
Gone with the wind 155, 163, 165, 166
Good-for-nothing 57, 58
Good for nothing but love 35
Goodbye 159, 160, 162, 163, 176, 179
Goodnight ladies 127
The goona goo 26
Gotta get some shuteye 35
The great lie 63, 82, 84, 85, 87, 150, 152, 154
Growlin' 15, 16
Gulf coast blues 83

Happiness is a thing called Joe 78
A hard day's night 177
Harlem nocturne 160
Harlem speaks 64
Harmony haven 58, 59
Harmony in Harlem 29
Haunted town 59, 60, 84, 85, 86, 87, 106
He walked right in 25
Hear me talkin' to you 152
Hear my song, Violetta 51
The heart you stole from me 63, 64
Heartaches 119
Hello baby blues 123
He's a Latin from Manhattan 56
He's A-1 in the army 69
He's home for a little while 93
High tide 26
Home for a little while 95
Honeysuckle rose 20, 26, 65, 69, 165, 166
Honorable rock of Hong Kong 169

Hoppy 158
An hour never passes 92
How am I to know? 87
How come 97, 99
How d'ya do do do 142
The hucklebuck 131, 133

I ain't got nothin' but the blues 94, 97, 99, 100
I believe in miracles 115
I cain't say no 116
I can't begin to tell you 105
I can't escape from you 20
I can't get started 57, 58,90, 114, 160, 175, 179
I can't get you out of my mind 103
I can't remember to forget 56, 58, 111
I cover the waterfront 113
I cried for you 35
I didn't know about you 84, 86, 92
I don't care 103
I don't know enough about you 109
I don't want anybody at all 71, 72
I don't want to be alone 81
I don't want to cry any more 51
I don't want to walk without you 69
I found my yellow basket 31
I get a kick out of you 140, 150, 152
I get along without you very well 33, 34
I got a right to sing the blues 153
I got it bad 105, 110, 113, 117, 164, 171
I got rhythm 68
I had the craziest dream 75
I hadn't anyone till you 155, 161, 162, 165
I hear a rhapsody 55, 60
I let a song go out of my heart 28
I like a man who makes music 83
I like to riff 70, 72, 74, 79, 81, 84, 86, 90, 93, 117
I lost my girl from Memphis 4
I love you 109, 145
I never knew 37
I only have eyes for you 116, 155, 165
I surrender dear 13
I want my share of love 35
I want you, I need you 10, 11
I wouldn't give that for love 35
If dreams come true 28
If I had a dozen hearts 102, 105, 107
If I loved you 103
If my heart had a window 119
If we never meet again 22
If you're ever in my arms again 27
Igor's dream 171
I'll be seeing you 84
I'll buy that dream 103, 104
I'll get by 84, 85, 86
I'll remember 39
I'll remember April 65, 97, 114, 158
I'll walk alone 86
Ill wind 132, 133
I'm a big girl now 110
I'm a dreamer aren't we all? 140
I'm an old cow hand 18, 19, 20, 22
I'm beginning to see the light 96, 97
I'm coming Virginia 65
I'm gonna laugh you right out of my life 152
I'm gonna love that guy 116
I'm happy about the whole thing 35
I'm just a lucky so-and-so 106
I'm keeping those keepsakes 16
I'm no angel 10
I'm prayin' humble 34, 35
Imagination 154
In-a-jam 29, 45, 90, 103
In a little wayside inn 18
In a mellow tone 82, 84, 87, 143, 154, 165, 166
In a mizz 35, 39
In a sentimental mood 100
In love in vain 111
In the moon mist 110
In there 82
In your own little way 24, 25
Indian love call 148
Indian suite 56
Indian summer 148, 151, 154
Inspiration 56
Into each life some rain must fall 90
Introduction to an ending 174, 175, 176
Iroquois 148
Is you is or is you ain't 89
Isle of pines 65
Isn't this a lovely day 153
Isola bella 55
It all begins and ends with you 22
It could happen to you 85
It had to be you 173, 175, 176, 178
It happened before 89
It must have been two other people 38, 39
It was a sad night in Harlem 22
It's a good day 117
It's a wonderful world 45, 46
It's easy to blame the weather 35
It's easy to fall in love 4
It's love I'm after 22
It's love, love, love! 84, 85
It's never too late to pray 104
It's only a paper moon 155, 165, 166
It's so peaceful in the country 65
It's the last time we'll fall in love 51
It's the talk of the town 22
I've got my love to keep me warm 175
I've got to be a rug cutter 39
I've had this feeling before 81
I've lost another sweetheart 11, 22, 26

Jangled nerves 22
Jazz marches on 21, 22
Jealousy 124
The jeep is jumpin' 82
Jeepers creepers 124
Jeep's blues 175, 176
Jive at five 165, 166
Joey 176
Johnny come lately 84
Joshua fit de battle of Jericho 125
Jubilee jump 105, 109, 113, 154, 161
Jubilesta 27
Juice head blues 113, 114
Jump jump's here 31
Jump session 34, 35
Jumpin' with Symphony Sid 146
Just a little fond affection 102
Just a little while 4
Just a-settin' and a-rockin' 108
Just as though you were here 72, 73
Just what we're doin' tonight 65
Just you, just me 97, 100, 102, 104, 111, 117

Kansas City 116
Keep on doin' what you're doin' 11
Keep the home fires burning 71, 85, 86, 90, 102, 103, 145
Keepin' out of mischief now 71, 72
King Porter stomp 19, 20, 21, 23, 45
Knockin' at the Famous Door 34

The lady is a tramp 164, 165
Lament for a lost love 38
Lament for May 49
The last jump 40
Laugh and call it love 29
Laughing boy 131
Laura 146
Lazy bug 37
Leapin' at the Lincoln 47, 48, 50
Lemon drop 130, 131
Lemon twist 151, 152, 154, 158, 161
Lester leaps in 158
Let the good times roll 164, 165, 166
Let's blow the blues 145, 155
Lilacs in the rain 41
Lingering twilight 4

Little dip 61, 62
Little green apples 178
Little island 168
Little John ordinary 59, 60, 61, 84, 85, 93, 120
Living from day to day 19
Lonely street 124, 126, 131, 133, 153
Lonesome as the night is long 110
Long ago and far away 19, 84, 85, 86
Lord Nelson 131
Love 154
Love grows on the white oak tree 40, 41
Love is a merry-go-round 24
Love is flying high 29
Love letters in the sand 154
Lover come back to me 111, 146
A lover is blue 42, 46
Lover man 162, 165, 166
A lover's lullaby 47
Lullaby in rhythm 29
Lullaby of Birdland 147, 150, 151
Lullaby to a lamp post 26, 27
Lumby 55, 59, 60, 152, 155
Lush life 134

Mab 66, 174, 175
Mab medley 175
Macumba 65, 66
Madame Butterball 104, 105
Main stem 167
Make believe ballroom 20, 21, 22, 23, 34, 39, 41, 46, 50, 51, 56
Makin' whoopee 115, 155, 165, 166
The man I love 80, 121
Manhattan blues 171
Margie 78
Marie 29
Me and the moon 20, 21
Meadowland 116
Melancholy mood 41
Mellow mood 93, 95, 98
Merry-go-round 59, 63
Merry widow on a spree 27
Midnight and you 21
A midnight masquerade 119
Midnight sun 160, 163
Midsummer matinee 72
Midweek function 37
The milkman's daughter 22
Milkmen's matinee 23
A million ways to forget 142
Miss a little miss 4
Miss Annabelle Lee 37
Mr five by five 74
Mr wonderful 151, 154
Mood indigo 75, 78, 107, 116
The mood that I'm in 24
Moods 120
The moon is crying for me 54, 59
Moon mist 75, 169
The moon of Manakoora 169
The moon was yellow 151
Moonglow 21, 150, 151, 152, 154, 155, 161
Moonlight fiesta 26
Moonlight in Vermont 166
Moonlight serenade 42
Moonshine over Kentucky 29
The moose 80
More and more 93, 94, 107
More moon 132
Moten swing 159, 161
Mother fuzzy 65
Mumbles 175
Murder at Peyton Hall 64, 115
Music to watch girls by 177
My blue heaven 19, 20, 50
My crime 140
My first thrill 17, 19, 20, 21
My heart has wings 39
My heart isn't in it 82
My heart keeps crying 41
My ideal 79
My melancholy baby 19, 20, 21
My old flame 120, 122, 126, 139, 150, 152, 161, 162
My old Kentucky home 49
My tane 169
Myna 151, 154, 156

Nagasaki 16
Nancy 106
Never in a million years 26
A new moon and an old serenade 35
The new Redskin rhumba 112
New York nocturne 41
Night after night 44
Night and day 20, 25, 34, 54, 105, 114, 116, 155, 165, 166
Night glow 43
The night is blue 13
Night of nights 68
Night song 36
No can do 114
No name jive 49
No pad to be had 108
Nobody knows the trouble I've seen 89, 113
Nobody loves a fat man 131, 133
Nostalgia 131
Now playing 124
Now you know 44
Nowhere 56, 57, 63, 85, 154
Number 5000 95

Obble-ee-eebop 93 ,94, 95, 99, 100
Ogoun badagris 42
Oh! Miss Jaxson 71, 72, 84, 85, 87, 94, 95
Oh, say can you swing 23
Oh you crazy moon 39
O'Henry 128
Ol' man Mose 108
Ol' man river 65, 146
Old fashioned love 13
The old payola roll blues 164, 165
Ole Miss 125
On a holiday 16
On a slow boat to China 125, 152
On bear hill 158
On the Atcheson, Topeka and the Santa Fe 100
On the sunny side of the street 96, 165, 166, 178
One for my baby 155, 156, 161, 164, 165, 166
One morning in May 125
One o'clock jump 86, 105, 160, 163, 179
Only a rose 36
Only forever 56, 57
Ooh, what you said 46
Open up your heart 150
Orchids for remembrance 53
Ornithology 132
Over the rainbow 131, 132, 154
Overheard in a cocktail lounge 27
Overtime 128

Pale moon 148
Pan Americana 127, 130, 132, 134
Para vigo me voy 60
Passe 115
Patience and fortitude 108
Pavanne 52
Peaceful valley 51
Peg o' my heart 124
Pennies from heaven 155
People will say we're in love 79
Perdido 117, 146, 149, 155
Phyllysse 56, 60, 61, 85, 95, 151
Pistol packin' mama 80
Please don't talk about me when I'm gone 95
Plowin' 63, 72
Poinciana 85, 86, 99, 169
Pompton Turnpike 52, 56, 65, 85, 87, 105, 108, 116, 117, 120, 122, 123, 124, 140, 159, 177, 178, 179
Ponce de Leon 62, 64
Poor little rich girl 92, 93, 94, 95, 103, 106, 107, 124
Poor Snoqualmie Joe 87
Portrait of Edward Kennedy Ellington 128, 131, 132, 133
Pow-wow 80
Power steering 113
Prelude in C# minor 28
Prelude to a kiss 31, 117
Pretending 116

Rabble rouser 173, 174, 175, 176, 179
Raffles 131
Rainbow on the river 22
Raincheck 85, 86
Rapscallion 158

Really? 133
Red silk stockings 119
Redskin mambo 148
Redskin Rhumba 55,59, 60, 69, 72, 78, 84, 85, 86, 87, 90, 92, 93, 94, 95, 96, 97, 98, 99, 100, 102, 103, 104, 106, 107, 108, 109, 111, 115, 116, 117, 118, 119, 122, 123, 124, 125, 126, 129, 131, 132, 133, 140, 141, 146, 147, 150, 151, 152, 154, 156, 159, 160, 161, 162, 163, 164, 165, 167, 168, 175, 176, 179
Reflections 64
Reminiscing 49
Return to paradise 168
The reverie of a moax 51
Rhapsody in blue 127, 128
Rhubarb 131, 145, 152
Rhumba fantasy 115
Rhumboogie 56
Riffin' 22
The right idea 43, 53, 69
Ring dem bells 52, 53
Robbins' nest 154, 161
Robins and roses 19, 20, 21
Rock it for me 29
Rockin' chair 133
Rockin' chair swing 25, 26
Rockin' in rhythm 50, 51, 72, 73, 85, 93, 94, 96, 120, 122, 127, 164
Rose room 145, 146
Rosetta 20, 21, 155, 165, 166

Safranski 127
A sailboat in the moonlight 25, 26
Sailing, sailing 23
St. Louis blues 145
Saltin'away my sweet dreams 82, 85, 86, 87
Sand in my shoes 168
Satin doll 173, 175, 176, 178, 179
Saturday night 93, 94
Say it isn't so 125
Say it with music 89
Say si si 116
Scotch and soda 37, 65
Scrub me mama with a boogie beat 56
Sea breeze 169
Seminole 148, 149, 152, 154, 171
Sentimental lady 84, 85, 103
September in the rain 25
Serenade in blue 153
Serenade to May 156, 159, 161
The sergeant was shy 52, 106, 107, 109, 110, 114, 115, 116, 121
720 in the books 45, 50
Shadrack 56, 65, 150
Shady lady 70, 72, 106, 109
Shame on you 27
Share croppin' blues 87, 88
She shall have music 21
The Sheik of Araby 41
Shoo, shoo baby 80
Since I fell for you 123
Sing, baby, sing 22
Sittin' home waiting for you 80
Six lessons from Madame La Zonga 49
Skyliner 84, 85, 86, 87, 88, 94, 95, 96, 97, 98, 99, 100, 102, 103, 104, 106, 107, 109, 110, 111, 115, 119, 123, 124, 125, 129, 139, 140, 141, 149, 150, 151, 155, 156, 158, 159, 161, 163, 164, 176, 177, 178, 179
Sleep 120
Sleepy lagoon 73
Sleepytime gal 145, 146
Sleigh ride in July 93, 94, 102
Smiles 29, 70. 89, 90, 93, 116, 123, 159, 161, 177
Smooth sailing 95, 97, 131, 132, 150
Snowfall 174
So far, so good 46, 47
So nice of you 20, 21
Solitude 65, 72
Some enchanted evening 131
Some like it hot 36
Some more jive 104
Somebody else not me 92
Somebody loves me 26
Somebody told me 44
Someone to watch over me 128
Something to live for 173
Sometimes I'm happy 154
Somewhere 59
Somewhere with somebody else 29
A song is born 118
Song of India 26
Song of the Volga boatmen 64
Sophisticated lady 19, 167
South Rampart Street parade 178
Southern fried 54, 120, 156, 159, 161, 177
Southland shuffle 45
Spain 140
Spanish kick 63, 156, 161
S'posin' 36, 155, 168
Spring in Venice 17
Star dust 65, 155, 160, 162
Star eyes 84
A star fell out of heaven 21
Stella by starlight 151, 154
Still the bluebird sings 38, 39
Stompin' at the Savoy 19, 20, 21, 22
Stop, look and listen 19, 21, 22, 23, 29
Stormy weather 122
The story of a starry night 69
The story of two cigarettes 94
Straighten up and fly right 84, 85, 86, 87,89, 95
Strange enchantment 36
Strange love 109
Strip city 171
Strollin' 80, 103, 104, 106, 115
Summertime 56
A Sunday kind of love 151, 152
Sunshine at midnight 17
Sure thing 151, 154
Surprise party 102
Surrealism 27
Sweet Genevieve 66
Sweet Georgia Brown 34
Sweet is the word for you 25
Sweet Lorraine 113
Sweet misery of love 21
Swell and super 131, 133
Swing it Mother Goose 66
Swing it Mr. Goose 66
Swing low, sweet chariot 25, 59, 60
Swing St. strut 35
The swing waltz 17
Swingin' down the lane 145, 146, 154
Swingin' on a star 85, 86
Swingin' on nothin' 64
Swinging down to Rio 24, 29
Swingtime in the Rockies 20, 21
Symphony 106, 107
Symphony in riffs 22

Tain't good 19, 22
Take a tip from the whip-poor-will 41
Take my heart 21
Take my word 24
Take the A train 93, 95, 98, 100, 106, 111, 115, 160, 162, 163, 165, 166, 178
Tangleweed 'round my heart 51
Tappin' at the Tapper 44, 50
T-bone for two 131
Tell it to a star 101, 102, 103, 104
Tenderly 155
Tennessee waltz for fun 141
Terry tune 121, 123
Thank your stars 44
That feeling is gone 29
That lucky old sun 134
That old black magic 71, 105, 146
That old devil moon 121
That old feeling 166
That real romance 70, 72
That warm and tender glow 176
That's for me 52, 56, 57
That's my desire 117
That's right, I'm wrong 37, 39
That's where I came in 119
Theme for Cynthia 140
Then you'll remember me 66
There will never be another you 165
There'll be some changes made 133
There's a lull in my life 26

There's a small hotel 96
There's no you 95, 96, 98, 99
These foolish things 19, 20, 22, 142, 155
They can't take that away from me 26
They're either too young or too old 80
Things ain't what they used to be 71, 72, 78, 81, 94, 102, 105, 114, 123, 148, 165, 166, 177, 179
The things we did last summer 116
This is madness 30
This is my last affair 25
This is no dream 37
This is no laughing matter 69
This is our last night together 12
This is the army 74
This is the night 116
This night 35
Three little words 4, 21, 22, 155
Through the courtesy of love 22
Tiger rag 4
Time on my hands 156
Time waits for no one 89
Tin roof blues 34
Tomboy 13
Too good to be true 17
Toodle-oo 20
The toy brigade 4
Trees 25
The trolley song 92
Trumpet typhoon 74, 75
Tulip or turnip 117, 122
Tutti frutti 75, 78, 79
Two hearts are better 43

Undecided 35
Until my baby comes back to me 87
Until the real thing comes along 19, 20, 21, 23
Until today 20
Upper Manhattan Medical Group 174, 175, 176
Uptown blues 58

The very thought of you 92
The victory walk 71, 74

Wahoo's lament 148
Walkin' my baby back home 146
Wanderin' blues 46, 47, 50, 167, 171
Warm valley 154, 171
Washington whirligig 71, 72, 87, 98, 99, 111
Wasn't it you 63
Way down yonder in New Orleans 21, 23
Wedding of the birds 4
West End blues 82, 90, 93
What a diff'rence a day made 88, 93
What is sweeter 10
What is this thing called love 154
Whatcha know Joe 55
What's new 40
What's the matter with me 46
What's this 132
When did you leave heaven? 20
When I'm with you 19, 20, 21
When love is young 26
When Sunny gets blue 166
When the one you love 106, 107
When the organ played at twilight 4
When the spirit moves me 48
When the sun comes out 63
When the world was young 174
When you wish upon a star 50
When you're low 18
Where can she be 35
Where do you keep your heart 49, 52
Where is my heart 19
Where was I 47
Wherever there's you there's me 111
Whispering grass 54, 56, 57
Who's sorry now 145, 152
Who's your Hoosier 148, 150, 152, 154
Why 61
Why don't you do right 75
Wichita windstorm 72
Wild Mab of the fish pond 54, 61, 156
Will you still be mine 156
Wilson that's all 131
Wings over Manhattan 54, 57, 61, 84, 94, 95
Without love 116
Without the shadow of a doubt 19, 22
A wonderful day like today 176
Wosie posie 145, 146, 150, 152, 154
Would you 20
Wrap your troubles in dreams 117
The wrong idea 42

Xango 101, 102, 103, 104, 105

Ya lu-blu 68
Yalta 104, 107
Yeah man 19, 21, 22
Yesterdays 97, 99
You always hurt the one you love 90
The you and me that used to be 25, 26
You and who else 49
You call it madness 156
You can depend on me 64
You do 122
You do the darndest things baby 22
You go to my head 28, 151
You got me 30
You keep coming back like a song 114, 115
You may not love me 111
You must have been a beautiful baby 30
You stepped out of a dream 161, 162
You talk too much 62
You walk by 60
You was right baby 100
You were meant for me 150
You were there 65
You, you darlin' 116
You'd be so nice to come home to 109, 110, 150, 151, 154, 161
You'll never know 78
You're a sweetheart 114
You're being followed 155
You're blasé 156
You're driving me crazy 132, 155
You're just in love 140
You're looking for romance 24, 26
You're lovely and I'm lonely 51, 53
You're my thrill 58, 115, 155, 161
You're not the kind 19, 20, 21
You've got me crying again 109
You've got me out on a limb 46, 47, 58
You've got me voodoo'ed 47, 48

Zamboanga 106, 107
Zanesville Zohiozzz 110
Zing went the strings of my heart 155

Name Index

Aarons, Al 178
Abbott and Costello 50
Abrams, Art 153, 162
Adams, Edie 171
Adler, Henry 38
Adrian, Iris 66
Albam, Manny 154, 156, 127, 128, 129, 130, 131, 132, 133, 134, 136, 150
Albright, Max 113
Alexander, Ray 168
Allen, Dorothy 87
Allen, Henry Red 24
Allen, Huffert 4
Allison, Tommy 125
Alley, Vernon 148
Alpert, Mickey 15
Alvarez, Chico 118, 126
Amarel, Frank 17, 18, 22, 24
Ammons, Gene 132
Amsterdam, Chet 147
Anderhold, Olin 69
Anderson, Cat 177, 178, 179
Anderson, Leroy 152, 153
Anderson, Roy 150, 151
Anderson, Stew 9, 10
Andrews, Huck 70, 71, 72, 73, 74
Andrus, Chuck 140, 146
Anthony, Leo 172
Anton, Artie 147
Arabia, Phil 146
Armstrong, Louis 71, 118
Ashby, Harold 177
Ashby, Irving 117
Atwood, Harlow 3, 10, 33, 50
Auer, Mischa 36
Auld, George 82, 147, 148
Audino, John 150, 162, 171, 177
Audino, Eddie 101

Babasin, Harry 100, 101, 118, 149, 150, 155, 157, 158, 160, 162, 167
Bagley, Don 171
Bailey, Buster 27
Bailey, Mildred 10, 139
Bain, Bob 118, 119, 151
Bakaleinakov, Mischa 83
Baker, Cy 64, 65
Baldwin, Dick 119, 121, 122
Ball, Chet 137, 138
Balm, Warren 112
Bank, Danny 74, 75, 76, 78, 82, 88, 110, 125, 126, 128, 129, 130, 147, 158, 159, 160, 174
Bannister, John 157, 158, 167
Barbour, Dave 95, 99
Barcroft, Lois 145
Barnet, Charles Daly, Jr. 67
Barnett, Giff 90, 91, 92, 95, 96
Baron, Paul 90
Barrios, Gil 133, 134, 136
Barron, Wally 9, 10, 11, 68, 69, 70
Barton, Phil 89, 92, 93, 94, 95, 96, 97, 98, 99, 100, 101, 102, 103, 104, 105, 106, 107, 109
Basie, Count 42, 50, 68, 76
Basso, Guido 178
Bauduc, Ray 112, 125
Beach, Frank 164
Beau, Heinie 164
Bello, John 159, 160
Bellson, Louie 118, 149
Bennett, Max 167, 169, 170, 171, 173, 174, 177
Benny, Jack 15
Benson, Edward 122
Beraidi, Frank 25
Berg, George 149
Berger, Irving 69, 70, 73, 74, 75
Berger, John 143
Berigan, Bunny 10, 23, 28
Berman, Marty 172
Bernardi, Noni 44, 45
Bernhardt, Milt 147, 148
Bert, Eddie 76, 78, 79, 80
Berteaux, Bob 165
Best, John 11, 24, 118, 147
Betts, Harry 132
Biagini, Hank 5
Bigard, Barney 26
Biggadike, Rupert 15
Blanche, Jeanne 114
Bloch, Rene 139, 140, 141
Block, Martin 56
Block, Sandy 37
Bloom, Kurt 22, 24, 25, 26, 33, 37, 38, 44, 51, 54, 56, 58, 62, 64, 65, 68, 69, 70, 73, 74, 76, 78, 79, 82, 83, 87, 88, 92, 95, 96, 99, 101, 103, 105, 107, 108, 109, 110, 113, 114, 115, 116, 117, 122, 125, 126, 128, 129, 132, 134, 136, 143, 144, 145, 146, 158, 159, 160
Bloom, Mickey 64, 65
Bloom, Mike 5
Bode, Frank 139
Bone, George 13, 15, 68, 69, 70, 73
Boone, Chester 25
Bose, Sterling 23
Boyd, Nelson 125, 126
Boza, Jean 25, 26
Bradley, Frank 107, 108, 109, 110, 113, 114, 115
Bradley, Nita 73, 74, 75
Brady, Willard 4, 11, 17, 18, 19, 22
Brauner, Buzzy 149
Brecker, Randy 174
Brewster, Ralph 19
Briggs, Bunny 100, 117, 118, 119, 120, 122, 123, 126, 127, 128, 129, 145, 159
Brisbois, Bob 167, 168, 169
Britt, Marty 11, 12
Brock, Jeri 142
Brooks, Randy 101

Brown, Ada 14
Brown, Jimmy 122
Brown, Lawrence 110, 177
Brown, Marvin 157
Brown, Nat 11, 12
Brown, Pete 27
Brown, Russell 69, 70, 73
Bruce, Hazel 66, 69, 70
Bryant, Willie 44
Budwig, Monty 178
Bullock, Chick 11
Bundock, Rollie 172
Bunker, Larry 169, 170, 171, 177
Burgess, Bob 129, 131, 150, 151, 152
Burnet, Bob 28, 29, 33, 34, 37, 38, 39, 40, 41, 44, 45, 56, 58, 59, 60, 63, 64, 65, 68, 69, 89, 90, 103, 113
Burnett, Joe 169, 171
Burns, Dave 126
Burns, Ralph 71, 74, 76, 78, 80, 82, 85, 86, 87, 97, 99, 100, 102, 105, 112, 116, 122, 127, 154
Bushkin, Joe 125
Butterfield, Billy 112, 147
Byers, Billy 158, 159, 160, 173, 174, 175, 176
Byrne, Bobby 56, 158

Cadena, Joe 163, 169, 170
Callender, Red 117
Camarata, Toots 11, 12, 13, 15
Campbell, Jimmy 118, 119, 122
Campbell, Norman 4
Candoli, Conte 141, 147, 173, 174
Candoli, Pete 148, 164, 173, 178
Canvin, Bobbie 65
Cappola, John 138, 139, 141
Carney, Harry 26, 177
Caron, Fern 126
Carpenter, Ike 149
Carr, Helen 138, 139
Carrell, Harry 26
Carroll, Bob 55, 56, 57, 58, 59, 60, 61, 62, 63, 64, 65, 66
Carroll, Johnny 69
Carter, Benny 9, 10, 11, 12, 13, 14, 16, 22, 24, 29, 31, 34, 35, 45, 68, 117
Carter, Bob 146, 149
Casino, Del 41
Castagnino, Bill 143, 146
Castle, Lee 149
Castleman, Jeff 177
Cates, George 2
Caudle, Charles 143, 144
Cavallaro, Carmen112
Cave, John 168, 169
Cedeno, Joe 158
Ceroli, Nick 172
Cesana, Otto 49, 51, 52
Chaloff, Serge 132
Chance, John 89, 91, 92, 95, 96
Chartrand, Pat 167
Cheifetz, Sam 147, 148
Chernap, Harvey 125
Chevalier, Maurice 3
Chiaveri, Guy 110
Childers, Buddy 139, 141, 147, 148, 149, 152
Choate, Ted 10, 11
Christian, Charlie 45
Christian, Tommy 8
Christleib, Pete 177
Christy, June 155
Churchill, Jane 29
Cicalese, Andy 141
Cipriano, Gene 172
Circirello, Pat 11
Claire, Dorothy 116
Clapp, Sonny 5
Clark, Bob 151, 153, 154, 157, 162
Clark, Garnet 12
Clarke, Chuck 125
Clarke, Harriet 51, 52, 53, 56, 67, 80, 81, 82
Clayton, Buck 6, 142
Clinton, Larry 55
Cleveland, Jimmy 174
Cohen, Paul 74, 76, 77, 78, 79
Cohen, Porky 82, 83, 88, 91, 92, 95, 96, 99, 101, 102, 103, 105, 107, 108, 109, 110, 121
Cohen, Zolma 119
Cohn, Al 131, 145, 152
Cole, Cozy 24
Cole, Nat 137
Cole, Steve 73, 74, 76, 78, 79
Comfort, Joe 169
Condon, Eddie, 110
Conlon, Jud 164, 165
Connors, Chuck 177
Constanzo, Jack 148
Conte, John 90
Conway, Billy 19
Cook, James 177
Cooper, Buster 177
Cooper, Les 13, 15
Copeland, Alan 156
Cottler, Irving 168, 169
Cradit, Don 178
Crain, Malcolm 24
Crawford, Jimmy 147
Cuomo, George 26
Curry, James 24
Cusumano, Bob 9,10

D'Agostino, John 26
Dale, Joe 11,12
D'Amico, Hank 147
Davidson, Don 143, 144, 145, 146, 157, 162
Davis, Frank 10
Davis, Maxwell 168, 175
Davis, Mort 73
Davis, Sammy, Jr. 171
Dawes, Bob 99, 101, 103,105, 107, 108, 109, 110, 112, 113, 114, 115, 117, 118, 119, 122, 123, 137, 138, 139, 140, 141, 142, 144, 147, 148, 150, 151, 152, 153,154, 155, 156, 158, 160, 162
Dean, Chasey 140
Dean, Vinnie 125, 126, 128, 129, 131, 132, 149, 158
Dean, Wesley 28, 33, 37
Deane, Laura 18
Decker, James 168, 169
Deems, Barrett 137, 138
DeFranco, Buddy 79, 80, 82, 83
De Geer, Rae 79, 82, 83, 88, 91, 92, 95, 96, 99, 100, 101, 103, 104, 105, 107, 108, 109
Dehlin, Kenneth 107
De Julius, Rudy 13, 15
De Karske, Karl 123, 142
Del Simone, Al 139, 141
Dell, O'Neill 142
Delta Rhythm Boys 108
Dennis, Clark 124
DeParis, Sidney 69
Depew, Art 153, 155
Derisi, Al 160
De Rosa, Vincent 168, 169
Derry, Bill 138, 139, 140, 141
De Rubertis, Vincent 112
Deutsch, Irving 62
Deutsch, Murray 62
Diaz, Horace, Jr. 4, 9, 10, 11, 17, 18, 19, 20, 21, 22, 23, 39, 46, 50, 51
Diaz, Vincent 157, 162
Dickenson, Vic 117
Dickinson, Hal 19, 21, 22
Dillard, Johnny 9, 10
Dinardi, Tony 126
Diven, Ernie 26
Di Vito, Harry 149
Di Vittorio, Vinnie 132, 134, 136
Dixon, Mort 12
Dolney, Bill 144
Dominick, Rocque 28
Donegan, Dorothy 102
Dorsey, Jimmy 11, 67, 112, 124, 125
Dorsey, Tommy 57, 58, 101, 112, 115, 118
Dottore, Salvatore 119, 122
Douglas, Bill 157
Douglas, Paul 8
Doyle, John 17, 18, 19, 22
Downing, Ken 149, 150, 151, 152, 155 Drelinger, Art 24
Duke, Paul 48
Dutton, Laura 103
Duvivier, George 160
Dweck, Dave 141

Eardley, John 140
Eberle, Ray 9
Echols, Wes 6

Edmonson, Bob 153, 155, 166, 167, 169, 171
Edson, Stan 174
Elden, Bob 24, 25, 28, 71, 73
Eldridge, Roy 51, 82
Ellington, Duke 4, 26, 29, 32, 34, 35, 36, 37, 38, 42, 44, 52, 64, 76, 101, 117, 120, 123, 142, 143, 172, 177
Ellington, Judy 31, 33, 34, 35, 36, 37, 39, 40, 41, 42, 43
Ellington, Mercer 177
Elliot, Lloyd 171, 172
Ellis, Don 156
Ellis, Herb 177, 178
Elman, Ziggy 45, 65, 112
Elmer, Ziggy 140, 141, 142
Ericson, Rolf 128, 129, 131, 132, 133, 136
Esposito, George 56, 58, 61
Estes, Bud 52, 53, 54, 55, 56, 57, 58, 59, 60, 61, 63, 85, 87, 115, 120, 124, 125, 131, 136
Estren, Joe 24, 25, 28
Estrin, Harvey 168
Etri, Bus 33, 34, 37, 38, 39, 40, 41, 44, 51, 53, 54, 55, 56, 58, 62, 63, 64, 68
Etter, Charles 133, 136

Fagerquist, Don 167, 177
Falco, Gil 162, 170
Falensby, Fred 147, 148, 164
Farnon, Dennis 131, 132
Faso, Tony 63
Fatool, Nick 112
Feather, Leonard 27, 80, 89, 130, 172
Feldman, Victor 168
Fellensby, Fred 15, 24
Ferguson, Flem 5
Ferguson, Maynard 128, 129, 130, 132, 133, 136,147, 148, 152
Ferrante, Joseph 68, 69, 70, 73
Fielding, Jerry 94, 96, 97, 98, 99, 104
Figueroa, Ernie 92, 95, 96
Firmature, Sam 156
Fishel, Bob 24, 25, 26, 28
Fishelson, Stan 132
Fisheer, Johnny 5
Fishkind, Arnold 113, 114
Fite, Charles 149
Fitzpatrick, Bob 168, 172, 173
Flanagan, Billy 19, 22
Flanagan, Ralph 83
Flato, Ludwig 26
Flory, Med 167, 169, 178
Flynn, Frank 168, 169
Forbes, Graham 28
Foster, Gerald 113
Foster, Jerry 86, 87
Fowlkes, Charlie 149
Frances, Adele 140, 141
Franklin, Lynn 150, 151, 152,154, 155, 156, 158, 161 162, 163, 165, 166, 167, 169, 170, 172, 173, 174,
Franz, Arthur 112, 169
Franzella, Sal 27
Frazier, George 24
Freberg, Stan 164, 165
Freeman, Ernie 170
Friley, Vernon 171
Fritz, Roscoe 35, 37, 40, 65
Fromm, Ed 76, 78, 79, 82, 83, 88, 92, 95, 96, 99, 103, 105, 107, 108, 109, 110
Frommer, Gay 149
Frye, Don 27
Fuller, Gil 127, 128

Gabe, Gelinas 4
Galbraith, Barry 159
Garber, Jan 7, 125
Garberg, Rollo 99, 100
Garcia, Russ 150, 151, 152, 154, 156
Gardner, Juliet 168
Gary, Vin 17
Gastel, Carlos 172
Gentry, Chuck 147, 148
Gibbons, Bob 168, 169
Gibbs, Terry 132
Gibson, Andy 21, 28, 29, 30, 33, 34, 39, 44, 60, 62, 64, 65, 68, 70, 71, 72, 73, 74, 75, 78, 79, 81, 82, 83, 84, 85, 86, 87, 89, 90, 92, 93, 94, 95, 96, 97, 98, 99, 100, 102, 103, 104, 105, 106, 107, 108, 109, 110, 111, 112, 113, 114, 115, 116, 117, 119, 120, 121, 122, 123, 124, 125, 126, 131, 133, 136, 139, 145, 146, 148, 150, 151, 152, 154, 156, 158, 159, 161, 162, 170, 172
Gilbert, Dick 89
Gillespie, Dizzy 66
Gillum, Richie 149
Gilroy, Claude, 138
Glenn, Tyree 142
Gold, Shelly 140, 146
Goldberg, Mike 76, 78, 79
Goldstein, Chuck 19
Gonsalez, Babs 91
Gooden, Joe 162
Goodman, Benny 45, 68, 69, 118
Goodman, Irving 19, 22, 23, 24,
Gordon, E.K. 8, 9
Gordon, Harry 57
Gordon, Justin 168, 169
Gormley, Paul 157
Gotwalls, Dave 24, 25
Gozzo, Conrad 148, 151, 171, 172
Graham, Claude 114
Graves, Joe 119, 121, 122
Gravine, Mickey 168
Gray, Billy 45
Greene, Kelly 172
Greer, Sonny 26
Griffin, Chris 10, 12, 13, 15
Gubin, Sol 140, 146
Guerin, John 177
Guiffre, Jimmy 132
Gussack, Billy 9, 10, 13
Gussack, Max 73, 74
Gustafson, Gus 148
Guinn, Jimmy 176
Guy, Bobbie 172
Guy, Fred 26
Guy, Joe 66
Guyat, Dick 138

Haden, Charlie 170
Hafer, Dick 128, 129, 132, 134, 136, 138, 141, 158, 159, 160
Haggart, Bob 45, 69, 125
Hahn, Harold 79, 82, 83, 87, 88, 89, 91, 92, 95, 96, 99, 101, 103, 105, 141
Haig, Al 101, 103, 104
Haines, Connie 178
Hall, Ben 28, 33, 37, 38, 41, 43
Hall, George 25
Hallac, Bill 103, 105
Halleck, Ted 99
Hallett, Dave 86, 87, 88, 91, 92, 95, 96
Hallett, Mal 11
Halstead, Henry 19
Hampton, Lionel 112, 118
Hanna, Jake 156, 162
Hanna, Ken 134, 135
Hanson, Jack 116, 117, 123
Hardaway, Bob 172
Hardwick, Otto 75
Harper, Herbie 118, 119, 123, 132, 141, 143, 147, 148, 172
Harrington, Bob 141, 142, 143, 147, 148
Harris, Bill 83, 132, 171
Harris, Phil 112
Hartford, Buddy 90
Hawkins, Coleman 50, 57
Hayes, Peter Lind 143
Heath, Helen 111
Hefti, Neal 68, 69, 116, 117, 118, 121, 122, 123, 124,137, 147, 151, 161, 170, 172
Heider, Wally 153
Henderson, Fletcher 13, 19, 20, 21, 22, 24, 32, 45, 130
Henderson, Horace 20, 26, 34, 57, 59, 60, 61, 62, 63, 64, 65, 72, 84, 85, 93,
Henderson, Jack 13, 118, 119, 122
Hendrickson, Al 118, 164, 168, 172
Hensel, Wes 83
Herfurt, Skeets 164
Herman, Woody 32, 101, 132
Herth, Milt 65
Herzon, Hal 87
Higginbotham, J.C. 68
Higgins, Joe 11

Hill, Teddy 80
Hilliard, Harriet 66
Hing, Kenny 149
Hinshaw, William 168, 169
Hinton, Milt 159, 160
Hitchcock, Jack 146, 147
Hoagland, Everett 6
Hodges, Johnny 157, 177
Hoffman, Dick 146
Holiday, Billie 37, 50, 57, 127
Holland, Peanuts 5, 69, 70, 71, 72, 73, 74, 75, 76, 77, 78, 79, 81, 82, 83, 84, 85, 86, 87, 88, 89, 90, 91, 92, 93, 94, 95, 96, 99, 100, 101, 102, 103, 104, 105,
Holman, Bill 139, 140, 141, 142, 143, 150, 151, 152, 154, 156, 158, 159, 160, 161, 162, 163, 170, 172, 173, 174, 175, 176, 179
Holman, Jack 150, 153
Holman, Willis 151
Hood, Ernie 99, 101, 102
Hopfner, Ray 63, 64, 65
Hopkins, Claude 11
Horne, Lena 56, 57, 58, 59, 60, 61, 70, 105, 106
Hostetter (Hoste), Joe 10, 17, 18, 19, 20,
House, Art 82, 83
Howard, Joe 172
Howell, Art 172
Howell, John 126, 127, 129, 132, 133, 136, 138
Howland, Art 171
Hucko, Peanuts 125, 149
Huffine, Charles 33
Huggins, Frank 167, 169
Humphries, Conn 55, 56, 58, 60, 62, 64, 65, 68, 69, 70, 71, 97
Hundling, Lloyd 62, 65
Hunt, Pee Wee 124, 125
Hurst, Ted 11
Hutton, Marion 75
Hyde, Michael 173, 177

Ibana, Diego 126

Jackson, Chubby 73, 74, 75, 76, 78, 79, 158
Jaffe, Nat 32, 33, 34
Jameniz, Ivar 128
James, Harry 66, 69, 112
Jarvis, Jack 69, 70, 71
Jeffers, Jackie 174
Jenkins, George 110, 113
Jenner, Russ 10, 13, 15
Jenney, Jack 13, 45, 69
Jerome, Jerry 119
Johnson, Bobby 13
Johnson, Burt 86, 87, 113, 114, 115, 117, 118
Johnson, Money 177
Jolly, Pete 177
Jones, Eddie 174
Jones, Hank 145
Jones, Herbie 177
Jones, Jo 146, 147
Jones, Rufus 177
Jung, Bob 149, 150, 154, 155, 157, 158, 159, 160, 162, 163, 167, 169, 170, 171, 172, 173, 174, 177, 178

Kahn, Tiny 131, 132, 134, 136, 154
Kamuca, Richie 174, 178
Kapp, Jack 111
Kasper, Jerome 164
Katzman, Lee 169
Kaye, Danny, 50, 118
Keene, Kahn 68, 69, 70, 73
Kelly, Peck 5
Kelly, Red 134, 136, 138, 153
Kennedy, Charlie 141, 167, 169
Kennedy, George 19, 22
Kenney, Dick 125, 126, 127, 128, 129, 132, 133, 136, 138, 139, 143, 144, 145, 146, 167, 168, 169
Kenton, Stan 132, 172, 179
Kernan, Jack 149, 150, 153, 155, 157, 158, 160, 162
Kessel, Barney 87, 88, 103, 105, 112, 113, 114, 115, 120, 152, 153
Key, Guy 133, 134
Kiffe, Karl 146, 176
Killian, Al 76, 77, 78, 79, 83, 99, 101, 103, 105, 107, 108, 109, 110, 113, 114, 115, 139
Killian, Bob 162
King, Bill 9, 10
King, Peggy 155
King Sisters 150
Kinsey, Gene 33, 37, 38, 41, 44, 51, 54, 88, 91, 92, 95, 96, 99, 101, 103, 105, 107, 108, 109, 110, 113, 114
Kirby, John 26, 27, 32, 55, 68
Kirk, Andy 50, 73
Kirkeby, Ed 24
Kitzmiller, Don 158
Klee, Harry 169
Klein, Manny23, 65, 164
Klein, Ray 162
Klinger, Frank 17, 18
Koffman, Moe 141
Koven, Jack 26
Kramer, Maria 55
Kress, Carl 11
Krupa, Gene 11, 45, 50, 68, 69
Kublin, Sam 74
Kusby, Ed 164

Lacey, Jack 24
Lagasse, Benny 73
Laine, Frankie 117, 124
Laird, Jack 139, 141
Lala, Tony 73, 74
Lamare, James 28, 33, 37, 38, 39, 40, 44, 51, 53, 54, 56, 58, 62, 64, 65, 68, 69, 70, 73, 74
Lambert, Dave 129, 131
Lamond, Don 145, 159, 160
Lamour, Dorothy 36, 38
The Lancers 156
Lane, Alan 62, 66, 68, 69,114, 115, 116
Lane, Frank 150, 160, 162
Lane, Kathleen 24, 25
Lang, Irving 107, 108, 110
Larson, Kent 132
Lasky, Allen 173
Lathrop, Jack 19
Laubach, Jack 168, 171, 173
Laufer, Milton 112
Lawrence, Jerry 89
Leary, Ford 55, 56, 58, 62, 64, 65, 66
Lee, Peggy 108
Lee, Sonny 22
Lee, Teddy 158
Leeman, Cliff 44, 51, 54, 56, 57, 58, 62, 63, 64, 65, 66, 69, 70, 73, 74, 75, 125, 126, 128, 129, 131
Le Maire, Jack 65, 66
Leon, Reuben 129, 132, 134, 136
Leonard, Harvey 146
Leonetti, Tommy 176
Leshin, Phil 146
Levy, Lou 132, 167, 168
Levy, Stan 164, 165
Lewis, Irving 112, 113, 114, 115, 116, 117, 123
Lewis, Mel 167
Lincoln, Abe 10
Lindsay, Mort 178
Link, Ernie 7
Little, Steve 168, 174, 177
Llewellyn, Frank 15
Lloyd, Shirley 23
Lodice, Don 112
Logan, Ella 96
Lombardi, Art 25
Lombardo, Guy 3, 7, 16, 33
Long, Bill 9, 10
Long, Huey 15
Loring, Michael 66
Lorraine, Betty 31
Louise, Jean 118, 119, 120, 121, 122, 123
Lowe, Mundell 145
Lyman, Abe 52
Lynne, Frances 125, 126

Mack, Lee 149, 153
Madden, Dave 150, 160
Maddox, Don 142
Magnante, Charlie 11
Maiden, Willy 173, 174
Maini, Joe 171
Maisel, Jack 9
Malzahn, Walt 150, 155, 158, 160, 162
Mangano, Vito 164, 172

Mann, Carol 117
Manne, Shelly 132
Manning, Don 153, 154
Manone, Wingy 22, 52, 66
Markham, John 138, 140, 141, 142, 162
Markham, Pigmeat 14
Markowitz, Marty 158
Marks, Franklyn 27, 62, 63
Marlow, Al 163, 166
Marlow, Mac 73, 74, 75, 76
Marmarosa, Dodo 79, 80, 82, 83, 87, 88, 91, 117
Marowitz, Sam 132
Marshall, Jack 164, 165, 169
Marshall, Jerry 146
Marshall, Wendell 160
Martel, John 86, 87, 88
Martin, Freddy 112, 155
Martin, Jackie 11, 12
Martin, Mary Lou 150, 151
Martin, Skippy 29, 41, 42, 43, 44, 45, 46, 47, 48, 49, 51, 53, 54, 56, 57, 58, 69
Martlock, Ken 125, 126, 128, 129, 132, 133, 136, 138, 139
Massey, Fred 154,155, 156
Massingill, Obie 126, 127, 128, 129, 132, 144, 146, 149
Matthews, Dave 87, 88, 103, 109, 110, 125, 126, 127, 128, 131, 132, 133, 134, 137
Mattison, Bill 162, 163
Matlock, Matty 5
Maxey, Virginia 79, 80, 124
Maxwell, Jimmy 160
May, Billy 29, 30, 35, 36, 37, 38, 39, 40, 41, 42, 43, 44, 45, 46, 47, 48, 49, 50, 51, 52, 53, 54, 55, 56, 57, 58, 59, 60, 61, 62, 65, 72, 73, 74, 75, 78, 79, 85, 87, 89, 92, 93, 94, 95, 96, 97, 99, 105, 106, 107, 108, 109, 110, 111, 112, 114, 115, 116, 117, 120, 121, 122, 124, 127, 132, 133, 139, 140, 141, 148, 149, 150, 151, 152, 154, 158, 159, 164, 165, 168, 169, 170, 172, 176, 177, 178, 179
McAfee, Johnny 110, 111
McBeath, Carlton 139, 140, 141, 148, 149, 150, 151, 152, 153, 154
McCall, Mary Ann 43, 44, 45, 46, 47, 48, 49, 50, 51, 61, 76, 78, 79, 80
McCarter, Don 4
McCook, Don 33, 37, 38, 41
McCoy, Paul 65
McCreary, Lewis 139, 140, 141, 150, 167, 171
McDaniel, Ernest 176
McDaniel, Sam 92
McDonald, Everett 103, 105, 107, 108, 109, 110, 113, 114, 115, 116, 117, 118
McDonough, Dick 23, 24
McEachern, Murray 155, 156, 164
McGarity, Lou 147
McGhee, Howard 73, 74, 75, 76, 77, 78, 79, 80, 103, 104, 106, 115
McGrath, Fulton 11
McGuffin, Walter 73, 74
McGuire, Larry 173, 177
McHugh, Mary 30
McIntyre, Hal 75
McKinley, Barry 24
McKinney, Fred 149
McNellis, Maggie 89
McQuinness, Henry 68, 69
McReynolds, Gus 114, 115
McVeigh, Bill 15
Mease, Art 141
Meisel, Ken 99, 101
Meissner, Joe 87
Meldonian, Dick 138, 139, 140, 141, 142, 159, 160, 174
Mendell, John 28, 33, 34, 37, 38
Mendelson, Jules 17, 18
Menza, Don 178
Meredith, Buzz 2
Merritt, Rita 141
Meyers, Peter 173
Michaels, Ray 38, 41
Mihelich, Ed 115, 117, 139, 140
Milazzo, Jimmy 26
Miles, Hal 140, 146
Miles, Tommy 24
Miller, Ann 77
Miller, Bill 13, 37, 38, 41, 44, 51, 56, 58, 62, 63, 64, 65, 68, 69, 70, 72, 73, 82, 97, 109, 110, 112, 113, 114, 115, 116, 117, 118, 120, 151
Miller, Eddie 45
Miller, Eric 148
Miller, Glenn 38, 39, 42, 54, 56, 58
Millinder, Lucky 30
Mills, Irving 26
Mills, Jack 68, 69, 114, 117, 150, 151
Mills Brothers 155
Mitchell, Lennie 157, 159, 162, 167, 170, 171, 173, 174
Mitchell, Ollie 150 , 152, 153, 154, 162
Moe, Hal 142
Mondello, Pete 158
Mondello, Toots 24, 45
Mondragon, Joe 148, 164
Monroe, Vaughn 116
Montoya, Ray 91
Moore, Bill 4
Moore, Billy, Jr. 33, 50, 63, 64, 65, 80, 84, 85, 86, 87, 88, 94, 95, 96, 97, 98, 99, 100, 101, 102, 103, 104, 106, 109, 110, 111, 115, 119, 123, 124, 125, 129, 139, 140, 141, 149, 150, 151, 156, 158, 159, 161, 169, 172, 179
Moore, Marilyn 144, 145, 146
Moore, Phil 42
Moore, Skip 87
Moore, Tom 69, 70 73
Mootz, Jack(ie) 86, 87, 88, 92, 95, 96, 99, 100, 101, 152, 155, 157, 170, 171
Morgan, Lanny 149, 150, 153, 155, 158, 160, 162
Morgan, Tom 24
Morris, Don 13, 17, 18, 19, 22
Morse, Ella Mae 156
Morton, Benny 125
Most, Abe 172
Motsinger, Buddy 150, 153, 155, 158, 160, 162, 167, 169, 170
Mullens, Diz 149
Mullins, Ralph 150, 151, 152, 153, 154, 156, 157, 158, 160, 162
Mundy, Jimmy 20, 21, 25, 36
Murphy, Claude (Spud) 43, 44, 50, 51, 54, 56, 58, 62, 64, 65, 68, 79
Murphy, Lyle (Spud) 7, 43
Murray, Ken 65
Myrow, Joseph 27

Napoleon, Marty 92, 95, 96, 99, 101
Nash, Dick 148,151, 152, 158, 167, 177
Nash, Ted 168, 169, 178
Nelson, Ozzie 12, 19, 22
Nestico, Sam 110
Newton, Frankie 26, 27, 37
Nichols, Bobby 144, 156, 168
Nichols, Dave 123
Nichols, Marion 13, 15, 16
Nichols, Wayne 145
Nicolini, John 24, 25
Nida, George 11
Nimitz, Jack 169, 172
Nixon, Marni 168
Norell, Della 114
Norman, Loulie Jean 169
Norvo, Red 10, 13, 147
Nottingham, James 159
Novack, Rudy 73
Nugent, Helen 9

Oberstein, Eli 15
O'Day, Joyce 17
Oliver, Mert 132
Ortez, Anita 175, 176
Ottinger, Walt 4
Owens, Johnny 28, 37, 38, 41, 44, 54

Pagani, Lou 141
Page, Lips 57
Paich, Marty 168
Pal, George 108
Paladino, Dick 15, 21, 53, 142, 143, 144, 145, 146, 150, 151
Pappalardo, Frank 115, 117, 118, 123

Parker, Del 73
Parker, Delores 137
Parker, Patsy 96
Parker, William 120
Parks, Bob 17, 18, 19
Parson, Jack 51
Payne, Danny 110
Payne, Don 149
Pedersen, Tommy 82, 88, 102, 103, 105, 107, 108, 109, 110, 112, 113, 115, 147, 148, 164
Pell, Dave 172
Pena, Ralph 14, 164, 165, 168, 169
Perissi, James 169
Perkins, Bill 158, 169, 171, 172
Perri, Danny 147
Perry, Betty 98, 113, 114, 115, 116
Peterson, Bob 144, 145
Peterson, Chuck 117
Peterson, Pete 12, 13, 15
Petrillo, James 54, 56
Pettiford, Oscar 74, 76
Pickering, Ben 82
Pierce, Dale 141
Pierce, Nat 158, 159, 160, 168, 170, 172, 174, 175, 177
Pino, Andy 82, 83
Pockrandt, Norman 150, 151, 152
Poland, Bob 83, 87, 92, 95, 96
Pollack, Ben 172
Porcino, Al 132, 138, 144, 145, 146, 150, 158, 160, 167, 169, 173
Potter, Freddy 171
Powell, Ginny 94, 95, 96, 97, 98, 99, 102
Powell, Mel 118
Powell, Specs 127
Powell, Teddy 66
Prell, Don 141, 143, 154
Price, Bob 61, 64
Price, Ruth 173
Price, Walter 62
Prince, Paul 24
Pripps, Eddie 87, 88, 91,92, 95, 96, 99, 101, 103, 105
Privin, Bernie 51, 54, 56, 58, 62, 65, 147
Procope, Russell 177
Proser, Monte 62, 63
Ptachek, Buddy 149, 150, 151, 152
Pupa, Jimmy 79, 82, 110
Purvis, Jack 5, 6, 9, 10

Raboy, Art 125, 126, 128
Rader, Don 174, 175
Raetz, Carl 141
Rafell, Don 113, 114, 115, 117, 118, 119, 170
Ramirez, Ram 12
Ramirez, Roger 74
Ramsay, Bill 99
Randall, Herb 125
Raskin, Milt 165
Raye, Martha 113
Rayman, Morris 103, 105
Reasinger, Clyde 174
Reed, Neil 12, 13
Reese, Gail 25, 26
Rehak, Frank 140, 159, 160
Reilly, Betty 150
Reis, Herb 73
Reo, Tommy 62, 64, 65
Resnick, Eph 156
Rey, Alvino 68, 69, 168, 169
Reynolds, Tony 43
Riccardi, Andy 82
Rich, Buddy 101, 125
Rich, Sonny 125, 146
Richards, Ann 147
Richards, Emil 168, 169
Richards, Johnny 127, 128
Richards, Trudy 127, 128, 129, 131, 132, 133
Richman, Boomie 147
Richmond, Bill 151, 155
Riley, Roy 5
Rips, Tiny 95
Rizzi, Tony 147, 148, 172
Roberts, George 171
Robertson, Bill 33, 37, 38, 41, 44, 51, 54, 56, 58, 62, 64, 65, 68, 69, 70, 73
Robey, Art 107, 108, 109, 110, 111, 113, 114, 115
Robbins, Billy 79
Robbins, Ruth 13
Robinson, Bill 1, 100
Robinson, Les 103, 104, 113
Rodgers, Harry 84, 85, 86, 87, 89, 95
Rogers, Shorty 113, 114, 115, 116, 131, 132
Rogers, Will 15
Roland, Gene 139, 145
Rollini, Adrian 11
Romer, Milton 16
Romero, Raoul 176
Rosen, Marvin 138
Rosolino, Frank 168, 171
Ross, Arnold 139, 149, 165, 170
Roten, Ray 163, 165
Roth, Lillian 1, 62
Rowles, Jimmy 164, 168, 169, 171
Royal, Ernie 132, 137, 149
Rugulo, Pete 127, 128, 129, 131, 132, 133, 134
Rumsey, Howard 83, 84, 87, 88
Ruppersburg, Don 28, 33, 37, 38, 41, 44, 51, 54, 56, 58
Russell, Ann 116
Russell, Eleanor 141
Russell, Percy 73

Sacramento, Paul 141, 142, 149
Safranski, Eddie 126, 127, 128, 129, 131, 132, 134
Salco, Jimmy 141
Salinas, Harold 5
Salter, Harry 12
Saltman, Henry 24, 25, 28
Sandole, Dennis 109, 110
Sarnelli, John 25
Sarracco, Frank 158
Satterwhite, Tex 142
Saunders, Carl 176
Sauter, Eddie 10, 12, 13, 15, 16
Savitt, Buddy 132
Savitt, Jan 51
Sayres, Dean 74
Scala, Edward 68
Schatz, Ziggy 141
Scherzer, Hymie 10
Schiffman, Frank 43
Schlicting, Sam 149
Schlinger, Sol 146
Schmidt, Harry 112
Schreber, Henry 5
Schutz, Buddy 24, 25
Schwaltz, Wilbur 168, 169, 173
Scott, Carolyn 118
Scott, Hazel, 75
Scott, Thomas 177
Scrima, Mickey 107, 108, 109, 110
Seaburg, George 103, 105
Seckler, Stan 144, 145
Serra, Hal 140, 146
Severinsen, Carl (Doc) 119, 121, 125, 126, 127, 128, 129, 132, 133, 136, 145, 146, 149, 159
Shaine, Munroe 146, 147
Shanahan, Dick 115, 116, 117, 118, 119, 120, 22, 123, 162, 170
Shank, Bud 111, 121, 122, 123, 137, 144, 177
Shannon, Linda 142
Shavers, Charlie 101, 125, 145, 14, 158, 159, 1609
Shaw, Artie 13, 23, 24, 147
Shaw, Rita 25
Shaw, Terry 12
Sheldon, Jack 178
Shelladay, Nelson 99, 101, 113
Sherman, Dick 140, 141, 144, 145, 146
Sherman, Norman 4
Sherock, Shorty 77
Sherwood, Bobby 128, 129
Shevak, Iggy 118, 123
Shirley, Ann 83
Shirley, Frances 91, 92, 95, 96, 99
Shore, Dinah 61
Shore, Rita 114
Shu, Eddie 137, 138
Simmons, Kermit 17, 18, 19, 22
Simon, George T. 26
Simpson, Don 155, 172
Siravo, Frank 112
Siravo, George 71, 76, 78, 79, 82, 84, 85, 86, 87, 88, 90, 92, 93, 94, 95, 98, 100, 102, 103, 105, 107, 111, 112, 113, 114, 115, 124
Skinner, Sanford 157, 158, 160, 162

Skolnick, Sam 51
Small, Ernie 149, 150, 151, 152, 156
Smith, Allen 148
Smith, Arthur C. 112
Smith, Beasley 5
Smith, Buzz 17, 18, 19
Smith, Carson 162, 163
Smith, Dalton 173
Smith, Howard 69, 149
Smith, Paul 164
Smith, Sheldon 104, 105, 107, 108, 137, 138
Smith, Stuff 31
Smith, Vernon 141, 142, 143
Smith, Willie 143, 147, 148, 151, 152, 173, 174
Snyder, Terry 158, 159
Solloway, Ann 79
Soltaine, John 144, 145, 146, 149
Southern, Jerei 158
Spangler, Ralph 4, 5, 10
Speer, Billy 9
Spencer, O'Neil 27
Sperling, Jack 150, 158, 160, 170, 172, 173, 174, 178
Spivak, Charlie 45
Stampe, Otto 142
Starr, Kay 83, 84, 85, 86, 87, 88, 89, 90, 91, 92, 93, 94, 99, 100, 101, 124
Stein, Lou 147
Stephens, Phil 33, 37, 41, 42, 44, 51, 54, 56, 58, 62, 63, 64, 65, 66, 68, 164
Stevens, Leith 27
Stewart, Al 158
Stewart, Buddy 1219, 131, 132, 133, 134, 137
Stewart, Freddie 107, 108
Stewart, Rex 26, 116
Stines, Boone 149, 151
Stoller, Alvin 147, 148, 152, 153, 164, 172
Strayhorn, Billy 172
Stress, Ed 101, 103, 107, 108, 109, 110
Stuart, Al 24, 25, 146
Sues, Leonard 112
Swift, Bob 74, 76, 78, 79
Swope, Earl 132

Tack, Ernie 171, 173
Tatum, Art 112
Taylor, Billy 26
Taylor, Dick 143, 144
Taylor, Larry 38, 39, 40, 49, 51, 52, 53, 54, 55, 69, 70
Teagarden, Charlie 125
Teagarden, Jack 45
Teele, Philip 177
Terry, Clark 119, 120, 121, 122, 158, 174, 175, 177
Thompson, Jack 76
Thompson, Sir Charles 146, 147, 157
Thomson, Scoop 4, 5,9, 10, 22
Thornhill, Claude 223, 24
Timbrell, H.J. 169
Tizol, Juan 26, 27, 104, 150, 153, 158
Todd, Tommy 99, 137
Tole, Billy 174
Torme, Mel 158
Towell, Ron 176
Tosti, Don 118, 119, 120, 122
Touff, Cy 162
Trenner, Don 138, 139
Triffon, George 174
Triscari, Joe 150
Triscari, Ray 150, 158, 171, 172, 177
Trujillo, William 152
Tucker, Ben 157
Tucker, Tommy 66
Tully, George 2, 4,
Turner, Buford 15, 19
Tuttle, George 74
Tynes, Gwen 82

Ulyate, Bill 164
Usher, Billy 116, 117, 118

Vance, Dick 76
Van Cleave, Nathan 9, 10, 11
Van Heusen, James 13, 27
Van Lake, Turk 76, 78, 79, 80, 82, 83, 89
Varsalona, Bart 132
Vaughn, George 17, 18, 19, 22
Venuti, Joe 69
Vidoloff, Robert 114
Villepigue, Paul 109, 124, 126, 129, 131, 133, 145, 146, 147, 148, 152, 154
Vincent, Romeo 150
Vohs, John 141
Von Zell, Harry 8, 10, 11
Vunk, Lyman 41, 42, 44, 51, 54, 56, 58, 62, 75, 79, 82, 83, 86, 87, 88, 91, 92, 95, 96, 109, 110, 131, 141
Vydal, Carlos 126, 129, 131, 134

Wade, Eddie 4
Wade, Johnny 91
Wagner, Russ 79
Wald, Murray 117
Waller, Fats 16
Walp, Charlie 132
Walter, Wallace 108
Ward, Helen 75
Warren, Fran 101, 102, 104, 105, 106, 107, 109, 110, 111
Washburne, Phil 115, 117, 118, 123
Wasserman, Eddie 140, 141
Wasserman, Herbie 168
Waters, Howard 4
Watson, Leo 27
Wayland, Hank 13
Wayne, Frances 70, 71, 72, 73, 108, 137
Webster, Paul 107, 108, 109, 110, 146
Weidler, George 112, 117, 118
Weidler, Walt 117, 118, 119, 122, 123
Weidler, Wolfgang 122
Weintraub, Charlie 55, 66
Weiss, Seymour 16
Weiss, Sid 17, 18, 19, 22, 24
Welk, Lawrence 112
Wells, Dave 138, 139, 140, 141, 143, 150, 151, 152, 153, 155, 158, 160, 162, 167, 168
Welsh, Chauncey 159, 160
Wetzel, Ray 127, 129, 131, 132, 133, 134, 136, 137, 138, 141
White, Bob 10
White, Jesse 164, 165
White, Leo 51, 54, 56, 58, 62, 63
Widder, Frank 146
Wiggins, Jerry 171
Willard, Pat 4
Willett, Chappie 28
Williams, Cootie 68, 177
Williams, John 146
Williams, Murray 22, 71, 73, 74
Williams, Tex 156
Williamson, Claude 119, 120, 122, 123, 125, 126, 127, 128, 129, 132, 133, 140, 141
Williamson, Stuart 142, 143, 158, 160, 162, 167, 169
Wilson, Curry 122, 139
Wilson, Jack, Jr. 173, 174
Wilson, Oliver 117, 118, 132
Wilson, Roy 89
Wilson, Teddy 13, 50, 57
Winding, Kay 178
Windsor, Joy 153
Wine-gar, Frank 4, 5
Winslet, Kenny 141, 143, 144, 146
Winters, Jack 114
Wied, Eddie 176
Wise, Herb 174
Woodman, Britt 178
Woods, Phil 140, 146, 147, 159, 160
Wootten, Red 150, 151, 152, 153
Wright, George 157
Wright, Harry 9
Wright, Lammar 123, 124, 125, 126, 128
Wyands, Richard 148
Wyder, Bill 4

Young, Evan 49
Young, Lester 34, 50, 57
Young, Snooky 174, 176
Young, Trummy 76, 78, 79

Zentner, Si 147, 148, 164
Zimmerman, Charles 62, 70, 73, 82
Zito, Freddie 118, 119, 121
Zito, Jimmy 118
Zucca, Joe 93
Zurke, Bob 5